Essays in Comparative Social Stratification

Essays in Comparative Social Stratification

Leonard Plotnicov *and*

Arthur Tuden

EDITORS

University of Pittsburgh Press

Contents

Tables

Essays in Comparative Social Stratification

Leonard Plotnicov / Arthur Tuden

Introduction

For more than a year, beginning in the spring of 1966, twelve distinguished sociologists, historians, and anthropologists presented public lectures at the University of Pittsburgh on the general topic, "Emerging Patterns of Social Stratification in Developing Nations." The stimulus for the lectures was an increasing interest in the areas of comparative social stratification and modern change in non-Western societies among many social science faculty members at the University of Pittsburgh, several of whom had previously organized and participated in an informal seminar on the subject. This experience revealed that (1) the published literature in this area was sparse, with the result that efforts to make substantive and theoretical comparisons frequently met with frustration and that (2) the long-neglected comparative study of social stratification was rapidly drawing serious attention and wider interest, manifest in the number of symposia on the subject at professional meetings of social scientists. The organizers of the Pittsburgh lecture series, therefore, arrived at what seemed an obvious conclusion: that our colleagues in other disciplines and other institutions currently involved in this area should be invited to Pittsburgh to discuss their recent work.

Invitations were extended on the basis of firsthand research in various major culture areas of the world, primarily in societies which traditionally did not have clear-cut class structures. Contemporary North America was excluded from consideration because an abundance of relevant published

This collection of essays derives from a series of lectures sponsored by the Department of Anthropology and supported with funds from the University of Pittsburgh's International Studies Program, for which thanks is gratefully extended.

3

material already exists on this region, and one paper, dealing with Latin America, unfortunately failed to arrive in time for publication. It may be of interest to note that, in choosing participants, the organizers of this symposium sought the widest practical range of theoretical perspectives. The contributors to this volume represent not only several academic disciplines but also—through training or affiliation, past or present—a variety of academic institutions in Germany, South Africa, Britain, Australia, the West Indies, and the United States.

In the past, research on social stratification has stressed one particular type: social class. For a variety of theoretical and practical reasons, scholars generally have not devoted comparable effort to other forms of structured social inequalities. Furthermore, the literature on the subject has tended to neglect historical perspectives. Therefore, within the general subject of the comparative study of social stratification, the speakers were asked to deal with their respective topics historically, to try to make the processes of change intelligible in terms of a continuity or discontinuity between past and present conditions. While the editors of this volume have their own theoretical frameworks, biases, and research interests, they made no attempt to suggest to the participants any particular theoretical position, as the essays in this volume, we believe, demonstrate. They did, however, urge that some consideration be given to related contemporary problems, such as economic development and nationalism, as factors influencing the changes in the patterns of social stratification.

Such a broad mandate might well have resulted in a disparate and unrelated selection of papers and, ultimately, in what is now fashionably called a non-book. Fortunately, however, the essays do provide a unity: while the authors do not agree theoretically, they treat similar situations, and all raise crucial problems of comparisons.

*   *   *

Social stratification, as most of the authors note, is a fundamental feature in the organization, maintenance, and changes of a complex society. Stratified societies display a distinctive structural anatomy. Characteristically, each has *social groups* that (1) are ranked hierarchically, (2) maintain relatively permanent positions in the hierarchy, (3) have differential control of the sources of power, primarily economic and political, relative to their rankings, (4) are separated by cultural and invidious distinctions that also serve to maintain the social distances between the groups, and,

(5) are articulated by an overarching ideology which provides a rationale for the established hierarchical arrangements. Since these features vary in different societies, it is difficult to construct an ideal model of a stratified society which can incorporate all varieties.

Not all societies, however, are stratified. In unstratified societies individuals are ranked merely on the bases of sex, age, and kinship statuses. Unstratified societies fall into two general categories. One is structured primarily upon age, sex, and—perhaps—shifting and temporary nonkinship solidarities. These criteria determine the allocation of tasks within the society and the modes of deference. Individuals eventually achieve, according to sex, whatever status positions of age exist within the society and move out of them without being able to block the same movements in other individuals. The second type of society, more complex but still unstratified, is differentiated on the basis of corporate kinship groups. Each kin group replicates the others and has relatively equal access to the economic resources in the environment. The units, therefore, are relatively equal in economic and political power; if one kin group becomes politically dominant, its position is temporary, for it is sooner or later replaced by another group based upon the same principles. It is a case of *primus inter pares.*

Having distinguished between unstratified and stratified societies, we may turn our attention to some general problem areas of the latter. First, it is interesting to note that the role of economic and political factors, as fundamental determinants of social stratification, is considered repeatedly in the essays which follow. Several authors are also concerned with the use of legitimate force as an essential element in maintaining the separation of social strata. Particularly, they point to its use in supporting the differential access to wealth and economic resources in a society. While this stress is in contrast to previous studies which have tended to ignore the brazen use of force to maintain the structure of the system, the concern with economics and politics as basic determinants of social stratification may, perhaps, indicate a return to past theoretical interests.

Second, most of the writers examine the heuristic limitation of stratification models when they discuss plural societies or slavery or other systems that manifest considerable variation. Thus it appears that the definitions and models available to us are singularly lacking in elements and constructions that make them applicable to situations of change.

Third, in their concern with change from one system to another, many of the authors raise such relevant questions as the comparability of social mobility between different systems, analysis of the stratum or structural area in which change occurs, or the discernible continuities between systems of the past and those which have subsequently emerged.

Finally, each paper stresses the effect of external influences or impingements upon a system of stratification as a basic determinant of change. This concern enlarges the usual parameter of the study of changes in stratification insofar as systems are more realistically analyzed within a wider systemic context.

*   *   *

All the papers deal with social change, but there is no intrinsic rule governing the order in which they appear. The chapter by Bendix, which concludes the volume quite justifiably could have been placed first. It raises theoretical issues of the most fundamental nature, namely, the continuities and discontinuities between traditional and contemporary societies and the history of intellectual thought regarding social change in the area of stratification. Although the reader may profitably start the volume with that chapter, we chose not to begin with it because its radical departure from conventional perspectives might have presented the reader with distorted expectations of the other contributions. We felt, too, that the issues raised by Bendix provided an appropriate conclusion to this book, which is intended, after all, to be exploratory. For similar reasons—that is, because the author raises questions concerning the fundamental universal principles of social stratification—the chapter by Southall could very well have served as an entrée. In the interests of overall organization, however, it has been placed in the second part with other essays devoted to the themes of historic continuities and discontinuities. Although many of the papers in Part II deal also with conditions of sociocultural pluralism, we have singled out—in Part I—those essays whose focus is specifically on social pluralism because of the current lively interest in this theoretical issue.

Nodding acknowledgement to the pioneer work of Furnivall has become customary in formal discussions of pluralism, and our contributors are no exception. Here, however, convention ceases. Burton Benedict and Raymond T. Smith review the concept of pluralism as it has been applied to a variety of cultural and social conditions, but they question its heuristic utility. While Benedict seeks to sharpen the analytical usefulness of the concept, Smith rejects it entirely in favor of social class.

Stated succinctly, Benedict's position is that social pluralism is a useful concept whereas cultural pluralism is not. In his opinion, scholars of pluralism have tended to concentrate on the analysis of cultural groups in plural situations and, as a result, have been diverted from studying social structure and institutions. They have been more concerned with investigating cultural differences within a society than with examining its economic or political structure. To analyze a system of social stratification one must determine the relationships between the society's structural categories, and those categories are not determinied by cultural differences. One must answer the question, "Who controls the economic and political machinery?"

Using Mauritius as his prime example, Benedict points out that Europeans in this nation (like those in South Africa cited by Kuper in a later chapter) "hold their position at the top of the social hierarchy [not] because of their cultural characteristics but because they control the political, legal, and economic machinery of the society." Benedict concludes his essay with an analysis of political change in Mauritius, showing how cultural aspects of group identity—formerly ignored as politically irrelevant—have in recent times been manipulated for political ends. This example illustrates the value of analyzing stratification in terms of structure, and primarily in the differential control of political power, rather than in terms of cultural pluralism.

Smith's paper on the Caribbean, an area almost synonymous with studies of pluralisms, like Benedict's, regards pluralism as a basically political phenomenon. Smith also argues that Furnivall's original ideas about pluralism were modified and misapplied by those who related them to Caribbean societies. Furnivall's main theory, according to Smith, is that ethnic distinctions in Burma and Java were breaking down with colonial rule and the imposition of a modern capitalistic economy. This process, he believes, was leading to a condition of social atomization or individualism and, as a paradigm, provides a better appraisal of the Caribbean situation than the modified interpretations of Furnivall's argument which have been more commonly applied. Smith's paper, which provides an economic history encompassing the periods of slavery and post-emancipation, shows how the cultural tradition of pluralism has obfuscated the fact that the political, economic, and social organization of Caribbean societies had been controlled "by a class of nationally oriented persons seeking to maximize profits in an established export sector of the economy." Smith does not commit the error forewarned by Benedict—that of thinking that a group, ethnic or class, holds power when, in reality, only certain sections or families within the group actually do so. This control is documented by

Smith in his discussion of how formal education developed and how it both reflected and, in turn, helped to crystallize the emerging class structure.

Of central importance to the history of the Caribbean is the place of the plantation system, which, Smith points out, resembled a total institution in which primary acculturation took place and which impressed its image upon the surrounding society. For this part of his analysis, Smith turns to Weber's concept of class as seen in terms of the individual's economic life changes. But it is not the author's intention to explain Caribbean social stratification solely in terms of this concept; the consequences of racial distinctions and discriminations preclude this. In attempting to relate social class with race, he finds Weber's concept of status group most helpful, and he directly confronts the controversy over pluralism. To what extent do the separate status groups "constitute separate social sections with no values in common"? To answer this question, Smith turns once again to Weber and applies the concept of political party, for not all the relevant conditions of stratifications can be subsumed under the categories of class and status group. His conclusion: In the way the concept has been used, "Caribbean societies are among the worst examples of plural societies."

The question of pluralism can be reduced to whether plural societies are structurally distinctive and require a special theory of stratification for their analysis. Our first two contributors answer negatively, while Kuper, the third, seeks to retain the concept by applying it to the white settler societies in Africa.

Like the previous authors, Kuper views the political system he studies as central to social stratification, but he also points out that the plural (ethnic or racial)sections of society are not coterminous with the stratified sections. "There are differences in class situation among members of the same race," he writes, "and a common class situation among members of a different race." In other words, the present-day societies of southern and central Africa have complex systems of social stratification wherein ethnic groups as well as classes are accorded unequal worth.

Weber's influence on studies of social stratification is again manifest in Kuper's use of the distinction between class, status, and power. But whereas Smith employs Weberian analysis to demonstrate its superiority over the pluralism model, Kuper attempts to show how it strengthens the validity of a pluralistic approach.

For Kuper the basic characteristic of a plural society is the differential incorporation of groups—ethnic and/or racial—in hierarchical relationships in which the groups form distinct strata. In an extreme form of plural society, structural divisions coincide with cultural distinctions. White settler societies in Africa are plural in form because the component groups are differentially incorporated into the central political system. But by "differential incorporation" Kuper does not mean that some groups are not fully a part of the total society, only that they have less access to the exercise of political power. The political structure, however, in turn, determines the nature and extent of participation in the economic sectors of the society. As we mentioned above, Kuper indicates that there are many examples of deviation from this ideal construct in the disconformities between class and status group. The association between these categories and the control of political power is far from perfect. To take the extreme of whites and blacks, we find that while the former occupy the topmost positions in the economy, they also "as individuals are distributed through all layers of the economic structure." In fact, the majority of whites "must be described as proletariat or petite bourgeoisie." Black Africans, on the other hand, not only occupy intercalary positions linking the racial groups, or the interstitial positions between them, but they are also to be found in small, though increasing, numbers in retail trade and in the liberal professions. This upward occupational and social mobility among blacks evident in South Africa, however, involves a cultural transformation which differentiates them from the mass of their people. Is it not theoretically inconceivable that this should take place without a concomitant development of black political participation? Kuper answers that a measure of economic advance is quite compatible with apartheid; continued high rates of economic growth need not inevitably alter the ideology and policies of the South African government, for, compared with the common market situation (class), race is the more compelling basis for social mobilization. The Government responds to economic advance by increasing political repression.

South African society, however, has hardly reached a state of stable equilibrium. "The tensions between class, status, and power," he states, "are a stimulus to dynamic change in the system of stratification."

Paula Brown Glick's chapter concludes the section on pluralism and deals with the port town of Vila, New Hebrides, in the Pacific, a major culture area which only recently has begun to provide comparative data for studies of social stratification. Her study, along with a wider increase in our knowledge of pluralism and stratification in this region and southeast Asia (where Furnivall developed his ideas), will serve to challenge conceptions now held about the associations between pluralism and stratification. Cases like Vila, though typical in this region, are very different from what we are accustomed to expect with large mainland societies. Glick points out the important but somewhat neglected aspect of stratification and pluralism here; namely, that the local systems can be understood only in terms of a wider context. This issue is raised as a basic argument by Bendix in the last chapter.

Vila is built and depends upon special political circumstances for its existence and is, therefore, both an interesting and an important case for comparative study. It is under joint French and British rule, with each government holding sovereignty over its own nationals. Non-nationals must choose to be under French or British law, and natives are under a joint District Administration considered neither French nor British. Political support and reinforcement of hierarchical relationships between groups comes from outside the local context. Its population looks to metropoles and external cultural centers as essential reference points, and even the natives seek higher education and cultural stimulation outside their territory. "Vila is an outpost of many different cultures," according to Glick, who suggests that plural societies may always have an outpost character, that they may be, like Vila, "a medley of strangers imposed upon the local population." The impact of colonialism in the history of plural societies is apparent, but one questions whether independence and political autonomy for the New Hebrides would result in any radical change. Glick thinks that the heterogeneity of the native population is sufficient to maintain a condition of pluralism even then.

However, Glick considers Vila an example of social pluralism for reasons other than its multiple administration. Life in Vila comes very close to our general concepts of sociocultural pluralism because of its highly heterogeneous population, apparently determined to maintain its culturally distinct parts. It seems to provide a perfect example of Furnivall's classic model, which Glick extends by remarking that mingling without mixing occurs in sports and, to a lesser extent, in dances. The organization of these recreation activities is an interesting parallel to Furnivall's market situation.

It is curious to note that each of the four chapters dealing directly with pluralism provides its own variation, however slight, on Furnivall's concept. By contrast, Weber's concepts of class, status group, and power, or political party, are employed by the contributing authors with little or no variation in meaning.

India, with its religious, ethnic, and caste division, has been viewed at times as representing a form of sociocultural pluralism,[1] but China normally is not regarded in this light. Why, then, were not Robert Marsh's chapter on China and Bernard Cohn's on India placed among those dealing specifically with the issue of pluralism? To have done so, would imply that these, as well as other papers in this volume, might all be covered under this rubric and that, indeed, the designation of an example as "plural" is arbitrary and subjective. With the definition of pluralism, to our present knowledge, so uncertain, we thought it best to let the responsibility of appropriate designation rest with the contributing scholar. We have, therefore, grouped the final seven essays around a focus on historical problems.

Part II begins with India, which is normally regarded as the model of a traditional and rigid caste system. In contrast to this general image of Indian caste permanance, Cohn points out that, on the other hand, constant and complex change has been an ever-present feature of the system. India was not the structurally and culturally stable society nineteenth-century scholars were led, on the basis of their studies of the sacred texts, to believe it was. Cohn's essay focuses on the emergence of new stratified groups, particularly elites, in response to European contact. Since the late eighteenth century these contacts, including British colonial rule, have accelerated social mobility. Abundant evidence indicates that, of the several developing elites, no single type—such as a Western-educated bureaucracy—was especially favored.

Some can be regarded as political or administrative elites, others as business or commercial elites, and they were drawn from different sectors of the traditional society: from humble backgrounds and from elite aristocracies, from rural areas and from cities. Some elite groups maintained traditional life styles: others participated in modern society, helping to develop modern Indian institutions. And some did both.

Marsh attempts to analyze changes in Chinese social stratification on the basis of theories and generalizations developed from Western experiences. Particularly, he bases a social hierarchy on the ranking of occupational roles. The editors would question the cross-culture applicability of what might be culture-bound analytical models, but Marsh's rigorous

---

1. Berreman, G. D. (1967) "Stratification, Pluralism, and Interaction: A Comparative Analysis of Caste," in *Ciba Foundation Symposium on Caste and Race: Comparative Approaches,* ed. A. V. S. de Reuch and J. Knight. London.

research methodology and closely reasoned argument compel those of us with a bias toward cultural relativism to examine our position. Later in this Introduction we will return to this problem.

In a quite different sense, Marsh's method is an example of controlled comparison. Using the Ch'ing period as a baseline, Chinese society is defined as an historical continuity within which variation is explored through time and space. The two Chinas of the present are contrasted and, in turn, compared with the past. By this means Marsh is able to show how status incongruence was socially beneficial in Ch'ing times but dysfunctional in contemporary Taiwan and mainland China.

In the earlier era, Marsh points out, "sumptuary laws rigidly and precisely defined the style of life and status-honorific rewards that each legal category of persons could display and enjoy." Wealth, however, did not initially confer prestige; the latter derived from scholarship and administrative office. Marsh hypothesizes that the desire to acquire prestige motivated the wealthy to seek office and thereby "to direct their leisure and their capital into system-problems instead of into exclusively private uses," and thus resulting in wider societal integration.

In Communist China, status incongruence lies in the conflict between ideologues and technocrats, on the one hand, and between real and ideal status evaluation, on the other. These conditions show no signs of resolution. In Taiwan the conflict is between the native Taiwanese and the alien mainlanders, who maintain political control through the military regime. Here a resolution would lie in the removal or assimilation of the mainlanders or the achievement of greater political and economic controls by the natives.

Marsh also characterizes stratification changes in Taiwan as "evolutionary" and those on the mainland as "revolutionary." By "evolutionary" he means following those patterns generally common to modern urban-industrial societies. On the mainland where, by contrast, developments with implications for stratification have been directed and imposed, the changes are radical and "revolutionary" to the extent that the ideologies of the Chinese Communist Party have been accepted.

Finally, we may note the structurally similar political situations between Taiwan and the white settler societies in Africa, described by Kuper, or indeed, within the framework of comparative studies, the position of Negroes in the United States. Nor should we avoid serious consideration of Kuper's and Marsh's conclusions and prognostication; they may well apply closer to home.

No volume surveying contemporary social change is complete without considering "the case of Japan." The use of quotation marks here is intended to remind the reader that the history of Japan's modernization, and many features of contemporary Japanese social organization and culture, appear to defy categorization. Japanese data have the reputation for providing exceptions to generalizations. With regard to modern social stratification, Japan again appears true to form.

Edward Norbeck surveys the problems associated with defining Japanese social classes. Some of these, however, are not unique to Japan but, rather, are common difficulties found in defining social stratification phenomena anywhere. Norbeck critically reviews Japanese census and other statistical data normally employed in analyses of social change in complex societies and points out the dangers inherent in uncritical acceptance of official administrative sociological categories. These can often distort historical and sociological reality. For example, the traditional status of farmers in Japan cannot be a meaningful category for a scholar uninitiated in the complexities of Japanese culture. As in the traditional Chinese system, described by Marsh, the Japanese had an idealized ranking of occupational roles and assigned farmers a position higher than merchants. This viewpoint becomes understandable if we know that, traditionally, farmers could be enormous land-holders. However, as one might expect, poor farmers and landless tenant farmers made up the bulk of the category, and even persons who worked at agriculture part-time could be considered farmers.

The problems of defining Japanese social strata are compounded in a diachronic study. Not only does the system change with time, but the terms used to designate categories also change in meaning. As Norbeck states, "assignments in social status that might appropriately be given . . . in 1867, 1967, and various points of time between these dates are surely not identical." Like Cohn, Norbeck attempts to deal with the problem of social mobility over a long period of time. There has been relatively little mobility at the extremes of the social hierarchy, but in between—in the middle strata—there has been great mobility. Thus, while most Japanese business leaders come from traditionally elite families, there are some exceptions, such as tenant farmers who rose to become owner-operators as a result of the post-World War II land reforms.

The outcaste groups, traditionally known as Eta, represent another problem in describing and analyzing change. During the past century, this group has increased at least five times faster than the general population—partly by natural increase and partly by drawing members from outside. They no doubt have lost some members as well, although this information is not available, and—lacking indications to the contrary—we must also presume that natural increase can account for only a fraction of this phenomenal growth. If this group were racially or ethnically distinct, a parallel with pluralism might be suggested. Perhaps the concept of caste is applicable here, but Norbeck does not directly deal with this question.

He does, however, touch on some areas that most scholars of social stratification have preferred to avoid: the dimensions of ethic or ideology and social psychological factors concomitant with stratification structures. At some point these facts must be analyzed, not ignored.

Most contributors to this volume have pointed out the importance of the political system to social stratification; yet few have dealt at length with the symbols and behavior that, on the one hand, reflect the unequal distribution of power in a society and, on the other, express the ideology of inequality. Abner Cohen's paper, analyzing the social stratification of a Moslem Arab village in Israel, illustrates the importance of marriage in this context.

Since the choice of spouse is generally acknowledged to be a fundamental index to relative standing in any hierarchical social ordering, it is curious that most writers of comparative studies have seriously neglected to analyze marriage. The works of Lévi-Strauss and Leach, among others, have drawn attention to the fact that judicious marriage choices constitute political facts of life among tribal peoples, just as they do in the modern Western industrial and commercial elite and as they did in the royal families of a past era in Europe. Cohen applies this type of analysis to peasants. He shows how marriage is directly involved with the distribution of economic and political power and, hence, how essential it is to our understanding of stratification in this part of the world. In a manner of speaking—reminiscent of Lévi-Strauss and Leach—women are used like counters in a game of family honor. A woman's marriage is an indicator of the family's social status. Since social status is never to be taken lightly, or placed in jeopardy by the local Romeos and Juliets, it is carefully supervised by the men of consequence in the family.

Cohen directs his attention to the basic social unit of the Middle East—what he terms the "patronymic group," otherwise more loosely called lineage. Tracing its function and relation to the social context of historic periods and the present, he shows how the traditional Arab norm of first-cousin marriage has sometimes strengthened the political unity of the groups and how it also gives the lineage a greater chance for survival as a discrete social group in the face of modern changes. He also notes how this principle of endogamy can conflict with the principle of status equality between the spouses in marriage. For example, during the Mandatory Period, men of wealth married their daughters to families of equal status to uphold their own greater honor, at the same time, however, denying their lineage obligations.

Sydel Silverman's essay has a salutary value for the entire collection in that it raises questions about the boundaries of the unit of study. The two Italian regions of her study, she declares, are not typical of Italy or of the Mediterranean area. They are, however, no less "typical" than any other regions there. That the part cannot stand for the whole is an important theme of this essay, as it is to a lesser extent in the previous chapter by Cohen. This raises another issue: should the unit of comparison be the culture area or a subdivision within the culture area? Cautioning against an indiscriminate generalization on the basis of culture areas, the author shows how Italy, usually regarded as typical and illustrative of a pattern of social stratification common to Mediterranean Europe, contains contrasting systems from region to region. In this study she limits her examples to central and southern Italy, and even within these areas marked differences are evident in the criteria of social status, the structure of the lower class, and the relations between persons of different strata. These distinctions are interwoven with differences in kinship, political behavior, life-styles, and world view.

These regional variations are accounted for, ecologically, in the organization of agriculture and labor and in settlement pattern. In Central Italy they result in the formation of discrete and stable subgroups, but economic arrangements preclude such development in southern Italy. Here no sharp boundaries exist between economic or social categories, with the result that stratification more closely resembles a system of ranking—but ranking of families, not individuals. The two systems, of course, carry very different implications for social mobility. Silverman's chapter demonstrates her concern with inter-relating social class, status group, and political behavior, a concern she shares with several other authors mentioned earlier. Wider generalizations are not precluded by a recognition of regional variations, as

Silverman notes when she states, "In both regions, conformity to urban patterns [of behavior] . . . is perhaps the single most useful measure of one's position among the social classes."

Aidan W. Southall's paper, which follows Silverman's, deals with various types of social stratification traditionally occurring in black Africa and some structural and cultural implications for these and modern developments. Perhaps the essay's greatest value lies in the high level of its theoretical discussion. From his survey of traditional African societies, Southall concludes that two complementary orders are integral to all social systems: an ideological one and a socioeconomic one. The former encompasses moral, sacred, and ethical justifications for the social structure; the latter is the harsh reality of political and economic inequalities. "The two orders need not coincide," the author writes, "but [they] cannot diverge beyond a certain critical point in any system without radical change." Further, he continues, "it is realistic to envisage continuous changes occurring in either order, as well as interaction and accommodation between them, so that some divergence and inconsistency between the two is always likely to remain. . . . The phenomena of stratification and social change cannot be understood unless these two orders are kept conceptually distinct."

Applying these principles to the changes in Western societies over the past few centuries, Southall observes an ideological shift from a premise of inequality to one of equality and an erosion of the ideological order by changes in the socioeconomic order, "so that the former seem to have lost much of the autonomy which it possessed in former ages." Southall, in singling out the symbolic representation and ritual coordination of society to stratification systems, has chosen the most important general issues. In this respect he departs from other writers, most of whom closely examine the relationships between invidious social distinctions and the organization of unequal access to the control of persons and economic resources. While he justifies his unconventional strategy by asserting that all forms of stratification may ultimately be reduced to a binary structure (a structure basic to the nature of human social life), he is not unaware of the limitation of such gross dichotomies. He admits that binary division is merely a useful starting point for further analysis and that it frequently conceals ternary oppositions as well as more complex sectional divisions. These distinctions, it must be understood, are at the level of symbolic representations—namely, culture, which is but one dimension of reality. The other dimension, and not to be confounded with culture, is society, or social structure.

As editors, we admire Southall's courage and willingness to treat such fundamental issues, but we have some reservations about his position. His distinctions between culture and society are not always clear, and his dichotomous divisions may be in complementary and non-hierarchic relationships, which would invalidate them as examples of stratification. Finally, we maintain that the ranking of social roles or statuses is not in itself so indicative of stratification as it is of ranking, as in the case of hunters and gatherers and most pastoralists.

On a more substantive level Southall devotes some attention to the traditional conditions of slavery in Africa. The contrast between the position of slaves there and in Caribbean societies (as described by Smith in chapter 2) raises the question of whether the term "slavery" is sufficient and valid for dealing with the variety of conditions subsumed under this form of servitude. As we are concerned with the influence of traditional systems of stratification on subsequent developments, we may find it helpful to contrast the contemporary conditions of the descendants of slaves in Africa and the Americas.

Although the legal emancipation of slaves occurred about half a century later in Africa than in the Americas, descendants of African slaves suffer no particular stigma, except in those rare cases involving ritual or cult slavery (*osu*). Some individuals, indeed, take pride in their slave ancestry, especially when the forebearers held important slave positions in the political or military establishment. American descendants of African slaves, on the contrary, have yet to lose the mark of ignominious ancestry. Southall explains this contrast in part by pointing out that nowhere in Africa "did slaves in the stricter sense form a distinctive stratum of the population, as in the less elaborated traditional systems." With time, the status of slaves approached more closely that of their masters. In general, he concludes, "the more kin-bound a society is . . . the more fully strangers and captives have to be incorporated and the fewer their practical disabilities."

Finally, Southall cites several reasons why the development of class divisions and class consciousness were inhibited in traditional and modern African societies. In the past, he writes, "the vertical distinctions of lineage might override incipient horizontal divisions," even in hereditary kingdoms. Today, these distinctions are poorly developed because hierarchical ethnic stereotyping—that is, tribal stratification—has assumed widespread and greater importance.

In the concluding essay Reinhard Bendix attempts to revise contemporary views of the development of modern stratification. His scheme lays out the basic form taken by social stratification, calling attention to the variation which occurs within it as a result of late eighteenth-century revolutionary developments.

Professor Bendix reviews the history of ideas connected with modernization and shows how these ideas influence our conceptions of social stratification. In examining the intellectual climate within which our views evolved, he helps us both to appreciate the extent of Marx's influence and to understand the limitations of the Marxian framework when it is applied to modern conditions. One of these limitations is the functionalist view of modern, or modernizing societies, as self-contained structures; a second, stemming from the first, is the belief that modernizing societies recapitulate the developmental steps which first evolved elsewhere. Bendix's implication is that the framework for analysis today is the entire world, either as a single social system or one which has become increasingly unified in modern times as a result of the technological and political revolutions of the eighteenth century.

For Bendix, the characteristic economic basis of modern society originated in the Industrial Revolution in England and continues to develop wherever this technological revolution has penetrated, which, in one form or another, is nearly universal. Equally diffused is the modern political ideology, which began its spread with the French Revolution. For linguistic convenience the English and French models are used, but the origins of these basic transformations of modern social life have wider and deeper roots. As Bendix states, "A basic element in the definition of modernization is that it refers to a type of social change since the eighteenth century, which consists in the economic or political advance of some pioneering societies and subsequent changes in follower societies." It is, therefore, analytically unsound not to consider a society's external setting when dealing with social changes of such magnitude as modernization and its concomitant changes in social stratification. The influence of international communication, for example, is so great as to transform radically conditions in developing nations, thereby precluding the view that they are analogues of western European countries in the late eighteenth century. This being the case, the important role of intellectuals and government officials in transforming the economy and social structure of their developing countries is clear. The part they play in the development of social stratification in the new nations is equally important, for government employment is one of the major avenues of social mobility and thus "becomes a major basis of social stratification."

Bendix regards the search for a single or unified theory of social stratification as fruitless; the phenomenon is simply too complex. He and other contributors to this volume do, however, deal with several closely related issues. .These include the relative rates of social mobility between different strata at different periods of a society, or between different forms that stratification has taken in it, and the status incongruities or inconsistencies that occur within a relatively stable system of stratification or, under conditions of change, inconsistencies that indicate cultural lags or retentions. Our tendency is to assume that a concordance must exist between economic and political controls so that those who hold power in one sphere do so equally in the other, and that social mobility is a sum-zero game in which upward and downward mobility are counterbalanced. But these theories are inapplicable to conditions of change. Cohn reminds us that a society is not a closed system that requires some men to fall if others rise, and Bendix points out the discordance between economic and political controls in the course of European industrialization when, for some time, government employment remained the birthright of a traditional elite, the nobility. European aristocrats lost their economic preeminence to the rising bourgeoisie, but they retained political dominance long after the erosion of the economic foundations upon which their authority was established.

*   *   *

The contributors to this volume have dealt with different parts of the world and various forms of stratification, but the collection of papers, viewed as a whole, also displays some convergences on future research problems and theoretical agreements.

To the editors, one salient generalization emerges: that rarely does a society exhibit only one form of stratification or a single means of recruiting individuals into its component strata. Only incompletely and inaccurately can societies be described as "caste" or "class," "ascription-based" or "achievement-oriented." In India, Japan, Africa, and, many would argue, the United States, castes co-exist with other forms of socially structured inequalities such as social classes. In some of these societies, social classes co-exist with racial or ethnic discriminations, a situation taken as the hallmark of sociocultural pluralism. Even when a society can be characterized by a single system of stratification, variations within the system are found from region to region (as in Italy) or between town and country. Directly or indirectly, about half the contributors have stressed the importance of examining the rural as well as the urban areas of a society. In the past, studies of social stratification have been too heavily oriented to cities, a trend which overlooks the variations and, more specifically, the relationships between the two ways of life. The studies by Marsh and Norbeck attest to the importance of including rural areas in our investigations, and Cohn specifically states that to restrict the study of elite recruitment to cities is to ignore significant factors.

The number of societies exhibiting two or more types of social stratification is considerable and, according to Bendix's implications, may indeed be on the increase. The variations of one type of stratification—be it class, caste, or pluralism—among different societies can often be attributed to difference of autonomous development, but it is not so easy to explain regional variations in the same type of stratification within a single culture, as in Italy. Here, we think, Silverman's analysis of human ecological factors is a significant contribution. Certainly we must admit that it is insufficient to attribute such conditions solely to external circumstances such as conquest and the imposition of alien cultures and organization.

These papers underline the need for further research into the factors which produce variations within a type—whether these are regional, urban-rural, or coextensive within a single population of one locality. Even the limited examples provided by the contributors to this volume clearly demonstrate that many factors are involved, among them different ecological conditions and different regional histories. Another factor also may be significant: the degree of political control. A weak central government with diffuse political controls (as in Italy and India) apparently encourages local variation; a strong state government (as in the Republic of South Africa), on the other hand, seems to minimize it, even under conditions that would lead us to expect great regional variation.

On the other hand, some modern societies with widely differing cultural heritages and histories share, in their own variations, a common form of stratification—social class. What is the significance of the similarity in the hierarchy of occupational evaluations among Taiwan, Japan, the Philippines, and Western Europe? Bendix, certainly, does not suggest that this is a simple case of diffusion. Does it mean that, when a society imports a particular economic organization, certain cultural concomitants must necessarily follow? If so, is this the result of historical coincidence or a close correspondence between forms of structure and culture? To what extent may these factors vary independently? This general problem area is currently attracting the attention of social scientists, and we expect it to become increasingly significant in comparative studies of stratification.

Studies of social change and social mobility are respectable as areas of theoretical research, and we do not foresee that they will be neglected by scholars in the future, but the articles in this volume suggest other specific problems and research areas. The historical dimension, in particular, may be crucial for some areas of analysis.

The influence of past systems on subsequent developments, for example, is a probable factor in the contrasting conditions of the descendants of slaves in Africa and in the New World. Here the different systems of slavery must be given prominent consideration.

A second research problem area deals with the existence and extent of status continuities during periods of system change. This was a primary concern in the essays of Cohn and Marsh, and it was central to Norbeck's study. Blessed as we are with such folk wisdoms as "plus ça change, plus c'est la même chose" and "the rich get richer and the poor get poorer," we have as yet no precise generalizations which apply to changes in systems of stratification. It appears that in most cases members of the elite in a former system become the elite in a new system. Norbeck tells us that there is relatively little change in the extremes of the hierarchy but much movement in between. Although we know that Indian castes elbow one another for room near the top so that over a period of time castes change position, we recognize that this does not involve a change of system. And even in the Industrial Revolution, the rising bourgeoisie did not replace the traditional aristocracy; rather, Bendix reminds us, the two groups shared the uppermost class to their mutual benefit, performing complementary functions.

The example of European aristocrats' retaining their high position shows that, even when a system changes, a group can preserve the same relative position within the new hierarchy. Problems of conceptualization and explanation, however, arise when a group undergoes changes of function so that it cannot be identified readily by its former characteristics. As an example Cohn reports the disappearance or elimination of landlords as a traditional class. The ex-landlords, in a new role as entrepreneurs in urban industry and commerce, retain their former stratum position relative to other groups. This transformation makes it very difficult to classify the group, either as ex-landlords, a new stratum, or as new bourgeoisie.

A related problem concerns the conditions of social mobility. The editors believe that this concept should be restricted to individual or group changes in stratum position within a system but not to changes between systems or under conditions of social change. To illustrate, let us take, as a hypothetical example, a low-caste Indian who emigrates as a plantation laborer to Africa or the Caribbean, subsequently becoming a wealthy trader in his new location. In the new society he may, by virtue of being a wealthy businessman, hold one position in its system of stratification, but should he return to his natal society, he would revert to his low-caste position. This example is analogous to changes in the system of stratification within a society.

One of the problems in attempting to view mobility *between* systems is the non-comparability of different systems. The structures are different; the shapes of the pyramids are different. Nonetheless, we might well probe the question of whether different rates of mobility are associated with different systems: Are mobility rates, for example, highest in a system of social classes because its ideology is achievement-oriented? Evidence now shows that this is not a sound conclusion. Although the theoretical problems pertaining to comparative mobility rates have yet to be satisfactorily resolved, there is strong indication that mobility rates—including the social mobility of slaves—were much higher in traditional African systems of stratification than in modern industrial societies.

Possibly the mobility rates within a particular system change with the development or evolution of the system, showing a greater degree of flux in the early stages than in the later and more mature form of the system. Finally, we may note here an observation of Benedict's: "The more rigid the stratification, the more culturally distinct are its strata because mobility and communication between members of different strata are restricted." This suggests a circular, or feedback, process between mobility and the form of the stratification system, a possibility that might well be examined in future research. Hopefully, one would find a cause-and-effect relation in addition to concomitant variation.

Motivation, ideology, and the social psychological dimensions of social stratification are research areas that merit—even demand—more serious attention in future studies. We also recognize that these non-structural aspects resist easy handling, a reason, perhaps, why so few of our contributors have attempted to come to grips with these problems. These fundamental issues may be postponed, but they cannot be avoided.

Political and economic coercion alone cannot hold a system together. To some extent, every system of social inequalities must be "sold" and accepted ideologically. How people are motivated to accept inferior positions or to seek and work for superior ones and even how they come to reject the ideology of one system in favor of another are all relevant research problems for which we lack adequate empirical and theoretical material. The task is by no means easy; in some cases, where the types of stratification vary, we find that the basic ideological principles can be contradictory. How, for example, can social class and caste or pluralism co-exist when the principles of status recruitment are as mutually opposed as achievement and ascription? The general theoretical view of such circumstances, that of incompatible pattern variables, is interpreted as an indication of change from one type of stratification to another. Yet, such conditions may indicate something entirely different: that, perhaps, a society may accommodate a greater variety of structures and ideologies than has been assumed possible. People are probably more flexible in compartmentalizing their lives and adjusting to complex conditions than we would believe.

In the earlier discussion of Cohen's paper on Arab villages, several issues relating to the study of marriage as an aspect of social stratification were raised as possibilities for future research. In addition we note here another. Although one assumes a high degree of endogamy within a social stratum, there have been few comparative studies to provide quantitative data on this aspect. We know that, even when there is good reason to believe that the statistical norm will closely approximate the cultural norm of endogamy, as in India, there are exceptions to the rule, but we do not know the implications for social stratification of exogamy. When people marry out, they usually marry up or down, although marrying out may also involve a horizontal move. In any case, a study of marriage may provide useful insights into fundamental structural aspects of stratification. One problem which bears exploring is whether different forms of stratification—slavery, pluralism, and social class, for example—are related to stratum endogamy —and if so, in what respect. The implications and consequences will surely be quite different from system to system.

Turning to problems of research methods, we observe that the authors, with the exception of Glick and Marsh, seem to lack concern for considerations of research techniques and related matters. In general they provide neither a detailed explanation of how they derived the outlines of the hierarchical divisions they describe nor the criteria used in defining these social groupings. These omissions may be largely attributed to the fact that their papers were prepared for a symposium, for the authors are not remiss in this regard in their other publications. Certainly, considerations of methodology and the quantification of description may not be neglected; indeed, they can be quite instructive. For example, Marsh's construction of an index of perceived social usefulness for various occupations is a relatively simple procedure that can be employed for both comparative synchronic studies (between contemporary societies) and historical comparisons. In this study Marsh, in focusing on problems of change, has arrived at some stimulating hypotheses regarding expanding and contracting occupations. As he says, "societal prestige is a conservative force, while self-evaluation of occupational utility is a more sensitizing predictive factor."

Our final point for discussion, which could very well have come first, is the basic question of whether social stratification is a universal human phenomenon. Sociologists tend to think it is; anthropologists tend to think it is not. In support of their position, sociologists cite ethnographic examples of stratification among primitive people, usually hunters and gatherers. Anthropologists, in response, declare that these are examples of social ranking, suggesting that sociologists lack a command of the anthropological literature. To this the sociologists counter with the accusation that anthropologists do not know the sociological publications, especially the theoretical works. The controversy appears to boil down to the claim that anthropologists have the comparative empirical data, while the sociologists control the relevant theory. Seen from the perspectives of the opposing camps, the anthropologists fail to recognize stratification in their own research provenances, while the sociologists are either culture-bound or cannot distinguish between stratification and social ranking. The editors, speaking from more than a disciplinary allegiance to anthropology, regard the distinction between stratification and ranking as valid and important.

One contributor, a sociologist, illustrates the issue with his definition of social stratification as "the structure of differential evaluations of, and attached to, roles in the division of labor." According to this definition social stratification would indeed be universal, for even the most simply organized societies have a division of labor based on age and sex, the roles differentiated by those axes are evaluated and given unequal esteem, and rewards are allocated accordingly. Yet one cannot discern strata based on these distinctions unless they are sex-specific (that is, all men rated superior to all women). And even this condition is not analogous to one in which social groups are given hierarchical positions within complex societies.

This issue leads to our concluding point, which—unlike that of other recent symposia—is *not* an optimistic resolution to pursue further research in some interdisciplinary fashion with the hope of reaching an otherwise unattainable degree of understanding. This idea, we feel, is seductive, unrealistic, and—possibly—detrimental. No amount of further research will resolve the theoretical question of whether social stratification is a universal phenomenon, but an increased amount of cross-disciplinary communication is certainly a move in the right direction. Our point is that, while it is indeed quite desirable to join forces, we must be prepared to disagree.

One discipline's theories and methods may be more effective than another's for dealing with the particular problems in studying social stratification, but we must recognize also the possibility that different disciplinary perspectives may serve only to complement one another. For example, the traditional anthropological interest in comparative studies has influenced other social sciences, just as the topic of social stratification and the concerns with quantification of data, long the bailiwick of sociology, are attracting the attention of anthropologists and other social scientists.

We do not foresee—nor would we invite—a future of amalgamation of the social sciences. While we think there will be continued overlapping of interests, we believe that the principal concerns and methods of these individual disciplines will remain distinct. We do hope, however, that the studies in this volume will encourage an objective and realistic appreciation of the respective strengths of history, anthropology, and sociology so that these may be employed most beneficially in further interdisciplinary efforts aimed at the comparative study of social stratification.

Part I

Social Pluralism

Chapter 1/ Burton Benedict

Pluralism
and Stratification

The concept of social or cultural pluralism has its champions (e.g., Rex 1959; M. G. Smith 1960, 1965a; Berreman 1967; van den Berghe 1964) and its detractors (e.g., Braithwaite 1960; Benedict 1962; Morris 1957, 1966; R. T. Smith 1958, 1961). The former see it as an analytic tool of some importance, possibly defining a separate type of society. The latter see it as a label of convenience which can lead to considerable confusion. Clearly the usefulness of the concept depends on the kind of problem one wishes to investigate. It may be more useful for work on cultural differences within a society than for examining the political and economic structure of that society. In this paper I shall examine the ways in which the concept of pluralism has been used by its proponents, particularly in relation to social stratification.

The term "plural society" came to the attention of anthropologists through the writings of J. S. Furnivall, who served for twenty years in the civil service in Burma and wrote extensively on that country and on what was then the Netherlands East Indies. The idea of the plural society derived from the work of Dutch economists, notably J. H. Boeke (1953). Boeke

---

Since this paper was written, a number of important works on pluralism have appeared, for example, L. A. Despres (1967) *Cultural Pluralism and Nationalist Politics in British Guiana;* L. Kuper and M. G. Smith, eds. (1969) *Pluralism in Africa;* P. L. van den Berghe (1967) *Race and Racism.* They have not been taken into account in this article.

29

proposed the notion of a dual economy consisting of capitalist and pre-capitalist parts, the latter having low or non-existent economic values, an idea which has been firmly refuted by Firth (1929) and many later economic anthropologists. Furnivall developed the plural society concept in such works as *Netherlands India: A Study of a Plural Economy* (1939), "The Political Economy of the Tropical Far East" (1942), "Some Problems of Tropical Economy" (1945), and *Colonial Policy and Practice* (1948). He set out the following as the general characteristics of a plural society:

1. The plural society is a result of colonialism, that is, the imposition of alien rule.

2. The sections of a plural society are defined in ethnic terms.

3. The sections are separate. They are held together only by a Western administrative system which had either abolished or fatally weakened the indigenous administrative system.

4. The only interaction between members of different sections of the population is in the market place. An economic division of labor, defined by racial lines, evolved because of the conquest situation and expediency. (The British found it easier, for example, to use Indian labor in Burma than to train Burmans and learn Burmese. And the Indians were cheaper, especially if they were convicts. The Burmans were left as cultivators, and the Indians went into trade. Elsewhere the Chinese filled this role.)

5. There is a lack of what Furnivall calls "a common social will" (1942:202 f.) or "social demand" (ibid., 200 f.). Each section has its own values and standards which do not extend across ethnic barriers. Consensus is difficult, if not impossible, to obtain. There are no agreed goals or common social or moral standards. Hence exploitation of one section by another is rife since there is no common social demand against it. Market relations are what Rex calls "raw" (1959:115).

6. Each section is incomplete: It is not a corporate or organic whole. The life of the colonial administrators centers in the club. The home, wives, and children are missing as are most home institutions. The immigrant communities are also incomplete, lacking the cultural and structural features of life in their homelands. Even the native life is incomplete due to the breakdown of indigenous social structure. (It seems not to have occurred to Furnivall that these might be indications of the development of new institutions.)

The feature of Furnivall's theory which attracted M. G. Smith and Rex was the idea of the lack of a common social will. This they have used to attack Parsonian theories (1953) of the integration of society through a common institutional structure and common values. P. L. van den Berghe (1964) also attacks this idea in his study of Caneville, a pluralistic community in Natal (p. 243 f.) although he admits that Caneville does constitute a social system and that people interact in a well-structured, predictable fashion and are interdependent (p. 244). Rex, on the other hand, sees a plural society as showing endemic imperfect institutionalization and maintains that it is a laboratory for studying social change and race relations. He asks whether Weber's and Parsons' functional integrative theories of a society are correct or whether theories of social conflict are more appropriate.

A major trouble here is a confusion of levels of abstraction. Weber's and Parsons' theories are *general* theories of society. They deal with society at a highly abstract level, with its functional prerequisites (Aberle et al. 1950). At this level one can talk about a society as an integrated whole in the sense that the war of all against all is precluded and that certain society-wide institutions are functioning. This still leaves room for conflict—but at a lower level of abstraction. It is perfectly possible to focus attention on conflict without assuming a total lack of consensus in the society. I think it can be shown that in situations of conflict, except perhaps truly revolutionary ones, there is a good deal of consensus about goals even though there may be considerable disagreement about how to reach them or who is to reach them.

Failure to appreciate this point is very clear in the work of M. G. Smith. In *Stratification in Grenada* (1965b) Smith takes the system of social stratification in this small West Indian island to "prove" that a plural society is a different species of society and one to which Parsonian concepts of consensus do not apply. He runs into three difficulties: (1) the definition of society, (2) the degree of consensus about a common value system, and (3)—really an aspect of (2)—the notion that stratification implies radically different values in each stratum. Let us examine these "difficulties" in detail:

1. *Definition.* Most social anthropologists would agree with Nadel (1951:183–88) that ultimately a society must be defined in political terms. Nadel defines society as "an aggregate of human beings who co-ordinate their efforts for the employment of force against others and for elimination

of force between them and who usually count as their principal estate the possession and utilization of a territory" (p. 187). As Mintz (1966) points out in his review of Smith's book, *The Plural Society in the British West Indies,* if one defines a society as a political unit then plural societies are societies by definition, that is, units only in a political sense.

2. *Consensus about a common value system.* The second difficulty involves the question of how separate the sections are in a plural society. Do they really meet only in the market place? Are the institutional complexes of each section so different that we can really treat them as separate entities or are there important areas of interrelations between them? Are there institutions which transcend individual sections and are common to the whole society?

A number of anthropologists and sociologists (e.g., Rex 1959; Morris 1957, 1966; Braithwaite 1960; Benedict 1962; R. T. Smith 1958, 1961; Belshaw 1965) have criticized Furnivall's contention of the separateness of the ethnic sections. Rex states that there is insufficient analysis of the market. Furnivall, he believes, does not show how far ethnic groups are economically specialized and how far they are integrated to form new groupings and institutions. Rex cites Malinowski (1945) who, in a three-column approach, saw new institutions arising as a result of contact between indigenous and European institutions in Africa. Belshaw (1965) shows that people in all sections of a plural society are interested in maximizing profits, although profits may be variously defined, thus leading to different kinds of maximization. Yet once this is granted, we have a wide variety of institutions which may not be congruent with ethnic groups. Since members of various ethnic sections participate in the market, one must turn from an analysis of ethnic sections to an analysis of the economic structure as a whole. The question becomes how far different groups (and we must not beg the question by defining them ethnically) participate in different kinds of economic institutions. We may find different types of economic institutions characterizing different sections of the population, but sections may have to be defined as cash and subsistence or rural and urban or commercial and non-commercial. In this way we would be defining the sections structurally and not by cultural criteria. The fact that in some societies the sections can be distinguished ethnically or culturally does not assist us in the analysis; on the contrary, it hinders us by leading us to categorize individuals in one or another ethnic or cultural section rather than attempting to fit them into a particular economic sphere.

The points at which such economic spheres interact are highly significant. It is at just such points, as Barth (1966:18) stresses, that entrepreneurs operate and that bridging institutions develop. A good example of entrepreneurs who perform bridging transactions between spheres of economic activity is Epstein's account (1964: 58 ff.) of To Dungan, who bridged the shell money and cash spheres among the Tolai of New Britain. A plural society with Chinese, Europeans and Tolai, New Britain, according to Epstein, has an economy composed of three sectors: subsistence, shell money, and cash. While it is true that the Chinese and Europeans operate almost entirely in the cash sector and the Tolai largely in the subsistence and shell money sectors, this does not carry our analysis very far. We need to look at the economy as a whole, to see the ways in which the cash, shell money, and subsistence sectors interact. Only then can we understand why shell money persists and the ways in which cash penetrates into the ongoing economy of the Tolai. The cash sector, in other words, does not have ethnic boundaries.

My point is that concentration on pluralism diverts attention away from an analysis of the economy as a whole. Entrepreneurs in plural societies compete for laborers or customers from all ethnic sections. The effects of urbanization show the many ways in which members of the various ethnic sections of a plural society are interrelated in economic institutions. It is difficult, if not impossible, to do an economic analysis of a plural society without analyzing the society as a whole.

3. *Differing values.* It is in the system of social stratification that the proponents of the plural society concept see the real challenge to Parsonian theories of a common value system. In his book, *Stratification in Grenada,* M. G. Smith tries to show that Grenada is a plural society because of differing values and institutions among the elite. He shows that 403 individuals listed in the *Grenada Handbook and Directory for 1946* are divided into four ranked strata by cliques, clubs, occupations, income, landholding, color, marriage, and kinship patterns, etc. He claims these four ranked strata represent "two antithetical and dissonant sets of value orientations" (p. 251). The high strata stress ascriptive values such as descent, color, and the inheritance of property. They form themselves into exclusive cliques. The lower strata stress individual achievement. This sounds very much like the differences between the "haves" and the "have-nots" and can hardly be said to prove that the society is plural, unless we grant that all stratified societies are plural. (This points to one of the greatest pitfalls into which

the plural society concept can lead.) Similarly Berreman (1967) maintains that India is a plural society because castes are culturally distinct (p. 48). But the same point might be made about class stratified societies—as indeed it has been made by Weber—for this is just the distinction between class and status group. As I tried to show in an earlier paper (1962), when we talk about stratification, we are talking about structure. When we talk about plural societies, we are talking about ethnic or cultural categories. In that paper, using Mauritius as an example, I tried to show that we could not distinguish strata on the cultural bases of language, nationality, and religion alone. If I had used associational or kinship institutions peculiar to each section as a basis for the study, I still would not have been able to define a system of social stratification. A description of cultural categories is not an analysis of the relations between the categories; rather, one must turn from an analysis of the cultural traits in each section of a plural society to the major political and economic institutions of the total society. Europeans in Mauritius or South Africa hold positions at the top of the social hierarchy not because of ethnic or cultural characteristics but because they control the political, legal, and economic machinery of the society.

The confusion attendant in inserting ethnic criteria in an analysis of stratification can be seen in *Ethnic Stratification* by Shibutani and Kwan. At one point the authors state, "In a stable system of ethnic stratification there is no direct competition among people in the different ethnic categories" (p. 261). But the ethnic distinctiveness of the strata is not material to the analysis. The estate system of medieval Europe eliminated competition between strata, but it was not a plural society. Similarly India is not generally regarded as a plural society; yet the caste system, classically described, eliminated competition between strata. The important variable here is the type of stratification rather than the cultural or ethnic distinctiveness of the strata. The more rigid the stratification, the more culturally distinct are its strata because mobility and communication between members of the different strata are restricted. The definition of strata by ethnic criteria is only one of a number of possibilities, and of course ethnic differences in a society do not necessarily mean that social strata will be defined ethnically.

But let us return to the question of the presence or absence of a common social will in a plural society. Let us hypothesize a rigid system of social stratification with marked cultural (and ethnic, too, if you like) differences between the strata. How far do individuals in such a system lack a common social will?

Shibutani and Kwan stress that a stable system of stratification rests on consensus and that, even in situations of social change, members of the lower strata aspire to the values of the higher strata. A good deal of evidence supports this view although a cultural lag may cause the lower strata to adopt values which are already being rejected by the higher strata. For example, studies of upwardly mobile Negroes in the United States and the West Indies (e.g., Dollard 1937; Clarke 1957) have revealed an adoption of Victorian middle-class standards which had already been rejected by upper- and middle-class whites, and studies in India have shown lower castes sanskritizing their rituals at a time when upper castes were rejecting these rituals in favor of Westernization (Srinivas 1962). It appears that lower strata rarely challenge the system as such—but only their place in it. In any situation short of a revolutionary one, there must be a large measure of agreement on the goals for which individuals are striving. Despite Smith's protestations to the contrary, this would seem to be the case in Grenada.

I think much of the trouble here lies in such vague phrases as "common social will," "social demand," and "common values." What does Furnivall mean by such phrases? In the 1942 article he gives two examples, both from Rangoon. In the first he cites sanitary arrangements: People were in the habit of using a patch of jungle as a public convenience, but, when fuel became scarce, they cut trees from this patch—and persisted in doing so even after the Commissioner, in response to agitation by Europeans, passed orders that no one should cut fuel near the town. This, he says, is an instance of individual demand prevailing over social demand. In the second example Furnivall maintains that rickshaws persist in Rangoon because "all classes alike have an economic interest in the retention of rickshaws, but there is no common standard of social decency, no social demand that can be mobilized against them" (p. 201). He contrasts this with England, where "the individual demand for cheap conveyances is overborne by the social demand for human decency" (ibid.). Apart from his obvious ethnocentrism, what makes Furnivall so sure that the demands for fuel and rickshaws are not social demands? Or is he really saying simply that they are not the social demands of twentieth-century England? How are we to estimate, let alone measure, social demand or common values? In England, as Furnivall admits on the same page, this factor is measured in elections. If this is the measure, he can hardly complain that disenfranchised Burmans lack a common social will when they fail to carry out the Commissioner's order not to cut fuel. And, if all classes have a common economic interest in the retention of rickshaws, does this show a lack of common values? The fact that the Burmese lack what Furnivall considers a common standard of social decency is not relevant to the question. If they shared Furnivall's values, they clearly would not tolerate rickshaws; they appear, however, to have values which not only tolerate but actively demand rickshaws. An analysis in terms of common values, it seems to me, is bound to run into serious difficulties. Not only is it difficult to identify the values—let alone a common social will—but it is even more difficult to measure them. As social anthropologists, we should look not at common social will but at common social interactions.

Any discussion of the plural society and its relation to the system of social stratification must focus largely on the political system. Furnivall predicated the existence of the plural society on the imposition of alien rule. The degree of mobility permitted between sections of a plural society, stratified or not, is a function of the type of political system. And when Furnivall was writing about common social will, as we have just seen, he took elections, a political manifestation, as the means of determining it.

Those who claim theoretical importance for the plural society concept see the political dimension as crucial. The plural society is a society held together by force exercised by a ruling minority, typically an imperialist power, as opposed to a society held together by consensus. These may have some use as polar models, but it is clear that known societies fall between the two extremes. South Africa is more nearly the plural society held together by force while the United Kingdom more closely resembles the consensus model; yet we find some consensus in South Africa and some force in Britain. The important point, however, is that a society need not be plural to fit this model. Nazi Germany and Fascist Italy were held together by force, yet they were hardly plural. Switzerland, the Lebanon, Brazil, and Belgium approach the consensus model but a case could be made for calling them plural societies. Even Britain has Scottish and Welsh nationalists who occasionally resort to violence. This again points to the danger in viewing all differences as evidence of pluralism. What we need to consider is not the degree of pluralism but the type of political structure. Social mobility is a crucial variable. When little mobility is permitted, the separation of sections is preserved and strengthened, thus requiring more and more force to hold the society together. Here a good example is South Africa, where laws and rights differ for Europeans, coloreds, and Africans, intermixing is severely discouraged, and wages, occupations, voting rights, and residence are all strictly defined by ethnic group. Other types of political systems also operate in this manner. Property qualifications on the franchise, prevalent in many British colonies and, indeed, in many Western countries not so long ago, separated sections of the population. Ethnic and cultural differences between the poorer and the wealthier sections also strengthen the distinction between them. The system of indirect rule, found in many former African colonies, also fosters pluralism by establishing different sets of rights for tribal and non-tribal peoples.

You will note, however, that even in these variants of what might be called an estate system (that is, a system of stratification in which the strata are legally defined), we are looking at the whole system, not just one section within it. All systems of social stratification are *systems* and could not function if there were no common understandings (Berreman 1967:53). In all systems of social stratification the allocation of power is crucial, but it is an error—and one into which concentration on pluralism can lead—to think that the power is held by the members of a single ethnic or cultural group. It is held not by an ethnic group as a whole but by certain sections or families within the group (Parsons 1940).

I maintain that when we examine societies in terms of pluralism we are looking at differences in culture, not in structure. A structural analysis must determine whether any cultural traits in a given section of the population favor or militate against its members' participation in the political or economic structures of the society as a whole—for example, the prohibition of usury for Christians in the Middle Ages, the prohibitions against caste Hindus becoming butchers or shoemakers or against Muslims dealing in pork products. These are all examples of cultural features which affect the occupational structure of the whole society.

In examining the power structure of a plural society, we will want to see how far the ethnic sections within the society are groups and for what purposes they act corporately. This is apt to be a concomitant variation of the political structure itself and will vary from society to society and over a period of time.

As an example let me cite my own field work from Mauritius (Benedict 1961, 1965). A small island in the Indian Ocean about five hundred miles east of Madagascar, Mauritius had no indigenous inhabitants. Today it contains over three-quarters of a million people in an area of 720 square miles. Ethnically and culturally, the population can be divided into Indians, both Muslim and Hindu of many castes, several sects, and five linguistic groups who together make up two-thirds of the population; Creoles of mixed African or Indian and European descent, both Catholic and Protestant, and with many social distinctions based on skin color and education (28 per cent); Chinese, both Hakka and Cantonese speakers, practicing Chinese and Christian religions (3 per cent); and Europeans, mostly of French extraction but including a number of Britons (2 per cent). Traditionally these sections were stratified with the Europeans owning the sugar estates and having top managerial and governmental positions, the Creoles in the white-collar occupations and working as artisans, the Chinese in retail trade, and the Indians as agricultural laborers. This is very crude delineation, and one could find a large number of exceptions. Even at an early date many Indians were traders, large numbers of Creoles were laborers and poor fishermen, and by no means were all the Europeans rich and powerful. The ethnic sections of the population were not corporate groups, but *most* retailers were Chinese, *most* laborers were Indians, and *most* estate owners were Europeans. I have analyzed elsewhere (1962) how, in the course of time, this structure underwent a change and class strata appeared within each ethnic section. This did not at first necessarily diminish the pluralism of Mauritius, but it produced parallel strata within each section. Upper-class Indians, Creoles, and Europeans, however, began to find that they had economic and political interests in common, and this tended to break down the barriers between them. Lower classes found similar common economic and political interests. In the middle strata, on the other hand, where competition for upward social mobility was greatest, there was a tendency to symbolize competition in ethnic terms. Nevertheless, if we look at the economic structure of Mauritius, we do not find that the sections of the plural society form corporate groups (Benedict 1965: chap. 3). There is economic mobility, sometimes even accompanied by a change of community.

Changes in economic stratification took place during a period when the power situation remained more or less constant. Mauritius was a Crown Colony, ultimately controlled from London. In 1967 Mauritius became an independent nation within the British Commonwealth, a parliamentary democracy based on the Westminster model. In this form of government obtaining office depends upon the number of supporters a candidate has, and Mauritian politicians are now appealing to electors along those lines which they hope will win them the greatest numbers of supporters. Consequently ethnic, cultural, linguistic, and religious criteria are becoming important symbols for political affiliation. A brief historical résumé of the political development of the island will show the ways in which this situation has arisen.

The constitution of 1831 provided for a Council of Government composed of seven official members and seven non-official members, all of whom were chosen by the Governor. They were mainly Europeans, chosen from the planter and commercial class, and they tended to be re-appointed. (One served for twenty-four years.) Under this constitution, which remained in force for fifty-five years, all power rested with the Europeans, in effect with the British administrators. The most effective political opposition came from European and Creole planters and professionals, who in 1882 petitioned Queen Victoria for an elective element in the constitution. In 1886 a new constitution was granted, providing for a council of eight official members, nine nominated members (some of them officials), and ten elected members. Power still rested with the administration. The franchise was restricted to males who had an income of at least Rs.50 per month or who owned or rented substantial property, leaving the vast majority of the Indians and most of the Creoles without the vote. As far as politics was organized, in ethnic terms it was a struggle between the Creoles and the British, who were supported by many wealthy Franco-Mauritian planters, but the restriction on the franchise meant this was a struggle between the relatively well-to-do. In 1891 the population of Mauritius was 370,588, but the total electorate was only 5,164 and only 298 Hindus and 103 Muslims voted (*Mauritius Blue Book,* 1892, p. J.1).

Sixty-two years later, in 1948, a new constitution was introduced. This provided for a Legislative Council of three officials, twelve non-official nominees, and nineteen elected members. The franchise, with a simple literacy or property-holding qualification, was extended to both sexes, and the electorate increased from about 12,000 in 1946 to nearly 72,000 in 1948. This brought a radical change in the political situation. Creoles and Franco-Mauritians became less concerned with their position vis-à-vis the British administrators but more concerned with their position as ethnic minorities faced with an overwhelming Indian electorate. Thus ethnic identity took on a new meaning. While some Creole intellectuals and Creole workers joined the Indians in the Labour Party (which had been founded by Creoles), others drew closer to the Franco-Mauritians. Creole and Franco-Mauritian newspapers began to print articles about "the Hindu menace" and to appeal to common cultural, linguistic, and religious traditions binding Creoles and Franco-Mauritians together. This process, which has been accelerating, also made Indians more aware of their cultural distinctiveness. It is a process which Bateson (1935) long ago termed schizomogenesis. Muslims, fearing for their minority status vis-à-vis Hindus, formed their own party. In the 1963 elections, in which there was universal adult suffrage, some Hindus began to make appeals on the basis of still narrower cultural criteria. Tamil and Telugu organizations appeared, and the low castes were urged to organize against the high castes. Thus we see that a wide variety of cultural symbols are available for use in a political context. Prior to 1948 the ethnic sections of Mauritius were mere categories or, perhaps, what Ginsberg (1934) has called quasi-groups or potential groups with no corporate functions. In the political climate after 1948 and increasingly with the approach of independence, these quasi-groups became corporate in a political context. Cultural criteria such as caste, which had been all but ignored previously, are becoming important symbols of political alignment. It is on this level that pluralism becomes important in ethnically diverse societies such as Mauritius, Malaysia, Guyana, and Fiji, but it is also important in Belgium, the Lebanon, and Canada. In the first instance it is not the pluralism but the politics we must examine.

REFERENCES

Aberle, D. F., A. K. Cohen, A. K. Davis, M. J. Levy, Jr., and F. X. Sutton (1950) "The Functional Pre-requisites of a Society," *Ethics* 60:101–11.

Barth, F. (1966) *Models of Social Organization.* Royal Anthropological Institute Occasional Paper No. 23. London.

Bateson, G. (1935) "Culture Contact and Schizomogenesis," *Man* 35: 178–83.

Belshaw, C. S. (1965) *Traditional Exchange and Modern Markets.* Englewood Cliffs, N. J.

Benedict, B. (1961) *Indians in a Plural Society: A Report on Mauritius.* London.

———— (1962) "Stratification in Plural Societies," *American Anthropologist* 64: 1235–46.

———— (1965) *Mauritius: Problems of a Plural Society.* London.

Berreman, G. D. (1967) "Stratification, Pluralism and Interaction: A Comparative Analysis of Caste," in *Ciba Foundation Symposium on Caste and Race: Comparative Approaches,* eds. A. V. S. de Reuck and J. Knight. London.

Boeke, J. H. (1953) *Economics and Economic Policy of Dual Societies as Exemplified by Indonesia.* Haarlem.

Braithwaite, L. (1960) "Social Stratification and Cultural Pluralism," in *Social and*

Cultural Pluralism in the Caribbean, ed. V. Rubin. Annals of the New York Academy of Sciences 83, art. 5, pp. 816–31.

Clarke, E. (1957) *My Mother Who Fathered Me.* London.

Dollard, J. (1937) *Caste and Class in a Southern Town.* New York.

Epstein, T. S. (1964) "Personal Capital Formation Among the Tolai of New Britain," in *Capital, Saving and Credit in Peasant Societies,* eds. R. Firth and B. S. Yamey. London.

Firth, R. (1929) *Primitive Economics of the New Zealand Maori.* London.

Furnivall, J. S. (1939) *Netherlands India: A Study of Plural Economy.* London.

————— (1942) "The Political Economy of the Tropical Far East," *Royal Central Asian Journal* 29, pts. III and IV:195–210.

————— (1945) "Some Problems of Tropical Economy," in *Fabian Colonial Essays,* ed. R. Hinden. London.

————— (1948) *Colonial Policy and Practice.* London.

Ginsberg, M. (1934) *Sociology.* London.

Malinowski, B. (1945) *The Dynamics of Culture Change: An Inquiry into Race Relations in Africa.* New Haven.

The Mauritius Blue Book. (1892) Port Louis, Mauritius.

Mintz, S. W. (1966) Review of M. G. Smith, *The Plural Society in the British West Indies, American Anthropologist* 68:1045–47.

Morris, H. S. (1957) "The Plural Society," *Man* 57:124–25.

————— (1966) Review of M. G. Smith, *The Plural Society in the British West Indies, Man,* n.s. 1:270–71.

Nadel, S. F. (1951) *The Foundations of Social Anthropology.* London.

Parsons, T. (1940) "An Analytical Approach to the Theory of Social Stratification," *American Journal of Sociology* 45:841–62.

————— (1953) "A Revised Analytical Approach to the Theory of Social Stratification," in *Class, Status and Power,* eds. R. Bendix and S. M. Lipset. Glencoe, Ill.

Rex, J. (1959) "The Plural Society in Sociological Theory," *British Journal of Sociology* 10:114–24.

Shibutani, T., and K. M. Kwan (1965) *Ethnic Stratification: A Comparative Approach.* New York.

Smith, M. G. (1960) "Social and Cultural Pluralism," in *Social and Cultural Pluralism in the Caribbean,* ed. V. Rubin. Annals of the New York Academy of Sciences 83, art. 5, 763–85.

————— (1965a) *The Plural Society in the British West Indies.* Berkeley and Los Angeles.

————— (1965b) *Stratification in Grenada.* Berkeley and Los Angeles.

Smith, R. T. (1958) "British Guiana," *Sunday Guardian of Trinidad,* April 20, pp. 25–59.

————— (1961) Review of V. Rubin, ed., *Social and Cultural Pluralism in the Caribbean, American Anthropologist* 63:155–57.

Srinivas, M. N. (1962) "A Note on Sanskritization and Westernization," in *Caste in Modern India and Other Essays,* ed. H. N. Srinivas. London.

van den Berghe, P. L. (1964) *Caneville: The Social Structure of a South African Town.* Middletown, Conn.

Chapter 2/ Raymond T. Smith

Social Stratification
in the Caribbean

The main interest held by the Caribbean for the comparative study of social stratification is in the processes by which peoples of diverse social, racial, and cultural origin are incorporated into one social system. It is important, however, to recognize certain peculiar features of the Caribbean which must be taken into account in any comparison. Students of the region are sharply divided on the value of the concept "plural society" for understanding status differentiation. Like the United States, most Caribbean countries have adopted a national motto which seeks to express the idea of unity: Jamaica's is "Out of Many, One People"; Guyana's, "One People, One Nation"; and the slogan of Trinidad's ruling party is "All o' we is one." On the other hand, the image of a "plural society"—the obverse of the unity theme—is a very pervasive part of the culture. Some years ago Jamaica's evening newspaper started a beauty contest which was to have ten winners spanning the whole racial spectrum of that island, and its slogan was "Ten Types: One People." Apart from being intrinsic to the culture of the various territories, the idea has been developed in a more academic version which runs something like this: A plural society is a *special type* of society which is composed of cultural sections, each of which is really a little society in itself with its own basic institutional patterns. Each has its own kinship, family, and mating system, its own religious beliefs and practices, socializa-

I am grateful to Professor Lloyd Fallers of the University of Chicago for his very useful comments on an early draft of this paper.

tion system, recreational activities, values, and language variant. The whole thing is held together by the political domination of one section.

In its application to the Caribbean the plural society theory was developed mainly by Dr. Michael G. Smith in a series of works published between 1953 and the present.[1] The stimulus for that development was a book by J. S. Furnivall, *Colonial Policy and Practice: A Comparative Study of Burma and Netherlands India* (Cambridge, 1948). That book was intended, in part, as a critique of the then-current policies of colonial development and welfare, and its basic thesis was that the free play of economic forces has brought into being in the tropics multi-racial societies with no common standards and no common culture, whose members have in common only animal existence on the one hand and economic competition on the other. In one passage he does say that tropical societies are plural societies in which each racial section "holds by its own religion, its own culture and language, its own ideas and ways." In some ways this is an accurate description of Burma and Java to which it was applied, but this is the section of Furnivall's work that has been developed into a full-scale model of the very different Caribbean societies. The main argument of Furnivall's book, however, points in a different direction; laissez-faire economics and colonial rule, he says, combine to act as a "solvent" of traditional cultures and values, creating a situation of social atomization in which *individualism* is the main driving force. Inadequate as it may be, this seems to be a better appraisal of the situation than the more recent modified version of the theory.[2]

This paper is not intended as a critique of Dr. M. G. Smith's work nor of the plural society concept; the issue is raised at the outset because the term "plural society" has been widely used in relation to the study of social differentiation in developing societies, and it is in relation to the Caribbean data that it has been most fully developed.[3] It is also raised because it points to a series of real difficulties in the interpretation of empirical materials. These difficulties involve such questions as the following: How does one determine when one is dealing with a "society" and not simply a mechanical aggregate of discrete groups? And, if a society is more than a mechanical aggregate of groups, then what is it? In its simplest form the problem can be stated by asking whether the members of the society share any common basis for judging social worth or whether the "society" is merely an arena within which groups compete with each other for the power to dominate others. Stated in this way, the problem is almost as old as human thought itself and is not a peculiarity of some particular kind of state, old or new. It is discussed at some length in Dahrendorf's book and is the focus of much of Max Weber's political sociology.[4] Neither Weber nor the writers reviewed by Dahrendorf were concerned primarily with "underdeveloped" or multi-racial societies; their focus of attention was industrial society and the great world civilizations. Nevertheless, their ideas are relevant, and Weber provides a series of analytic categories which can be applied to the study of new states, as a growing body of work testifies.[5] In the analysis of social stratification, his distinction between "class," "status group," and "party" is particularly useful and does not prejudge the issue of "pluralism" or "unity."[6]

As we have said, the Caribbean exhibits peculiar features which must be taken into account in comparative analysis. The main one is the almost complete absence of an indigenous population, or its relegation to a position of extreme marginality as in the case of the Amerindians of the Guianas. In this respect the Caribbean resembles the United States more than it resembles Latin America or the new states of Africa and Asia; we are dealing with societies composed of immigrants who had their traditional cultures sharply modified by the transfer to the New World and who were unable to maintain traditional forms of social structure. Secondly, one must recognize the dominating position of plantation agriculture. In many territories the societies were established as plantation colonies, while in others, such as Cuba, Puerto Rico, and Spanish Santo Domingo, plantation agriculture intruded into a mixed farming complex of small- and medium-sized farms. In both types of situation there was a convergence toward a common system of interdependent plantation and small-farming sectors as the old slave plantation colonies threw off communities of small farmers after emancipation. There is some reason, then, for speaking of these Caribbean territories as plantation societies, for even those who were not directly incorporated into plantation life were affected by it and the plantation did much to shape the general features of the overall society.[7] It is important to begin with this observation since it provides some counterweight to the image of a collection of different races. A very high proportion of immigrants experienced plantation life as their initiation into the region. The plantation was more than a market place in which people met to exchange goods and services; in many respects it was more like a "total institution" in which primary acculturation took place and which impressed its image upon the society which existed around it.[8] Even for those who were not residents, the plantation was the major instrument through which the whole population became involved in a system of market relations which stretched around the world, and it was the initial framework for a system of graded occupational categories. Whereas in parts of Africa, for example, one might be able to think of a tribal population being drawn into an occupational system from which they might periodically or permanently withdraw, occupation in the Caribbean is a primary social identity. Terms such as "small farmer," "rice farmer," or "cane farmer" are usually more appropriate than "peasant," for farming is an occupation rather than a way of life. There are exceptions to this generalization, of course, especially in the Spanish-speaking territories which have a long tradition of independent farming. But even there, the tendency to romanticize the *jíbaro*—the peasant folk-hero—is more a matter of national symbolism than a description of current realities.[9] The main point to be made, then, is the appropriateness of the concept of class in Weber's sense:

(1) a number of people have in common a specific causal component of their life chances, in so far as (2) this component is represented exclusively by economic interests in the possession of goods and opportunities for income, and (3) is represented under the conditions of the commodity or labour markets.[10]

The Primary Structure of Stratification

We begin, then, with a discussion of the division of labor, of the occupational system, or as Fallers terms it, the primary structure of stratification.[11] This discussion must be brief and highly schematic, and although a wide-ranging comparison would be desirable, Jamaica and Guyana will be used as the main examples, with some reference to Puerto Rico. The bulk of the working population of all Caribbean societies traditionally has been engaged in agriculture—as plantation laborers, small farmers, or both. There has been a trend toward the development of a symbiotic relationship between plantation agriculture and small farming, with political power usually being deployed to favor the continued profitable operation of the plantation sector. The distinction between small farms and large farms (or plantations) has generally been great, and the discrepancy between the "life chances in relation to the market" of the large and small farmers was similar to that between the employer and the laborer; in fact, the small farmers were frequently part-time laborers on the plantations. Some intermediate positions developed in Jamaica with the establishment of banana farming, in Cuba and Puerto Rico with tobacco farming, and in Guyana with the growth of the rice industry. Sometimes it appears that the development of such crops as rice has provided the economic base for a counter-movement back to a less differentiated economic system; rice especially has been used as the foundation for an essentially domestic mode of production. Certainly this is so to some extent, but two trends should be taken into account: the growth of a group of medium-sized rice farms using machinery and the tendency for rice cultivation to be used as a part-time activity which really masks a growing unemployment problem.[12] In Guyana, rice farmers are organized into a Producers Association and all marketing is carried out through a central statutory board, so that despite the domestic nature of production there is still a large element of bureaucratization in the industry.

Over the past hundred years or so there has been a reduction in the proportion of the population engaged in agriculture. This was not simply the result of a process of industrialization or modernization. Sometimes it merely reflected a trend toward a more normal population structure as the reduction in infant mortality rates increased the proportion of children in the population. In other cases, where there was an actual shift in the deployment of the labor force, the growth of numbers in domestic service or in small shopkeeping and other kinds of trading was an indication of increasing unemployment rather than a voluntary shift. More recently there has been an increase in the number of unemployed, who are now beginning to recognize themselves as a class, and an increase in the proportion engaged in industrial occupations of one kind or another.[13] The first complexes of occupations to develop outside agriculture were trading and those occupations associated with government and the professions. The trading network distributed imported goods on the one hand and locally produced foodstuffs on the other. The patterns by which locally produced commodities are distributed within Caribbean territories have attracted anthropologists' attention because they constitute informal networks of considerable importance and interest which have been ignored by economists.[14] They also indicate the strength of institutionalized patterns of behavior among the "folk" and illuminate patterns of social integration which are outside the normal framework of the colonial society. Although these marketing patterns are of intrinsic and comparative interest, they are certainly no more important than the network of small retail shops which covers each Caribbean territory. Many of these shops are so small that they represent nothing more than a part-time activity which brings in very little money; others support an influential village elite and provide sufficient income to enable their owners to send their children to secondary school and up into higher status white-collar occupations. The growth of an indigenous entrepreneurial class out of this kind of shopkeeping has been rather limited; at the upper end of the scale the really profitable import-export and wholesale trade was dominated by a class of merchant planters, while at the bottom the proliferation of small shops kept growth limited. The planter-merchant fusion at the upper levels was the result of the close dependence of planters upon those who advanced money against their crops or took over their plantations when they went bankrupt. Booker Brothers of Guyana is the best example of a large plantation trading combine controlled from Europe, but in many other territories there was a similar aggregation of control into the hands of a small number of firms or families, frequently related through intermarriage.

Since World War II the field open to enterpreneurial activity has gradually expanded, and this has affected the whole Caribbean. The fostering of economic development and social welfare (the reasons for which we need not go into here) has resulted in an increase in production and in productivity in the traditional export agricultural sectors, an increase in the level of exploitation of primary products such as bauxite and oil, some degree of industrialization, and an increase in expenditures on services such as education, medicine, and public works, partly through aid from outside sources.

Puerto Rico, which has provided the model for other countries hoping to develop themselves by attracting foreign enterprise and foreign capital, is worth a brief examination. Puerto Rico's experience is unique in many respects, especially insofar as it derives from its dependence upon the United States, and yet the general pattern of development is not dissimilar to the rest of the Caribbean in its effects upon the primary structure of stratification. (Cuba must be excepted from that generalization since it has embarked upon an entirely different course, and one which other countries find it increasingly difficult to follow in view of United States intervention.) The main relevant feature of the Puerto Rican experience is the emergence of a new class, oriented to consumption and the emulation of an American style of life. Gordon Lewis has characterized the economic development of Puerto Rico as follows:

The industrializing process is not of the classic North American–Western European variety centering around the mass production of goods with a heavy industrial base. It is, rather, a basically distributive entity, characterized typically by the proliferation of companies undertaking the sale and consumption of goods produced by the United States economy. Its "new men" are clerks, managers, salesmen and advertising publicists rather than production technicians; and their work largely concentrates upon sponsoring and catering to, the new consumption habits of the Puerto Rican buyer.[15]

Exactly the same could be said of the "industrial development" of Trinidad or Jamaica or Guyana, or any other society in the region where development of any kind has taken place. Even such seemingly heavy industries as oil refining are often just a piece of automated window-dressing tied to a system of distributive outlets for refined automobile gasoline. Jamaica is far less advanced in these developments than Puerto Rico, and Guyana has hardly begun, but the direction is clear. There is emerging a whole new complex of Jaycees (Junior Chamber of Commerce), Rotarians, Lions, and other "young businessmen's organizations" often affiliated with parent bodies in the United States.[16] Salesmanship is the new road to sucess, although it is a very bureaucratized type of salesmanship, operating through exclusive agencies which receive a great deal of guidance and, sometimes, direction from parent corporations in the form of packaged sales campaigns, service training, and even supervisory personnel. The products sold are the trappings of mass consumption society: automobiles, refrigerators and similar appliances, television sets, phonographs and hi-fi equipment, rotisserie barbecues, household fittings, and even Kentucky Fried Chicken. The workers who sell, service, and sometimes assemble, these products live in new housing areas outside San Juan, Kingston, and other capitals. They are also among the main consumers of what they sell. Although a mass market has not developed, the change in consumption patterns goes fairly deep into these societies.

Some of this new business activity is in the hands of the old merchant class, but opportunity exists, too, for new elements to move into positions of considerable affluence. In Jamaica this is particularly evident in the increased wealth and entrepreneurial activity of families with Syrian, Lebanese, Chinese, and Indian origins, some of whom go considerably beyond the traditional shopkeeping field. Although such activity is in no sense monopolized by groups of a particular racial composition, it is still generally true that Negro and colored persons tend to seek upward mobility through governmental or professional activities.

Official Development and Welfare Policies have brought a commensurate expansion of opportunity in the governmental and professional fields. Educational facilities have been expanding throughout the region, with the possible exception of Haiti (although there has been *some* expansion even there), partly because of a general policy shift toward providing increased educational opportunity and partly to meet an increased demand for persons with higher educational qualifications. New branches of government, particularly those concerned with economic development, have emerged. Planning Units, State Banks, and Ministries of Finance have replaced the old Colonial Secretary's Office as the hub of government, and they are staffed by young local men with degrees in economics or political science rather than by expatriate career officers.

All this adds up to a significant shift in the structure of the occupational system, but many of the old distinctions remain. The stress on formal education as the criterion of mobility into white-collar occupations, coupled with the new emphasis on consumption, provides indicators of status which are of great symbolic significance. The aphorism that the rich are getting richer and the poor are getting poorer is probably true at the ends of the occupational scale: the merchant class at one end and the unemployed and semi-employed at the other. It is also true that small farmers are experiencing a relative deprivation vis-à-vis both urban workers and the higher income groups. But in the middle range of the occupational system there appears to be a more continuous income gradient than is commonly perceived. Here the workers variously described as "skilled manual" or as "craftsmen" are important; although they are not large in number, they constitute a reference group for those who wish to escape from low-wage employment in agriculture.[17] The Jamaica Labour Force Survey of 1957 reported that 17.8 per cent of the active labor force are skilled craftsmen. Many of these may have nominal rather than real skills, but the post-war expansion in building, in automobile servicing, and in light manufacturing has created a demand which has remained fairly high through the constant drain of migration.

Skilled manual workers are sharply differentiated from the lower grades of white-collar workers even though they frequently earn more. It is true that such workers do not constitute an alienated proletariat in the way that the European working class was thought to do, but as a potentially important element in social change, they have not been given the attention they deserve. Although the traditional status gap between manual and white-collar workers still exists, the two groups tend, to some degree, to act together in demands for higher income or in exerting political pressures of one kind or another. Cumper's work in Barbados has pointed to a real difference in style of life and social orientation which occurs as persons enter the skilled worker category,[18] and it does seem that, in class terms, one must distinguish this type of worker rather than regard him simply as part of an undifferentiated lower class. More research is needed, but—in Jamaica, for example—it is clear that new, higher income groups within the manual worker category are separating out and can be distinguished in such terms as religious affiliation, family pattern, and consumption habits as well as income.

In summary, one can say that, while the pyramidal class pattern—with a broad base of poorly paid workers and small farmers and a small, wealthy elite at the top—is typical of underdeveloped countries, recognizable patterns of change seem to be taking place. The change from individual to corporate ownership of plantations, combined with the corporate character of mining and oilfield operations, means that there is no longer as much inherent importance in a resident landowning group.[19] A high proportion of those in the high income sector receive salaries or wages of one kind or another; many are executives of foreign firms rather than capitalists, and the local capitalists are members of the commercial classes, only recently emerging into prosperity. At the lower end of the class scale is a rapidly expanding group of unskilled workers who have to make out by "scuffling." This highly expressive Jamaican term refers to any activity by which people are able to make some money or, as they put it, "to get a bread," and it encompasses such diverse activities as porterage, begging, minor trading (such as buying and selling empty bottles), odd-job work in suburban gardens, washing cars, or petty theft. The gap between high and low income sectors is bridged somewhat by the emergence of a higher-paid group of skilled workers in construction, light industry, and service occupations and by the existence of a group of prosperous operators of middle-sized farms. Despite these trends and the rise in the absolute level of living of the lowest status groups, an increasing gap is developing between the level of living of the high and low income sectors.

Gordon Lewis' descriptions of Puerto Rico catch the essence of the changes that are taking place throughout the region, even though the stage of development differs among the territories. He writes:

There has been taking place, in fact, a very real structural transformation of the economy and its work structure. . . . The capital basis is shifting from the ownership of land to industrial, bureaucratic, and commercial activity as preferred styles of economic activity. . . .

Puerto Rico . . . is a classic example of the materialist appetite run riot. Its very proximity to the North American world and its unprotected exposure to the psychologically clever advertising of the "hidden persuaders" and the "image merchants" of that world has made it a ready victim of the disease. . . .

As the struggle for economic survival thus proceeds, the society will discover that in the place of the myth of social unity . . . there has been unleashed a Pandora's box of competing class and group aspirations it may take more than the emotional invocation of *puertorriquenidad* to assuage.[20]

Although much of this is peculiar to Puerto Rico, the trend is quite general throughout the Caribbean.

Processes of Allocation

Delineation of the changing occupational structure is a complex undertaking in the sense that it requires the collation and interpretation of a great deal of factual information, but the problem of understanding the way in which people evaluated the social status of different occupations and the processes by which individuals were allotted to them is complex in another sense. It is complex in the sense that the information is difficult to come by at all. A constant theme running through all discussions of Caribbean society, and particularly the non-Hispanic Caribbean, is the paradoxical opposition between ideas of equality on the one hand and the gross differences in the social position of black men and white men. So long as slavery existed, the problem could be resolved (or, at least, ignored); slaves were a different category of being, and their position was defined by law. Similarly, free persons of color and Jews were subjected to specific legal disability.[21] In 1834 Jamaica had 311,100 slaves, approximately 15,000 whites, and 45,000 free persons of color, the majority of the latter being of mixed African and European ancestry. At this time the difference in legal status among these groups was beginning to dissolve and by 1838 it had disappeared completely, but even when those legal distinctions were in full effect, there was no simple direct correlation between legal standing and social class. The whites included persons who were poor and ignorant while some of the colored were men of property and education and some slaves were moderately well-off.[22] During the slavery period it was the whites who expressed those attitudes of independence and egalitarianism which struck visitors from Europe, causing them—however inaccurately—to return with the tale that a man could come penniless to the colonies and end up with a fortune and a seat in the mother of parliaments.

Emancipation destroyed all that for the whites; the number of planters diminished rapidly, and those who survived were forced to operate larger units and increase their efficiency, with corporate ownership of plantations eventually becoming the general rule. Here the convergence between the Spanish and non-Spanish areas is seen again; in Cuba, Puerto Rico, and the Dominican Republic the penetration of North American-owned corporate plantations gradually displaced or overshadowed the individually owned smaller plantation. In the British territories the post-emancipation planter faced the problem of obtaining sufficient labor to keep going. Technically all men were now free and equal agents in a market situation, but the planters had, or obtained, sufficient power to modify that situation in their favor.

In trying to understand the way in which persons were allocated to roles within this system, one must take into account two sets of factors, each one complex enough to fill several volumes. There is, first, the desire to maintain or, in the case of Cuba and Puerto Rico, to expand a plantation agricultural system. This led to the restriction of development in other directions and the growth of mechanisms ensuring the allocation of labor to plantation work rather than to any other kind of activity. Secondly, although all civil disabilities were removed by the emancipation acts, a cultural image of a "plural society" was institutionalized, and one aspect of that image was the idea that different races had different aptitudes for various occupations. These factors are empirically intertwined, of course, as are those involved in the analytical categories of status group and party; in Faller's terminology, they all constitute the secondary structural and cultural aspects of the stratification system.

Let us deal briefly with the first set of factors. During the nineteenth century the British territories gradually expanded the institutions of civil society under the system of Crown Colony Government.[23] Enlightened Governors (and even unenlightened ones) spoke endlessly of "development," "progress," and "upliftment." They encouraged agricultural diversification, the improvement of peasant agriculture, the establishment of schools and stressed the importance of education, the improvement of water supplies, and the importance of better housing. "Community development" has a long and unimpressive history in the Caribbean. No matter how enlightened the Governor or his principals in London, he operated within the framework of an ongoing system, the basis of which was plantation agriculture. The local legislatures were dominated by planters or their agents, and they devised all the standard methods of coercing labor; they imposed poll taxes, placed large import duties on necessities, restricted access to land, introduced indentured servants to force down the price of free labor, and applied the law of Master and Servant in such a way that it almost recreated the master-slave relationship.[24] All this restrained the emergence of any major differentiation of an occupational kind within the working class. There was little technological improvement until the twentieth century, save in the factory processing of sugar and in sugar agronomy—and that hardly affected the labor situation. In Puerto Rico the trajectory of development was different but tended in the same direction. The means by which labor was constrained followed a more Latin American pattern involving paternalism,[25] until the period of American occupation after 1898 when the full development of the corporate plantation took place.[26]

It is important to stress that the general economic backwardness of Caribbean societies was not simply due to the persistence of tradition; it was at least partially induced by the manipulation of society by a class of rationally oriented persons who sought to maximize profits in an established export sector of the economy and who often sincerely believed that if their efforts failed, the countries concerned would degenerate into chaos. The overall class structure was different from that found in most traditional societies with a two-class system.[27] Here the upper class is not an administrative, priestly, warrior, or leisure class living off surpluses from a relatively self-contained peasant sector; rather, it is a foreign, or metropolitan, managerial class actively controlling the whole economic process and depending upon the labor, rather than the produce, of the lower class. Perhaps the only territory for which this generalization would require really serious modification is Haiti, where the breakdown of the plantation system after the first period of independence was only partially restored, leaving a large population of small farmers living a precarious existence on farms too small to provide much more than a bare subsistence. And, of course, the generalization should not obscure the fact (mentioned earlier) that some counter-differentiation emerged toward family production in the small farming sector—a fact which some analysts, concentrating their attention at that level, might consider to be the major fact of Caribbean social stratification —especially if their vantage point happens to be a small island or a remote area of a large territory.

I have found it convenient to use a model of "creole" or "colonial" society which distinguishes it rather sharply from that complex of relations previously referred to as "plantation society."[28] The model distinguishes those relations which arose when the ex-slaves were incorporated into civil society: a process most clearly seen in the British territories. Although the planters dominated the political process after emancipation, the intervention in colonial affairs by the imperial government was not without consequences. It defined the formal nature of civil society and developed the notion that merit should be the basis upon which men are judged and allocated to positions within the society. This idea was not, of course, new; we saw it in white society during the slavery period and it spread ever more widely after the French, American, and Latin American revolutions.[29] The ideal found objective expression only insofar as objective conditions required it, but it was still an important principle which could be invoked by all kinds of groups struggling to assert their own interests within the system. Conditions did require the training and appointment of local people to positions of intermediate status; teaching, the churches, the police, and civil service all recruited individuals from the local population for their lower ranks. Preference was given to whites—and to their kin, the colored— partly because of prejudice and partly because these groups generally had prior access to education. By the 1870's Jamaica's colored population was well represented in the white-collar occupations, and the formally open policy of the imperial government gave a semblance of democratic participation to the whole scene. Trollope remarked that "the coloured people in Jamaica have made their way into society," but he qualified it by adding: "Into what may be termed public society they have made their way. Those who have seen the details of colonial life will know that there is a public society to which people are admitted or not admitted, according to their acknowledged rights. Governor's parties, public balls, and certain meetings which are semi-official and semi-social, are of this nature."[30]

One of the interesting things about these intermediate status positions is that they required formal education of a literary or cultural type. Such education, hardly available in the colonies during slavery, was expanded only after the missionaries became active. An integral part of the missionary process was to teach people to read, and emancipation was followed by considerable spread of basic education in the three R's, actively encouraged by the imperial government. The planters' initial alarm at the spreading of such a "civilized" skill gradually turned to confidence that the right kind of training would make for a peaceful, contented, and God-fearing lower class.

Secondary education grew very slowly and was almost exactly gradu-
ated to meet the needs of the occupational system. It has been customary
in the West Indies to complain about the inappropriate content of education: an excessive emphasis upon literary and classical subjects and a
neglect of science and the practical arts. But this was the result of demand.
Agriculture declined in status as an occupation while the professions, and
particularly medicine and law, increased. More generally, it seems that the
educational system was really a part of a wider apparatus through which
ideas and sentiments were disseminated. Whether this apparatus is called
an ideology-imposing or a value-disseminating mechanism does not matter;
the point is that its effect was to institutionalize the idea of the English language and English culture as correct for the whole society. Similar mechanisms apparently were in operation in the non-British regions, although, of
course, they varied in their operation just as they vary from island to island
within the British Caribbean. Surinam is probably the least developed in this
respect, with a linguistic differentiation which is rare even in the Caribbean.

By the end of the nineteenth century the British territories had a three-
tiered educational system very closely related to the occupational structure
but also functioning as a part of the "pattern-maintenance" system of the
whole society. At the bottom were the primary schools, reaching the mass
of the people in varying degrees. In mountainous country like Jamaica or
in countries like Guyana and Trinidad where indentured immigrants still
were locked in the residential plantation system, a relatively small proportion
of children were even registered; in Barbados and in the Guyana Negro villages, both enrollment and attendance were high. According to a generous
definition of literacy, it is estimated that the proportion of literate Jamaicans
over five years of age was 52.5 per cent in 1891 and 60.9 per cent in 1921.
In 1931 more than 80 per cent of Guyanese Negroes were literate while
the East Indians were only 25 per cent literate in English. But whatever
their shortcomings, the primary schools did provide a steady trickle of
persons into teaching, the police, nursing, or—through scholarships—into
the secondary schools.

The secondary education system was usually dominated by one or two
schools which were either part of the government establishment or dependent upon government financial support. In addition there were a number
of endowed, church-run, or private secondary schools of varying degrees
of competence. Access to secondary education depended upon the parents'
ability to pay fees or the child's ability to win scholarships, the latter being
affected by the quality of primary education he had received. This led to a

selection of children whose parents were already of higher income and status, and in some territories the schools were notoriously monopolized by the children of expatriate civil servants. In most of the territories formal rules required open access on the basis of ability, but various means existed to keep out lower-class children, including such devices as refusing to admit children born out of legal wedlock.

The third tier of the educational system involved travel to Europe for university education, for only the Spanish-speaking territories found it worthwhile to start local universities.[31]

The post-war period has seen considerable change in the structure of the educational system, most notably improvement at the primary level and increased enrollment, a trend particularly noticeable among East Indians in Guyana and Trinidad. Secondary education has expanded considerably, and new measures are correcting the biases in selection which favored children of wealthier parents. Jamaica, for example, has made it mandatory that the bulk of scholarships to secondary schools be given to children from government primary schools rather than from those private preparatory schools which can afford to prepare their pupils more efficiently. The growth of local universities or colleges in all the major territories is making higher education available to people from poor families and opening more avenues for upward mobility. While it is true that this process is nowhere very advanced, it does make for a significant break with the past, and in Puerto Rico, where the trend is the most marked, it seems clear that education is now regarded as one of the most important, if not *the* most important, status indicator.[32] Education may be simply the badge or symbol of an hereditary class, but here it is becoming much more widely accessible so that the new elites may well become a meritocracy.

Status Groups

Max Weber defines status groups as follows:

In contrast to classes, *status groups* are normally communities. They are, however, often of an amorphous kind. In contrast to the purely economically determined "class situation" we wish to designate as "status situation" every typical component of the life fate of men that is determined by a specific, positive or negative, social estimation of *honor*. This honor may be connected with any quality shared by a plurality, and, of course it can be knit to a class situation. . . . In content, status honor is normally expressed by the fact that above all else a specific *style of life* can be expected from all those who wish to belong to the circle.[33]

As it stands this definition is not very illuminating, but Weber elaborated it in relation to a large body of empirical data drawn from the world civilizations. In the process he allows the concept of status group to take on many new dimensions of meaning (which are not always consistent), but there seem to be two main types of situation to which it can be applied. In the first place Weber seems to visualize social orders tending toward a stable state in which groups will separate out into distinctive entities arranged in a hierarchy of social honor. In the limiting case when such a state approaches stability this hierarchy will correspond rather closely to the class order, or will be based upon it, for "the road from this purely conventional situation to legal privilege, positive or negative, is easily travelled as soon as a certain stratification of the social order has in fact been "lived in" and has achieved stability by virtue of a stable distribution of economic power."[34] But he uses the idea of status group in a much more dynamic sense approximating Marx's conception of a revolutionary class. In this sense the term is applied to groups which develop and extend new ideas (usually in response to changing material circumstances), but in pursuit of their own ideal *and* material interests. If such a group is successful *their* ideas and values come to be dominant, along with their bearers, and may eventually come to be accepted by other groups outside their immediate circle. The element of contradiction in these two formulations really springs from Weber's method of ideal type analysis and can be resolved only by reference to empirical situations for which the models provide the means of understanding.

In our discussions of Caribbean societies we have found it necessary to refer to race as a factor affecting the allocation of persons to positions within the primary structure of stratification. Race has always been a primary datum for Caribbean societies, as it could hardly fail to be when it had been so closely linked with the difference between slave and free. During the late slavery period in the British territories, one writer stated the position as follows: "In the West Indies, the complexion of the slave is a real distinction which will always work strongly on popular prejudice; and even on those who make, as well as those who administer, the laws. Hitherto, at least, both prejudices and laws (at least in vulgar intendment) presume that every black man is, or ought to be, a Slave."[35] The phrase "ought to be" is important because it indicates that there was not then, and never has been, a simple direct correlation between race and status. The development of the idea of European superiority and African inferiority was a slow and complex process which is now beginning to be documented in such works as Philip Curtin's *The Image of Africa* (Madison, Wis., 1964). Elsa Goveia's *A Study of the Historiography of the British West Indies* (Mexico City, 1956) shows how changing conceptions of racial inferiority and superiority worked out on a more restricted canvas. The conception that "every black man . . . ought to be a slave" changed with a growing revulsion against slavery, but the general structure of the idea system has been carried forward to the present day. Even where the realities of power and formal position have placed Negroes at the top of a social hierarchy, there has always been a wider world in which they have felt constrained to try to *prove* that they are not inferior. In the new international stratification system, race is clearly a factor.

In the Caribbean there were varying developments of this system of ideas about the significance of race; in the Spanish-speaking areas, slavery —although it lasted longer—was not so extensive, and Roman Catholicism combined with a different pattern of exploitation to produce less clear-cut racial attitudes.[36] After emancipation in the British territories one can see the development of a widely shared image of a "plural society," an image which served different groups in different ways. The basic idea that each person has a "primordial identity"[37]—as a European, African, East Indian, Chinese, Mulatto, or whatever it might be—was combined with the idea that all persons should be in a process of "becoming." The goal toward which this "becoming" was directed was "civilization." Here is a potential contradiction, especially when one considers that race was often equated with mental capacity, especially in the minds of the Europeans. But civility demanded different things from different men, and there was room for disagreement over the question of who had the capacity for becoming what. There was no doubting the fact that all evolution was tending toward the superior life style of the European, and so the question resolved itself into how far and how fast it would be possible for non-Europeans to attain a European level of civilization and refinement. Africans, and the other non-Europeans, were willing to go along with this "civilizing" process up to a point. The whole crux of the problem of understanding these societies lies in the question of where this civilizing (or more properly Europeanizing) process stopped. Did these groups *really* retain their own institutions, somewhat modified by the new environment, and simply submit politically when the alternative of rebellion failed or appeared profitless? Why did some stop at one point and others continue? And what does one make of the fact that some groups appear to value more than one institutional pattern simultaneously?

Space does not permit of an adequate treatment of these questions; for adequacy would involve the discussion of a long period of changing development. The shortest way to summarize the situation is this: The dominant status groups in the Caribbean were traditionally European, and they emulated a European feudal aristocratic way of life while at the same time developing local characteristics of their own which varied from territory to territory. The lowest status group was either enslaved or bound to the dominant group in some other way. That binding varied from a kind of personal paternalistic relationship to one based on direct physical coercion, indirect coercion through the labor market, or some combination of these three. The life style of the lowest status groups was affected by three factors: their pattern of daily activities (their ecological situation), their historically derived cultural heritage (with its own internal variations), and their relationship to the dominant group. In terms of the interplay of these factors various kinds of segmental divisions arose, the boundaries of which shifted with time. For example, tribal distinctions between Africans and caste distinctions among East Indians gradually (or sometimes suddenly) disappeared, while new distinctions based upon occupational or urban rural differences appeared. In Puerto Rico the characteristic type was the *jíbaro,* the creole peasant, sturdy, independent, wise, happy, and poor. Although African subcultures developed, particularly in Cuba, the general life style of the Spanish-speaking territories has been that of the creolized European peasant. The rest of the Caribbean has been typified by a creolized African culture, varying according to the operation of the three factors mentioned above. Guyana is peculiar in having a population majority which is of East Indian descent, although there are large Indian minorities in Trinidad and Surinam, and lesser ones in Guadeloupe, Martinique, and Jamaica. Although East Indians in these places tend to have a more sharply differentiated subculture based upon the more recent influence of their historic cultural tradition, the same process of modification is at work and tends to vary with the factors of ecological situation and relation to other status groups.

That lower status groups exist, that they have their own life styles based upon historic cultural traditions, and that they have been influenced by their relation to the Europeans is beyond dispute. What is perhaps disputed is the extent to which they constitute *separate* social sections with no values in common.

Particular interest attaches to the emergence of groups corresponding to the second of Weber's meanings of "status group"—that is, groups which are innovating and disruptive of the established social order. To avoid misunderstanding, let us state at once that the term "established social order" is used in a relative sense and does not ignore the fact that the "social order" was perpetually being challenged. Slaves, indentured workers, and common laborers were in an almost constant state of rebellion and developed various modes of passive resistance against plantation managements. The frequent outbreaks of violence against shopkeepers testifies to the profound dissatisfaction of large numbers of lower status people.[38] However, since these manifestations of unrest could always be brought back under control by the application of force, it must be assumed that a social order was established which was accepted to some degree by everyone in it—whatever their reason for acceptance might have been.

Assuming that the established social order drew a sharp distinction between black and white, slave and free, and that it was stabilized and integrated in some way, the first group to emerge as an important contradiction of that order was the free colored. Special terms such as *gens du couleur* and Free People of Colour were used to designate these people, who were, in the main, offspring of white men and slave women. As is widely known, they came to occupy an intermediate position in the status system, emphasizing their distance from the blacks and emulating the life style of the whites. But they also became the main bearers of the idea that they had the right to access to high status positions and to better life chances in relation to the market *in spite of color.*

As European civilization was substituted for color as the formal qualification for status and as opportunity for mobility developed, there was a growing contradiction between the aspirations of the colored elite and the continued monopolization of key positions of control by white groups which remained privately exclusive whatever the nature of public society might have been. The British made masterly use of selective rewards, and what has become known as "one spookism" or "tokenism," to maintain a minimum of satisfaction within the major organizations of society. By the judicious distribution of awards in the sovereign's Birthday and New Year's Honours Lists, invitations to public functions at Government House, and the creation of "advisory" positions within government, the structure of colonial government and society were maintained while at the same time an illusion of "democratic participation" was created.

Challenges to the stability of colonial society came from two sources:

from the disorganized violent protests of the lower classes and from those members of the creole elite who had an independent economic base from which to operate. The latter were the lawyers, doctors, dentists, journalists, and some of the lesser merchants who had conflicts of economic interest with the planter group.[39] It was men such as these who developed ideas of nationalism, pan-Caribbean unity, Garveyism, and pan-Africanism and who were receptive to socialism, trade unionism, communism, and a host of other doctrines flowing in from abroad. They were a minority within the broad body of the middle class, but they eventually became its spokesmen as a conservative adherence to the old order became less feasible. More significantly, perhaps, they constituted themselves the leaders of lower-class protest, a phenomenon we shall later consider in more detail. The important point here is that the middle status groups can be viewed in two ways. From one point of view, they all shared a similar life style based upon an emulation of the manners of the whites and differentiation from the lower stratum, but they were fragmented into a hierarchy of subgroups or cliques, membership in which was determined by particularistic criteria. Thus, there were separate cricket clubs for the light- and the dark-skinned people, for East Indians and Chinese; Free Masons lodges and hosts of less formal cliques and networks were similarly segregated. From another point of view, the members of this elite—or some of them—came to challenge the very existence of such an order, couching their challenge in terms of the pro-claimed values of white culture. Paradoxically, they argued in effect that cultural "whiteness" rather than ethnic whiteness should be the criterion of high status, but even this proved to be an unattainable goal; while all were, indeed, members of the British Empire, none could be truly *English*. Even the French, who made a real effort to do so, did not succeed in making French West Indians into Frenchmen. However much the life style of this broad middle status group converged toward that of the English Colonial Servant group, they did not become members of the "expatriate" elite.

The position today is changed in several important respects, some of which we have already touched upon. For years the dominant group consisted of the Governor and his civil servants of the Colonial Service, and together they directed a bureaucracy staffed by local people. They set the style of life for the civil servants beneath them, not so much by mixing socially but through the general pattern of bridge parties and drinking, of dances and receptions which filtered down through the hierarchy of cliques and clubs. To maintain such a life style required money of course, but the money was spent mainly on such things as entertaining, education for children, travel (to Europe preferably), and clothes for the womenfolk. Houses were large by modern standards and required servants; furnishings were solid but often modest, and the mark of respectability was not so much what one had as the way one could use it and approximate an English style. All this is rapidly disappearing. Except in the French Antilles, the old colonial European elites are mainly gone, but there are more Europeans and North American whites around than ever. Foreign businessmen, visiting technical "experts," and staffs of foreign embassies and missions, along with the tourists, set the new standards for elite behavior. The style, no longer British, is international bureaucratic and North American. Some ties with Europe remain of course. The Dutch and French Antilles still have formal ties with their old metropoles, and the Queen of England still reigns over Jamaica, Trinidad, Guyana, and Barbados, while the smaller islands and British Honduras are only semi-independent. The Governor of Jamaica is a black man, but—to the amusement of some Jamaicans and the annoyance of some others—he still wears the ceremonial dress of the old British Governors. Government House, however, is not what it used to be. The focus of attention has shifted to the Prime Minister's residence and to the receptions at foreign embassies and missions. To be able to do one's shopping in Miami or New York is more important than to go "home" to England on leave. The most important thing is to have a good education, a good job, and a nice home in the suburbs. Status groups now separate out on the basis of residential area and pattern of expenditure just as they do in more "modernized" countries.

The major cleavage is between earners of high and low incomes, and this is most evident in Jamaica where that line tends to coincide with a line of cultural differentiation. The upper status groups, which are referred to as "middle class," view the "lower class" as a large, black, threatening mass of lazy, immoral, and violent people who would destroy the developing prosperity of Jamaica if given half a chance. The archetype of the middle-class nightmare is the Rastafarian: the man who rejects Jamaican society completely and yet expresses in his doctrine of glorification of Africa, in his physical appearance which stresses and flaunts its "black" characteristics, in his refusal to be intimidated by the law, the potential rebellion of the whole lower class.[40] Of course it *is* a nightmare and not a view of reality, but there is enough power in the symbolism of blackness to make it important.[41]

In Jamaica as in Puerto Rico the manual worker and the white-collar worker are separated by a gap which is wider than the difference in income would suggest. In Jamaica that gap tends to be symbolized in terms of color, especially since the blacks virtually monopolize lower status occupations and experience a *felt* deprivation accompanied by a negative evaluation of blackness itself—despite all the efforts to reverse that state of affairs. This attitude is reflected in a story of the reaction in Morant Bay to a new statue of Paul Bogle, working-class hero of the 1865 rebellion. The statue, executed by Mrs. Norman Manley for the centenary celebration of that event and erected before the courthouse in Morant Bay where Bogle was hanged, was designed to express the power, the strength, and the righteousness of the ordinary Jamaican in his long fight against injustice and oppression. Curiously, it was not at first very popular with the common people of Morant Bay, and their objections were summed up by one spectator who observed, "Them would never have mek' him so black if him was not a black man."

Only one of the many Caribbean territories, Jamaica is typical only in the growth of its middle class and in the increasing gap between its high and low income sectors. Even that may differ radically in Cuba, where the experiment is too young to draw many conclusions. In Guyana the picture is complicated by the less advanced development of the class division and a major segmentation between Negroes and East Indians which cuts across class boundaries. However, these status group differentiations are far more complex than a simple division into racial groups would suggest. In order to clarify that situation let us move into the final topic of party differentiation, which in Guyana interacts in particularly interesting ways with status group differentiation.

Parties

The Marxian theory of social class, especially in its more vulgar interpretations, has tended to equate class and status group and to view classes in their fully developed state as politically organized groups. To avoid this fusion and confusion of elements, Weber devised the categories of class, status group, and party, even though he was well aware of their frequent empirical coincidence. Parties orient their action, he believes, toward "the acquisition of social 'power,' that is to say, toward influencing a communal action no matter what its content may be."[42] The applicability of the concept of party is also made conditional upon other factors, for although parties may represent class or status group interests they do so in an orderly and societalized manner by influencing or controlling a staff of persons who are available for the enforcement of the party's wishes.

Examination of nineteenth century Caribbean political life shows that what were there termed "parties," if they existed at all, were loose coalitions of individuals competing for political office in a situation where those offices were mainly honorific. This was not uniformly so, but the establishment of Crown Colony Government in the British territories tended to transform them into centralized authoritarian states structurally similar to, though certainly not identical with, those of the Hispanic Caribbean. The extent to which the creole population could influence the course of government was limited everywhere except in Haiti, or where the creole population included a planter class of European descent. Political offices, where they existed, were mainly honorific, and policy was determined for the most part in the metropolitan capitals. Lewis, writing of Puerto Rico, states in general terms some of the directions in which the relationship between colony and metropolitan center could move when he says:

Classically, the anatomy of colonial nationalism passes through various and successive stages. It begins with a stage of psychological dependence upon the governing power; affiliates itself to the progressive and friendly elements of that power; assumes that the solution to the colonial problem involves merely the transplanting of the best in the metropolitan culture to the dependent society. The strategy of the *turno en el poder,* used by Muñoz Rivera during the last decade of the Spanish regime, was founded upon this frame of reference; and in the British Caribbean a generation later it was reflected in the well-known slogan of Captain Cipriani in Trinidad that "what is good enough for the British Labour Party is good enough for me." A further stage is reached when these great expectations are disappointed, either because the progressive forces in the metropolitan society fail to come to power or because, once in power, they are tempted to forget their colonial allies. When this point is reached the colonial nationalist movement must accept the alternative of dying a slow death or of seeking out new sources of support in the mass base of its own society. It no longer sees itself as a suppliant begging aid from the sovereign power but as a nationalist task force, secure in mass support, demanding that charity be replaced with justice. If the demand is refused, the situation can rapidly deteriorate into the ugly arbitrament of armed conflict, as in the cases of post-war Indonesia and Algeria. If it is met with real sympathy, it can set the stage for a policy of statesmanlike accommodation between both sides, as in the case, most famously, with the withdrawal of the British Raj from India in 1947.[43]

Carribbean societies represent a range of variation in their stage of development: the French Antilles are a part of metropolitan France; the

Netherlands Antilles, Puerto Rico, and now the smaller British Islands are in special relationships of various kinds; Jamaica, Trinidad and Tobago, Barbados, and Guyana are independent members of the British Commonwealth; Cuba, Haiti, and the Dominican Republic are Republics. In all of them the pattern has been for power to pass from the metropolitan center (usually preceded by its passage from one metropole to another) to one or another party within the creole elite. As Gordon Lewis indicates, those parties begin by seeking their support within the metropolitan society and then tend to shift toward seeking a popular base, and more recently they have often been obliged to supplement that support by making alliances with one or another protagonist in the "cold war." The outcome of party struggles and the exact shape taken by them is dependent upon a wide range of factors and is partly determined by the structure of the society and the nature of the political tradition it inherits.

The territories of the British Caribbean have made the transition to independence by a series of stages which were intended to pave the way for some form of parliamentary democratic system in which formally organized parties would play an important part. The various constitutions drawn up by Colonial Office officials in preparation for, or following upon, special conferences held in London, sought to provide a legal framework for this transition, on the assumption (one supposes) that respect for legitimacy would contain the acquisition and exercise of power. Formal party organizations were thus partly a response to constitutional planning, but once formed they became the vehicles for personal and group interest. The earliest parties were, as stated earlier, simply loose associations of individual political virtuosi. This was partly due to the fact that the structure of *government* was such that elected legislators could only influence its course by individual persuasion, if at all. The earliest real political parties were formed for the purpose of taking over a new structure of government and succeeding to positions of power. The form and sequence of stages of that transition helped to shape the nature of party alignments, but the inclusion of universal adult suffrage as the formal means of selecting political successors to the imperial power guaranteed that populism must be an element in the party struggle.

Leadership of West Indian parties has always been mainly drawn from the higher status groups, and as power became more securely lodged in the hands of local politicians, party affiliation became a possible means of preferment of advancement for supporters as well as leaders. Politics as a form of vocational activity brings ample rewards, but the right choice of party can also affect the life chances of supporters. Nor is this simply a matter of class position or class conflict.

Jamaica can serve as an example. The People's National Party was formed in 1938 as an instrument for nationalist activity. Its inaugural meeting was attended by Sir Stafford Cripps of the British Labour Party, and in 1940 the party adopted an official "socialist" policy. The party leader was Mr. Norman Manley, Q.C., leading criminal lawyer, ex-Rhodes scholar and Oxford Blue. Alexander Bustamante, a fair-skinned small businessman who had spent a great deal of his life abroad, had already emerged as a charismatic leader of the lower classes during the riots of 1938 and had become the founder, leader, and life-president of the Bustamante Industrial Trade Union, a position he has consistently refused to give up even at the cost of having to forego the honor of becoming Jamaica's first Governor General. Imprisoned during the war by the British for "subversive activity," he came out of detention to form the Jamaica Labour Party in 1942 and to win the elections in 1944.

The curious cross-cutting of support for these two parties is noteworthy, as is the manner in which they have developed over the years. The J.L.P. was originally a populist party through which scattered and peripheral groups of lower-class persons, and particularly sugar workers, were drawn into closer contact with the central institutions of the society through Bustamante's personal activities and charismatic leadership. Gradually the party changed because of the demands that were imposed upon it by the requirements of office and the need to work with the civil service. Even so, it was long assumed that the Jamaica Labour Party leadership was really incapable of running the country and would eventually give way to the more "competent" leadership of the People's National Party. The J.L.P., despite its labor base, was essentially a conservative party which intended to improve the condition of the working class within the economic and social framework of the existing system, and for this reason it was preferred by the old upper classes and by the sugar companies. The P.N.P. was led by a group of left-wing intellectuals, ranging from moderates of a Fabian Socialist or Labour Party inclination, to more extreme Marxists, and they sought to build up a party structure which would serve as the vehicle for a demand for immediate independence and which could be used as the instrument for bringing about a radical transformation of the existing social structure. The extent to which the P.N.P. leadership was dedicated to such a radical program varied, and after Manley expelled a group of left-wing "extremists" in 1953 the general tone of party policies was more moderate and, in fact, Puerto Rico was taken as the model for Jamaican development. The important thing is that this party was essentially an urban movement and drew its main support from the middle class, to whom Manley represented the very ideal of a successful man. It had to work very hard to build up support in the rural areas while retaining the backing of the urban population.

With the passing of time the Jamaica Labour Party has undergone the greatest transformation by attracting into its leadership members of the "intelligentsia," by retaining most of its mass support, by adopting a similar policy program to that of the P.N.P., and by being able to win support among the middle class simply by being in office. As the P.N.P. developed a fairly successful labor wing and acquired some mass support in the rural areas, the two parties tended to become more alike. Interestingly enough, conflict between them has intensified at two levels: within the middle class and, in many areas, within the lower class. The parties approximate only very loosely "class" or "status group" divisions, and in fact other class-based movements are developing, among them the Unemployed Workers Council and status group movements such as the Rastafarians which tend to regard both major political parties as being middle-class and/or "anti-black."

The stability of the "two-party democratic system" rests upon the ability of the two parliamentary groups to recognize the legitimacy of each other's actions and to confine their supporters' activities to the polls without permitting or encouraging physical violence, and—most important—upon the ability of the government in power to cope with outbreaks of violence from a growing population (which is being frustrated in its aspirations) while at the same time maintaining democratic institutions intact. In this inherently unstable situation signs of strain are already evident in the violence which preceded the 1967 election, in charges of patronage, in suppression of freedom of movement, and in the number of strikes. But with all that the situation is far from chaotic.

Jamaica has been discussed at some length because it provides an interesting comparison to Guyana, where the dominant motif in politics has been generally perceived to be "racial." Guyana has an East Indian population which in 1964 numbered 320,070 (estimated) or 50.2 per cent of the total population, while Negroes numbered 199,830 (estimated) or 31.3 per cent of a total population of 638,030 (estimated).[44] The rest of the population is composed of Mixed, Amerindians, Chinese, Portuguese, and other

Europeans. Space does not permit us to recount the history of political development in Guyana over the past fifteen years, but the salient points are these: In 1953 the country held its first election under a system of universal adult suffrage and under a constitution which was designed to be transitional to eventual independence. The prospect of change called forth two main parties, the People's Progressive Party and the National Democratic Party. The elements of the population that had been important in Jamaica were here arranged in somewhat different fashion. The peripheral rural groups of plantation workers had been organized under the leadership of Cheddi Jagan, an East Indian dentist who, unlike Bustamante, was a left-wing radical reformer. The urban middle class tended to support the National Democratic Party, which was led by a diverse group of lawyers, dentists, doctors, journalists, and small businessmen, and which favored a moderate program of reform but concerned itself mainly with "Guyanization," or the replacement of foreigners by local men in positions of prestige and control. Forbes Burnham emerged during the election campaign as the leader of the long unionized urban lower class. The sugar interests and more conservative members of the old creole elite tended to keep aloof from the election and to support any party other than the People's Progressive Party. The P.P.P. won the election under the joint leadership of Jagan and Burnham, embarked upon a course of precipitate reform, and was thrown out of office by the British Government after only a few months.[45] It was a fact in 1953, and has continued to be a fact, that the majority of rural sugar workers are East Indians and a majority of lower-class urban workers are Negroes, and it was natural, though by no means inevitable or universally the case, that Indian candidates would stand in Indian areas and Negro candidates in Georgetown. The consolidation of Jagan as an "Indian leader" and Burnham as a "Negro leader" did not take place until they began to compete with each other for power.

That competition for power began not too long after they had been removed from office on the charge that they were subverting the constitution and seeking to establish a communist government. Jagan had already been identified as the acknowledged leader of the left-wing group within the party and various individuals had left rather than be associated with anything vaguely associated with "communism," especially in view of the attitude of the United States toward that doctrine. It seemed to many people unlikely that Jagan would ever be allowed to assume the leadership of an independent Guyana and certainly not without a complete *volte-face* on the ideological level. Whatever the exact reason for it, a split (thereafter increasingly defined as a racial split) took place in the party, with Burnham as the leader of one section and Jagan, the other. After a very complex series of developments, which included outbreaks of violence and, according to Arthur Schlesinger, Jr., an indication to the British Government that the United States would prefer to see Burnham in power,[46] the country became independent under the Prime Ministership of Forbes Burnham. The three parties of present importance in Guyana are the People's Progressive Party (the East Indian and left-wing rump of the old P.P.P.), led by Jagan in opposition, the People's National Congress (the Negro wing of the old P.P.P. combined with the N.D.P.) led by Burnham, and the United Force led by Peter D'Aguiar. The latter is a small conservative party representing mainly urban middle-class and lower-middle-class groups, and forms an uneasy coalition with the P.N.C. against Jagan's party.

Now, there is no doubt that the pieces in this jigsaw puzzle are racially cut; nor is there any doubt that the outbreaks of violence which occurred in areas where the political struggle was most intense, were felt to be, and came to be defined as, racial incidents. People were murdered or raped or wounded for no reason other than the fact that they belonged to one race or the other—Negro or Indian. But in addition to, or under-lying, the racial confrontation is the same range of factors that exist in Jamaica. Competition for posts and promotion in the bureaucracies and rising levels of aspiration among the lower classes exist here as elsewhere; race merely provides another channel into which conflict can flow. It is not in itself the *cause* of the conflict. The three parties represent three segments of the political elite which are by no means simply racially differentiated. Each party is multi-racial by design in its top leadership. It is the electoral support which is racially divided, and, as in Jamaica, each party has to reward its supporters to some extent, when it can, by the distribution of offices, work, or other benefits. This consolidates support but it can also lead away from a strict racial division; Indians who saw a personal advantage in supporting Burnham and held little hope of Jagan's being elected might well have switched allegiance, provided, of course, they could do so with some measure of self-respect. The same was true with the many non-Indians who supported Jagan, some for ideological reasons and some out of self-interest. The difficulty was that there was always doubt as to whether outside forces would permit Jagan to retain power. It is very difficult to imagine, in the near future, development in Guyana of a two-party democratic system with an orderly transfer of power and office from one to the other. It is doubtful that either of the main parties as presently constituted would recognize the legitimacy of the other as the sole ruling power. The best that could be hoped for would be the creation of some form of government to which both Indians and Negroes can accord legitimacy. Even if that could be achieved, the potential imbalances which operate in Jamaica will come into play: a rapidly growing population and an inadequate rate of economic growth. Outbreaks of violence may flow in many possible directions, and—while race has provided one set of channels in recent years—it is just as likely that class-based movements will develop.

It should be clear from this discussion that the dimension of "party" —especially in the context of a modern state structure—differs markedly from the other two categories. In the Caribbean parties have their own logic of development which passes through a series of phases depending upon the stages of the relation to a colonial power and of the development of an internal political situation. They serve to aggregate a range of interests, and even when they confront each other, as in Guyana, as the organized political embodiment of one kind of status group differentiation, one must realize that they operate within a framework of relationships which provides the occasion for conflict as well as the means for resolving it.

Conclusion

The Caribbean societies are among the worst examples of "plural" societies in spite of their diversities of race and consumption levels, and of culture. Compared with many Latin American countries, where the problem of peripheral traditional sectors which have not been drawn into the central institutions of the society is combined with the problem of growing urban slum populations and gross disparities in income level, the Caribbean is rather less depressing. Nor does it have the problems of traditionalism one finds in Asia or Africa. Ironically, in societies with the least "racial" diversity the contrast between center and periphery (to use Shil's terms) has been most marked. Cuba, Puerto Rico, Haiti, and the Dominican Republic probably had more marked regional subcultural differences than did those countries where colonial rule created conditions which knit together the various sectors of the society. That knitting has created problems of its own, of course, including political conflict, but underlying all the manifestations of unrest and disturbance is a new set of factors increasing in importance, factors which derive from the very nature and pace of social, cultural, and economic change.

The drive toward nationalism which characterized the 1930's and 1940's faced all the problems involved in creating communities out of "plural" units—the divided, colonial societies inherited from the nineteenth century. But, despite appearances, nationalism has not been a really strong force. The key issues have revolved around economic development and the means of raising the standard of living of the growing population; nationalism to most people simply means better standards of living. As the early charismatic leaders like Bustamante, Muñoz Marin, Manley, Grantley Adams, and others leave the scene, the old national struggle against imperial domination will be forgotten. The problem now is: What aspirations will the people of the Caribbean develop? The malady of Puerto Rico has been diagnosed as a growing restlessness as the old bonds of kinship and neighborhood, of patron and client, and of cultural participation are abandoned in favor of status-striving within a new consumption-oriented, "Americanized" way of life.[47] One Puerto Rican delegate to a recent conference likened the new society to a basket of crabs, in perpetual movement, clawing and climbing upon each other without any sense of direction or purpose. Critics of such an interpretation argue that "modernization" produces benefits that the majority of people really want, and that it results in higher standards of living, better health, housing, and education. It is difficult to decide just what are the inevitable cultural concomitants of economic development, more universal education, increased levels of living, and increased occupational mobility. Whatever the answer may be, it is clear that in Puerto Rico "modernization" is closely bound up with "Americanization"; this is the case for most Caribbean societies, even in the absence of direct political ties, simply because of proximity and growing involvement in the hemispheric economic and communications system. The image of the "admirable man" toward which everyone strives, each in his own way, is increasingly the man who lives the good life of mass consumption society in the way depicted by advertising agencies. Commercial television, films, and newspaper and magazine advertising all try to give a local cast to "the image" but it comes out basically North American.

It can be argued that the drive for "progress" is inherently good and that a measure of cultural Americanization is a small price to pay for fundamental improvement in the general welfare of the population of the region. Some would argue that developing countries could follow no better model than the United States, a sentiment widely disseminated in the Caribbean. However, it is clear that the matter is not a simple one of choosing to adopt or not to adopt an "American way of life." The fundamental problem is how to provide an economic base capable of sustaining rising expectations while at the same time creating a new sense of community. The divisions and identities inherited from the past are, of course, incorporated in the present, but the structural base of contemporary conflicts is not explicable in terms of the past alone. The *techniques* of modernization themselves may produce conflict if they result in the achievement of a high level of consumption by one segment of the population while others are frustrated in their aspirations. It could be further argued that the particular pattern of economic development produced by the Puerto Rican model is bound to produce such conflicts.

East Indians and Jews, Chinese and Negroes, and other elements in these complex societies each have their own self-image and differentiated conceptions of the good life; it is true that for many people in the Caribbean being French, or British, or Spanish, or Dutch, or American is a value to be cherished, but it is also true that these symbols are manipulated in accordance with interests which arise in the arena of the contemporary class and power system, and all these factors must be taken into account.

NOTES AND REFERENCES

1. M. G. Smith, *A Framework for Caribbean Studies* (Kingston, Jamaica, 1955); "Social Structure in the British Caribbean about 1820," *Social and Economic Studies* 1, no. 4 (1953); "Ethnic and Cultural Pluralism in the British Caribbean," working paper for the thirtieth study session of the International Institute of Differing Civilizations (Lisbon, Portugal, 1957); "Social and Cultural Pluralism," in *Social and Cultural Pluralism in the Caribbean,* Annals of the New York Academy of Sciences 83, art. 5 (1960); *The Plural Society in the British West Indies* (Berkeley and Los Angeles, 1965); *Stratification in Grenada* (Berkeley and Los Angeles, 1965).

2. R. T. Smith, "People and Change," in *New World: Guyana Independence Issue,* ed. George Lamming (Georgetown, Guyana, 1966).

3. See for example such works as P. D. Curtin, *Two Jamaicas* (Cambridge, Mass., 1955); Burton Benedict, *Indians in a Plural Society* (London, 1961); S. N. Eisenstadt, *The Absorption of Immigrants* (London, 1954).

4. R. Dahrendorf, *Class and Class Conflict in Industrial Society* (London, 1959); R. Bendix, *Max Weber: An Intellectual Portrait* (New York, 1960).

5. See C. Geertz, ed., *Old Societies and New States* (New York, 1963); T. Parsons, *Structure and Process in Modern Societies* (New York, 1960); E. Shils, "Political Development in the New States," in *Comparative Studies in History and Society*, 2 (1960): 265–92, 379–411; S. N. Eisenstadt, *Modernization: Protest and Change* (Englewood Cliffs, N. J., 1966).

6. H. Gerth and C. W. Mills, eds., *From Max Weber: Essays in Sociology* (New York, 1946).

7. There has been a tendency to suppose that the form taken by slavery, and the degree of its harshness, was dependent upon whether the slave owners were Catholic or Protestant. Tannenbaum, Elkins, and Klein have argued in this vein but Elsa Goveia, in a critical review published in *Comparative Studies in Society and History* 8, no. 3 (1966) shows that the critical variable involved here is not religion but the form of plantation organization involved.

8. See R. T. Smith, "Social Stratification, Cultural Pluralism and Integration in West Indian Societies," in *Proceedings of the Third Conference of Caribbean Scholars* (Puerto Rico, 1967).

9. See G. Lewis, *Puerto Rico: Freedom and Power in the Caribbean* (New York, 1963); M. Tumin and A. Feldman, *Social Class and Social Change in Puerto Rico* (Princeton, 1961).

10. Gerth and Mills, *From Max Weber*, p. 181.

11. L. A. Fallers, "Equality, Modernity and Democracy in the New States," in *Old Societies and New States*, ed. C. Geertz (New York, 1963).

12. The situation is not dissimilar to that described by Geertz for Indonesia where he describes increased production and yields of rice which just keep up with population increase as "water-treading." See C. Geertz, *Agricultural Involution: Processes of Ecological Change in Indonesia* (Berkeley and Los Angeles, 1963).

13. It is extremely difficult to arrive at any exact measure of the level of unemployment and under-employment since so many people are seeking work, but many of them would not be prepared to work full-time. This is particularly true of women. On the other hand there are large numbers of people who may not be enumerated as "unemployed" but who shift from one form of casual labor to another, sometimes having as many as three or four different "jobs" in one day.

14. S. W. Mintz, "The Jamaican Internal Marketing Pattern," *Social and Economic Studies* 4, no. 1 (1955); M. Katzin, "The Business of Higglering in Jamaica," *Social and Economic Studies* 9, no. 3 (1960).

15. Lewis, *Puerto Rico*, p. 183.

16. Again this follows the Puerto Rican pattern. See Lewis, ibid., p. 249.

17. See M. G. Smith, "Education and Occupational Choice in Jamaica," *Social and Economic Studies* 9, no. 3 (1960).

18. G. E. Cumper, "Household and Occupation in Barbados," *Social and Economic Studies* 8, no. 2 (1959).

19. In particular localities within the framework of individual societies landowning elites may still be of critical importance. This is so in parts of Puerto Rico and certainly in the rural areas of Jamaica and in many of the small islands. In Martinique and Guadeloupe an old French landowning class is still of considerable importance even at a more inclusive level.

20. Lewis, *Puerto Rico*, pp. 244, 256–59.

21. See D. G. Hall, "Slaves and Slavery in the British West Indies," *Social and Economic Studies* 11, no. 4 (1962).

22. Particularly tradesmen who operated independently and paid a fixed proportion of their earnings to their owners.

23. See R. T. Smith, "Social Stratification, Cultural Pluralism and Integration in West Indian Societies," pp. 236–39, 246–50.

24. See C. Jayawardena, *Conflict and Solidarity in a Guianese Plantation* (London, 1962); J. Beaumont, *The New Slavery* (London, 1871); P. Curtin, *Two Jamaicas* (Cambridge, Mass., 1955); D. G. Hall, *Free Jamaica* (New Haven, 1959).

25. See E. Wolf and S. Mintz, "Haciendas and Plantations in Middle America and the Antilles," *Social and Economic Studies* 6, no. 3 (1957).

26. J. H. Steward, et al., *The People of Puerto Rico* (Urbana, Ill., 1956).

27. See T. Parsons, "Some Reflections on the Institutional Framework of Economic Development," in *Structure and Process in Modern Societies* (Glencoe, Ill., 1959).

28. R. T. Smith, "Social Stratification, Cultural Pluralism and Integration in West Indian Societies," pp. 233–44.

29. As Anthony Trollope pointed out in his book *The West Indies and the Spanish Main* (New York, 1860), the Governor had a fairly free hand to run civil society as he wished, and could even be sure of planter votes for his policies—on one condition. Here, in speaking of Guyana, he reports a planter's conversation with the Governor: "We are not particular to a shade in what way we are governed. If you have any fads of your own about this or about that, by all means indulge them. Even if you want a little more money, in God's name take it. But the business of a man's life is sugar: there's the land; the capital shall be forthcoming, whether begged, borrowed, or stolen;—do you supply the labour. Give us Coolies enough, and we will stick at nothing" (p. 197).

30. Trollope, *The West Indies and the Spanish Main,* p. 99.

31. Various institutions of higher education were started soon after emancipation, mainly for the training of clergy. This was partly because of the difficulty of recruiting suitable clergymen from Europe, though the Jamaican Baptists had the positive notion that a local clergy was necessary and not simply a matter of not being able to get outsiders. During the nineteenth century various suggestions were put forward and some starts made toward the creation of a West Indies university but these efforts came to nothing until the foundation of the University of the West Indies in 1948.

32. See Tumin and Feldman, *Social Class and Social Change in Puerto Rico.*

33. Gerth and Mills, *From Max Weber,* pp. 186–87.

34. Ibid., p. 188.

35. W. Dickson, *Mitigation of Slavery* (Pt. 2: Letters to Thomas Clarkson) (London, 1814), p. 512; cited in D. G. Hall, "Slaves and Slavery in the British West Indies," p. 314.

36. See Goveia's comment referred to in note 8 above for an important qualification to the view of religion as the key variable here.

37. See C. Geertz, "The Integrative Revolution," in *Old Societies and New States.*

38. As recently as 1965 there were widespread and apparently irrational outbreaks of violence against Chinese shopkeepers in Jamaica.

39. See R. T. Smith, *British Guiana* (Oxford, 1962), pp. 49–57.

40. Rastafarians are members of a cult, begun during the Italian-Ethiopian war, which proclaims the divinity of Haile Selassie and demands repatriation to Africa for its members. It is closely related to similar movements among New World Negroes but is distinguished by its asserted rejection of Jamaican society and its laws. Many

Rastafarians engage in such conspicuous actions as growing their hair long in accordance with their idea of East African styles, and some smoke marijuana in defiance of Jamaican law. Although the actual number of Rastafarians is quite small, they represent a much more widespread dissatisfaction among lower-class Jamaicans.

41. See a very interesting article on this subject by James A. Mau, "The Threatening Masses: Myth or Reality?" in *The Caribbean in Transition,* ed. F. M. Andic and T. G. Mathews (Puerto Rico, 1965).

42. Gerth and Mills, *From Max Weber,* p. 194.

43. Lewis, *Puerto Rico,* p. 143.

44. *Report of the British Guiana Commission of Inquiry Constituted by the International Commission of Jurists: Racial Problems in the Public Service* (Geneva, 1965), p. 32.

45. For a fuller account of the events of this period see R. T. Smith, *British Guiana,* pp. 163–83.

46. A. M. Schlesinger, *A Thousand Days* (New York, 1967), pp. 708–13.

47. See Steward et al., *The People of Puerto Rico,* pp. 500–02.

Stratification in Plural Societies: Focus on White Settler Societies in Africa

In this paper, I deal generally with stratification in plural societies and specifically with stratification in the white settler societies of Africa. Both terms, *plural societies* and *white settler societies,* require some definition. I shall follow M. G. Smith in regarding the differential incorporation of groups in hierarchical relationships as characteristic of plural societies.[1] The joint stock company may serve as an analogy, with its differential incorporation of categories of stockholders and preferential and ordinary shareholders. The forms of this incorporation are exceedingly varied, including slavery, serfdom, tributary relations, castes, estates, and parliamentary systems. The differentially incorporated groups generally have different cultures and are of different racial or ethnic stock. In an extreme form of plural society, structural divisions coincide with cultural and racial or ethnic distinctions.

The white settler society is a plural society in which domination and settlement by whites is associated with great cultural diversity of the plural sections. If independence is stipulated as necessary to the constitution of white settler societies, then only South Africa—and perhaps Rhodesia— among all the states of Africa have moved to white settler status. I shall use white settler society in its pure sense to denote an independent society under white settler domination, and I shall deal primarily with South African society, but—to extend the range of comparative material—I shall also use the term loosely to include colonial African societies with "appreciable" white settler populations.[2] Differential incorporation is effected in the constitution of white settler societies, ramifying from the central political system through other institutional structures. Constitutions tend to be parliamentary, with the result that provision for categories of persons with full franchise, or restricted franchise, or under total exclusion from the franchise provides a rough index of differential incorporation.

From the wide range of problems and perspectives relating to stratification in white settler societies, I have selected for analysis some of the relations between class, status (in the sense of position resting on estimation of honor), and power, and some processes of change in the resultant systems of stratification. I shall examine these relations at two different periods of time, a hypothetical pre-industrial or early industrial period, and a period of advanced industrialization; and I shall consider how they are expressed at collective and individual levels, and how they are affected by criteria of ascription and achievement.

I

I assume that differential incorporation in the central political system is the primary basis of stratification in white settler societies. To an appreciable extent, there is a determinism by political factors. This is not to suggest that white settler societies emerge as fully constituted states, suddenly and without preamble. Antecedent factors influence the modes and conditions of incorporation. There may be a preliminary period of contact, leading to the negotiation of a protectorate relationship under treaty; or hostile frontier relations and intermittent wars may precede incorporation which develops in a quite variable way as the area of domination extends; or there may be an early direct group confrontation and conquest, but this occurs rarely without prior contact and interaction. To describe the political incorporation as primary and determining no doubt exaggerates its significance, but it is certainly central to the system of stratification and is so perceived by both white settlers and native peoples. Restratification is essentially a struggle between subordinate groups seeking to change the terms of political incorporation and dominant groups using the power of the state to maintain differential incorporation.

This process may be traced in any of the white settler states. In South Africa, the Act of Union in 1910 structured the racial hierarchy by a graded system of parliamentary participation and exclusion, and many of the later constitutional changes were directed to revision of this system, so as to perpetuate white dominion more effectively; apartheid itself, far from effecting a separation of groups, integrates them more rigidly by differential incorporation in the central political system, as well as in the political systems of other institutional structures. In Rhodesia, the struggle by white settlers to maintain racial domination is expressed primarily at the constitutional level, in a conflict over conditions of parliamentary participation, and in the Government's unilateral declaration of independence. In Kenya, the racial composition of the Legislative and Executive Councils early became the focus of a constitutional struggle, in which Africans were the final victors; contemporary African rule derives in large measure from evolutionary constitutional change in the conditions of incorporation. In Algeria, by contrast, revolutionary change followed on the failure of constitutional reforms. In all these cases, the relationship to the means of government is the crucial variable in the system of stratification. Differential incorporation gives a central role to the political institutions, channeling social mobility mainly through processes of political change.

By reason of the dominance of the political structure, the market situation is neither free nor competitive; in particular, participation of subordinate groups is severely controlled. Not all strata are drawn into the market economy. There is, in fact, a quite variable relationship to the market situation and its life chances. Many Africans continue a modified form of traditional subsistence economy and tribal organization. They have experienced enclosure of land by white settlers, and they often live overcrowded, in great poverty, on the deteriorating lands which remain theirs under communal forms of ownership or occupation. At this level, Africans and whites are dialectically opposed in the sense that the increasing affluence of white farmers confronts the growing misery of African peasants, seemingly as cause and effect.[3] Presumably the collective organization and material deprivation of these African peasants should provide the social conditions for political mobilization and revolutionary action, but in general they seem more inclined to a persistent conservatism.

The many Africans living and working on white farms are almost equally detached from the market situation. Their conditions vary from forced labor and near serfdom to contracted employment. Low and unregulated wages may be combined with the right to farm a small piece of land in exchange for months of service to the white farmer. Wives and children are often committed to labor in these service obligations. The poverty of the farm worker is perhaps as great as that of the peasant, and his mode of life is similar, but the social context is profoundly different. In contrast to the collective organization of peasant society, farm workers are fragmented in segregated clusters of subordination to individual masters, a situation of disconnected living which impedes collective political action.

The strata most engaged in the market economy are the urban industrial and commercial workers, but even here there is variability. At one extreme are workers permanently settled in the cities with their families; they are the descendants of peasants, pried out of their traditional settings by the negative inducements of taxation and poverty, and the positive attractions of new needs and desires. At the other extreme are migrant workers, converting urban wage into traditional subsistence. Even in South Africa, the most highly urbanized and industrialized of the white settler societies, insulation from urban life may be considerable, as for example, in the compounds of the gold mines, where colonies of mostly pagan workers are collectively housed in ethnic enclaves; or the insulation may be quite voluntary and derive from commitment to tradition, as among Red Blanket Xhosa in the port town of East London. But in general, African townsmen follow an urban mode of life, under the conditions of a racially regulated market situation, which nevertheless exposes them to an ethnic diversity of contact. These are circumstances which might be expected to promote movements of African nationalism or economic radicalism.

The market situation, as it affects the occupational structure of white settler societies, may be described in general terms, first, as confining Africans to unskilled manual work while reserving skilled, clerical, professional, and managerial work for whites; second, as monopolizing for whites leading positions in all political structures, of state, church, education, economy, and recreation; and third, as imposing an extreme inequality in wage by reason of the convergence of economic, political, and other institutional expressions of racial stratification. These general terms, however, somewhat distort the actual situation in the direction of conventional stereotypes. Some Africans are engaged in semi-skilled and skilled manual occupations, and in clerical and professional occupations which link the racial groups or arise in the interstices between them. I have in mind, for example, the auxiliary African elite of evangelists, priests, court officials, interpreters, and teachers, on whom white missionaries and administrators have always depended; and to these must now be added the African incumbents of many positions in intercalary structures designed to regulate the racial order, such as tribal authorities and school boards. In interstitial occupations are agents who mediate between the dominant and subordinate sections, assisting fellow Africans to comply with oppressive bureaucratic rule. There are honorific occupations, such as Prophet or Bishop in the Zionist Churches or President of an independent Ethiopian Church, in which Africans may rise above the racial confinement of life chances and human dignity. And there are small but increasing numbers of Africans in the independent liberal professions of law and medicine and in retail trade. Restriction of Africans to the lowest levels of employment is the general, but by no means the exclusive, mode of economic incorporation.

Conversely, while it is true that whites as a group occupy the main positions in the economy of the society and reserve for themselves most of its opportunities, whites as individuals nevertheless are distributed through all layers of the economic structure. If they are to be classified in relation to ownership of the means of production, then the majority must be described as proletariat or *petite bourgeoisie*. The conventional view of white settlers as a class of *grande bourgeoisie* derives from the attribution of certain qualities of the collectivity to all its individual members. To be sure, white settler communities vary in their patterns of recruitment and of class structure; Kenya settlers, in the early days of settlement, for example, were recruited quite appreciably from upper- and middle-class strata. But there is inevitably structural diversification in the movement from colonial administration to white settlement, from a sprinkling of civil servants and missionaries to substantial communities of farmers, artisans, traders, industrialists, and professionals.

Characteristically, white settler societies of a sometime English persuasion include not only white settlers and African peoples but also third groups imported for labor in the colonies. The conception of a British Empire encouraged the planned interchanges and labor migrations of peoples within its widely extended boundaries. The effect was further to complicate the plural complexities and tensions of the societies. As to the system of stratification, political, academic, and lay intelligences often locate these introduced groups in a middle stratum of a three-tier structure, with white settlers at the apex and Africans at the base. This can greatly misrepresent the facts, again by a process of stereotyping which converts collective achievement into individual attribute. Where the introduced group is numerous, its members are certain to be distributed over the entire range of occupations. For example, although it is true that Indians own many retail shops in several South African cities, most South African Indians are working-class, living in great poverty quite comparable to that of Africans. They are conveniently, but falsely, described as traders in the sacrificial rites of scapegoating.

I have been defining the system of stratification thus far in terms of the market situation of the different racial groups. I make the assumption, following Weber, that a common market situation represents a possible and frequent, but not inevitable, basis for communal action. Whether communal action will result depends upon, among other factors, the nature of the contrasts and the transparency of the connections between the life chances of different classes, upon the opportunities for mobilizing the members of a class, upon the presence of other bases for communal action, and upon the salience and appeal of these other bases for leaders and followers. I do not mean to imply that there must be a realistic basis for communal action, nor that communal action is most likely to develop from the basis which seems most compelling and promising, objectively considered. The situation is indeterminate, leaving scope for "false consciousness" and other forms of human choice, and for political initiative and distortion.

The two major bases for communal action in white settler societies are race and the market situation, conceived in terms of opportunities for goods and income or of the relationship to the means of production. They do not coincide; as I have shown, there are differences in class situation among members of the same race, and a common class situation among members of different race. Race is clearly the more compelling, or opportune, basis for social mobilization. Indeed, it is only in abstraction from the differential political incorporation of the races that it is possible to speak of whites and non-whites as sharing a common class situation. The market situation seems to derive from the racial situation, and market competition readily converts to racial conflict. From the earliest days, whites have imposed a specifically racial regulation of the market situation in their own interests at all levels, and communal action between whites and non-whites, directed to shared market interests, has been minimal. As between African and Indian workers in South Africa, and under the influence of common elements in their political and market situation, there have been clear intimations of communal action but precarious, threatened by racial antipathy and competition. In the case of African traders, however, the competition with Indian traders has tended to take a racial and scapegoating form.

Corresponding to the limited communal action, there appears to be little consciousness of common class interests. I do not mean to imply that class consciousness automatically arises out of the objective situation; on the contrary, it is a product of intellectual formulation, acquired by training in the home, in school, in workers' colleges, and in country clubs as well as through mass media and in political and trade union organizations. In white settler societies, sensitivity training in class perception is limited by the preoccupation with race. The racial definitions are elaborated and inculcated, and the racial perspectives are primary, with classes seen as divisions within each racial group and not as drawing together members of different racial groups.

The general pervasiveness and dominance of race rests on the differential incorporation of the groups in the political structure of white settler societies, which enables the dominant group to seek regulation of the market situation toward consonance with political and other institutional stratification. It has not been greatly challenged by industrialization, which is still of modest proportions—even in South Africa, the most highly industrialized of the African states—and has not generated a volume of contact and interaction in any way comparable with race relations which are societal in extension. However, before I consider the possible consequences of a high level of industrialization in white settler societies, I want to comment on concepts of honor, as they affect the system of stratification.

II

I use the term *honor* to refer to both positive and negative evaluation of social positions, social strata, and racial groups. In some contexts, it is of relevance only to the minutiae of stratification; in others, it affects the very structure of the system. I shall consider three aspects: (1) What are the various conceptions of the prestige of occupations within the context of the market situation? (2) To what extent has there been a formation of status groups? (3) Related to the second point, to what extent does the hierarchy of race rest upon a recognized entitlement to honor? Here I have in mind Weber's discussion of the transformation of horizontal and unconnected coexistences of ethnically segregated groups into a vertical social system of super- and subordination, and his explanation of their different consequences. "Ethnic coexistences condition a mutual repulsion and disdain but allow each ethnic community to consider its own honor as the highest one; the caste structure brings about a social subordination and an acknowledgement of 'more honor' in favor of the privileged caste and status groups."[4] To what extent, then, have elements of consensus emerged in the acknowledgment of racial claims to honor?

There has been little research on the prestige of occupations in African societies. This has not inhibited scholars, however, from concluding that Africans greatly honor education and accord highest prestige to the professional occupations, and the available evidence does, indeed, support the conclusion that the professions are highly rated. Since education and income are equally characteristic of the professions, however, it is not clear which quality commands the greater esteem. African evaluation may reflect the values of the dominant group since the professions are highly regarded in Western industrial society. But again, the occupational values of white settlers are not really known and may be quite distinctive. Entrepreneurial activity in developing economies holds such promise for social mobility and is so rewarding even for those of modest and untutored accomplishment that it may well be accorded very high prestige; and white settlers may have a greater affinity for occupations of virile moneymaking than for those of genteel learning. There may be differences, too, between sections of the white population; thus, I have the impression that in South Africa, education stands in higher repute with the Afrikaners than it does with the English.

The pluralism of white settler societies enters most intricately into the evaluation of occupations. It patterns occupational opportunity and experience differently for the various groups, perhaps excluding Africans from such occupations as engineer, accountant, financier, and industrialist, or channeling Indians into manual labor and retail shopkeeping, or reserving senior civil service, managerial, and executive positions for whites. Presumably the perception of occupations is related to this variant experience.

Occupations take on coloration from the broader system of stratification. Characteristically manual labor becomes associated with Africans and falls into disrepute amongst whites; so, too, occupations concerned with Africans, such as white superintendents of African locations, are diminished in status by what is seemingly perceived as a contagion of contact. Conversely, Africans in occupations generally reserved for whites may enjoy an exaggerated esteem.

Reactions to racial domination affect the prestige of certain occupations and the esteem for style of performance in these occupations. In a white settler society where restrictive legislation against Africans and convictions for petty offenses are common—as they are in South Africa, the profession of law can offer some protection against persecution. Hence, Africans may give high honor to an African lawyer who performs as a "lion in the courts." They will also honor a white lawyer in the same role, which is, however, likely to draw upon him the opprobrium of his own racial group. An African doctor demonstrates by the very fact of his qualification that the African race is entitled to honor and equality; the President of an Ethiopian Church asserts African independence and equality, perhaps playing the role of a Daniel for his people.

In terms of the relevance of race relations to occupational prestige among Africans, I distinguish several categories. There is, first, the prestige of the African auxiliary elite, such as civil servants, which derives from their role in relation to white authority; ambiguity attaches to this form of prestige. Second, there is the prestige attached to positions in the interstices between the white and African sections, such as those of Bishop or Prophet in the Zionist Churches, honored mainly by lower-class strata and largely rejected by middle-class Africans. Third, there is the prestige of occupations, or esteem for style of performance in occupations, which challenge white authority: the "lion of the courts," for example. And finally, there is the prestige of occupations which enjoy high standing among whites, and even higher standing among Africans, because of the greater rarity of the achievement and its symbolic racial significance.

Prestige by ascription and prestige by achievement may be so interwoven as to produce extreme incongruity. I have referred to the exaggerated prestige enjoyed by Africans for achievement of professional status, as in law or medicine. This prestige often is acknowledged also by whites, for many of whom it may serve the function of reinforcing belief in African inferiority. By exaggerated praise of an African who achieves a professional status which is commonplace among whites, they assert the extraordinary quality of the achievement as transcending what they assume to be the limitations of African genetic condition.[5] Now African professionals combine in their positions this inflated prestige of achievement with the deflated racial status ascribed to them under the political constitution, a situation of intense incongruity. In the case of whites, low occupational position is particularly debasing because it challenges the ascriptive prestige of race. Thus, at the lowest occupational levels, whites combine negatively valued achievement with all the privileges attached to the ascribed high status of race, again a situation of incongruity. Maximum tension is engendered in the confrontation of these two categories of incongruent status.

Comments on the second problem I raised, concerning the formation of status groups in white settler societies, must be impressionistic, given the dearth of research. Status groups did form to a very limited extent across racial divisions. In some towns, there were interracial status groups of African, European, and Indian intellectuals and professionals, sharing a common Western culture combined with an emphasis on the exotic beauty of Indian civilization, which seemed to provide the core of associational interest and enrichment. The presence of a third (middle) ethnic section may be an important stimulus to the growth of interracial groups of high status. Presumably these groups may serve as an index of the state of divisive pluralism within a society. Where they flourish, this perhaps indicates a societal trend toward integration.

For the most part, status groups form within ethnic and racial divisions. They are clear at the extremes of high and low status, which is perhaps usually the case in systems of stratification. I have the impression, however, that clarity of definition is sharpest in subordinate groups. Here there seems to be a greater awareness of high status and a greater gulf separating high and low status groups. If this is, indeed, the case, I suggest the following explanation. In the dominant section, there is so much opportunity, and so little restraint on action, that class structure and status order tend to be continuous. Moreover, there is the common ascribed prestige of race and an appreciable diffusion of the resources and styles of bourgeois life. In the subordinate sections, by contrast, the great majority subsist in relatively undifferentiated poverty. Emergence from this poverty to high professional status effects a profound transformation in economic condition, in style of life, and in life chances; it involves also a cultural transformation. Hence, members of the emerged elite are greatly differentiated from the mass of their people, and this differentiation is increased, I would suppose, by the adoption of some of the extreme forms of social distance current in the society and expressed in the relations of the dominant toward the subordinate racial groups.

Within the dominant white group, the extremes correspond to what French writers describe as *grands colons* and *petits blancs*. The upper status group of white settlers may be characterized by the magnificence of its possessions, the abundance of its servants, the leisure of its women, and the display of its prestige. Among the English in South Africa, this upper stratum combines something of the style of life of the master of a Virginian plantation with that of an English aristocrat as set forth in the pages of fashionable journals. The lowest status group is perhaps best characterized by the ambiguity of its interstitial position in the structure of racial domination. By its very presence, it challenges the ascribed prestige of the white race. This ambiguity is most clearly illustrated by the status group described as "poor whites" in South Africa. The term itself conveys that two incompatible qualities, poverty and whiteness, are being combined to constitute an unnatural and grave problem. And, indeed, the state of poverty within a dominant group, as in the case of the "poor whites" among the Afrikaners of South Africa, may be conducive to political extremism, physical brutality, and social disorganization.

African status groups within the exchange economy may also be defined in terms of their interstitial positions between Africans and whites, or between traditional and Westernized African communities. I have already commented on the ambiguous position of the African educated elite, combining high status by achievement with low status by race. Even among Africans, the very high prestige accorded the educated elite is affected by distrust of their often instrumental role in racial domination, and of their general alienation from many traditional values. This elite may be characterized by standard of living, modest but elevated above that of the common man, a somewhat bourgeois style of life within the limits permitted by grave discrimination, some freedom of occupational expression, and an acknowledged right to leadership. At a different status level, and intermediate between the traditional African and the Western urban sectors, are the migrant groups. They move between town and country, maintaining many traditional customs; they show an affinity for Zionist type prophetic religions, which effect a syncretism between Christianity and ancestral beliefs; and they have little knowledge of Western civilization and technology. Some of these groups so insulate themselves, so strongly reject the West, and so insistently assert traditional values that they can hardly be regarded as part of a status order which includes both the educated elite and themselves.

Discontinuity in values is most marked in the evaluation of racial status. I suppose that the dominant group perceives the racial hierarchy as a status order resting on legitimate claims to honor. There seems to be a general, though not universal, consensus among white settlers that they form a racial elite, not merely by reason of political differentiation but by right of racial superiority; and there seems to be a general denigration of African racial status, though again not universal and varying in content from conceptions of ineradicable inferiority to paternalist conceptions of underprivilege. An idealization of Africans may also be found in white settler attitudes, but rarely, and I take the norm to be one of contemptuous rejection on grounds of alleged biological inferiority.

African reactions, both to their own status and to the status of whites, are more complex, and different aspects must be distinguished, relating not only to race but also to culture and political domination. It is customary to say that Africans accepted from whites the image of their own inferiority. Certainly, many texts convey the repugnance felt by educated African Christians for the traditions of their people; but there was also repugnance for aspects of Western life and, in particular, for what was conceived as a lack of humanity. Subordinate groups, under conditions of extreme discrimination, often react to the humiliations of their inferior status in the society by asserting their superiority in human quality, as of intellect among Jews, or of humanity among Africans, or of religious state of grace, as among many deprived groups. Perhaps African reactions combined sentiments of both inferiority and superiority. It should be remembered that contact between Africans and white settlers takes place in a situation in which Africans are moving toward the increasing adoption of many elements of Western culture. They cannot fail to recognize the military, technological, and scientific power of white settlers and the efficiency of their formal educational systems; and there are no doubt many other aspects of Western culture which have a strong appeal. But all this relates to culture, not to the intrinsic qualities of the person, and it becomes difficult to disengage sentiments of cultural superiority or attraction or shame, and reactions to domination, from sentiments of racial dignity or contumely.

I do not know to what extent whites are perceived as a single social unit, "the white man." Certainly there are terms for the white man in African languages. But in the first place, whites occupy very different positions in the class and status structure of the society, and Africans are aware of this diversity. This, indeed, is one source of acute conflict, since the lowest strata among whites most aggressively assert white domination. In the second place, whites are of different ethnic background, and knowledge of this difference is crystallized in African linguistic concepts, as for example in Zulu and Swahili, or in words introduced into the language of the colonial power. Thus, in research among Zulu-speaking people in South Africa, I found a distinction drawn between *abelungu* (white man) and *amabunu* (Boers or Afrikaners), and, in a sample population of African school teachers, the English were highly rated on certain qualities of character in sharp contrast to the Afrikaners. It is probably in the first stages of contact and later, only in the racist ideologies of conflict, that whites are most readily perceived in any such unified way as "the white man."

I think that I can best suggest some of the complexity of the evaluations of whites by reference to religious affiliation in response to Christianity. I offer this only by way of analogy, drawing on South African patterns. Traditional ancestral beliefs persist among a third of the African population, indicating not only commitment to tradition but some rejection of Western culture and its white bearers. The Zionist churches, effecting a syncretism between Christianity and ancestral worship, express repugnance both for white men and for their ways. The Ethiopian churches, like the Zionist, assert African independence from white control, but they take over the dogmas and rituals of the parent church, thereby affirming the religious beliefs introduced by white men while rejecting their domination. Finally, there are the large numbers of Africans (over two-fifths of the total population) in the mission churches, relating to Christian doctrine and white leadership within the institutional framework of a common religious domination, albeit under the most varied arrangements of segregation and accommodation.

Perhaps these responses convey some of the dimensions of the reactions to white claims of entitlement to honor. They must also be interpreted within a time perspective, differentiating, for example, periods of a qualified franchise in which many educated Africans saw their life chances as resting on personal acquisition of Western culture, from periods of disenfranchisement, collective commitment, and revolutionary challenge to white domination.

III

I turn now to the final problem, the effects of advanced industrialization on the relations between class, status, and power. As I have sketched these relations, there are many deviations from the general tendency for class situation and political power to coincide. They are particularly marked in the dominant group, whose members are distributed throughout most levels of the occupational structure. Deviations from close correspondence between the distributions of social honor and of political power in the dominant group are even more marked. The variable estimation by white setters themselves of the honor due to their own members contrasts sharply with their equality of power under the constitution of the state. There are white status groups accorded the highest prestige and others, interstitial in the structure, whose very pressence undermines claims to racial excellence. As to Weber's approach to the transformation of the horizontal and unconnected coexistences of ethnically segregated groups into a vertical social system of super- and subordination, I am sure it is safe to say, however reluctant I am to be dogmatic, that in contemporary African white settler societies, white settler claims to "more honor" are widely rejected.

The tensions between class, status, and power are a stimulus to dynamic change in the system of stratification. Industrialization may be expected to act in the same direction. However, the relations I have been discussing between class, status, and power are quite consistent with a level of industrialization characterized by a high rate of economic growth and of capital investment, as in South Africa. In saying this, I do not mean to imply that the industrializing process has not engendered pressures toward racial restratification. Quite apart from other consequences, it creates a social basis for movements of African nationalism and revolution. But in the first place, the economic relations in industry are regulated to conform as far as possible with the political structure of stratification; the collective barriers of racial ascription are raised against individual mobility by achievement. In the second place, the structure of power is such as to provide ready means for equilibration. In general, the greater the tendency for industrialization to modify the extreme inequality of racial stratification, the more rigid and unequal become the conditions of differential incorporation in the polity.[6] In South Africa, the enactment of a wide range of laws to control occupational mobility, to restrict interracial contact and to curtail and abolish the non-white franchise coincided with high and sustained rates of industrial growth.

The initial consequences of industrialization are thus an increasing political racial extremism in the attempt to maintain a dynamic equilibrium of class, status, and power in the system of racial stratification. The sources of this extremism are the monopoly of constitutional political power by white settlers and the structure of the economic system. Since most white settlers are distributed toward the base of the white occupational structure, there is in the class situation of these settlers, who constitute a majority of voters and are most exposed to competition by subordinate groups, the social basis for politics of racial extremism.

Let me suppose that we now leap over a period of years. Industrialization is much advanced. National income has more than doubled, return on investment attracts local and international capital to new enterprise, and high rates of economic growth are maintained. In the process, the market situation is transformed for white settlers. They do not experience industrialization as a dialectical process, and the standard of living of all sections rises. There is a redistribution toward middle-class occupations, so that the occupational structure of whites becomes more diamond-shaped; but this does not mean that they are insulated from competition, which is likely to be directed by subordinate groups at different levels; low and intermediate. White occupational distribution becomes more continuous and less stratified, though there are still strata of lumpenproletariat, and of relatively unskilled manual and clerical workers.

Among Africans, large numbers remain in their traditional subsistence economies, politically controlled under direct or indirect rule, but otherwise, somewhat marginally incorporated in the larger society. Agricultural production in white farming areas becomes more efficient and mechanized to meet the increasing demands of industrialization, and there is some employment for Africans at higher levels of farming skill, including managerial responsibility. Farming is more fully integrated into the industrial economy. Migrant strata are absorbed into the large and growing African urban proletariat. For Africans, too, industrialization is not a dialectical process. They are not depressed into ever greater misery, but, on the contrary, their living standards also rise, albeit slowly and laboriously. More opportunities open at higher levels, increasing the number of professionals, retail traders, and embryonic industrialists. There are African chambers of commerce, finance corporations, building investment and insurance societies, and growing sophistication in the channeling of African purchasing power toward African bourgeois aggrandizement. In general, class structure becomes more pronounced among Africans as it becomes more tenuous among whites, and there is an increasing area of overlap in the market situation of the two groups.

I assume that changes in the distribution of honor within each of the racial groups will follow much the same pattern, namely dispersion among whites and concentration into status groups among Africans. The reason for this lies in their different opportunities for distinction under conditions of economic expansion. Lacking an aristocracy and greatly appreciative of wealth and its manifestations, so that there is a close correspondence between class and status (in the Weberian sense), members of the white group experience great social mobility, which renders both the class and status structures more fluid and continuous. However, low marginal status groups persist, this being characteristic, so it seems, of plural societies. By contrast with whites, the more limited opportunity for Africans in a racially controlled market situation, encourages the formation of high status groups, with a distinctive Westernized upper-class style of life.

As for the distribution of honor between racial groups, I assume that in a world with independent African states and an international ethos of racial equality, white settlers increasingly abandon claims of entitlement to racial honor, and Africans more universally reject any such claims. The system of racial domination, that is to say, is stripped of any pretensions to moral legitimation.

Assuming such changes in the class and status orders as I have sketched above, there remains the problem of the consequences of these changes and of advanced industrialization for the political system of stratification. I am sure that they are indeterminate. They depend on the actions of African nations and of the United Nations, on the state of the Cold War and the policies of the great powers, and on the choices of Africans and non-Africans—rank-and-file and leaders—within South Africa itself. The survival of the system is contrary to reason and morality, but clearly this is not an adequate basis for predicting its demise. The political institutions may have generated so much power—by increase in organizational capacity and skill, by multiplication of structures of control, by fragmentation of subordinate groups, and by mobilization of naked force—that they are able to maintain an equilibrium of class, status, and power. The social system may be viable for many years.

If the system is changed by revolution, I would expect the form of that revolution to be racial radicalism rather than economic radicalism. I do not think that black and white proletariat will come together as long as whites enjoy a franchise from which Africans are excluded. It seems almost inevitable that white workers should seek economic protection by political means on grounds of race, so that racial membership would retain its crucial significance. In any event, Africans themselves must perceive the social system in racial terms. By reason of the differential incorporation of the races in the polity, it is race, not class, which is the main determinant of their life chances. Racial status becomes continuously more salient, since the political system has a dialectical quality in terms of race relations; the more white settlers increase the power of the central political institutions to counter changes in the class and status orders, the greater is the deprivation of power experienced by Africans. They are thus driven to challenge the specifically racial constitution of the society, and they cannot fail to be attracted by the possibility of a reversal of the racial order, by which they would control the industrial and other resources in their own interests, rather than share control with their former exploiters. The revolutionary challenge is all the more likely to take the form of racial radicalism since, I assume, the African proletariat will need assistance from the African bourgeoisie. They can come together on the basis of common race but not of common class; and leadership for racial causes should be readily offered by members of a bourgeoisie, experiencing both a material enhancement and a racial frustration of their life chances.

There is also a possibility of evolutionary change in response to revolutionary challenge. The social basis for this evolutionary change would be the dependence of white industrialists on African labor, and common interests between sections of the African and white bourgeoisie. Differential incorporation of the racial groups in the political structure might be progressively abolished by a series of constitutional reforms. Since political equality would not eliminate the unequal command over resources by the racial groups, the effect might be to transform a system of racial domination into one of class domination in which, however, there would be a high correlation between race and class. Hardly conducive to stability, this might be expected to activate new movements of racial radicalism unless industrialization rapidly resulted in the distribution of abundant gratification throughout the society.

NOTES AND REFERENCES

1. See M. G. Smith, "Institutional and Political Conditions of Pluralism," in *Pluralism in Africa,* ed. Leo Kuper and M. G. Smith (Berkeley and Los Angeles, 1969).

2. See my paper "Political Change in White Settler Societies," in *Pluralism in Africa.*

3. Ibid.

4. H. H. Gerth and C. W. Mills, eds., *From Max Weber: Essays in Sociology* (New York, 1958), p. 189.

5. Whites do not accord Indians this exaggerated prestige. On the contrary, their achievement is resented.

6. See my paper, "Political Change in White Settler Societies," cited above, and Pierre L. van den Berghe, *South Africa* (Middletown, Conn., 1965), chap. 8.

Melanesian Mosaic: The Plural Community of Vila

Furnivall (1948:304) characterized plural society as a medley of peoples who mix but do not combine. The term, variously specified or refined, can be applied not only in Southeast Asia, but widely in colonial and immigrant countries. Throughout the Pacific Islands, Europeans came in the nineteenth century as traders, then as missionaries, planters, men of commerce, and finally as the administering power. Asians entered these territories from the late nineteenth century onward as laborers and later as small shopkeepers and artisans. Islanders migrated to work in European enterprises. In every center of economic and political development, the local islanders were soon outnumbered by immigrant islanders from more distant places seeking employment. Nearly everywhere in the South Pacific such a mixture of peoples can be found. Indigenous political and economic development has not yet displaced the dominance of Asians and Europeans.

While the phenomenon of plural society has been widely observed, as

The research was supported by the Australian National University and included funds for field assistance and data analysis. Marney Anderson and several other assistants worked in Vila and in Canberra. Later data analysis was made possible by the British Ministry of Overseas Development and the State University of New York, Stony Brook. Suzi Matoba, Paula Weinstein, and Hal Levine helped with data analysis and tables.

yet few studies have been made of plural communities. In this paper I discuss Vila, in the New Hebrides, which has an exceptional variety of ethnic, racial, and national peoples and yet is one of the smallest capital towns in the Pacific. We shall look at Vila as a community and consider whether the persons in its several ethnic categories form social strata or other subdivisions with separate religious, cultural, economic, political, or social institutions. This is a case study of a small multi-ethnic community. The town can be treated as a social system, but I hope to show the great importance of ties outside. Vila does not have the protective and political associations found among ethnic groups where economic and power competition between groups is high, even though most of the townspeople are immigrants. Yet the ethnic categories are highly visible racially, linguistically, and culturally; the categories are also differentiated politically and economically; and mixing is selective and present in some institutional contexts only.

I shall here report on part of a study which I carried out with H. C. Brookfield in 1964 and 1965. No single theoretical approach is appropriate for this analysis. The discussion touches on several of the common topics of contemporary anthropology and sociology—urbanization, social stratification, and plural societies. The paper begins with a description of the town and its growth.

A century ago the Vila area was the home of several Melanesian villages, some of them located on small islands with gardens on the main island of Efaté. The area which became the town was the garden land of the people of Fila Island (Ilôt Vila) in the bay.

As a colonial community, Vila owes its origin to the French coconut planters' and traders' decision to place their economic interests at Port Vila in the 1880s and 1890s. At first French and British commercial interests were protected by a joint Naval Commission. An Anglo-French Convention was signed in 1906 establishing the New Hebrides Condominium and providing for a joint administration. The Condominium has a unique legal system: each government retains sovereignty over its nationals, and resident subjects of other powers must opt to be under either French or British law. In Vila and elsewhere, the New Hebrideans are under District Administration and considered neither British nor French. However, the two police forces and District Administrations are responsible for New Hebridean affairs.

By 1900, Vila was a social and political center with a Catholic mission, a school, a hospital, and shops. There were 143 French colonists.[1] In 1907, the Anglo-French Condominium was proclaimed with its capital at

Port Vila. Government buildings followed with offices and residences for officials and ever-increasing building for commercial activities, schools, churches, and private residences. Some small service industries—bakeries, butcher, tailor, and repair shops, etc.—were soon established. By 1914 Vila was a small colonial town, and soon more government departments, the wharf, radio and telephone services, military forces, public school and roads were established. Several thousand Vietnamese from Tonkin were brought in the 1920s and 1930s as contract laborers to work on French plantations. When their contracts expired, most of them were repatriated, and after 1940 most of the remaining Vietnamese were in the towns engaged in skilled occupations, selling vegetables and market gardening, running taxis and shops. Immigrant Chinese established shops, mostly in towns, from the 1920s onward.

Efaté was an American base from 1942 to 1945 with a naval station at Port Havannah and, in the Port Vila area, a military hospital, many new roads, and an air field. Since 1946 Vila has continued expanding its population, commerce, and governmental activities. To replace the departing Asians and to fill new needs for skilled personnel, other islanders have come to Vila. They can be distinguished as Polynesian (Tahiti, Wallis and Futuna, Tonga), Melanesian (Fiji, Solomon Islands, New Caledonia), or Micronesian (Gilbert Islands), but a more important distinction is between those from French or British colonies or protectorates, since the immigrant islanders are of French or British nationality, speak French or English, and work for French or British employers. In recent years there has been a growing population of mixed race, locally known as Métis.

Vila remains the commercial center of the Southern and Central Islands of the New Hebrides and the capital of the Condominium, but Santo in the north, which developed from an American base established in 1941, is of considerable commercial importance. In Vila new buildings of cement have gone up, a few new industries (such as meat freezing and canning and cement-block making) have been established, and there is much increased building and shipping. Tourism has hardly begun.

Vila has become an urban community through its settlement by foreigners—first the French traders and planters, and later more Europeans as missionary, government, and commercial personnel. The expanding town drew Asians and Islanders from distant places, and New Hebrideans from all parts of the New Hebrides group. Vila has not become a great population concentration—the whole New Hebrides island group in 1967 had a population of 76,582 people, with 9,452 in Efaté, 3,072 in the urban area of Vila town, and 7,738 in the Vila area (McArthur and Yaxley 1968).[2]

On the other criteria of urbanism, Vila presents a peculiar situation. As an urban community, Vila is neither very large nor densely settled, and it has not grown spectacularly. The technology and degree of occupational specialization are typically urban. It is the seat of government and the center for overseas transportation and for social life. But for its sophisticated segments of population, outside cultural centers are essential reference points. Vila is a cultural center (Redfield and Singer 1954) mainly for its own immediate hinterland and, to some extent, for the New Hebrides Group.

From an anthropologist's viewpoint, Vila is small enough to be studied without relying entirely on such techniques of urban study as questionnaires and sampling. Vila is most interesting when examined as a distinctive case of a plural community—ethnic relations and stratification taken together.

Studies of urbanism stress the cultural influence of cities as centers for the development and spread of new ideas, technological, and moral transformations. Redfield and Singer also point out a secondary pattern of urbanism: the folk society is "urbanized by contact with peoples of widely different cultures" (1954:61). They further note that colonial cities have developed as outposts of imperial civilizations and have culturally diverse populations. If we add to this a recognition of these plural communities as medleys, we may then ask whether the city has the same meaning and focus for all people in the community and its hinterland. My observations of Vila suggest that, in this small and minor colonial center, the city has not all the functions of an urban center for all of its people. It is a center for diffusion of Western ideas only for the indigenous people of its hinterland and the immigrating population from its outlying area; for that group, the New Hebrideans, it is a place of cultural diffusion in which nationalistic movements, education, technology, political and economic developments, etc., originate. Yet even the New Hebrideans know that they must look outside their territory for higher education and stimulation. Vila town, for all its population, including the diverse Melanesians, is a place where peoples mingle; the language used at home is hardly ever the main language spoken with work-mates or school-mates or in commercial activities.

The diverse ethnic categories are not true groups (Morris 1967:173); I shall refer to them as sections of the population. There is no way to classify them exclusively or exhaustively. Vila is a place of interaction for these sections, but it is not a center of development of any cultural tradition; it is an outpost of many different cultures. The many ethnic sections each look outside for the new ideas of their cultural tradition: to France, New Caledonia, England, Australia, New Zealand, China, Vietnam, Tahiti. In the Pacific region, New Caledonia is an outpost of French culture, Australia and New Zealand to a lesser extent of British culture, and these are Western, as opposed to Pacific Island or Asian. "Pacific Islander," which is not a true ethnic category, encompasses the separate categories of Tahitian, Fijian, etc., while "Asian" comprises Chinese, Vietamese, and others in smaller numbers. For most residents of Vila, outside reference groups and cultural traditions are of great importance. France or England is "home" to most of the Europeans. Many of them, especially the government employees, see their time in Vila as an interval between periods of home leave. The European plantation-owning families have their interests centered upon the New Hebrides and New Caledonia more than do the business or professional people of the town.

The population associated with Vila includes that of a number of Melanesian villages and the rural fringe from which town workers and school children commute daily or weekly. The connections between these people and the town is multiplex. They sell agricultural products, both consumable foods in the town market and tree products for export, and they buy food, clothing, and household goods in the town shops. About 46 per cent of the village men work in Vila, and villagers depend upon town commercial, governmental, educational, health, social, and other services. Yet the villages are self-contained communities in many respects. Further, there is no clear line between town and country, and participation in the community is not a simple function of distance. Some communities at a considerable distance from Vila participate more than some nearer villages (Brookfield, Brown Glick, and Hart, 1969). The rural area also contains European-owned plantations of mixed coconut and other tree crops, cattle, and some market gardens; the residents may have many or few ties to the town.

The Locality

Vila is focused upon the bay and rises steeply from the shore; commerce and shipping activities occupy the central part along the water. On prominences above, the Catholic church, Joint Court, and French and British Residencies were early established. Residential land has filled in the spaces between and above these, and all have encroached upon the former agricultural land—originally sparse native gardens which were later more

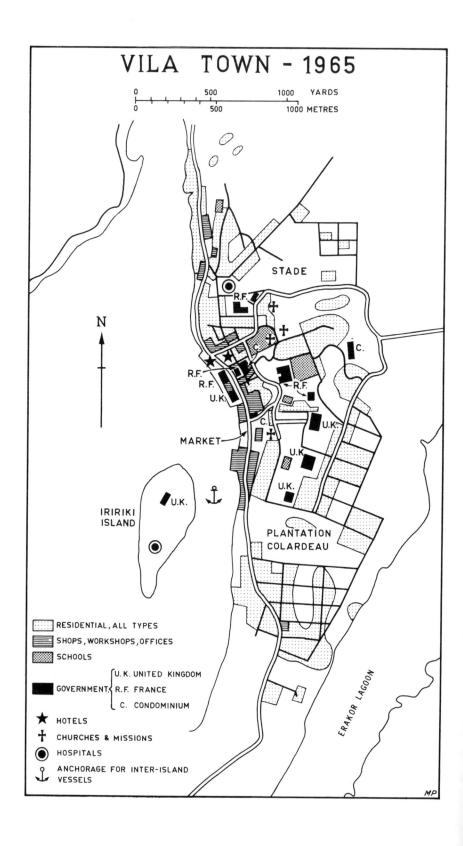

VILA TOWN - 1965

```
0          500        1000    YARDS
0          500        1000 METRES
```

N

STADE

R.F.

C.

R.F.
R.F.
U.K.

R.F.

C.

MARKET

U.K.

U.K.

U.K.

IRIRIKI
ISLAND

U.K.

PLANTATION
COLARDEAU

ERAKOR LAGOON

RESIDENTIAL, ALL TYPES
SHOPS, WORKSHOPS, OFFICES
SCHOOLS
GOVERNMENT { U.K. UNITED KINGDOM
             R.F. FRANCE
             C. CONDOMINIUM
HOTELS
CHURCHES & MISSIONS
HOSPITALS
ANCHORAGE FOR INTER-ISLAND
VESSELS

MP

densely planted with coconut trees, both by the villagers of Fila Island and two European plantations established in the 1880s. The region around Vila is now mixed: native village gardens and coconut groves, European plantations, Islanders' and Asians' market gardens, and various modern installations such as the airfield, schools, builders' workshops, and peri-urban housing all intermingle in the hinterland. Title to land in the town and its immediate environs has been completely taken over by non-Melanesians: individuals, commercial companies, governments, and churches.

The town has no fixed boundaries, save that it is a dog license area and a garbage collection district.[3] The main street, Rue Higginson, named after an Irish partisan of French interests, runs along the shore through a dense area of new and old Chinese shops, a taxi parking lot, the bank, two hotels, French and British District Agency offices, the Cultural Centre, Post Office, several large general stores controlled by outside French New Caledonian and Australian interests, the site of the weekly fresh foods market, mechanics' workshops, and dock installations. Little land is occupied by warehouses since copra, the largest export, is mainly stored in an old ship permanently moored in the harbor. Both north and south of the town area this road leads out to residential and agricultural land.

Iririki Island in the bay is the site of the British Resident Commissioner's house and the Presbyterian Mission hospital. The Melanesian community, which once owned Vila's land, has houses and gardens on Fila Island. Many Fila Islanders hold regular jobs in the town; their canoes pull up on the beach, and the women sell produce and cooked food in the market. There is regular launch service between both Iririki and Fila Island and the town. The harbor is used by government ships which tour the island group and by commercial copra and trade ships. Overseas cargo and tour ships call regularly, bringing imported goods and food, taking away produce, and allowing passengers and crew a brief visit ashore.

Although the town has no zoning or regular plan, some areal differences can be noted. Along the shore to the north, on low-lying land, are small houses mostly occupied by New Hebrideans who have come to Vila seeking employment. Some of these houses were first built in 1956–1962 for Vietnamese awaiting repatriation; when most of them left in 1963, the houses were occupied by Melanesians. In the central section of the town, in or near the shop buildings, are concentrated residences of Chinese and some Vietnamese. The central and north shore part of Vila is the most ethnically mixed area.

The northern section of the town stretching inland on rising land is private residences, mostly single-family houses of wood, occupied for the most part by French but with some others, including a cluster of Vietnamese around their Catholic Church. In the same area is the French hospital, police barracks, French Public School, Catholic Church and School, and Bureau de la Résidence de France. Still further out is the sports ground (Stade) and the Tennis Club. Scattered south of these on hills are the Joint Court buildings and some offices and residences of the Condominium service intermingled with private houses. Further south is the British Paddock, consisting of the United Kingdom government offices, police barracks, residences of officials, and a greensward laid out as a golf course. Nearby are the Presbyterian Church and pastor's residence, the British Ex-Servicemen's Association clubhouse, and private houses mainly occupied by British subjects, including Australians, New Zealanders, and Fijians.

The Colardeau plantation borders this area and now includes a settlement of New Hebrideans and other residents. Beyond it is a new suburban residential area. Some land here is used for market gardening, shops, and workshops; then begin the native lands of Erakor and Pango villages. A few suburban houses are on the lagoon or waterfront. In all residential areas servants' quarters are attached to the dwelling house. Frequently, Melanesians living in these quarters outnumber the residents in the main house. Also throughout the area are buildings used as barracks or dormitories for groups of men, some maintained by an employer, others by a group of friends.

The Population

New Hebrideans are the largest section of the population in all but two of our census divisions: the central area where Asians are most numerous, and the hill area of private houses where Europeans predominate. The ethnic segregation is due partly to the provision of housing by employers— the governments and, to some extent, missions and business establishments.

The census covered a larger area than is shown on the Vila Town map, which includes only the urban area plus some of the sections we have classified as peri-urban and some of the institutional population (in schools, hospitals, jails, and missions). The rural areas and the villages are not shown. (For purposes of tables, broad racial or ethnic categories were distinguished.)

TABLE 1
POPULATION BY ETHNIC CATEGORY

	European			New Hebridean			Other Pacific Islander			Asian			Métis			All Races		
	M	F	T	M	F	T	M	F	T	M	F	T	M	F	T	M	F	T
Urban	279	251	530	584	470	1,054	102	97	199	128	97	225	150	139	289	1,243	1,054	2,297
Peri-Urban	39	36	75	565	421	986	31	29	60	38	43	81	72	76	148	745	605	1,350
Institutions	32	60	92	335	204	539	14	11	25	4	3	7	11	16	27	396	294	690
Rural	22	20	42	130	46	176	12	7	19	0	0	0	6	6	12	170	79	249
Villages	4	3	7	935	903	1,838	2	1	3	4	2	6	19	19	38	964	928	1,892
Total	376	370	746	2,549	2,044	4,593	161	145	306	174	145	319	258	256	514	3,518	2,960	6,478

Table 1 shows that the races in the Vila region are not evenly distributed in the urban, peri-urban, rural, and village divisions. New Hebrideans predominate and comprise 71 per cent of the total, but less than half
of the urban division. The only significant sexual disproportion is among
New Hebrideans, reflecting the migration of men to Vila for work.

Table 1 was also broken down into our census divisions, and percentages of the several ethnic categories in the divisions were calculated. New
Hebrideans are especially concentrated in the peri-urban area north of the
town center. Europeans, 11.5 per cent of the total, are concentrated in the
town residential area. Asians, who form 4.9 per cent of the total, are concentrated in the town center and in a mixed peri-urban area to the south,
but some Asians live in nearly every area. Immigrant Pacific Islanders and
Métis (people of mixed ancestry) who comprise 4.7 and 7.9 per cent,
respectively, of the population, are widely scattered in the urban and
peri-urban areas.

These broad racial or ethnic categories can be further distinguished by
nationality and specific ethnic category. The largest groups of white race
are French (468) and British (246); others number 32. European settler
families, including plantation owners, businessmen, and some government
employees, are now the permanent residents of town and country with
much intermarriage and relations throughout the New Hebrides, in New
Caledonia, and in Australia.

On the basis of place of origin (that is, the home country or island
group) and nationality, we can make some important distinctions within the
racial categories. Of the Melanesians, the 13 New Caledonians are French,
15 Solomon Islanders and 66 Fijians are British. Fijian adults are mostly
employed by the British in clerical and skilled occupations. Eleven Tongans
(Polynesians) are also associated with the British. Of other Polynesians,
the 37 Tahitians and 162 Wallis and Futunans are French in nationality.

Among the Asians the majority (211) are Vietnamese, very few of
whom have French nationality. The 82 Chinese include some of British and
a few of French nationality. A few Japanese, Indonesians, and Indians, of
varied nationalities depending on their place of origin, make up a total of
319 Asians, of whom 120 were born in Asia, 161 in Vila, the remainder in
other places.

In using a mixed race and ethnic category, Métis, we attempted to
distinguish the various components for one or two generations past and
discovered that every possible combination of the elements in the popula-

TABLE 2

POPULATION BY AGE GROUP

	0–14			15–29			30–44			45–59			60–74			75+			Total		
	M	F	T	M	F	T	M	F	T	M	F	T	M	F	T	M	F	T	M	F	T
Europeans	126	128	254	42	61	103	122	116	238	57	37	94	26	18	44	3	10	13	376	370	746
New Hebrideans	897	822	1,719	942	707	1,649	367	283	650	213	138	351	61	50	111	70	44	114	2,549	2,044	4,593
Other Pacific Islanders	52	59	111	43	47	90	45	23	68	16	9	25	3	3	6	2	4	6	161	145	306
Asians	54	51	105	47	50	97	21	24	45	44	20	64	6	—	6	2	—	2	174	145	319
Métis	193	180	373	29	39	68	25	22	47	9	10	19	2	4	6	—	1	1	258	256	514
Total	1,322	1,240	2,562	1,103	904	2,007	580	468	1,048	339	214	553	98	75	173	77	59	136	3,518	2,960	6,478

tion is present, including mixed Asians and mixed Islanders. The largest number are part European and of French nationality. While most of the ethnic categories are also in some sense ethnic sections of the population, with a common language and culture among each group of Asians and Islanders, this is not the case for the Métis. We can speak of ethnic sections or ethnic categories for those of French origin or ancestry, for the British and Australians and New Zealanders combined, and for the Vietnamese, the Chinese, the Tahitians, the Wallis and Futunans, the Fijians, the Tongans, but we cannot fit the Métis into this type of classification. A high proportion of them is young (Table 2), and their place in the social system of Vila is yet to be established.

Age and sex (Table 2) show some significant differences. Males outnumber females among the New Hebridean urban and peri-urban population. There are few New Hebridean children in town, especially in the 10 to 14 age group, and a predominance of men 20 to 24 years old. All these indicate the migration of men to work. The very low number of 15 to 29-year-old Europeans, and especially of 15 to 24-year-old males, is a measure of the numbers who have left their families for school and other occupations, and the predominance of older persons employed, especially by the governments. Pacific Islanders and Asians have so recently migrated to Vila that hardly any are found in the older age groups. The Métis are especially young: the median age is 10, 72 per cent are under fifteen, and 86 per cent were born in the New Hebrides.

Quite different educational patterns are followed by the people of Vila. Education is not compulsory, and the schools use different languages for instruction and curricula (Table 3). The French public and Catholic schools in Vila have European, Asian, Pacific Island, Métis, and New Hebridean pupils. The British have three small schools at the lower grades used almost exclusively by the children of British government officers, both Europeans and islanders. They also support village mission schools and a teacher's training college for New Hebrideans, but make no provision for the general town population. A number of English-speaking white families in Vila send their children to the French public school, where the curriculum is the same as in metropolitan France.

Before 1966, the upper levels of high school were not taught in Vila. Many French-speaking children, both French and Vietnamese—but rarely others—went to Nouméa, New Caledonia. Older British children are commonly sent to boarding schools in Australia, New Zealand, or the United

TABLE 3
SCHOOL PUPILS: SCHOOLS ATTENDED BY ETHNIC CATEGORY

Schools Attended	European			New Hebridean			Other Pacific Islanders			Asian			Métis			All Races		
	M	F	T	M	F	T	M	F	T	M	F	T	M	F	T	M	F	T
French Government	45	45	90	194	160	354	12	16	28	20	18	38	55	45	100	326	284	610
Catholic-French	17	28	45	94	92	186	13	14	27	16	14	30	44	39	83	184	187	371
All French-Speaking Schools	62	73	135	288	252	540	25	30	55	36	32	68	99	84	183	510	471	981
British Government	26	23	49	55	13	68	2	3	5	1	1	2	6	5	11	90	45	135
Protestant: English	—	—	—	233	183	416	2	2	4	—	—	—	2	7	9	237	192	429
All English-Speaking Schools	26	23	49	298	196	494	4	5	9	1	1	2	8	12	20	327	237	564
All Schools[a]	92	100	192	597	459	1,056	29	35	64	37	33	70	121	104	225	876	731	1,607

[a] Includes ten students of Condominium Agricultural School and some on leave from schools outside the Vila area.

Kingdom. Most Chinese children go to school in Singapore, Hong Kong, or Australia. A few selected New Hebridean children are sent to English-speaking schools in the Pacific Islands or elsewhere by the British government. New Hebridean pupils are numerous at the lower grades in the French-speaking schools but often drop out after a few years. Some young Asians have gained sufficient education to obtain skilled and clerical jobs at levels unavailable to most of the older generation of Asians.

Relations between Ethnic Categories and Occupations

Occupational stratification in Vila is highly correlated with the ethnic categories: Europeans predominate in the high-status occupations, and the intermediate-status occupations are held by members of all ethnic categories, but Asians, Métis, and Pacific Islanders are especially numerous in crafts, and Asians in clerical and sales occupations. The owners and managers of all the large businesses and most small ones are European. Sales and clerical workers are mostly Europeans, but some are Asians and Métis. In these relationships, the Chinese often work in British firms and the Vietnamese in French firms. Artisans of various sorts are frequently a mixed group of people—Europeans, Asians, Métis, and Islanders. These specialized skills are often acquired through an informal apprenticeship within the organization. Builders employ Vietnamese as masons, carpenters, painters, etc., in the building trades, and in mechanics' shops a mixed group of people are occupied in various specialties. Interviews with employers indicated a widespread opinion that the Vietnamese became capable artisans in the course of working at a trade but that New Hebrideans have not the background or the native ability to acquire these skills very rapidly. Nonetheless, the building and mechanics' workshops employ a large number of New Hebrideans as unskilled or apprentice labor, usually at low wages. On ships, many of the seamen are Islanders from various parts of the Pacific. Employment in food establishments of all sorts is mostly New Hebridean, but the owners are predominantly French or, sometimes, Chinese. Small and large shops have mixed sales and clerical staffs, and multilingual clerks are required to deal with customers.

The relations between occupations (Appendix), ethnic categories, and sex (Table 4) show many differences. The professional and semi-professional category has a high proportion of Europeans although New Hebrideans are commonly nurses, teachers, and ministers of religion.

TABLE 4

OCCUPATIONS BY SEX AND ETHNIC CATEGORY

Ethnic Category	Professional			Administrative			Clerical			Sales			Agricultural			Transport			Crafts			General Laborer			Services			All Gainfully Employed		
	M	F	T	M	F	T	M	F	T	M	F	T	M	F	T	M	F	T	M	F	T	M	F	T	M	F	T	M	F	T
Europeans	50	59	109	79	3	82	23	58	81	14	8	22	17	1	18	18	1	19	28	–	28	–	–	–	–	9	9	229	139	368
New Hebrideans	82	47	129	19	–	19	31	6	37	55	1	56	424	134	558	227	–	227	244	5	249	70	–	70	117	298	415	1,269	491	1,760
Pacific Islanders	4	5	9	1	–	1	1	6	7	1	1	2	10	1	11	29	–	29	32	1	33	8	–	8	5	22	27	91	36	127
Asians	2	3	5	2	–	2	4	15	19	25	22	47	10	2	12	12	–	12	45	9	54	–	–	–	6	1	7	106	52	158
Métis	1	4	5	6	–	6	1	8	9	4	4	8	6	2	8	11	–	11	27	–	27	1	–	1	–	10	10	57	28	85
All Groups	139	118	257	107	3	110	60	93	153	99	36	135	467	140	607	297	1	298	376	15	391	79	–	79	128	340	468	1,752	746	2,498

Administrative and managerial occupations, in which European men over-
whelmingly predominate, do, however, include some New Hebridean police
officers. The clerical and sales category includes a large number of New
Hebridean men and somewhat fewer European and Asian men. Among
women, most clerks are European, many are Asian, and a few are of
other ethnic categories.

New Hebridean men are employed chiefly in agriculture, transport,
crafts, service, and general labor. They most often hold unskilled and semi-
skilled jobs. New Hebridean women are most often domestic servants when
they are not at home and engaged in farming. Among New Hebrideans, the
men hold more white collar occupations, mainly in government but also as
sales clerks in shops, than do the New Hebridean women.

A closer look at some categories is revealing. Chinese men and women
are most often shopkeepers, but the Vietnamese are divided: Vietnamese
women are often in sales and clerical occupations while Vietnamese men
are predominantly skilled craftsmen and farmers. The white collar occupations are means of mobility. Vietnamese girls employed in town are often
closely associated with French men with whom they work and cohabit.

A few Métis are distributed in all occupational categories, with a pre-
predominance of men in crafts and transport. Métis women are teachers,
clerical and shop workers, and servants. European women are mostly professional and clerical workers, while men are most often professionals and
administrators.

These differences between men and women of the same ethnic category
indicate the training opportunities available to different groups. European
women may have some professional training, but even without it they work
as clerks, saleswomen, kindergarten teachers, etc. No European men are
laborers or service workers. Asians often have enough schooling for a clerical job, as do the Vietnamese women. The men, through an informal
apprenticeship, become carpenters, masons, mechanics, etc. Other Pacific
Island men who, in most cases, have come to Vila with training in skilled
trades or as clerks, hold jobs in crafts and transport.

Avenues of training open to New Hebrideans are few. Under special
circumstances—until recently only through mission auspices—boys may
be able to move from village schools to district schools and more advanced
training for positions as medical aides, teachers, or clerks. Some get jobs
which lead to proficiency as mechanics, ship's crewmen, builders, and
drivers. Both governments are increasing educational facilities for New

Hebridean men, but their greatest opportunity would have been to take over skilled jobs left by the Vietnamese in 1963. Now many of these posts have been filled by Métis, other Pacific Islanders, and the remaining Asians. Very few New Hebrideans had the skills at the time, and employment opportunities have not increased very much since then. The governments do not discriminate against the New Hebrideans, but they have not provided the necessary training and have had to—reluctantly—bring in skilled and semi-skilled workers from outside. Plantation owners and employers in town, especially the dock managers who need many workers for short periods, complain that New Hebridean workers are untrained and unreliable. Our interview sample of 38 New Hebridean men employed in Vila revealed that they had held an average of 4.8 jobs each; sixteen had had jobs lasting four years or more, but all had some jobs for short periods only.

The economy has little potential for growth; copra, coffee, cocoa, and beef are the main agricultural export products, and the local market is too small to support more than a few consumer industries. The two specialized export industries, manganese mining and fishing, do not use Vila facilities. Vila trade mostly serves the government and shipping personnel and their families in Vila and the agricultural people, both on plantations and in native villages, in the environs. Agricultural production cannot expand very far, and industrial development has few prospects. Much can be done to improve the standard of living and efficiency, but the present division of labor and social strata are likely to remain. Regardless of skill, there is a high correlation of nationality of employer and employee, with very few French people working for British employers, or British for French.

Representation of Ethnic Categories in Vila Activities

Some councils and committees function for the whole of the New Hebrides. The Advisory Council has functionary, titular, and elected members intended to insure some representation from all segments of the population. In this complex political situation, it has little power and is not concerned with Vila town but with the entire island group. Committees with specific responsibilities, e.g., medicine or agriculture, are similarly made up of a representative group of those with these specialities. Committees usually include an ethnic cross-section of the community: French, British, and New Hebrideans are usually included, but rarely those of the smaller ethnic minorities.

Important occasions—the inauguration of institutions and buildings, national holidays, and official visits—bring out a representative crowd of government officials and private citizens to ceremonies. Receptions and cocktail parties are held to celebrate national occasions (the Queen's Birthday, the Fête Nationale) and to honor distinguished visitors. The guests at such occasions always include government officials and important private citizens—professionals, the managers of businesses, and owners of plantations. Europeans predominate, but there are nearly always some representatives of the other races of Vila. The most prominent local professional and business people are regularly invited while others are rarely seen. The group recombines frequently for public and private affairs. After three months in Vila, one of our team members could name most of the people present at a cocktail party of 200 people.

Certain organizations for the town and the island group show a similar representation. The Chamber of Commerce is island-wide and includes among its members the prominent men of commerce, industry and agriculture including French, British, Chinese, Vietnamese, Métis, and a few prominent New Hebrideans.

The predominance of French culture and interests is always evident. Associations take a characteristic French form and title, and Frenchmen outnumber all others in membership and as officers. The two most frequently elected British men are married to French women and participate equally in French and British society.

Also prominent in Vila's social life are veterans' organizations. The Anciens Combattants and Association des Français Libres, with a few non-French members, conduct memorial ceremonies and occasional social actvities. The British Ex-Servicemen's Association has a building for meetings and parties, a bar, a pool table, and coin gambling machines. Its members include British, Australians, New Zealanders, and Fijians, of whom perhaps twenty-five men use this as a regular club. The membership list includes a few Frenchmen. On such occasions as ANZAAC Day and the Queen's Birthday, dances are held at the clubhouse.

The British Red Cross, composed mostly of British wives of government officials, operates quite separately from the French Red Cross. A Catholic charitable organization is French. A Chinese club doubles as a residence place for single Chinese men in the center of Vila and contains what may be the only ping-pong table in town. One native club with about two hundred members, including natives from a number of islands, participates in some sports and holds social gatherings from time to time.

A wide range of sports are pursued in Vila by different sections of the population. The schools, especially the upper grades, participate in team sports and also in individual competitions. European football is the most popular sport with teams drawn from town and village groups, the police forces, schools, and clubs. Most of the organizing is done by Frenchmen, but the players are largely New Hebrideans except for a few Asians and Métis. Trophy cups are provided by prominent business organizations, and the games are played at the Stade or on playing fields in native villages.

French sports for young people are organized partly through the French schools. Committees promote athletics, basketball, volleyball, handball, and some other team sports. A large and more inclusive committee was established to encourage participation in many sports at the South Pacific Games, held periodically in different centers in the Pacific Islands. Basketball and field athletics have a few enthusiastic European adherents who both participate in and coach these sports. Most of the judges in athletic events are Europeans, and in the athletic competitions a few sportsmen—Europeans, Métis, and Islanders who are practiced sprinters, jumpers, etc.—often win repeatedly. The British Ex-Servicemen's Association provides a basketball cup, and the British Government offers prizes at athletic competitions on the Queen's Birthday. Fund-raising and social events sometimes are sponsored by athletic groups, and these are among the few occasions for the mixing of all races in Vila.

Golf and tennis, chiefly European sports, are highly segregated; the British, for the most part, play golf, the French, tennis. A golf course has been laid out on the grounds of the British Residency, and a small committee of British women organizes golf competitions here for both men and women. The same area is sometimes used for cricket games. The tennis club, near the Stade, has mostly French members and officials but includes a few active British players. Competitions are frequent and the club has some social events.

The one special cultural event which I witnessed was a ballet with choreography by the French school headmaster. The corps de ballet was mostly from the French schools and included some young teachers and a number of French, Vietnamese, and Métis young people. Pétanque (boule) is played often in one or two empty lots in the center of town late in the afternoon. The players include Vietnamese, Métis, and New Hebrideans, many of them men who work in the town as taxi drivers or in hotels and shops. Sports bring together persons of different ethnic sections but rarely encompass all.

Both informal and public social activities are largely unilingual and limited in the social strata involved. Parties among friends are commonly within occupational groups—the British Office, young French-speaking white-collar workers, members of the faculty at the teachers' college, etc. The French-speaking young people, especially when the Nouméa High School is on vacation, congregate in the one night club and the snack bar. Public dances are well attended, often by numerous groups of three to six couples, associates in business or government offices. Tables are sometimes purposely organized to bring together French and British officials. These monthly or bi-monthly dances are at the British Ex-Servicemen's Association, the new hotel, the nightclub, or on the cargo and passenger ship from Australia. Since most European young people over fifteen are away at school, those who attend the dances are mainly Vietnamese and Métisse girls and Métis boys of lower socioeconomic position than the older French and British couples who attend. The boys and girls go separately, largely, in groups—the girls sitting at tables and the boys circulating among dance partners. New Hebrideans often watch from the street. On the major holiday in 1965, the Fête Nationale, dances were held at the hotel on July 13 and 14 for Europeans, and another dance with no admission charge was held in a temporary hall on the waterfront for New Hebrideans and a few other Islanders. Racial mixing occurred only at sports activities, sports club dances, and a few official receptions and social activities for special groups, such as the teachers' college. Stratification is obvious—a few Europeans mix with Asians, Métis, and educated Islanders, who are an intermediate class, and some of these mix with New Hebrideans, but very few New Hebrideans associate with Europeans outside work and official activities.

The Bases of Diversity

Social differentiation in Vila chiefly follows ethnic categories, especially in occupation, housing, and social participation. This is clearest in the difference between Europeans and New Hebrideans, who meet mainly as master and servant, employer and employee, professional and client, or administrator and subject. The Asians, Islanders, and Métis are intermediate in social status and overlap with both groups. But while all live in this small town and share in its facilities, contacts among members of the several ethnic sections are limited. Some of the social segregation is along linguistic and national lines, and racial categories cut across these. Only those New

Hebrideans who have had an overseas education leading to a specialist occupation speak a European language fluently, and these few form the New Hebridean elite, members of committees and guests at official functions. Most New Hebrideans in Vila speak their home language with others of their island area and pidgin English with all others in Vila. Most Asians and immigrant Pacific Islanders are fluent in one European language but also use pidgin at work and their own language at home. Many of these immigrants live in small enclaves and rarely participate in town affairs. Young adults in these categories are fairly numerous, and they are more likely to participate in town affairs than are their elders.

The European category must be divided between French and British, and further between the settler families and government employees serving terms in the New Hebrides. The majority of the settlers are French; they often depend entirely upon their local town and plantation activities for their livelihood and have married members of other settler families. Many have family and cultural ties outside, in New Caledonia, France, and other countries. All Europeans have relations outside, and both government and the larger business firms provide periodic home leave for their permanent administrative employees.

Ethnic diversity and outside ties are especially evident in Vila because of the Condominium government and the language division between French and English. Furthermore, the division of language and nationality extends throughout the population—to Asians, immigrant islanders, and, to a lesser extent to the New Hebrideans who have become associated with one of the colonial powers by going to school, learning a European language, and working for European employers.

The small size of Vila, too, accentuates its outpost character: it is a small part of the British High Commission for the Western Pacific and a part of New Caledonia in some of its relations with metropolitan France. No ethnic section of the Vila population has any autonomy: each is so small that it can be hardly more than an enclave in a plural community. The Fijians, Tongans, Wallis and Futunans, Tahitians, Chinese, and Vietnamese are of such recent immigration that hardly any adults are Vila-born. Except for those of nearby villages, most of the adult New Hebrideans are also recent arrivals in Vila.

No section of the population is entirely focused upon Vila as its cultural center and source of knowledge, relationships, and values. Much of the diversity of Vila is due not to local conditions but to the diversity of ties and backgrounds of its inhabitants. However much they may mingle in the town, all look to larger societies elsewhere.

Plural societies may often be of this colonial outpost character—a medley of strangers imposed upon the local population. The local population may predominate numerically, but the dominant culture of the towns is imported. Western church and school are closely connected, and both have great influence upon the native people. The indigenous culture has little influence on the immigrants; they dominate politically and economically, and the indigenous people emulate them. Western influence is filtered through the immigrant Westerners and the other ethnic sections who take part in economic development. A pattern of stratification develops with the western people in control of wealth, power, and skills. An intermediate level of shopkeepers, clerks, and artisans is of mixed composition, and the indigenous population makes up the town's laboring class.

After colonial territories become independent, they incorporate Western legal systems, forms of government, and technology. They continue to depend upon external stimuli, even when they reject foreigners as leaders. In independent ex-colonial nations, plural society may be perpetuated by differentiation within the indigenous population and the continued participation of other ethnic sections in the community.

APPENDIX

OCCUPATIONS INCLUDED IN THE LARGER CATEGORIES

Professional: Engineers, surveyors, physical and natural scientists, physicians, nurses, midwives, teachers, religious leaders, lawyers, and artists.

Administrative: Government officials, police officers, directors, managers, overseers, foremen.

Clerical: Clerical workers.

Sales, Agencies: Shop workers, proprietors, securities and services employees.

Agriculture: Planters and managers, plantation workers, livestock workers, small farmers and workers, fishermen, foresters, other agricultural laborers.

Transport, Communications: Ship officers, ship crews, wharf and airplane workers, drivers, other transport, telecommunication, and postal employees.

Craftsmen, Production: Producers of clothing, wood, and metal; mechanics; electrical, building, and earthmoving and road-making workers; food and beverage producers.

General Laborers: Laborers, non-agricultural.

Service: Firemen, policemen, domestics, waiters, etc.; cleaners, janitors, hairdressers, launderers, photographers, and undertakers.

Not Gainfully Occupied: Domestic duties, students, retired, no occupation, patients, infants (0–4), children (5–14) not in school, unemployed, prisoners, N/S and unidentifiable.

NOTES

1. O'Reilly (1956) is the source of most of this historical information. Doumenge (1966) provides some useful data, but there is no full record of Vila history.

2. Most of the figures and tables to follow are taken from a voluntary census we conducted in the region including Vila in July 1965. The results will be more fully reported in Brookfield and Brown Glick (forthcoming). The New Hebrides census of 1967 is a more complete population count, but does not duplicate our questions.

3. Our best information on the town and occupants of houses was provided by the Sanitary Inspector.

REFERENCES

Brookfield, H. C., and P. Brown Glick (forthcoming) *The People of Vila.* Canberra.

Brookfield, H. C., P. Brown Glick, and D. Hart (1969) "Melanesian Melange: The Market in Vila," in *Pacific Market-places,* ed. H. C. Brookfield. Canberra.

Doumenge, F. (1966) *L'Homme dans le Pacifique Sud.* Société des Oceanistes Publication No. 19. Paris.

McArthur, N. and J. F. Yaxley (1968) *Condominium of the New Hebrides: A Report on the First Census of the Population 1967.* New South Wales.

Morris, H. S. (1967) "Some Aspects of the Concept Plural Society," *Man* 2:169–84.

O'Reilly, P. (1956) "Naissance et développement de Port-Vila, capitale des Nouvelles-Hébrides," *Missions des Iles* 74:56–67, 72.

Redfield, R. and M. Singer (1954) "The Cultural Role of Cities," *Economic Development and Cultural Change* 3:53–73.

Part II
Historical Perspectives

Recruitment of Elites in India Under British Rule

Elites in India: The Accepted View

In the study of stratification in any society, several attributes and functions are seen as requisites of elite status: the holding and exercising of political power; a disproportionate control of or access to the valued goods and services of the society; high control over ritual statuses; high access to the valued intellectual or cultural activities in the society; and a distinctive life style and consumption pattern aspired to by significant numbers in the society. Conventionally, the study of elites focuses on recruitment and socialization, and on the relationship between holding elite status and the exercise of political and economic power. The self-conception of elites and how they maintain the boundaries setting themselves off from the rest of the society have also engaged scholars.

At first glance, India, a caste society, would seem to be a relatively easy society in which to identify elites and map their social attributes and functioning. Defined rankings of closed corporate groups make up the caste hierarchy in any given locality, and there are region-wide agreements on the relative ranking of the cultural-occupational orders in the society. For example, all the local closed corporate groups made up of carpenters have a defined place within a local hierarchy and roughly the same position in all local hierarchies throughout a region. Finally, there is a civilization-wide set of cultural categories about the ranking of the four or five great orders

121

within the system: the famous *varna* classification of Brahman, Kshatriya, Vaishya, Sudra, and Panchama or Untouchable.

Recruitment to a corporate group (*Jati, Biradari*), a cultural-occupational order (*Jat*), and a civilization-wide cultural category (*varna*) is by birth. Recruitment by ascription and an immutable rank order within the society are the ethnographic hallmarks of traditional India.

European writers on India during the eighteenth and nineteenth centuries constantly referred to the position and power of the Brahman within the system. Certainly it was and, to some extent, still is held that in traditional India it was the Brahman who had all the power—political, ritual, and economic—which goes with elite status. James Mill's *The History of British India,* originally published in 1820 and widely regarded in the nineteenth century as the major work on Indian history, is typical of the century's literary treatment of the Brahman.

The Brahmens among the Hindus have acquired and maintained an authority, more exalted, more commanding, and extensive, than the priests have been able to engross among any other portion of mankind. As great a distance as there is between the Brahmen and the Divinity, so great a distance is there between the Brahmen and the rest of his species. . . . The Brahmen is declared to be the Lord of all the classes. He alone, to a great degree, engrosses the regard and favour of the Deity; and it is through him, and at his intercession, that blessings are bestowed upon the rest of mankind. The sacred books are exclusively his; the highest of the other classes are barely tolerated to read the word of God; he alone is worthy to expound it. The first among the duties of the civil magistrate, supreme or subordinate, is to honour the Brahmens. The slightest disrespect to one of this sacred order is the most atrocious of crimes. . . . Not only is this extraordinary respect and pre-eminence awarded to the Brahmens; they are allowed the most striking advantages over all other members of the social body, in almost everything that regards the social state. . . . Their influence over the government is only bounded by their desires, since they have impressed the belief that all laws which a Hindu is bound to respect are contained in the sacred books. (1820:159–62)

Not all European writers on India saw the system to be as pernicious as Mill did. William Robertson, one of the late eighteenth-century Scottish moral philosophers, was an ardent admirer of Indian society and the Brahman:

The object of the first Indian Legislators [Brahmans] was to employ the most effectual means of providing for the subsistence, the security, and happiness of all the members of the community over which they presided . . . they set apart certain races of men for each of the various professions and arts necessary in a well-ordered society, and appointed the exercise of them to be transmitted from father to son in succession. . . .

To this early division of people into castes, we must likewise ascribe a striking peculiarity in the state of India; the permanence of its institutions, and the immutability in the manners of its inhabitants. What now is in India, always was there, and is likely still to continue: neither the ferocious violence and illiberal fanaticism of its Mahomedan conquerors, nor the power of its European masters, have effected any considerable alteration. (1828:52–53)

An immutable and fixed hierarchy, an unchanging culture and society, and the dominance of the Brahman were the key ethnographic facts in the early nineteenth-century view of Indian society.

Another school of thought which developed in the nineteenth century, however, looked elsewhere for elites in traditional India. This school saw an aristocratic traditional elite, derived from the Muslim conquerors and/or from the control over land which princes and royal families exercised. A concern for Indian aristocracy had been closely related to British imperial policies since Lord Cornwallis' term as Governor General in the late eighteenth century. Cornwallis' crucial decisions about the levying and collection of land revenue and the establishment of title to lands grew out of his belief that the landed aristocracy were the natural leaders of the society. He thought that the Bengal landed aristocracy was in decline, and felt compelled to re-establish it in a position of control over the land and people of rural Bengal. Most of the great British administrators of the pre-Mutiny generation—Mountstuart Elphinstone, Charles Metcalfe, John Malcolm, and Henry Lawrence—identified with the Indian aristocracy and felt British policy and rule should be based on the loyalty and stability of the traditional aristocrats.

In the post-Mutiny period, as Thomas Metcalf and others have shown, British policy very consciously exalted the aristocracy and increasingly saw it as a political and cultural counterweight of the new English educated classes. Lord Lytton, Viceroy from 1876 to 1880, expressed this position in the extreme when he wrote to Queen Victoria:

Your Majesty's Indian Government has not hitherto, in my opinion, sufficiently appealed to the Asiatic sentiment and traditions of the Native Indian Aristocracy. That aristocracy exercises a powerful influence over the rest of the native population. (Gopal 1965:113)

Lytton wanted the Crown to turn the aristocracy into a feudal nobility. "The whole social structure of this Empire is essentially feudal and eminently fitted for the application of the salutary military principles of the feudal system" (ibid., 114).

The idea that the landed gentry and the princes were the natural leaders of Indian society grew through the nineteenth century under the twin pressures of colonial policy and British administrators' vision of their living a gentry-like, if not aristocratic, kind of life in India.

The British in the later nineteenth century were very much aware of the development in India of a new group, the Western-educated, frequently referred to scathingly as the "Babus." It is this English-educated group that twentieth-century scholars like B. B. Misra, Bruce McCully, A. R. Desai, and many others saw as the new elite of India. From this group the early nationalist leadership was recruited; and, as the administrative services were Indianized, the professions expanded, and modern industry and commerce developed, they manned the top levels of the emerging modern institutions. Their origins, their relation to traditional social structure, their life styles and assumed alienation from their traditional culture have received the most attention from observers and scholars of the modern Indian scene.

To summarize, the accepted picture of elites and elite formation shows India as a caste society which was stable, if not static, before the impact of British rule. Elite status traditionally rested in the Brahman—the center and head of the caste system and the monopolizer of ritual influence and power. Alternatively, and to some extent concomitantly, elite status also rested in the aristocracy, defined as the descendants of pre-British royal houses and the substantial landholders. The stability of the society was shaken but not destroyed by the consequences of British rule; and, particularly through the introduction of English education and new occupational opportunities for the educated in the modern segment of the society, a new Western-educated elite arose. In the remainder of this paper I shall turn to an examination of this view. The discussion will center on a series of questions: How stable or static was traditional Indian society? What was the nature of mobility? Did a unitary new elite emerge? What was its origin or origins? How did it exercise its influence? How did it maintain its position? What was its distinctive life style?

Brahmans and the Traditional Society

The assumption about the centrality of the Brahmans and their values is derived from the Brahmans' view of themselves, their culture and society. When one looks at eighteenth- and early nineteenth-century writings, or at the work of more recent scholars like Max Weber, it becomes clear that the picture being drawn is usually based on sacred texts. The texts and their interpretations were largely in the hands of the Brahmans and exalted the nature and position of the Brahman. A second problem with using the traditional texts as a basis for inference about Indian society and culture lies in the simple historiographic questions of when they were written, by whom, and for what purpose. Nineteenth-century scholars, assuming the static nature of Indian society, had little trouble with these simple questions. One could use the Code of Manu, a third-century A.D. text, to infer something about social relations in the nineteenth century. This is clearly untenable because Indian society and culture were far from stable or static through this fifteen-hundred-year period. Looking only at the period of 1500 to 1800, one sees a picture quite different from one of structural and cultural stability.

The Islamic invaders, by 1500, had established an elite life style (I would label it *Persianized*) which was highly attractive and readily accepted by many upper-caste Hindus, including Brahmans. One need look only at the Nehrus to see the importance of this Persianized culture, even for Brahmans. The conventional picture of Jawaharlal Nehru as a man between Brahman India and the rational West, a picture which he sometimes promoted, is to a large extent an oversimplification. Jawaharlal Nehru's ancestors moved from their native Kashmir in 1716 and for four generations had served as professional civil servants for the Mughal emperors in Delhi. The last important Nehru in Delhi was Jawaharlal's grandfather, who was Kotwal, a high police official, when the Mutiny broke out in 1857 (Nanda 163:18). As B. R. Nanda states in his recent joint biography of Nehru and his father, "The only surviving portrait of Ganga Dhar [Nehru's grandfather] shows him bearded, dressed like a Mughal Grandee, with a curved sword in his hand. There was nothing surprising in a Kashmiri Brahmin being turned out like a Muslim nobleman, if we remember that the conventions, the ceremonials and even the language, Persian, of the Mughal court had since the days of Akbar, set the fashion for the entire Indian subcontinent" (ibid., 19). The manners which a contemporary anthropologist doing field work throughout much of North India labels "traditional"—the courtly speech, the hospitality, the indirectness, the politeness toward strangers—are not Brahmanic or peasant but the courtly style of the Mughals.

The period from 1500 to 1800 was rich in the emergence of new religious sects: the Sikhs, the Lingayats, the flowering at the local level of Hindu-Muslim syncretic cults like the Pancho-Pir, and the culmination of the Bhakti movement—all, although Hindu in origin, were influenced by certain Islamic doctrines.

During the same period, one saw a circulation of political elites: the rise of the Marathas, the resurgence of groups like the Jats near Delhi, and the coming to power behind the Bengal throne of commercial families like the Jagat Seths. The political system of India through the end of Mughal rule was not an imperial despotic one, as conventionally seen, but rather a very complex political system in which the various levels were balanced against one another, and where there was conflict within levels. This system of balanced oppositions reached from the village to the imperial capital. The system furthered and rewarded individual and group mobility, and the fortunes of individuals, families, lineages, and sub-castes were constantly shifting. Even in the less Islamicized south of India, political changes frequently brought changes of caste status and intermarriage between castes (*Krishna* 1937:75).

Even the so-called isolated village, neither isolated nor self-sufficient in the eighteenth century, was very significantly penetrated by the outside world, as demonstrated by Thomas Coats' account about Lony, a village twelve miles from Poona in Maharashtra. Coats reported that in 1820, 68 out of 84 families of cultivators were in debt to the total amount of Rs. 14,532 or about Rs. 210 per household. These debts were in cash, incurred to defray the expenses of marriage or to purchase cattle or food (Coats 1823:226). There were five shopkeeping families in Lony, all foreigners— three Jains from the Carnatic (Madras) and two Marwaris from Rajasthan. In addition to money-lending, these shopkeepers sold grain, cloth, *ghi,* sugar, spices, soap, *bhang,* opium, salt, nuts, and pens and ink. The village supported a school. Land was bought and sold freely within the village, and Coats tells us that many of the villagers "are not without a tolerable knowledge of the leading events of the history of their own country. On the whole they are better informed than the lower classes of our own countrymen . . ." (ibid., 205). This account of Lony in 1820, two years after the British extended direct rule over Poona district, makes it sound like anything but an isolated place, an unchanging village.

Who Were the Traditional Elites?

Having rejected the notion of traditional India as a unitary society existing changeless through time, the question of who the elites were at a particular time becomes an empirical one. Let me briefly indicate who I think some of the elites were in the eighteenth century just before and during the time when the British were establishing their suzerainty over the south Asian sub-continent.

India in the eighteenth century was largely a peasant society and a caste society—that is, a relatively localized society within which groups were relatively fixed in their membership. In drawing a map of elites, I would start at the bottom—not, in the eighteenth century, at the village itself but rather at what I term the town fort. The basic political, social, and economic unit of the eighteenth century was the little kingdom, the territory controlled by a lineage, a patrimonial domain. To follow Eric Wolf's recent usage (1966:50), "Patrimonial domain over land is exercised where control of occupants of land is placed in the hands of lords who inherit the right to the domain as members of kinship groups or lineages, and where this control implies the right to receive tribute from the inhabitants in return for their occupance." The members of the lineages lived in forts or walled towns. Here they concentrated the surplus agricultural product from the rural areas and supported and consumed the products of specialists such as priests and craftsmen. At times, scholars and itinerant ritual specialists were imported, as were weapons and luxuries such as fine cloth. The members of the dominant lineage developed a distinctive life style, emphasizing military virtues and the gentlemanly courtly styles associated with the Persianized Mughal courts. They were *the* rural elite.

Another type of rural elite, in some respects indistinguishable from the controllers of patrimonial domains, were local chiefs who in their person and family were the controllers of the domain and not members of a lineage. Instead of a corporate group inheriting control over the domain, it was inherited by an individual chief or *raja*. These local chiefs often directly emulated the Mughal courts and had *divans* (prime ministers), military leaders, court priests, etc., who formed, on the basis of office, an elite for the domain.

Finally there were *prebendal* domains originating from grants to officials who drew tribute from the agricultural producer both on behalf of the state and as their salary (Wolf 1966:51). Theoretically, prebendal domains were granted only for limited periods and were not inheritable. By the eighteenth century, however, many prebendal domains owing their origins to the Mughals had become heritable and were on their way to becoming patrimonial domains. The significant difference in terms of elite formation was that holders of prebendal domains had fewer connections with groups under them. Sometimes the prebendal elites were Muslims in a predominantly Hindu area, or were Brahmans, a caste group not usually found as local landed elites, at least in north India.

In the eighteenth century, the Mughal court, which had controlled the Imperial level of the pre-eighteenth-century political system, rapidly declined in power. However, a number of regional cities, such as Murshidabad in Bengal, Lucknow in Oudh, and Poona in Maharashtra, replaced Delhi and Agra, the old Mughal capitals, as political and cultural centers. Regional elites grew up around the courts of the nawabs and rajas. These elites tended to be somewhat cosmopolitan in their recruitment and made up fairly diverse groups: the immediate relatives, agnatic and cognatic, of the ruling chief; some of his caste mates or cultural groups, usually important in the army; the international-Persianized civil servants who, because of their knowledge of Persian, the language of the courts and administration, and their administrative experience, could move from regional court to court in India, providing necessary administrative skills. In origin, this international-Persianized civil service group might be Persian or from other Islamic-professing groups domiciled in India. Often they were Hindu, frequently Kayastha, the traditional writing castes; Brahman, as in the case of the Nehrus referred to before; Prabhus, on the West Coast; and at times from merchant castes. In addition, these regional courts had poets, teachers, scholars, and jurisprudents forming a kind of intellectual/cultural elite.

These regional courts in Faizabad, later in Lucknow in Upper India, Murshidabad in Bengal, Mysore in the south, and Baroda in Gujarat, set the consumption style for the local elites, whose members frequently served for a time in the armies or revenue services of the regional chiefs. The courts were urban and had an urban way of life.

Linked to this urban-royal elite group, but not necessarily central to it, were commercial elites. Commercial activity and groups in Mughal and eighteenth-century India are usually seen as subordinate and dominated by the royal courts and the landed patrimonial and prebendal land controllers. I think this picture requires some modification. In western India, particularly in Gujarat and Maharashtra, the commercial castes appear to have been dominant in trade and craft centers like Ahmedabad. In other urban centers owing their origin to political function, the commercial groups shared political control of the towns with government officials (Gune 1953:12; Hopkins 1901:178–84). In some regions, commercial groups became very powerful and, in Murshidabad in Bengal, were really the power behind the throne, becoming king-makers in the revolutions of 1740 to 1765. Part of the significance and emergence of the commercial groups as a kind of elite was, of course, their relationship to the European powers, but this was at a time when the European powers were not in any sense dominant militarily or politically in the sub-continent, so that groups deriving advantage from their connection with the Europeans operated entirely in the indigenous society.

The interesting thing about the commercial elites was that they followed a much different life style than did the royal or local elites or the Persianized civil servants. Their consumption pattern appears to have been more austere; they were—as they are now—more religiously oriented, more likely to be vegetarian, and supporters of traditional ritual and religious activity. Their ethic, as befits commercial groups, seems to have been a conserving and saving one. Tending to be part of fairly widespread, well-organized networks found far from their traditional homes, the commercial groups still maintained ties with their home territories; Multanis from the Punjab, Marwaris from Rajasthan, and Chettiers from Tamilnad were found in enclaves over much of India.

In the eighteenth century, the top commercial groups were far from being mere sheep to be shorn by royalty, as is often asserted. Robert Orme, the first historian of British India, described the family of the Jaget Seths in the following terms:

There was a family of Gentoo merchants at Muxadavad, whose head, Jugguseat, had raised himself from no considerable origin to be the wealthiest banker in the empire, in most parts of which he had agents supplied with money for remittances; from whom he constantly received good intelligence of what was transacting in the governments in which they were settled; and in Bengal his influence was equal to that of any officer in the administration . . . and the great circulation of wealth he commanded, rendered his assistance necessary in every emergency of expence. (1778:29–30)

The final touch to this picture of the traditional elites was their recent rise to elite status and the often very humble origins from which they derived in a generation's time. Scindhia, the great Maratha chief of the mid-eighteenth century, came from a shepherd family; his father had been the slipper bearer of a local chief. Murshid Kuli Khan, the founder of the Bengal state, was believed to have been a Brahman who was purchased as a small child by a minor Mughal officer and brought up as his own son. No matter what his origins, Murshid Kuli Khan's rise to the nawabship was through skill in politics, military affairs, and as a revenue official (Karim 1963:15–16). The family of the rajas of Banaras derived from early eighteenth-century petty landholders, rising in one generation from this relatively low status to rajas of a major part of Oudh.

In summary, if—in referring to the traditional elite in India—we imply something about the actual social structure at the period before European domination and not just general statements about civilization-wide cultural values, we must look at a wide range of situations and groups in the eighteenth century, a time of change and circulation in the political and economic system of India. I have tried to indicate briefly some places where one would look for elites.

The Emerging Elites in the Nineteenth Century

In the beginning of this paper, I discussed briefly the commonly held model of elite formation in nineteenth-century India, in which access to Western education is seen as the key. The argument of this paper, however, is that the processes and results are much more complicated than those of one institution and one class emerging as the only elite formed under British colonial conditions. To find our new elites we must look at several places in the social system, beginning with the rural segment.

The British administrative frontier in India was continually moving during the later part of the eighteenth century, starting in Bengal and Madras and reaching the Punjab and Oudh in the 1840s and 1850s. The central aspect of this moving administrative frontier was the establishment of systematic means for assessing and collecting land revenue, the principal source of income for the British state in India. In order to assess and collect revenue in India, the British had to develop a basis for designating tax-payers. In developing this, they reached directly into the center of the Indian social network, where the key features are control of land and of followers and the relations among agricultural producers, those who control producers, and the state. British land revenue policies differed from region to region and from time to time. A considerable amount of time, energy, and scholarship has gone into study of changes in policy and the persons who made policy. In fact, except for the Mutiny, this subject has received the greatest attention in the study of modern Indian history. In all this study, however, little attention has been focused on what actually happened in the realignment, if there was one, in the distribution of land. Harold

Lasswell's famous question about politics—who gets what, when, and how?—hasn't been asked, let alone answered, so far as control of the key resource of nineteenth-century India—land—is concerned. By the later half of the nineteenth century, most parts of India—with the exception of Oudh and the Punjab—had a similar pattern of land distribution. Usually 30 or 40 per cent of the land in a given district or region was held by a very small number of large landholders; 70 per cent was held by thousands of petty landholders. If, for example, in a district in 1880 there were 100,000 landholders, 99,900 held 70 per cent of the land and 100 held 30 per cent.

In Bengal, where there was a landlord revenue settlement, the goal in 1793 was to settle landed rights with a small group, at best no more than several thousand landlords. In the middle of the nineteenth century— through land sales and the selling of certain rights to revenue collection— the number of landlords, individuals, and families had grown enormously. Let me illustrate with the district of Jessore, in East Pakistan. In 1790, there were 46 estates; in 1793, 122 estates; and, in 1875, 4,408 estates. Of these 4,408 estates, 3,790 were small and paid up to 500 Rs. revenue annually (53 per cent of the revenue); 485 medium-sized estates paid between Rs. 500–1,000 (26 per cent of the revenue); and 133 large estates paid over Rs. 1,000 annually (22 per cent of the revenue). In Bengal, as exemplified by Jessore district, a relatively tight control by a small number of families had shifted to a more diffuse system of land control (Hunter 1875:262–308). Muzzafapur, in Bihar, another permanently settled district, had 1,331 estates in 1790 and, by 1891, 21,346 estates with a total of 157,604 proprietors (Stevenson-Moore 1901:54–55, 290).

In the Zamindari areas—Bengal, Bihar, Orissa, Northern Madras, and Eastern U.P.—the process of fission is clear; inequities in assessment, skill in management, and differential access to the administrators enabled some to gain and caused others to lose land. In addition, given the rule of equal inheritance, some holdings got smaller and smaller. However, there were also processes of fusion. The only son of an only son could have a fairly large holding. Skill and luck could enable small holdings to become bigger. However, fusion seemed to occur most at the upper end of the scale. A very large landholder controlling thousands of acres, such as the Maharaja of Darbangha in Muzzafapur district, could, through purchase and chicanery, add to his holdings. Secondly, throughout the nineteenth century, urban-based individuals—civil servants, lawyers, and merchants—kept putting together large estates by transmuting their income from non-rural activities into land. So the process of fission and fusion went on simultaneously, and my guess is that some of the big got bigger and most of the small got smaller.

I think the pattern of distribution of land is fairly well established for Zamindari areas. Interestingly, *ryotwari* (or peasant settlement areas) appear to have followed the same pattern. The Madras settlement was supposed to have been made up of peasants; in 1827, over two million *ryots* (peasants) received rights to land. However, by the end of the nineteenth century, the pattern of a small number of large holders and a large number of small holders emerges. In all of Madras presidency (which includes several permanently settled districts), 804 *zamindars* paid over Rs. 1,000 revenue annually and held 40 per cent of the land. About three million *ryots* most of whom paid less than Rs. 10 annually, controlled the remaining 60 per cent of the land (Baden-Powell 1892:142).

The Land Controllers and their Significance for Elite Structures

Viewed from the late nineteenth century or the twentieth century, the large landholder looked like the long-established aristocracy of India. The British, largely for policy reasons, tried to treat the large landholders and the Princes as an ancient aristocracy. In reality, the large landholders, certainly throughout much of Bengal, Bihar, Uttar Pradesh, and parts of south India, were very much the result of the conditions of the late eighteenth century and the effects of British rule.

For example, in 1895, in four of the eastern districts of Uttar Pradesh, 134 revenue payers paid about one-third of the revenue of the districts; well over 100,000 others paid the rest. Most of these large revenue payers can be termed "new men"; 29 owed their rise to economic prominence to government service under the British as subordinate officials (head clerks) and judges; 36 of the new men owed their origins to commercial activity. Of the 75 families, few came from landed families in the area. Most came from outside or from towns and cities. The next largest group of landholders was what may be termed eighteenth-century aristocracy. The largest of these was the Raja of Banaras. Macaulay's rhetoric in his famous essay on Warren Hastings notwithstanding, the Raja of Banaras was not an ancient lord displaced by the rapacious Warren Hastings but very much a newly risen regional chief who rose in one generation from near peasantry to royalty. Others of the eighteenth-century aristocracy were recipients of prebendary domains distributed by the British for support received at the time of Chait

Singh's rebellion in 1781. Two old aristocratic families, paying 11 per cent of the large landholders' revenue, were from old families; however, their home domains were not in the Banaras region. The homeland of the Raja of Vizagapatam was more than a thousand miles away.

An important characteristic of the large revenue payers, regardless of their origin, was that by the end of the nineteenth century they were over-whelmingly urban-based. In 283 land sales records which I have found for the period 1795 to 1850 in the Banaras region, seventy per cent of buyers of lands at auction indicated urban residence. Therefore, if one is to argue that these large landholders are the natural elite of the countryside, it is clear they are an absentee rather than a resident elite.

In the late eighteenth and early nineteenth centuries, there emerged in the cities of India, including the European-established ones like Calcutta, a life style to which the newly arrived groups were central. Their origins, whether commercial, civil, and/or royal or aristocratic, were less important than the consumption style to which they aspired. The consumption style included both modern and traditional elements. For example, the biog-rapher of Dewan Krito Ram, a Kayastha of Calcutta who owned large *zamindaris* in Jessore, Birbhum, and Hughli in Bengal, wrote that:

In his retired life his attention was always directed to do such religious acts as would endear him to his countrymen. . . . He used to celebrate the Durga puja with great éclat and his charity on such occasions was almost unlimited. [At the festival] he used to distribute one rupee to every man who showed a big earthen pot full of water. . . . He established idols Madan Gopal Jew in Jessore and Radhaballah Jew in Birbhum and endowed the Brahmans of those places with sufficient lands for their support, dedicated temples to Shiva in various parts of Benares . . . constructed a road from Tara to Mothuabati. . . . (Ghose 1881:40–41)

The Raja of Banaras spent thousands of rupees each year in support of the Ram Lila, a festival eagerly anticipated not only by the Indians of Banaras but by the British as well. The life style included spending on traditional means of establishing or maintaining status but also spending on the more modern segment of the society. For example, Radha Kant Deb, the leader of the conservatives in Calcutta, gave a supper and grand ball for both British and Indians in 1858 in honor of the recapture of Delhi and Lucknow and the advent of Queen Victoria's rule in India. In 1860, the *Englishman,* one of the leading English language papers in Calcutta, described a dinner and ball at Radha Kant Deb's in the following fashion: "What with an excellent band, beautiful fireworks, and tastefully lighted gardens the *tout ensemble* of the Raja's mansion was almost like a dream of the Arabian nights." (ibid., 94). The urban landed elite in Calcutta and other cities as well, in the early nineteenth century, helped establish institutions central to modernization, such as the Hindu College and the Calcutta School Book Society, and served with distinction on the Committee on Public Instruction. In Bombay, Elphinstone College owed its origins to an endowment by wealthy residents of Bombay for three professorships. In a real sense, at one and the same time, the newly arrived landed and commerical groups maintained what is sometimes perceived as the traditional life style for the wealthy and also began to participate in the modern society and establish institutions central to the recruitment and training of new urban elites.

I have argued that in the eighteenth century there was a local elite—the members of the dominant lineages, the petty rajas, the descendants of prebendary dominion holders under the Mughals—and the regional elite, who were the town fort dwellers. It has been assumed that the latter group was reduced to poverty and peasantry by the effects of British revenue policies and the rise of the large landholders:

Millions of people were, by these settlements, deprived of rights that they had enjoyed for well over two thousand years, hereditary cultivating proprietors of land were turned into rackrented tenants-at-will, and conditions were thus created that led to continuous social discord and economic deterioration and the decay of agriculture. (United Provinces Report 1948:81)

This view of the rise of the new landed class shows the old local landed elite dispossessed of their lands and status, the villages of India without leadership, and the rural sector populated by a dispirited, rack-rented tenantry. The picture is most frequently portrayed by journalists and many Indian politicians, and it is accepted by some political scientists and historians, but it comes as a shock to anyone who has done anthropological field work in an Indian village. Anthropologists do not find Indian villages broken, leaderless, or dispirited. The dominant castes, sometimes Rajput, sometimes Brahman, Maratha, Ahir, Okkaliga, or Muslim, act as the political and economic center of the village society. They also set the cultural consumption standards for upwardly mobile groups in the village. In short, they are the village elite, in many cases the direct descendants of the lineage town fort dwellers of the eighteenth century. The nineteenth century contains much evidence that the old rural elite did not get wiped out and did not knuckle under to the new urban-based elite. The reasons why they did not become dispossessed are fairly simple. A society is not a closed system with a finite quantity of power, status, and goods and services so that if one group rises in status, income, and power, another group necessarily has to fall, as in some kind of hydraulic system. The rise of the new men does not necessarily mean that the old men fall or disappear. When new landlords did appear, what did they control? They did not really control the land, but they had some rights over it and its product. Most frequently, those who lost rights stayed where they were as permanent tenants, often at favored rates and still directly controlling the best land and most of the labor within the village. Their economic position did not necessarily deteriorate. In many parts of India, at least until the 1860s and 1870s, agricultural prices and production were rising. Commercial crops were introduced, and in some areas the producers of sugar cane, cotton, and some of the grain crops benefited as much as the new landlords. Therefore, even though one's legal status may have changed from "landlord" to "tenant," one was not necessarily worse off. Similarly, to a low-caste person in a village or to petty shopkeepers, it did not actually matter much whether the members of the dominant caste were legally landlords or tenants; they still exercised much of the authority and held the same position within the village and local society as they always had. Finally, as was pointed out, many of the new landed classes were urban dwellers and, hence, very often remote. So, through the nineteenth century and into the twentieth century, there was a highly localized but nonetheless clearly evident local elite, in some respects more immediately and directly involved in the villages than they ever had been.

The New Urban Elites

Thus far the argument of this paper has been that there was considerable continuity in the elite structure of rural India in the eighteenth and nineteenth centuries. The establishment of British rule, however, did provide a context for a new urban-based elite to develop in the major port cities and presidency capitals of Calcutta, Bombay, and Madras. This group is usually described as the Westernized elite who followed the new occupations of law and teaching in Western-style schools and who were increasingly important in the lower ranks of the British civil service.

In some respects the roots of Westernization in India go back to the sixteenth and seventeenth centuries when small but significant groups of Indians, particularly merchants and civil servants, began to attach themselves to the European officers of the Portuguese, Dutch, British and French companies. In the eighteenth century brokers and middlemen (*Gomashtas* and *Banyans*) had well-recognized roles in the trading networks which grew up in the European-Indian trade (Arasaratnam 1966:85–95). Little is known about the recruitment and origin of these commercial groups who fit into the interstices developing in the society. There is some evidence to suggest that, initially, those who took advantage of opportunities in the eighteenth century in the growing urban centers were to some extent marginal to the traditional urban social structures. The Parsis in Bombay, a group of Zoroastrians who had migrated from Persia after the Arab conquests of the seventh and eighth centuries, A.D., settled on the western coast of India as craftsmen and petty merchants. In the eighteenth century, through their relations with the British, their fortunes expanded greatly, and they found their way into a whole range of expanded commercial and craft opportunities.

It was not only religiously and culturally marginal groups, nor the traditional merchant-trading castes, who found new chances under the European-fostered commercial activities. The Setts of Calcutta illustrate another pattern. These were a weaving caste in Bengal who were able to monopolize for a time the brokerage function in the cloth trade of Bengal and who became wealthy through it (Ghosh 1960:42–55).

Although systematic research is yet to be done on the origins of these new Westernized elites, an impressionistic picture of some of the important Bengali families can be drawn from Lak-Nath Ghose's *Modern History of the Indian Chiefs, Rajas, Zamindars . . .* (1881). Ghose gives biographical and historical information for over sixty Bengali families. The method of selection for inclusion in this work is unclear, and the length of each entry may be related to the amount of money the families were willing to pay for inclusion in the work. However, although some prominent families may have been left out, most who are included are of significance in mid-nineteenth-century Bengal society.

In the eighteenth century, work in the civil service under the British, business in association with Europeans, tax farming, and landholding seem to have been primary sources of family wealth. Until the 1830s family fortunes seem to have expanded, with commerce and landholding the principal routes to success. However, the striking thing in the family histories is the diversity of occupations and sources of wealth, even within single generations. There is no simple pattern. Individuals made money as land-holders, then became civil servants under the British while their brothers might have entered commercial activity. The general traditional status of the families, such as caste or the specific status based on lineage and sub-caste, does not seem to have been crucial to success. Some upwardly mobile families, such as Digambar Mitra's, claimed descent from a very high Kayastha family twenty-three generations earlier (Chunder 1893:3). Other families appear to have had dubious status in the past. The Tagores, for example, were in effect outcast Brahmans. James Furrell, the writer of a memoir on the family, puts such traditional ambiguous status in a favorable light by stating:

While, however, the flaw thus introduced [by outcasting] into the pedigree of the family has in no degree affected the respect in which they are held by their countrymen, it has invested them with the right of making their own caste laws, and thus conferred on them an immunity from vexatious restrictions which they would not otherwise have enjoyed. (1892:19–20)

Many of the sixty families in Ghose's book seem to have been of quite obscure origin, whether they were Brahman, Kayastha, or Subrabanik. Some, though apparently few, owed their origins to service under the Mughals, such as Nava Krishna Deb who founded a distinguished north Calcutta family and who was an ancestor of Radha Kant Deb. The family had served as relatively high officials of Nawabs in Bengal, and by the middle of the eighteenth century served Lord Clive as Persian translators and on diplomatic missions.

In the eighteenth century there was constant connection of families with the British as *diwans,* translators, commerical agents, and revenue officials. In the early nineteenth century, commercial activity, speculation in East India Company bonds, military contracting, indigo and silk manufacturing, importing and banking all led to wealth. After the 1830s the legal professions seem to have attracted a good many sons of men who first made their fortunes at the turn of the century. Some idea of the income possible in law, even by 1850, is indicated by the statement that Prosunna Kumar Tagore made 20,000 pounds a year in his practice.

It is easy to oversimplify grossly the process of social change that was going on in Calcutta. Some structural changes did take place and new life styles emerged, but the conventional picture of a new urban class society, involved in the liberal professions and Western ideas, establishing new institutions to further Westernization, can be exaggerated. Like many views of Indian society current today, the picture drawn by Indian and Western scholars tells us more about the time when they are writing than about the past they purportedly are describing. One example of this need of scholars to see a glorious social and cultural revolution in nineteenth-century Bengal is given by Amiya Charan Banerji, who writes:

> Superstitions and cruel customs played havoc in Hindu society. The burning of widows in those days was a common practice. The poor meekly submitted to the tyrannies of the rich. . . . Modern science had not yet begun to dispel ignorance, superstition and blind faith. The Hindu orthodoxy formed an almost immovable barrier on the path leading to progress and development. This was the setup of the Hindu society, specially in Bengal when Rammohan Roy appeared on the scene. His was the mighty genius who tore to pieces the arguments advanced by orthodox pundits in support of idolatrous and superstitious practice and of the cruel custom of Satidaha. In religion, in education and in the political sphere he gave the start to national awakening about one hundred and fifty years ago. He was indeed the father of the Indian Renaissance. During the period of the Renaissance, a galaxy of inspired religious leaders, great social reformers, noble patriots, eminent political thinkers and mighty literary geniuses appeared in India and especially in Bengal. (Gupta 1958:79–80)

Banerji glosses over a wide range of cultural and social problems in his eulogy of Ram Mohan Roy and the New India. He elevates intellectual statements made by such reformers to the status of social fact; he continues to see India in the realm of values and culture rather than in behavioral and structural terms, and he confuses words with actions.

At the same time that Ram Mohan Roy was "causing" the "Renaissance" there were figures like Radha Kant Deb who, although consistently labeled "conservative" by scholars, may have been more representative of the Calcutta elites than Ram Mohan and his followers, or those, like the members of the Young Bengal movement, who were preaching radical cultural reform. The complexities of the movements for reform in the period 1820 to 1850 can be seen in the fact that Radha Kant Deb, often labeled an orthodox Hindu, nevertheless wrote and spoke English and was quick to utilize the newly available printing industry in Calcutta to publish the first Bengali spelling books and readers, following European models. He was a scholar of Persian, Arabic, and Sanskrit as well as English.

But it is interesting to note that, in the institutions which can reasonably be said to have underlain the self-conscious movements which aimed to change Bengali culture, the division into modern and traditional does not hold. In particular I would point to the establishment in 1817 of the Hindu College and the Calcutta School Book Society (Majumdar 1951; Basak 1958; Bagal 1962). In these two crucial institutions, Ram Mohan Roy and his followers, who are labeled the "moderns," have played but a minor role. It was Radha Kant Deb and the "orthodox" who raised the money and held the important offices in these modernizing institutions. From the end of the eighteenth century there were in Calcutta small private schools run by Britishers and Anglo-Indians to which some of the new urban Indians sent their children. Mr. Sherbourne's school had many of the Tagores as pupils between 1805 and 1815. Numerous richer families hired tutors to teach their children English. The motivation for sending children to these schools rather than to local religious preceptors or to indigenous schools was the obvious practical usefulness of learning English.

There was no means of carrying on English education beyond the rudimentary level until the founding of the Hindu College. Sir Hyde East, Chief Justice of the Supreme Court in Calcutta (1813–1821), was one of the Britishers most instrumental in founding the College. In his view the motivation for supporting the College was the desire among the Hindus of "rank and wealth . . . to form an establishment for the education of their children in a liberal manner as practiced by Europeans" (Majumdar 1951:44). The College was divided into two sections: the School, which taught Bengali and English grammar and arithmetic to boys from ten to thirteen, and the College, in which English, history, geography, chronology, astronomy, mathematics, and chemistry were taught (Presidency College 1956:1). On opening day there were twenty pupils, and within three months the number had grown to sixty-nine. By the late 1830s 500 students were enrolled in the College and almost 400 in the junior school. For forty years (1820–1860) the Hindu College produced most of the leaders in most areas of Bengali life. Ram Prasad Roy, son of Ram Mohan Roy, the first Indian to be appointed a judge of the High Court, was a product of the College. So were the linguist Krishna Mohan Banerji; Radha Nath Sikdar, the first person to measure the height of Mount Everest; Satyendra Nath Tagore, the first Indian to enter the I.C.S; Mohendralal Sarkar, the scientist and founder of the Indian Association for Science; and such writers, journalists, and polemicists as Peary Chand Mitra, Rajnarain Basu, Gourdas Basak, Michael Mahusdan Datta, Digambar Mitra, and Ramtaru Lahiri (ibid., 6–7).

The Calcutta School Book Society, which underwrote the costs of writing and publishing basic primary school textbooks in Bengali and English, was run by the same group of individuals who ran the College. Most of these books were simple readers, spellers, and arithmetic books, and the Society also produced *Digdarshan,* a newspaper for school children. By the middle of the nineteenth century, therefore, a small but significant group of Bengalis holding a wide range of religious views and differing in their attitudes toward change was emerging from the educational institutions. Because of the nature and content of their education and the occupations they fostered, these began to have an effect on the structure of Bengal. However, as with the rural segment of the society, the differentiation was by no means unidirectional or unrelated to the structural pattern of the traditional society.

Until the end of the nineteenth century the spread of college and university education was slow. Between 1858 and 1881 the Calcutta University produced only 1,701 graduates. (This calculation is based on Appendix D—"Occupations of Graduates of Calcutta University, 1858–1881"—of Pradip Sinha's *Nineteenth Century Bengal: Aspects of Social History.*) Table 1 summarizes the occupations of these 1,701 graduates. The immediately striking thing about the occupations of the graduates of Calcutta is the very narrow range of jobs which they represented. Legal practice or government employment as judicial officers and employment as teachers account for over half the positions held by the College graduates. The free professions other than law and teaching were practiced by very few Indians. Even more surprising, few of the graduates found occupations in commerce. Although more Indians were self-employed than were employed by the government, most of these were legal practitioners or teachers, both professions which depended on government activity or support.

Government employment, teaching, and law were the occupations into which the Western-educated were finding their way at the turn of the nineteenth century. What relationship did these newly educated have to the older elites discussed earlier in this paper: the old land controllers, the eighteenth-century commercial families and groups, and the new urban landholders, or the aristocracy of big landholders and Princes? Thus far there is little data on which to base an answer to this crucial question. There has been too little systematic work done, in a quantitative fashion, to provide more than a few preliminary suggestions. From government education reports collated and analyzed by Anil Seal on Bengal students in 1884–85,

Recruitment of Elites in British India

TABLE 1

OCCUPATIONS OF 1,701 CALCUTTA UNIVERSITY GRADUATES, 1858–1881

Occupation	# of Graduates	% of Total	# of Graduates	% of Total
LAW			776	45.6
Legal Practice	500	29.4		
Government Employment	192	11.3		
Law Students	84	4.9		
GOVERNMENT SERVICE OTHER THAN LAW			162	9.5
British				
High (e.g., deputy collector)	74	4.3		
Low (e.g., clerk, translator)	78	4.6		
Princely State				
High	7	0.4		
Low	3	0.2		
EDUCATION			358	21.0
Private or Government Aided	165	9.7		
Government	193	1.3		
COMMERCE, LANDHOLDERS, AND OTHER			30	1.8
OCCUPATION UNKNOWN, DEAD, OR ABROAD			375	22.0

SOURCE: Pradip Sinha, *Nineteenth Century Bengal: Aspects of Social History* (Calcutta, 1965), Appendix D.

it may be inferred that thirteen per cent of the students in college had fathers whose incomes amounted to over Rs. 5,000 per year, seven per cent of those attending high schools and only two-and-a-half per cent of those in middle English schools were within this range. The bulk of the college, high school, and middle English school students' parents had incomes between Rs. 200 and 5,000 per year (Seal 1968:63–64). Ellen Mac-Donald Gumperz's work (1968) on the records of Fergusson College in Poona, which analyzes the incomes of those who guaranteed the students financially in the period from 1885 to 1895, shows 66 per cent of the students' guarantors with incomes of less than Rs. 800 a year. In a study of 1,746 Indians who entered the Middle Temple Inn in London to receive legal training in the period from 1863 to 1944 (investigated by Peter McGregor, Thomas Kessinger, and Bernard S. Cohn), only 39 or 2.2 per cent of the students' fathers had hereditary titles such as Talukdar Rais

TABLE 2

OCCUPATIONS OF FATHERS OF MIDDLE TEMPLE INN STUDENTS
AND GUARANTORS OF FERGUSSON COLLEGE STUDENTS

	Fathers' Occupations: Entrants to Middle Temple Inn, London, 1863–1910 (N = 605)*	Guarantors' Occupations: Students at Fergusson College, Poona, 1885–1895 (N = 1,140)†
Law, Private	119 (20)	Not reported
High Court	*49*	
Other	*70*	
Government Service	85	414 (37)
High (Rs. 1,000 or more monthly)	*7*	
Medium (Rs. 500–999)	*38*	
Low (Less than Rs. 500)	*15*	
Scale unknown	*25*	
Princely State Service	45 (7)	102 (9)
Landholder/Agriculture	181 (30)	184 (16)
Commerce	70 (12)	96 (8)
Professional/Private (e.g., doctor, teacher)	55 (9)	200 (18)
Unknown/Other	50	35 (3)
Pension	Not reported	102 (9)

NOTE: Number in parentheses = per cent of each total.

* Calculations based upon Middle Temple Inn Register. Done by Peter McGregor, Thomas Kessinger, and Bernard S. Cohn.

† Calculations by Ellen MacDonald Gumperz based on Fergusson College records.

or Jagirdar, indicating officially recognized or hereditary landed status on an extensive scale.

The hypothesis, then, about students who received Western-style education late in the nineteenth century was that they did not come from the wealthiest Indian families nor from those groups in the society whom the British officially recognized as the traditional aristocracy. Table 2 provides data comparing the occupation of the fathers of students entering Middle Temple Inn during the years between 1863 and 1910 with Dr. Gumperz's data on the occupations of guarantors of Fergusson College students in the 1885 to 1895 period. The students at Middle Temple Inn were drawn from all over India but mainly from Bengal (127 or 21 per cent), Punjab and Delhi (103 or 17 per cent), Maharashtra (88 or 15 per cent), Bihar (86 or 14 per cent), and Uttar Pradesh (86 or 13 per cent). Students from the rest of India accounted for 111, or 20 per cent. The cost of sending a son to London to the Middle Temple was much greater than that of sending him to Fergusson College. Several of the categories used by Gumperz and by my associates in analyzing occupations are not comparable. Gumperz does not give separate figures for lawyers, and our category of landholders is not strictly comparable to hers. The comparison of the two sets of data, however, gives some idea of the range of status among boys receiving English education in the two differing situations.

In India more than in the West, "father's occupation" is not necessarily the best indicator of a family's status, in direct financial or social terms. A father's brother or father's father may be the crucial person in determining the status of a family in a local stratification system. I suspect the Gumperz data, which is based on occupation of the guarantor rather than on the father's occupation, may more clearly reflect the status of the boys involved. In terms of the two institutions, a college which drew on Maratha speakers in Bombay and the Middle Temple Inn of Court in London, it would be reasonable to assume that two different kinds of populations are involved. The Middle Temple population is drawn from a higher social and economic stratum—one which, given the prevalence of lawyers and government service at a higher level than in the Gumperz study, indicates a population which has been for two generations (father and son) operating in the Westernized segment of the economy and society. This assumption is strengthened when we consider the size of residence city reported by Middle Temple Inn boys. Among them, 36 per cent had residences in cities over 200,000 population, primarily Calcutta, Bombay, Delhi, Madras, Lucknow, and Hyderabad, with the vast majority coming from Bombay and Calcutta. Only nine of the boys' fathers resided in villages during the period of 1863 to 1888, and five per cent were in small towns (5,000 to 9,999 population). In the Gumperz study only two per cent came from Bombay itself, 30 per cent from Poona—and 15 per cent from villages. Even considering the prevalence of large cities in the background of the Middle Temple population, however, the bulk of the students (47 per cent) came from small cities and district towns. What can be inferred from our study and that of Gumperz is that the groups from which English-speaking students were drawn were fairly widely dispersed in India and reflected diverse social environments. Most of the students were recruited from the district towns and provincial capitals in which their fathers worked. Even though Calcutta, Bombay, and to a lesser extent Madras were the focal points of commercial, intellectual, and political activity engaging the most attention from the new elites, the students were drawn from a much wider social network than the metropolitan cities. Many were from the smaller cities and even the countryside and villages.

Although much research remains to be done on the students themselves to determine their occupations and where they worked, we can hypothesize that a view of the elite structure which focuses only on the Presidency capitals and the activities, life styles, and thought of the English-speaking populations of these cities will miss much that is significant in the stratification system.

It has been assumed that the newly educated elites in India in the late nineteenth century were drawn from a very limited portion of the Indian population. In Bengal, three caste categories tended to provide most members of new elites: the Brahmans, the Kayasthas, and the Vaids. These are the so-called *Bhadralok*—the respectable people. In Bihar and Upper India it was the Brahmans again, urban-based trading and writing communities, and Bengalis and other outside groups who sought English education. In the Punjab it was the commercial families. In western India it was the Prabhus, a writing caste, the Brahmans, and the Parsis, while in the south the Brahmans led in obtaining Western education.

In general, the systematic statistical work done so far on caste categories and education in the late nineteenth century seems to support this general picture (Seal 1968: chap. 2). Eighty-seven per cent of the students at Fergusson College from 1885 to 1895, as reported by Mrs. Gumperz, were Brahmans. The British often dismissed the newly educated as being unrepresentative of the population at large and as merely continuing the old structure in which, they believed, the Brahmans dominated the social system.

As with most other generalizations about stratification in India, this picture of dominance over Western education by a few castes, and, hence, of elite status in the Westernized segment of the society must be disaggregated, and we must direct our attention, instead, to the sociological reality of the situation. We must ask: In what sense did the fact of ascription to a caste category, such as Brahman or Kayastha or trading caste, have behavioral concomitants which would affect the stratification system? As we pointed out at the beginning of this paper, the effective social unit in the caste system is not the categorical level but the kinship and face-to-face grouping in the society—the *biradari* and *jati* levels, the endogamous and exogamous groups. Hence, what was important to Indians in the late nineteenth century was not the fact that someone was a Brahman, but that he was a particular *kind* of Brahman belonging to a particular *gotra* (clan) from a particular place—a Brahman descended from specific ancestors, whose kinship ties were with specific groups. Within the category of Brahman in any region was a tendency toward more conflict within the category over issues of social and ritual precedence, social standing, and economic power than existed between members of different caste categories. The same was true within caste categories, among larger groupings such as the Bhadralok in Bengal. Within this category there was competition for jobs and entry into schools; members fought out local politics so that, as an elite, they had little unity in the face of British or other groups in the society.

As can be seen, the newly educated elites clustered within a narrow range of occupations in the society. Law, teaching, and government service accounted for most of their activities. Yet there were other elites who did equally important things in the society. Commercial activity often rested with groups who were not highly Westernized. The cotton manufacturers of Ahmedabad tended not to be English-speaking until the late nineteenth century. The Marwari and Subarbaniks who controlled much of the real estate in Calcutta in the late nineteenth century were another group of non-Westernized, successful businessmen.

Conventionally the Muslims have been seen as a backward and deprived category in the society whose members failed to take to Western education with the speed and alacrity of the Hindus and others, and Muslim nationalism is thought to have been a direct outgrowth of the feeling of economic and political deprivation. However, like most generalizations about the nineteenth century, this view needs more careful examination. Among the 605 students at Middle Temple, 210 (or 35 per cent) were Muslim at a time when Muslims accounted for only about a quarter of the Indian population. Two provinces produced more than half of these law students: Uttar Pradesh and Bihar, both provinces in which the Muslims were in the minority. Interestingly enough, Maharashtra, which had less than five per cent Muslim population, produced ten Muslim law students in the Middle Temple population in comparison with only twenty-eight

Hindus and forty-six Parsis. Because of the highly selective factor governing those who went to the Middle Temple, this data cannot be taken as representative of the society; nonetheless, the significant number of Muslims attending school in London during this period is suggestive in a number of ways.

Those areas in which Muslims were numerically in the minority outproduce areas where they were in the majority, such as Bengal and the Punjab. In the minority areas, Muslims were influential as landholders and as ruling elites during the eighteenth century. Was there a continuity from the traditional ruling and landed elites of the eighteenth century among the Muslims as there was not with the Hindus? Or do these students, in origin, represent different groupings in Indo-Muslim society?

The question of the differentiation of elites becomes even more important in the twentieth century, with the rise of popular politics within the colonial system, in elections to local governing bodies and to legislative bodies, and with the rise of the nationalist movement. The tendency has been to see a direct continuity from the small, Westernized elite to the control of the Indian National Congress even though the political styles of many leaders, such as Gandhi and Patel, tapped traditional loyalties and identifications of Indians. In the twentieth century, the nationalist movement in India, both Hindu and Muslim, became the meeting ground for the old and new elites. As electoral politics developed and as the nationalist movement mobilized more and more support, drawing on the countryside, the leaders who were recruited from the English-speaking elites entered into alliance with the rural local notables and elites who were the descendants of the eighteenth-century land-controlling elites. It was this group of land controllers who continued to control the countryside and who provided the voting strength of the Indian National Congress from the 1930s to the late fifties. In reality, the English-educated were not a small, isolated group, as the British administrators described them. They were allied with the effective controlling elites of the countryside, while the British found themselves captive to their own theory of a landed aristocracy centered on the large landholders and the Princes, whom they thought to be the controllers of the rural society.

REFERENCES

Arasaratnam, S. (1966) "Indian Merchants and Their Trading Methods," *The Indian Economic and Social History Review* 3, 1:85–95.

Baden-Powell, B. H. (1892) *The Land Systems of British India,* vol. 3. Oxford.

Bagal, J. C. (1962) "Primary Education in Calcutta," *Bengal Past and Present* 81.

Basak, N. L. (1959) "Origin and Role of the Calcutta School Book Society in Promoting the Cause of Education in India," *Bengal Past and Present* 78, no. 1.

Chunder, Bholanauth (1893) *Raja Digambar Mitra: His Life and Career.* Calcutta.

Coats, Thomas (1823) "Account of the Present State of the Township of Lony," *Transactions of the Literary Society of Bombay.* London.

Furrell, James (1892) *The Tagore Family: A Memoir.* Calcutta.

Ghose, Loka-natha (1881) *The Modern History of Indian Chiefs, Rajas, Zamindars* . . . , pt. 2. Calcutta.

Ghosh, Benoy (1960) "Some Old Family Founders in Eighteenth Century Calcutta," *Bengal Past and Present* 79:42–55.

Gopal, S. (1965) *British Policy in India 1858–1905.* Cambridge.

Gumperz, Ellen (1968) "General Summary of Major Variables—Fergusson College Students, 1885–1895." Unpublished manuscript.

Gune, T. V. (1953) *The Judicial System of Marathas.* Deccan College Dissertation Series, no. 12. Poona.

Gupta, A. C., ed. (1958) *Studies in the Bengal Renaissance.* Jadavpur.

Hopkins, E. Washburn (1901) *India Old and New.* New York.

Hunter, W. W. (1875) *Statistical Account of Bengal,* vol. 2. London.

Karim, Abdul (1963) *Murshid Kuli Khan and His Times.* Dacca.

Krishna, M. H. (1937) "The Caste Changes in Indian History," *Man in India* 17:75.

Majumdar, R. C. (1951) "The Hindu College," *Journal of the Asiatic Society of Bengal: Letters* 21.

Mill, James (1820) *The History of British India,* vol. 1. London.

Nanda, B. R. (1963) *The Nehrus: Motilal and Jawaharlal.* New York.

Orme, Robert (1778) *A History of the Military Transactions of the British Nation in Indostan* . . . , vol. 2. London.

Presidency College (1956) *Centenary Volume, 1955.* Alipore.

Robertson, William (1828; originally written 1791) *An Historical Disquisition Concerning the Knowledge Which the Ancients Had of India.* . . . London.

Seal, Anil (1968) *The Emergence of Indian Nationalism.* Cambridge.

Sinha, Pradip (1965) *Nineteenth Century Bengal: Aspects of Social History.* Calcutta.

Stevenson-Moore, C. J. (1901) *Final Report on the Survey and Settlement Operations in the Muzzafapur District 1892–1899.* Calcutta.

United Provinces Zamindari Abolition Committee (1948) *Report,* vol. 1. Allahabad.

Wolf, Eric (1966) *Peasants.* Englewood Cliffs, N. J.

Chapter 6/ Robert M. Marsh

Evolution and Revolution: Two Types of Change in China's System of Social Stratification

Definition of Social Stratification

There is a great variety of approaches to the study of social stratification and class. There are the Marxists; the ecological school, such as Sahlins; the Warner school; the functionalists, such as Parsons, Davis, Moore, and Barber; antifunctionalists like Tumin and Buckley; multidimensional analysts like Weber and Lenski; and those like Duncan who argue that at least in the United States there are no definite social classes, only discrete differences in occupational status and income. One would have hoped that these approaches at least would agree substantially on the *definition* of stratification. But this is not the case. Probably the only common element in the various definitions is that stratification refers to societal rewards which are differentially distributed, with the result that there is some kind of institutionalized inequality.

Given this conceptual confusion, it behooves us to clarify our own definition. *Social stratification* is here defined in terms of three concepts: the division of labor, evaluation, and rewards. Every complex society has a *division of labor,* the major craft or occupational role specialties of the

149

members of the society. Roles are *evaluated* by the members of the society, and role incumbents are *rewarded* for role performance. Insofar as all functionally significant roles are evaluated as *equal,* and are *rewarded* equally, there is, by our definition, no social stratification. The division of labor has a purely *horizontal* extension in social space. Social stratification proper, then, refers to the differential evaluation and the differential rewarding of functional roles. The greater the *vertical* extension in social space of these invidious distinctions concerning evaluation and rewards, the greater the degree of social stratification.

To say that roles in the division of labor are evaluated on the basis of their "functional importance" is to speak elliptically. We mean that roles are evaluated by people on the basis of the degree of knowledge and/or responsibility which their successful performance demands. Those roles which require either an extensive body of ideas and skills or the control over a large number of other people's roles, or both, tend to be evaluated more highly by the members of any society than roles which require fewer ideas, skills, and smaller spans of control.

The kinds of rewards that are relevant to stratification are numerous indeed, but the most common and important are: authority and power, wealth and income, and prestige or "status honor."

Our definition of social stratification is, then, *the structure of differential evaluations of and rewards attached to roles in the division of labor.* This definition specifies the type of phenomena which we shall call "stratification." It does not attempt to *explain* these phenomena, for that is not the purpose of a definition. Nor does it attempt to answer such questions as: What is the relative influence of ecological, economic, and ideological factors upon stratification? To what extent does stratification impede intergenerational mobility? To what extent does stratification give rise to solidary social *classes?* These and other questions are problems for theory and research, not matters to be settled by definition.

Let us now examine the system of social stratification in China. We shall first describe the system as it operated in "late Imperial" times, that is, during the Ch'ing dynasty (1644–1912), the last dynasty before the overthrow of the monarchy. With that as our "baseline from which change took place," we shall consider the two main lines of development, both of which began during the Republican period (1912–1949) and continue today, one in Taiwan in Nationalist China and the other, in Communist China.

Social Stratification During the Ch'ing Period

We begin our analysis by dividing the functionally significant roles in Ch'ing society according to how highly evaluated and rewarded they were.[1] Three levels may be distinguished: highly valued roles, medium valued roles, and lowly valued roles.

Highly valued roles

The most highly evaluated and rewarded, functionally significant roles were those of the Emperor, the imperial family, the nobility, and the officials in the imperial bureaucracy. The functions fulfilled by these roles were primarily *integrative*. For one thing, the local community in China, though highly segmented in relation to other communities, was not self-sufficient or self-contained.[2] Villages were interdependent in many ways. Problems of irrigation, protection against floods and other natural calamities, economic interchange, social interaction—all required types of integration and regulation *above* the community level. Performance of the most highly evaluated roles of emperor and official gave all Chinese a membership in a larger state, with benefits ranging from hydraulic control to a political-religious world view. By thus producing a relatively unified empire, the emperor and the bureaucracy also functioned to suppress feudalism.

Medium valued roles

The functions of the above-mentioned bureaucratic roles were largely confined to high-level system problems, for example, tax collection and the maintenance of peace and order. A *hsien*—comparable in size to an American county—could have a population of several hundred thousand people; yet a single *hsien* magistrate was typically in charge of the administration of the entire area. In this sense, the arm of the imperial bureaucracy did not extend down to the primary structural units of the society: the marketing community,[3] the village, the patrilineage, etc. Imperial control, though despotic, was not tightly totalitarian in its actual operation.

The handling of *hsien*- and lower-level system problems therefore required an intermediate leadership elite, whose roles would complement those of the imperial bureaucracy. These roles included raising funds for financing and operating irrigation, granaries, and other public works, arbitration in settling local disputes, organizing and commanding local defense corps, acting as intermediaries between the government and the people, maintaining temples, performing ideological functions in ceremonies, philanthropy, and education. These roles were filled, first, by the local literati —men who held degrees in the Confucian examination system but who were not in the imperial bureaucracy; second, by those who assumed these roles because their income provided both the necessary leisure and the excess capital. The latter often did not hold degrees but were large landowners or wealthy merchants.

A given landowner or wealthy merchant could hold disparate positions: however great his *economic rewards,* his *prestige* would be low until he became involved in local leadership functions, at which time it would rise toward the level of his economic status. His prestige, however, would never become perfectly correlated with his high economic status until he, or a kinsman, achieved degrees and government office. This incongruity between the economic status and the prestige of wealthy landlords and merchants was functional for the society in that it motivated those who had the economic surplus to direct their leisure and their capital into system-problems, instead of into exclusively private uses.

Chinese Communist writers on the Ch'ing period emphasize the role of the elite as economic exploiters of the peasantry. Our analysis is closer to the facts. However important landownership and business may have been as *one kind of necessary condition* for membership in the local elite, the sufficient condition was the performance of roles dealing with the above-mentioned intermediate-level system-problems. These were positive inputs into the system, not simply aspects of "exploitation" in the sense of taking-out from the system. Moreover, many members of this local elite performed these medium valued roles not because they were or ever became wealthy landowners or merchants, but because of their prestige as degree holders and literati. As Weber and others have realized, the local elite in China was a *status group,* having honor and deference in common, rather than an economic class, having wealth as a common characteristic.

Lowly valued roles

The vast majority of the Chinese population performed the relatively lowly evaluated and little rewarded role of peasant-farmer, a role which clearly required less knowledge and responsibility than even the local leadership elite, let alone the imperial bureaucracy. The majority of merchants were small shopkeepers and peddlers and, as such, were also included in this group.

Cross-Cutting Aspects of Stratification: Ethnic and Legal

To this description of the system of differential evaluation and rewards during the Ch'ing period must be added two aspects which cross-cut the system. First, the Ch'ing rulers were ethnically Manchu, not Han Chinese. The traditional Chinese system of stratification thus had superimposed upon it an alien group, who preëmpted many of the most highly evaluated roles. The Manchus became more and more acculturated to Han Chinese ways during their three centuries of rule. Nevertheless, their presence at the top of the system of stratification as a conquest dynasty, and the belief among reform-minded Chinese at the end of the nineteenth-century that the stratificational rewards the Manchus enjoyed were undeserved in terms of their role performance, were factors making for change in the system.

A second cross-cutting factor was a legal one. Three legal categories carried invidious distinctions relevant to stratification. These categories were first, the elite (*kuei*), which included officials, holders of ranks, titles, and degrees; second, the commoners (*liang*), which included the mass of the population in the respectable occupations; and, third, the outcast or pariah people (*chien*). These three legal categories were directly but not perfectly correlated with the distribution of evaluation and rewards attached to major social roles.The elite included all the highly evaluated roles and some of the medium evaluated roles. However, landowners and merchants who performed medium evaluated roles but who lacked degrees and titles would be legally classed as commoners, not as elite. Sumptuary laws rigidly and precisely defined the style of life and status-honorific rewards that each legal category of persons could display and enjoy:

The houses, apartments, carriages, dresses, furniture, and other articles used by the officers of the government, and by the people in general, shall be conformable to the established rules and gradations. Accordingly, the individual who possesses any such articles for use, contrary to these rules and gradations, shall, if an officer of the government, be punished with 100 blows, deposed from his office, and rendered incapable of future service; if a private individual is guilty of this offense, the master of the family in which the article is used shall be punished with 50 blows.[4]

The lowest legal category of person—the pariah or "mean people" (*chien*)—included those in certain very lowly evaluated occupations: prostitutes, actors, lictors, odd-jobbers (*ku-kung-jen*), domestic and other kinds of slaves, musicians in certain areas, beggars, boat people, etc. These groups were often descendants of social deviants (e.g., criminals) and unassimilated conquered peoples within China. Two redeeming factors about this legally pariah group were that (a) it comprised an extremely small proportion of the population and (b) it offered some possibilities for legal re-classification as commoner and, eventually, even as a member of the elite.

The Breakdown of the Traditional Stratification System

When we compare the number and range of differentiated functional roles, the evaluation of their functional importance, and their rewards, in late traditional China on the one hand and in contemporary Taiwan and mainland China on the other hand, we cannot miss the fact that there have been basic changes. Before analyzing some of these changes, let us note their major causes.

First, the breakdown of the traditional stratification system was part of the whole process of change in Chinese society and civilization.

Second, and more specifically, the weakening or elimination of the landlord class has been perhaps the most crucial cause of change in the stratification system. The Kuomintang program for land reform was never carried out on the mainland, partly because, after 1937, with the loss of the modern cities of China to Japan, the Kuomintang "became increasingly dependent upon the rural economy and thus upon the support of the ultraconservative landlords in the hinterland."[5] It remained for the Chinese Communists to carry out the complete destruction of the landlord class. Local leadership roles then became the responsibility of Communist party cadres and peasants. In Taiwan, there has been a less radical, but nevertheless *de facto,* elimination of the landlord class through the quite effective Kuomintang-directed land reform program. Much of the money landlords received from the government for their land has been reinvested in urban industry and commerce.

Third, changes in China's educational system have had important consequences for stratification. In 1905, the Confucian civil service examination system was abolished, thereby further undermining the Confucian basis of education. A modern educational system developed. The sons of the old literary elite went in increasing numbers to Japan and the West for modern education and, at the same time, missionary schools and a growing network of public elementary education developed in China itself. Today, in both mainland China and in Taiwan, the educational system is a major vehicle for specifying new roles in the division of labor, training personnel to fill these roles, and diffusing through the population beliefs concerning how these roles should be evaluated and rewarded.

A fourth factor in change in the stratification system is the political revolution. Leadership has shifted from hereditary imperial rule, staffed by literary trained scholar-officials, toward greater power for military officers and businessmen in Republican-Kuomintang China and toward greater power for Communist party members, military officers, and Marxist-Leninist intellectuals in Communist China.

These and other changes have greatly influenced China's division of labor. Many new occupational roles have emerged or have increased in prestige evaluation: engineers, modern trained doctors, lawyers, nurses, brokers, seamen and railway workers, factory workers and party workers, leaders in modern business and finance. At the same time, occupations such as teacher are no longer the exclusive preserve of males.

Let us now examine these changes at the core of the stratification system, first in Taiwan and then in Communist China.

Social Stratification in Contemporary Taiwan

We begin our analysis, as before, by describing which occupational roles have the highest evaluation, which are intermediate, and which are at the bottom in this respect. A survey of a systematic, multistage area sample of 507 male Taiwanese household heads living in Taipei city in 1963, which I conducted, asked respondents to rate the standing of 36 occupations. These data, collected and analyzed by means of the N.O.R.C. technique, yield a prestige score for each occupation and provide us with quantitative data on the core phenomenon of social stratification. See Table 1.

The hierarchy of occupations in Taiwan very closely resembles that in the United States, Denmark, Japan, the Philippines, and other societies in which such studies have been done (Spearman rank correlation coefficient between Taiwan and the United States is .84; between Taiwan and Denmark, .85; between Taiwan and Japan, .80; between Taiwan and the Philippines, .79). Occupations which receive the highest evaluation in Taiwan are those which require either considerable education and specialized training (professor, physician, public prosecutor, chemist, civil engi-

TABLE 1
PRESTIGE RANKING OF OCCUPATIONS
(Taipei, Taiwan)

Rank	Occupation	Percentage of respondents using each category					Prestige score[a]	Percentage unable to rate occupation[c]
		Highest	*Fairly high*	*Middle*	*Fairly low*	*Lowest*		
1	University professor	56	31	11	2	b	88	4
2	Physician	49	40	9	1	1	87	4
3	Public prosecutor	46	37	14	2	b	85	10
4	Factory owner-manager	26	48	24	2	b	80	4
5	Chemist	18	53	27	2	b	77	5
6	Civil Engineer	18	53	27	2	b	77	4
7	Supervisor in board of education	15	44	37	3	b	74	9
8	General manager of a company	10	46	39	4	1	72	5
9	Executive secretary of a company	9	41	45	5	1	71	5
10	Building contractor	10	40	43	6	1	70	6
11	Shop owner (large scale)	11	32	48	8	1	69	6
12	Newspaper reporter	7	33	52	8	1	67	7
13	Middle school teacher	8	26	54	11	1	66	5
14	Accountant	1	18	64	16	b	61	5
15	Army captain	9	15	49	22	6	60	19
16	Political party worker	6	17	47	24	7	58	28
17	Clerk	1	9	60	29	2	55	5
18	Owner-cultivator	4	10	48	30	8	54	4
19	Retail merchant (smaller scale than 11)	3	16	42	26	13	54	7
20	Factory foreman	1	6	57	33	3	54	6
21	Policeman	4	10	45	31	10	53	6
22	Skilled laborer in a factory	1	7	42	41	10	50	4
23	Driver	b	5	38	45	13	49	4
24	Shop clerk	b	2	33	48	17	44	4
25	Carpenter	b	2	23	51	23	41	3
26	Army corporal	3	5	21	34	37	41	15
27	Repairman	b	2	15	47	35	37	4
28	Barber	b	2	18	44	36	37	4
29	Taoist priest	1	5	16	32	46	37	11
30	Street vendor	b	b	14	40	45	34	5
31	Pedicab driver	b	b	10	33	57	31	4
32	Farm laborer	b	1	8	31	60	30	4
33	Janitor	b	1	9	32	59	30	3
34	Servant	b	b	6	28	65	28	3
35	Unskilled laborer (e.g., coolie)	b	1	5	19	74	27	3
36	Rubbish collector	b	b	4	9	87	24	4

Table notes on following page.

neer) or a large degree of responsibility over subordinates or over capital (factory owner-manager, general manager of a company, executive secretary of a company). Medium evaluated occupations are lower in knowledge and responsibility: e.g., shop owner, school teacher, clerk, owner-cultivator, factory foreman, skilled laborer. At the bottom of the hierarchy are occupations that require little or no formal knowledge and responsibility: peddler, pedicab driver, farm laborer, servant, unskilled laborer.

Though new occupations have developed since Ch'ing times, the same invidious distinctions between "head" work and "hand" work—between mental and manual labor—underlie both Ch'ing and contemporary Taiwanese stratification systems. As we shall see, it is only in Communist China that a revolutionary attempt has been made to destroy this distinction.

Table 2 shows the results derived when the mean prestige scores are computed for the major occupational groups in Taipei.

How well does this societal ranking of occupational prestige correspond with self-evaluation of the usefulness of one's occupation in society? We asked all respondents: "Is your own occupation more useful to society than other occupations, neither more nor less useful, or less useful than other occupations?" There is a moderate positive relationship between prestige and perceived usefulness of occupations ($\gamma = .48$, see Table 3).

Notes to Table 1.

NOTES: Data were received in response to the following question: "People in society generally say occupations are divided into 'higher' and 'lower'. What do you think? If these occupations are rated in one of five categories, how would you rate each one? Highest, fairly high, middle, fairly low, or lowest?" The N.O.R.C. technique transforms these ratings into a prestige score by weighting the five categories 100, 80, 60, 40, and 20, respectively. The score of 88 for university professor is obtained by multiplying the per cent in each category by the weight, summing these five numbers, and rounding to two digits.

a Two or more occupations have the same prestige score (77, 54, 41, 37, and 30). When these scores are extended one decimal, these ties disappear, thus allowing us to rank the 36 occupations without ties.

b Less than 0.5%.

c The percentages in this table distinguish between (1) respondents who rated an occupation in terms of one of the five rating categories—"highest" through "lowest"—and (2) respondents who did not, the "don't knows". The five columns used for the former group total 100 per cent across the row (except for rounding). The last column is the percentage of the total sample (N = 507) who were unable to rate a given occupation. For example, there were 20 "don't know" responses, or four per cent of the sample, on the occupation of university professor.

TABLE 2

PRESTIGE OF OCCUPATIONAL GROUPS

(Taipei, Taiwan)

Rank	Occupational Group	Mean Prestige
1	Professional, technical, and administrative (1–3, 5–7, 12–14)[a]	75.8
2	Large business (4, 8–10)	73.3
3	Owner-cultivator farmers (18)	54.0
4	Small business (11, 19, 30)	51.0
5	Clerical (17, 24)	49.5
6	Skilled laborer (22, 23, 25, 27)	44.0
7	Semi-skilled, unskilled, service workers (21, 28, 31, 33–36)	32.4

[a] Numbers in parentheses refer to the rank of occupation in Table 1 and indicate which occupations were included in each category in computing the mean prestige.

Three-fourths of the Taiwanese in high-prestige occupations believe their occupation is *more* useful to society than other occupations; only one per cent believe their occupation is *less* useful. At the other extreme, of those in low prestige occupations, three-fourths believe their occupation is either "of the same usefulness" or "less useful" than other occupations.

We constructed an index of Perceived Societal Usefulness for each occupational group, by subtracting the per cent of the respondents in that

TABLE 3

RELATIONSHIP BETWEEN OCCUPATIONAL PRESTIGE AND BELIEF

IN THE SOCIETAL USEFULNESS OF ONE'S OCCUPATION

(Taipei, Taiwan)

Is your occupation:	Occupational Prestige					
	High		Medium		Low	
	%	N	%	N	%	N
More useful than others?	72	43	47	143	22	23
Same?	27	16	44	132	41	43
Less useful than others?	1	1	9	28	37	39
Total %	100		100		100	
Total N		60		303		105

group who say their occupation is less useful than others from the per cent who say their occupation is more useful. The greater the difference, the greater the index score, and the greater the perceived utility of that occupational group. The professional-technical-administrative group are highest in perceived usefulness (66.7), followed by large businessmen (50.0), clerical workers (49.3), skilled workers (16.6), small businessmen (12.3), and semi-skilled, unskilled and service workers (− 6.5). (See Table 4.)

TABLE 4

PERCEIVED SOCIETAL USEFULNESS OF ONE'S OCCUPATION
BY MAJOR OCCUPATIONAL GROUPS
(Taipei, Taiwan)

| | Is your occupation: | | | | | |
	More useful than others?	Same?	Less useful than others?	Total %	N	+% "more" −% "less"
Professional, Technical, Administrative	70.0%	26.7%	3.3%	100%	90	+66.7
Large business	54.5	40.9	4.5	99.9	22	+50.0
Clerical	55.6	38.1	6.3	100	63	+49.3
Skilled labor	52.2	43.5	4.3	100	46	+47.9
Farmers	33.3	50.0	16.7	100	6	+16.6
Small business	31.9	48.5	19.6	100	163	+12.3
Semi-skilled, Unskilled, Service	26.0	41.6	32.5	100.1	77	− 6.5

NOTES:
$\chi^2 = 61.338$ (12 d.f.) P > .001
$\gamma = .350$

Why do those classed as "large businessmen" have such a relatively low self-perceived societal usefulness? The rated occupations included in this category (see Table 1) are factory owner-manager, general manager of a company, executive secretary of a company, and building contractor. However, the respondents whom we have categorized as "large businessmen" (in terms of their own occupation) do not have really large-scale firms. In a cross-section sample of Taipei one does not find many businessmen with, say, 500 or more employees. Therefore, a more appropriate term for our "large businessmen" would be "medium scale businessmen." This is borne out also by data on mean income, to be presented below. When we use the term *large,* we really mean "large in relation to the small businessmen in our sample."

When perceived societal usefulness is compared with prestige evaluation (see Table 5), we observe some consistent patterns: the professional, technical, and administrative groups are highest in both prestige and usefulness, the large business group is second in both, and the semi-skilled, unskilled, and service group is lowest in both. There are also some discrepancies. Clerical workers and skilled laborers regard their occupations

TABLE 5

A COMPARISON OF THE RANKING OF OCCUPATIONAL GROUPS BY
SOCIETAL PRESTIGE, AND BY PERCEIVED USEFULNESS
(Taipei, Taiwan)

Prestige Evaluation by Society	X̄ Score	Self-Evaluation of Societal Usefulness	X̄ Score
1 Professional, technical, administrative	76	1 Professional, technical, administrative	67
2 Large business	73	2 Large business	50
3 Owner-cultivators	54	3 Clerical	49
4 Small business	51	4 Skilled labor	48
5 Clerical	50	5 Owner-cultivators	17
6 Skilled labor	44	6 Small business	12
7 Semi-skilled, unskilled, service	32	7 Semi-skilled, unskilled, service	−6.5

as more useful than the prestige allotted them by the members of the society warrants.[6] On the other hand, small businessmen and farmers perceive the usefulness of their occupations as lower than their occupational prestige warrants. If we consider the trends in the labor force in Taiwan, clerical and skilled workers are becoming a larger proportion, while farmers have been diminishing in proportion, and small businessmen are likely to follow suit. This suggests an interesting general hypothesis: among occupations that are expanding, e.g., clerical and skilled workers, society's evaluation of their prestige lags behind the self-evaluation of societal usefulness by members of that occupation. Among occupations diminishing in importance, e.g., farmers and small businessmen, members of the occupational group perceive their declining usefulness before societal prestige evaluation begins to fall. More generally, the perceptions of incumbents of any given occupation are more sensitive to underlying labor force trends than are the prestige evaluations of the members of the society in general. If an occupation is declining, its incumbents' perceptions will be the first to reflect this; likewise, if an occupation is in the ascendancy, the incumbents will be the first to reflect it through their perceptions of the usefulness of their occupation. Thus, with regard to occupations that are expanding or contracting in the labor force, societal prestige is a conservative force, while self-evaluation of occupational utility is a more sensitive predictive factor.

Allocation of Rewards

There is a significant positive relationship between the prestige evaluation of one's occupation and income: over half the high prestige occupations bring high economic rewards (NT$ 4,000 or more per month); middle prestige occupations bring mostly middle- or low-income rewards;

TABLE 6

RELATIONSHIP BETWEEN OCCUPATIONAL PRESTIGE AND INCOME
(Taipei, Taiwan)

Income	Occupational Prestige					
	High		*Medium*		*Low*	
	%	N	%	N	%	N
NT$ 4,000 or more	53	32	15	47	2	2
NT$ 2,000 to 3,999	38	23	42	134	26	29
NT$ 1,999 or less	9	5	43	140	72	82
Total %	100		100		100	
Total N		60		321		113

and 73 per cent of the holders of low prestige occupations receive low income (under NT$ 2,000 per month). (See Table 6.)

The occupational group receiving by far the highest median income is large businessmen (NT$ 5,701 per month); those in professional, technical, and administrative positions are next, although much lower in median income (NT$ 3,151); third are small businessmen (NT$ 2,221). These are followed, with smaller gaps, by clerical (NT$ 1,417), skilled workers (NT$ 1,138), owner-cultivator farmers (NT$ 1,001), and, at the bottom, semi-skilled, unskilled, and service workers (NT$ 984).

The main discrepancies in the ranking of these seven occupational groups between prestige evaluation and income are shown in Table 7.

TABLE 7

RANKING OF OCCUPATIONAL GROUPS BY PRESTIGE AND BY INCOME
(Taipei, Taiwan)

Rank on Prestige Evaluation of Occupation	Rank on Income	Rank Difference
1 Professional, technical, administrative	1 Large businessmen	1
2 Large businessmen	2 Professional, technical, administrative	1
3 Owner-cultivators	3 Small businessmen	3
4 Clerical	4 Clerical	0
5 Skilled workers	5 Skilled workers	0
6 Small businessmen	6 Owner-cultivators	3
7 Semi-skilled, unskilled, service	7 Semi-skilled, unskilled, service	0

Small businessmen are higher in income than in prestige, and owner-cultivators are higher in prestige than in income. All other occupational groups are either in the same rank in both income and prestige (clerical, skilled, semi-skilled, unskilled, and service workers) or different by one rank (professional, technical, and administrative; and large businessmen). There is, thus, a rather close overall relationship between prestige evaluation and income in Taiwan.

Ethnic Aspects Cross-Cutting Stratification in Taiwan

Ever since significant Chinese settlement of Taiwan began in the seventeenth century, there have been ethnic aspects of stratification. Initially, the Hokkien and Hakka Chinese from the mainland who settled in Taiwan were ruled by Dutch and Spanish overlords (1624–1662). After 1683, the Taiwanese were part of the Ch'ing realm and as such were subordinate to the Manchus. Then, from 1895 to 1945, Taiwan was ruled colonially by Japan. The re-integration of Taiwan into the Republic of China after the defeat of Japan got off to a very bad start and soon led to conflict between Taiwanese and mainland Chinese. As Meisner describes the situation:

When Kuomintang soldiers and administrators arrived to reassert Chinese sovereignty over the island province in October 1945 they were enthusiastically welcomed as liberators by the Formosans. Within a few months, however, the Kuomintang had succeeded in alienating virtually all segments of the native population by inaugurating a military regime that treated Formosa as a conquered territory rather than a liberated area. The mass pillaging, official corruption and political repression that marked the early period of Kuomintang rule in Formosa set in motion the tragic events that culmintaed in the revolt of February 1947 in the course of which at least 10,000 Formosans were massacred.[7]

Consider now how ethnic factors have influenced occupational distribution. During Japanese rule in Taiwan, "the economic life of the cities was dominated by 300,000 Japanese immigrants who filled virtually all government posts and occupied the choice positions in commerce, industry and professions."[8] Tables 8 and 9 document this assertion, by viewing the same facts from two different angles. Table 8 shows the breakdown of each ethnic group by occupation-industry; table 9 gives the breakdown of each occupation-industry by ethnicity. These two kinds of analysis can yield quite different results. For example, although only 1.8 per cent of the Taiwanese were in government and the professions in 1905 (Table 8), of those in government and the professions in that year, 62.2 per cent were Taiwanese (Table 9). The reason for this difference is of course that there were many more Taiwanese than Japanese in the labor force, and the total number of government and professional workers in 1905 was very small. Thus, the 1.8 per cent of the relatively numerous Taiwanese who were in government and the professions could actually comprise 62.2 per cent of all those in the category.

Table 8 reveals that the modal occupation of Taiwanese was agriculture, and that of Japanese was government and the professions, and that this pattern was quite stable from 1905 to 1930.

Table 9 shows that Japanese males in 1905 comprised 38 per cent of all government personnel and professionals, although Japanese made up

TABLE 8

OCCUPATIONAL COMPOSITION OF TAIWANESE AND JAPANESE IN TAIWAN
(Percentage of Occupied Males Reported in Each Occupation, 1905, 1920, and 1930)

Occupation	1905 Taiwanese	1905 Japanese	1920 Taiwanese	1920 Japanese	1930 Taiwanese	1930 Japanese
Agriculture	69.9	1.0	68.9	4.4	68.0	4.6
Fishing	2.8	0.6	2.2	2.0	2.1	2.1
Mining	0.5	5.0	1.4	1.9	1.3	0.5
Manufacturing	5.6	20.6	7.9	27.4	7.6	18.2
Commerce	7.4	16.5	7.6	15.0	10.2	14.6
Transportation and Communication	2.2	13.9	3.2	11.7	3.9	11.0
Government and Professions	1.8	41.3	2.2	37.2	2.7	45.6
Other	9.8	1.1	6.6	0.4	4.2	3.4
Total	100	100	100	100	100	100

SOURCE: George W. Barclay, *Colonial Development and Population in Taiwan* (Princeton, 1954), pp. 66–67, Tables 14 and 15.
NOTE: Domestic servants have been excluded. Occupations listed for 1905 and 1920 have been adjusted to be comparable with those for 1930.

OCCUPATIONAL DISTRIBUTION OF TAIWANESE AND JAPANESE MALES ACCORDING TO TAIWAN CENSUSES OF 1905, 1920, 1930, AND 1940, AND OF TAIWANESE AND MAINLAND CHINESE MALES IN 17 TOWNS AND CITIES IN TAIWAN, 1953

(Per Cent)

Occupation	1905			1920			1930			1940			1953		
	Taiwan-ese (97.4)[a]	Japan-ese (2.6)	Total (100)	Taiwan-ese (94.5)	Japan-ese (5.5)	Total (100)	Taiwan-ese (94.3)	Japan-ese (5.7)	Total (100)	Taiwan-ese (94.1)	Japan-ese (5.9)	Total (100)	Taiwan-ese (76)	Mainland Chinese (24)	Total (100)
Agriculture and Forestry	99.9	0.1	100	99.6	0.4	100	99.6	0.4	100	99.5	0.5	100	98	2	100
Fishing	99.4	0.6	100	94.9	5.1	100	94.1	5.9	100	89.8	10.2	100	89	11	100
Mining	79.0	21.0	100	92.9	7.1	100	97.6	2.4	100	95.7	4.3	100	75	25	100
Manufacturing	91.1	8.9	100	83.3	16.7	100	87.4	12.6	100	86.7	13.1	100	75	25	100
Commerce	94.4	5.6	100	89.7	10.3	100	92.1	7.9	100	92.9	7.1	100	74	26	100
Transportation	85.7	14.3	100	82.6	17.4	100	85.3	14.7	100	79.8	20.2	100	59	41	100
Government and Professions	62.2	37.8	100	50.1	49.9	100	49.8	50.2	100	61.6	38.4	100	57	43	100
Other (chiefly day-laborers)	99.7	0.3	100	99.7	0.3	100	95.4	4.6	100	99.8	0.2	100	84	16	100
Σ deviations from distribution of total occupied:	− 6.9 / +74.6 / +67.7 Σ = 81.5			−10.7 / +73.9 / +63.2 Σ = 84.6			− 9.7 / +62.8 / +53.1 Σ = 72.5			−12.7 / +59.5 / +46.8 Σ = 72.2			−43 / +39 / − 4 Σ = 82		

SOURCES: For 1905, 1920, and 1930, George W. Barclay, *Colonial Development and Population in Taiwan* (Princeton, 1954), Table 16, p. 71; for 1940, Taiwan Provincial Government, *Taiwan ti-ch'i-tz'u jen-k'o p'u-ch'a chieh-kuo piao*, (1953), Table 15, pp. 60–61; and for 1953, A. F. Raper, et al., *Urban and Industrial Taiwan—Crowded and Resourceful* (Taipei, 1954), p. 254, Table 24. Based on survey data collected in seventeen cities and towns. Data for 1953 include both males and females and are therefore not completely comparable to earlier data.

NOTE: "For comparability, domestic servants are excluded at all dates. . . . Salt workers are assigned to Manufacturing from Fishing in 1905, 1915, and 1920." Barclay, *Colonial Development.*

[a] Numbers in parentheses = of all gainfully occupied, per cent from each ethnic group at time of census or survey. Cell entries are per cent of all in a given occupational group from each ethnic group.

less than three per cent of the total labor force in Taiwan. Japanese were thus 14.5 times over-represented in government and the professions in 1905. The amount of over-representation dropped to 9.1 in 1920, 8.8 in 1930, and 6.5 in 1940.

When the Japanese left Taiwan, many of their positions were filled by mainland Chinese. The data for 1953—the most recent available—are not entirely comparable with the 1940 data, but there are indications of the following trends: First, Taiwanese are still under-represented in government and the professions and over-represented in farming, fishing, and manual labor, in relation to mainlanders. Second, if we compare the disparities between Taiwanese and Japanese in 1940 with the disparities between Taiwanese and mainland Chinese in 1953, we can say that the Taiwanese rose in representation in government, the professions, and manufacturing and declined in agriculture, fishing and mining. In commerce, transportation and communications, and other sectors, the distributions were about the same in 1953 as in 1940 (see Table 9).

For each year in Table 9 a summary figure is presented. If the Taiwanese and the Japanese were distributed in each industry in proportion to their numbers in the total labor force, this summary figure would be 0. In fact, the deviations from this random model in the several industrial categories are so great that they total 81.5 in 1905, 84.6 in 1920, 72.5 in 1930, 72.2 in 1940, and 82 in 1953. This suggests that when all industrial categories are considered together, the distribution is always affected by ethnicity and the degree to which this effect occurs did not decline appreciably between 1905 and 1953.

The cleavage between mainlanders and Taiwanese runs through many aspects of stratification and social life generally. In the remotest rural areas the local policeman—the symbol of political authority—tends to be a mainlander. The relatively few Taiwanese who belong to the Kuomintang, occupy official positions, or cooperate with the government in the local areas are often regarded by Taiwanese as lackeys of the mainlanders, as people who have lost their Taiwanese identity. Since Taiwanese have less access than mainlanders to government officials, wealthier Taiwanese who attempt to develop industrial enterprises find themselves especially fettered by government regulations and interference. The mass of the Taiwanese are heavily taxed, and part of this burden is then used for "the endless series of 'campaigns' to 'recover the mainland'."[9] Close friendships between the two groups are rare.

Despite these conflict-laden aspects of stratification, there are indications of the gradual evolution of greater integration of the Taiwanese and mainlanders. Barring the absorption of Taiwan into the Peking regime, the following trends are likely to continue: mainlanders will become an ever-smaller proportion of the population of Taiwan, through differential fertility and mortality and out-migration; as the old mainland generation dies off and more and more of their descendants are born and reared in Taiwan, their identification with Taiwan and the Taiwanese will increase, and consequently the rate of intermarriage and cultural assimilation will also increase; the Taiwanese will steadily penetrate the higher levels of the occupational, power, and wealth structures, and other aspects of society. Many "third force" elements, in Taiwan, Hong Kong, and elsewhere, "argue that the Formosans' independence movement is basically an anti-Kuomintang political struggle rather than a movement of the Formosan nation against the Chinese."[10]

Social Stratification in Communist China

The changes in stratification in Taiwan can be described as evolutionary, in two respects. The tendency is broadly toward the kind of stratification system common to urban-industrial societies. And the processes through which these changes have occurred are similar to those in the more industrialized societies. In both these respects Communist China is different. Changes in stratification there should be described as revolutionary rather than evolutionary. One must immediately distinguish the stratificational changes *intended* by Mao's regime from the changes actually *institutionalized*. The intended changes are radically revolutionary; they are aimed at developing a stratification system different in many ways from that common to industrial societies and brought about through processes which also differ from those in industrial societies. In contrast to these revolutionary intentions, it must be said that the changes already institutionalized in stratification are a complex and unstable combination of evolutionary and revolutionary elements.

To clarify these assertions, we must again analyze the components of stratification—the division of labor, occupational evaluation, and rewards —at this time in Communist China.

The peasantry constitutes at least 80 per cent of the work force in Communist China, in contrast to only 52 per cent in Taiwan.[11] It is likely that occupations in the non-agricultural sector are more differentiated in Taiwan than on the mainland.

One must distinguish ideal from actual evaluation of occupational roles. The order in which the major social groups were listed in the *Common Programme* of 1949 (Article 13) indicates the Chinese Communists' ideal hierarchy of evaluation:[12]

Working class

Peasantry

Revolutionary armed forces (People's Liberation Army, People's Security Forces, People's Police)

Intellectuals

Petty bourgeoisie

National bourgeoisie

National minorities (non-Han Chinese ethnic groups in China)

Overseas Chinese

Other patriotic elements

This ideal hierarchy of prestige evaluation reflects a combination of Marxist-Leninist ideology and the actual relative support given by different groups to the Chinese Communists in their thirty-year struggle for power. Although the urban working class was in fact less influential than the peasantry, the revolutionary armed forces, and perhaps even the intellectuals in bringing the Communists to power, they are accorded highest evaluation for orthodox ideological reasons. The national bourgeoisie, the minorities, and the overseas Chinese were less supportive and are therefore lower in *ideal* evaluation.

When one views stratification more objectively, and less through the eyes of the Chinese Communists, the *actual* hierarchy of evaluation is somewhat different from the ideal structure. Always at the top are the members of the Chinese Communist Party. Under them are the "red" cadres (*kan-pu*) and the "experts." The latter group includes professional intellectuals and others, such as clerical workers with middle-school or more education, who do not claim physical labor as their main activity. Below the red and expert are the national bourgeoisie, who have continued to occupy a highly ambiguous position. At the bottom of the stratification system comes the mass of the population, the peasants and workers, whose relative position has altered over time. In the early 1950s, workers were ranked above peasants (and workers in heavy industry above those in light industry). Since the "Great Leap" of 1958 peasants have been accorded higher status, and among workers, those in light industry have risen in status relative to those in heavy industry. Space does not permit a discussion of why these complex changes have occurred.

A key contradiction in role evaluation is that between "red" and "expert," that is to say, between political-ideological loyalty to the party and technical expertise. Although this "contradiction" can be found at virtually all levels of the stratification system, it is perhaps most intense among the 3,840,000 "intellectuals." The greater the intellectuals' expertise, apparently the more resistant they become to political indoctrination.[13] The problem, of course, is that for the present system to function adequately, *both* technical expertise and political-ideological solidarity are needed. Lacking technical expertise, China cannot become a modern society, but lacking "redness" it would cease to be a socialist society. This dilemma continues to plague the regime.

Since 1949, "red" elements have at times been evaluated above expertise, at other times below. A frequent manifestation of the primacy of redness over expertise is the requirement that government and party officials, cadres, and intellectuals must perform periods of duty as manual workers on farms and in factories, mines, and construction projects. The intent is to "strengthen the contact between the cadres and the masses, and to raise the mass and labor viewpoint of the cadres."[14] Between 1958 and 1960, about 1,300,000 functionaries were reported to have participated in *hsia-fang* ("sending down") and to have done labor service.[15] Another manifestation of the priority of redness is when technically incompetent cadres presume to tell experts how to solve technical problems on the basis of "the thought of Mao Tse-tung." This was symbolized by the slogan of the Great Leap Forward: Politics Takes Command (*Chengchih kua-shuai*).

The same evaluational conflict can be seen in regard to the national bourgeoisie. The functional knowledge of the large capitalists is still indispensable in Communist China. "They have been repeatedly attacked . . . but have always bounced back. After the eruption of the great economic crisis of 1960–61, the leadership acknowledged their importance, extended their 'fixed interest' payments, and let them improve their relatively high levels of living; they were given a major role in pulling the country out of the crisis."[16]

Allocation of Rewards

The problem of rewards for functional role performance has been an even less settled issue than that of role evaluation. During the anti-Japanese war, there were only slight differences in income and standard of living between commanders and troops in the Communist army. Since 1949, the regime has at times followed a policy of increasing wage-differentials, and at other times a policy of greater equalization. Individual material incentives have alternated with collective productivity as the form of reward for role performance. There does not appear to be any clear trend.

Conclusion

Following our definition of social stratification, we have analyzed the structure of differential evaluations of, and rewards attached to, roles in the division of labor, in late traditional China, in Taiwan, and in Communist China.

Important changes in stratification are evident. One change has been in the nature of the most highly evaluated roles. The change from Ch'ing times to contemporary Taiwan has involved a shift from the generalist administrative role of the scholar-official to the roles of modern-trained professional, technician, manager, and businessman. In Communist China the change has been toward a rather unstable combination of "red" and "expert" roles. The criteria underlying these most highly evaluated roles are more unstable in Communist China than in either traditional China or contemporary Taiwan.

The role of landlord and the landlord class—which formed one of the major bases of high stratificational position in Ch'ing times—has been eliminated or at least radically weakened in both Communist China and contemporary Taiwan.

The ways in which the traditional Chinese stratification system has been altered may be described as evolutionary in Taiwan and as revolutionary in Communist China. The system in Taiwan is tending toward the type common in Western urban-industrial societies and is doing so through processes of change common to other industrial societies. In Communist China, it was not enough to alter the traditional system and then let normal processes of professional and managerial expertise emerge as new bases of stratification. This direction of change was partially subordinated to the revolutionary criteria of the Communist party leadership which demanded "redness" as well as technical expertise. The Communists have sought to create a revolutionary system of stratification; how much of this will, in fact, be institutionalized remains to be seen.

In stressing the different directions of change from the Ch'ing "base-line," we should not lose sight of the important continuities between this "baseline" and both Communist China and Taiwan. First, in all three systems the prestige evaluation of roles is based upon the degree of knowledge and responsibility called for in role performance. The Communist cadre is generally better educated than the mass of workers and peasants, and clearly has much responsibility; in these respects he is formally similar to the Ch'ing scholar-official and the professional, official, or business leader in contemporary Taiwan. Second, in all three systems there are aspects of what may be called "status incongruence," that is, where the occupational evaluation of a group is out of line with its income, power, or ethnic status. In late traditional China, this was evidenced in the economically deprived literati and the wealthy landowner or merchant who were still commoners because they lacked a degree or title. In Taiwan we have the restrictions on occupational opportunity for the Taiwanese, first in relation to the Japanese and now in relation to the mainland Chinese in Taiwan. The version of this in Communist China is the conflict between one's professional or technical expertise and his "redness." Just as a mainlander is better off than a Taiwanese in the civil service in Taiwan, one is better off being "red" than expert, at least during some periods, in Communist China.

It seems clear that these aspects of "status incongruence" were functional—that is, increased the adaptation of the system—in traditional China, whereas they are, in varying degrees, dysfunctional in both Taiwan and Communist China. Economic development in both the latter cases is impeded by the status conflict. Furthermore, the dynamics of the incongruence differ in the three systems. In late Imperial China, the conflict between literati status and high economic status tended to be resolved by individuals and families by having the wealthy imitate the symbolic style of life of the scholar-official and seek degrees in the examination system. Thus, while the status incongruence between the literati and the wealthy remained at the level of the system, it could be and was often resolved at the level of the individual lineage or family. In Taiwan, the incongruence will be resolved in the long run by ever-greater participation of Taiwanese in all occupations and by the removal, or assimilation, of the mainlanders. In Communist China, the "red" versus "expert" conflict shows no sign of resolution.

NOTES

1. The analysis in this section follows closely that presented in Robert M. Marsh, *The Mandarins* (Glencoe, Ill., 1961).

2. Fukutake Tadashi, *Chūgoku noson shakai no kozo* (Tokyo, 1946), pp. 180–222. 476–89.

3. G. William Skinner, "Marketing and Social Structure in Rural China," *Journal of Asian Studies,* 24, pts. 1–3 (Nov. 1964 to May 1965).

4. Sir George T. Staunton, trans., *Ta Tsing Leu Lee* (London, 1810), p. 185.

5. Mary C. Wright, "Modern China in Transition, 1900–1950," The Annals of the American Academy of Political and Social Science, 321 (Jan. 1959), p. 5.

6. Since the prestige scores and the Index of Perceived Societal Usefulness scores were computed in different ways, the comparisons are based on rank order, not on scores as such.

7. Maurice Meisner, "The Development of Formosan Nationalism," *The China Quarterly* (July–September 1963), p. 91. See also Albert Ravenholt, "Formosa Today," *Foreign Affairs* 30 (July 1952), pp. 612–24. The Taiwanese had also rebelled against Japanese rule in 1895 and had fought as guerrillas against the Japanese for several years thereafter.

8. Ibid., p. 96.

9. Ibid., p. 101.

10. Ibid., p. 104. Among other possible signs of change is the fact that in the 1964 elections, while 17 of the 21 successful mayoral candidates were Kuomintang members, the four who lost were in the three large cities of Taipei, Tainan, and Keelung, as well as in Taitung *hsien*. This is a serious threat to Kuomintang power in the urban areas. See Joyce Kallgren, "Nationalist China: Problems of a Modernizing Taiwan," Reprint No. 152, Center for Chinese Studies, University of California, Berkeley. (*Asian Survey*, January 1965)

11. Department of Civil Affairs, Taiwan Provincial Government, *Household Registration Statistics of Taiwan, 1959–1961* (Taipei, July 1962), Table 6, pp. 306–07.

12. The Chinese Communists judged applications for membership in such organizations as the Red Guards on the basis of whether their family background is one of the five "pure" classes: workers, middle and poor peasants, soldiers, cadres, and revolutionary martyrs.

13. H. Franz Schurmann, *Ideology and Organization in Communist China* (Berkeley, 1966), p. xxx.

14. *Hung-ch'i (Red Flag)*, January 1960.

15. Ibid.

16. Schurmann, *Ideology and Organization*, p. 94.

Chapter 7/ Edward Norbeck

Continuities in Japanese
Social Stratification

This paper discusses social classes and social mobility in modern Japan, comparing present conditions with those existing a century ago and pointing out what is new and what represents continuities from the past. It is necessary at the outset to make clear that discussion of social stratification in modern Japan is attended by serious problems of classification. Social scientists who concern themselves with this topic clearly think that social classes exist. The Japanese Sociological Society has, since 1952, conducted various surveys of social stratification and studies of "the middle class." During the past decade, the designation "new middle class" has become increasingly common in writings of both Japanese and foreign scholars.[1] No agreement has been reached, however, as to the criteria of classes and which proportion or segments of the populations may properly be regarded as meeting them. Debate revolves around the validity in defining class boundaries of such criteria as income, occupations, and educational attainments, and the value of self-appraisals of social class versus non-subjective appraisals. Part of the problem of classification is a modern overlapping of indicators of status, such as property

I am indebted to the National Science Foundation for financial support of the field research upon which this paper is based. Library research used in this paper was funded by the Advanced Research Projects Agency under ARPA Order No. 738 and monitored by the Office of Naval Research, Group Psychology Branch, under Contract Number N00014-67-A-0145-0001, NR 177-909.

and prestige, and the fact that many of the formerly obvious indicators of class distinctions, such as differences in clothing, hairdress, dwellings, speech, and demeanor, are disappearing.[2] It is clear from numerous attitude surveys conducted by Japanese sociologists that the blurring of markers of social divisions also applies to attitudes and values, a circumstance that is not surprising in an industrial nation with particularly well-developed media of mass communication.

The problem of defining classes in Japan also reflects in part the fact that Japan has become socially fluid, a mobile society in which no prospect of crystallization into a hierarchy of stable classes is evident in the near future. A trend toward increasing opportunities for social mobility for the individual citizen, however, does seem evident. Certain noteworthy exceptions to this trend exist, and these will be given consideration later. What we may say with certainty is that the circumstances of social stratification in Japan have changed greatly during the past century.

At present, although fairly strong traces of the past social hierarchy are still evident in certain ways, the old structure of social classes based upon hereditary ascription has disappeared; barriers to upward movement in social status have weakened greatly; and the nation is in a state of flux with respect to social classes. In impressionistic terms, Japanese society today may be described as consisting of a small class of the highly elite— composed of members of the imperial family, members of the former nobility who have retained wealth, and some families with long-established wealth and power; a fairly large and growing upper (or upper-middle) class of professional men and administrators; a large and rapidly growing middle class with several substrata composed principally of urban "salary men" in administrative and clerical occupations; a large and growing lower class composed principally of an increasing number of industrial workers and a shrinking but still large number of farmers; and, at the very bottom, a relatively small caste of social pariahs. A scheme of classification formulated by the Japanese sociologist Kunio Odaka divides our middle and lower classes into three groups and fails to make explicit reference to the outcastes. Odaka gives the following strata and proportions in the total population of 1960: Uppermost Stratum, 3 per cent; Upper-Middle Class, 18 per cent; Lower-Middle Class, 19 per cent; Intermediate Stratum, 32 per cent; and Lower Class, 28 per cent.[3] The points of greatest disagreement among classifiers of the modern social strata are the composition of the middle class and, especially, the social placement of certain white-collar workers. Some opinion holds that many white-collar workers, who have usually been regarded as middle-class, might more appropriately be regarded as the modern proletariat and labeled as lower-class.[4]

Although it is not possible to define the social strata of modern Japan sharply, it is possible to offer much evidence of modern social mobility. At the end of the Tokugawa era, approximately one hundred years ago, the Japanese population of about thirty-three million people was divided into hereditary social classes, rigidly hierarchical, that were maintained by force of law as well as by other means. At the peak were 450 families of the nobility numbering less than three thousand persons. Below the nobility but still in the class of the elite were the *samurai,* retainers of the nobility, who with their families numbered about two million persons. The largest stratum was composed of about thirty million commoners, most of whom were farmers. At the bottom, and sharply separated from the rest of the populace, was another class of several hundred thousand persons, composed principally of a caste then called the Eta and including various smaller caste-like groups bearing other names, who were legally denied many of the privileges held by commoners and usually lived in segregated communities.

Occupations in Japan were hereditary and class boundaries were further defined and maintained by many sumptuary laws relating to dwellings, clothing, hairdress, and the like, and to privileges. Elaborate rules of inter-class etiquette also help to mark and maintain boundaries of social class. Economically, the nation depended upon agriculture, and over 80 per cent of the population consisted of farming families. (In 1872, 14,100,000 persons of a total labor force of 17,319,000, or 81 per cent, were farmers.)[5] Most of the nation lived in small rural communities and life for the average person revolved around the family and the community. The rules of the social order allowed no movement outside of class boundaries. Such exceptions as existed were principally among members of the small urban merchant class, some of whom had gained wealth in Tokugawa times and for this reason had prestige and power despite a nominal assignment, after the model of Chinese society, to a status below that of farmers. Merchants were sometimes able to arrange the marriage of their daughters and sons to members of the generally impoverished samurai class.

The Meiji era (1868–1912) saw the opening of Japan to Western science, technology, and civilization, the beginning of the modernization of the nation. Changes were many and swift. Some, such as abolishment of the samurai class and the granting of the status of commoners to the outcastes, were aimed directly at the social order. A vast number of additional changes that included industrialization of the nation, the establishment of a relatively democratic form of government, and the establishment of a program of compulsory education for all citizens had indirect but probably far greater effects upon the old scheme of social classes. Changes of these kinds involved in the modernization of Japan are recorded in many writings that are readily available. They may be summed up for our purposes here in the statement that Japan has been transformed from a culturally backward nation composed principally of peasant farmers united with a ruling class in a rigid hierarchical structure of hereditary social classes into a modern industrial, urban power in which social distinctions of individual and class status depend increasingly upon achievement rather than ascription. If the circumstances at the beginning and end of the past century are compared, the social changes are striking. Most remarkably, these changes have occurred without social upheaval, a subject to which we shall return. Although Japan during this time fought several wars with foreign nations, domestically it experienced peace without serious disruption beyond that caused by such modern social problems as growing rates of crime and juvenile delinquency that are also found in other industrial nations.

Direct and inferential evidence of modern social mobility is plentiful, and it is useful to review some of it. As might be expected, the nation has undergone extensive changes in its occupational structure and demography associated with industrialization and urbanization. The farming population, which had decreased to 48 per cent of the total labor force in 1920, declined more rapidly after World War II to a figure of 23.2 per cent in 1965.[6] Major concomitant trends of occupational movement during the past century have been a great growth of industrial laborers, principally skilled and semi-skilled, and of white-collar workers associated with industry; substantial but lesser increases in managerial and professional workers; and, after a period of increase during several decades, a moderate but growing decrease of entrepreneurs in small business enterprises.

The shift in places of residence and in occupations of farmers implies demographic changes elsewhere in the nation and a complex of social changes, including changes in familial structure, that bear upon social status. In the decade from 1950 to 1960, 26 of the nation's 46 prefectures suffered a decline in population, and the average size of the family dropped from 4.97 members in 1955 to 4.53 in 1960.[7] These trends of change have continued since 1960. An interim census of October 1, 1966, reports increases in population in only 21 prefectures and a decrease in the average size of the family to 4.05 persons.[8] The decrease in familial size is principally the result of the breakdown of the old extended family and of the migration of young men and women to industrial cities, resulting in small nuclear families composed of parents and offspring. Such two-generational families constituted 56.6 per cent of the total number of families in the nation in October 1966, representing a proportional increase since 1960 in the number of such families that is over three times as great as the increase in the population as a whole during the same period.[9]

A distinguished Japanese demographer refers to very recent demographic changes as "revolutionary." The national population of about one hundred million persons is shifting habitat increasingly to a swath of land stretching southwest from Tokyo and Yokohoma about 300 miles through Mie Prefecture and Nagoya and on to the Osaka and Kobe areas to form a giant industrial metropolis, given the name "Tokaido Megalopolis," which in October 1965, contained 48 per cent of the nation's people.[10]

Intergenerational mobility in occupations is predictably great, and is as high as that of other highly industrialized nations of the world including the United States, Germany, Sweden, and France.[11] A national sampling survey of succession in occupations from father to son conducted by the Japanese Sociological Society in 1955 showed a continuity from father to son of 48 per cent and from grandfather to father of 65 per cent.[12] A later survey conducted in 1960 among males 20 years of age living in Tokyo reported much greater occupational movement; only 15 per cent of the sample of 2,000 were engaged in the same occupations as their fathers, and every occupational category except farming had movement, in and out, of over 50 per cent.[13]

This statistical information provides ample evidence of shifting occupations but tells us nothing clearly or directly about the social distinction involved in occupational movements. Many shifts in occupation, such as from agriculture to employment as a factory worker, may involve little or no change in social status. Much evidence exists, however, of social mobility associated with occupational movements, and, by and large, the prestige accorded to occupations in Japan conforms with occupational rankings in other industrial nations.[14] A recent and noteworthy study of social mobility by Hiroshi Mannari concerns the social and educational backgrounds of nearly 1,000 men who were judged to be the most outstanding persons in industry and commerce in Japan in 1960.[15] The following table shows the occupations of the fathers of these business leaders:

	Per cent
Farm landlord and farmer	24
Owner and executive of large business concern	22
Owner of small business concern	22
Government official and professional man	21
White-collar worker	9
Laborer and other	2
	100

As a whole, this study of the elite of the business world presents ample data to support its conclusions that "the crystalline structure of Japanese society in pre-industrial times has softened if not entirely dissolved, and that a considerable degree of social mobility now exists."[16] Mannari also observes that opportunities for social mobility in Japan are not equally available to all. A large part of the business leaders of his study have occupational backgrounds on the parental level of high or fairly high prestige (landlords, owners and executives of large business firms, government officials and professional men). These circumstances are not at all surprising; similar observations have been made repeatedly by native and foreign scholars.[17] In general, other things being equal, the more favored one is in social prestige of family background, the greater his chances of movement upward. Yet positions of high status are not absolutely closed to aspirants from humble backgrounds, and in the majority of cases positions are not inherited. Among the business elite of Mannari's study, men who followed in their father's occupational footsteps tend to be heirs to property rather than inheritors of salaried positions. About 8 per cent of the business elite, who are classified as upper class, have parents whose occupations are judged as lower class (farming and common labor), and 31 per cent come from middle class backgrounds (owners of small business concerns and white-collar workers).

None of the circumstances described above with regard to social mobility are unusual in the United States. A primary difference is in degree: in Japan the patterns of traditional social assignment are still evident, and social mobility is as yet less pronounced. A strong trend exists toward continuity of status—if not occupation—over the generations in the top and bottom strata of society. The greatest social movement occurs among the strata that lie between, the descendants of the erstwhile commoners. These trends do not appear remarkable, but the details of the general trends describe patterns that are unique to Japan. These and other continuities that relate to social stratification will be discussed under the several headings that follow.

Survival of the Old Class Structure

Remnants of the social strata of the late Tokugawa era that are preserved today in something like their old form are limited to a few members of the old paramount aristocracy and a relatively large number of outcastes. The imperial family holds unquestioned prestige. Democratization is evident, however, in the recent marriages of members of the imperial family to commoners. The peerage, created during the Meiji era and extended to a few outstanding commoners as well as to members of the old feudal nobility, was abolished only after World War II, and it is not surprising that members of this former class continue to have prestige.

Descent from samurai ancestors carries no special prestige today and calling public attention to such ancestry has been bad form for three or more decades. A samurai background has, nevertheless, been clearly an important asset in gaining or maintaining statuses of social eminence in modern Japan. Scholars of Japan have long emphasized the role of the samurai and their descendants in the modernization of the nation. The topmost positions in Meiji times—as government officials, military officers, and even as entrepreneurs in business, positions that theoretically held low status in Tokugawa times—were held predominantly by men of the samurai class. A random sample taken from the Japanese *Who's Who* in 1903 included 37 per cent of ex-samurai and a similar sample in 1925 included 29 per cent.[18] Mannari's study of modern business leaders reports that nearly one-third (31.5 per cent) of his subjects identified themselves as being of samurai backgrounds.[19] The tendency among descendants of the samurai to retain high social status seems especially noteworthy because the samurai had controlled little wealth. Subsisting in feudal times principally on stipends from their lords, many were hardly favored financially over commoners. When the samurai class was abolished in 1872, its members retained official designations as ex-samurai (*shizoku*) for some years and were so identified in official records of birth, marriage, and the like, until well into the twentieth century. They retained lingering prestige for some decades, but it was necessary for them to find new occupations, and these were frequently those carrying the highest social prestige. No tendency seems evident among the descendants of the samurai to cling strongly to any single prestigious occupation. Rather, the whole range of such positions has been occupied and intergenerational shifts have been common. Modern descendants of samurai among the business elite frequently had grandfathers who were military officers, government officials, or in other occupations of medium or high prestige. Employment as a white-collar worker has often served as a transitional step to occupations of higher prestige by samurai descendants of the following generation, a pattern of occupational movement that is also common among the descendants of commoners.

Retention of class status through generations and recovery of status after social revolutions are not, however, remarkable phenomena in other nations of the world. Social classes everywhere tend to perpetuate themselves long after the conditions which led to their emergence have disappeared. The samurai of Japan had high prestige and a bright aura of glamour which attracted the attention of scholars as well as novelists, playwrights, and the general population—with the result that we are better informed about their descendants than we are about the descendants of less colorful folk. Other occupational groups socially favored in late Tokugawa times have also been similarly "perpetuated." Mannari informs that approximately 1 per cent of the business elite claim descent from noble families, a figure that is disproportionately high in comparison with the probable number of modern descendants of the old nobility.[20] Other scholars have pointed out the importance to industry and commerce of members of the wealthy merchant class of Tokugawa times and their descendants and the influential role of wealthy farmers in the development of the textile industry.[21] Although neither samurai nor nobility, both of these occupational groups held prestige and power.

The tendency toward perpetuation of social assignment is perhaps strongest at the bottom of the social scale, but information available on this subject leads to many questions to which no clear answer can be given. The social assignment and the degree of social mobility among the farming populations during the past century are cases in point. The modern opinion which tends to identify farmers as lower class has probably prevailed for many years. In feudal times, however, farmers held at least nominal statuses of honor, below warriors (samurai) but above merchants.

In attitudes and values, most of the modern farming population seems most appropriately assigned to the middle class; however, other circumstances suggest that national opinion ranks them somewhat lower. Urban residents of Japan have long looked upon farmers as people apart, uncouth and of low social order. The traditional and once honorable word for farmer, *hyakusho,* has long been a demeaning word and is not used in official records or in conversation in the presence of farmers.

But the foregoing statements greatly oversimplify the circumstances. Many social distinctions which existed among the mass of farmers a century ago continued until very recent times. These were primarily social distinctions related to wealth. The category "farmer" ran a range from rich and powerful landlords—who did not themselves engage in agriculture —through owner-operators of small holdings of land, to impoverished tenants who owned no land. Social status seems generally to have accorded with wealth, and thus assigning farmers to a single social stratum is inappropriate. The land reform conducted after World War II put an end to the class of farm landlords and essentially put an end to farm tenancy. Nearly all farming has since been done by owner-operators. These developments in themselves are indicators of some social mobility; becoming owner-operators brought rises in social status as well as in income to the large number of former tenant-farmers.

Movement from agriculture to industry as a primary economic base strongly suggests concomitant social mobility. We have already noted the great occupational movement away from farming, a decline of approximately 60 per cent of the total labor force in about a century. As industrialization proceeded, the industrial labor force was for many years drawn principally from among the surplus farming population, and young migrants from farm to city still form a very important part of industrial personnel. Japanese statistics on agricultural employment are, however, deceptive and make it difficult to formulate statements about the occupational mobility of the descendants of farmers. As we have already suggested in our references to farm landlords of the past, appropriate identification of farmers as an occupational category has always been a problem. The factors of sex and age of the modern farm force must be considered in making statements about social and occupational movements, as must a long-established tendency among farming families toward compound occupations. For about a decade, Japanese farming has been conducted chiefly by females and aged males, the wives, mothers, and fathers of the male heads of households. Many household heads are included among the farming population in statistics but are employed part-time or full-time in other occupations, principally industrial. Part-time employment of farmers in non-farming occupations has long existed, and able-bodied males have recently tended to take on full-time employment elsewhere, working only occasionally on the farms. In 1965, 60 per cent of the farm labor force consisted of women, principally wives and aged mothers of household heads; 29 per cent, males over the age of 60; and 78.5 per cent of the members of farm families had dual occupations.[22] In view of these facts, it seems reasonable to state that the official farm population figure—23.2 per cent in 1965—is unrealistic and that the occupational mobility of farmers is in fact greater than the statistics indicate.

The question of the social mobility of the erstwhile farmers is equally troublesome. In discussing the parental occupational categories from which Japan's business leaders have come, Mannari bases "expectations" upon the national distribution of occupations in 1920, as given in the national census of that year, a time when the parents of most of his subjects were alive and actively employed and when the average age of the businessmen was about 22 years. He reports that 24 per cent of the business leaders of 1960 had fathers who were farmers, of whom about two-thirds (17.3 per cent) were non-farming landlords, and states: "Only 24 per cent of the 1960 business leaders are sons of farmers, who constituted 48 per cent of the 1920 population. The ratio is thus one-half that expected. However, if we look at landlords and operating farmers separately, we see that the former more than doubles the expectations, but the latter is far below expectation."[23]

This report appears to support our view that social mobility among people identified as being of farming backgrounds follows fairly well the general tendency toward perpetuation of social status through the generations. Nevertheless, there has been considerable upward social movement among descendants of working farmers. If persons more than one generation removed from farming backgrounds are considered, the movement upward seems greater. Among paternal grandfathers of the business elite, 14.9 per cent were operating farmers (and 33.4 per cent were farm landlords).[24] A look at gross statistics, of course, points to upward social mobility during the past century among descendants of working farmers. If the ratio of farmers in 1867 (80-plus per cent) in the population represents the proportion of their descendants in the nation today, the upward movement to middle class has been very considerable, since most of the nation is today regarded as middle-class (and relatively few of the farmers were landlords).

Social mobility is least pronounced among the socially lowest segments of the Japanese population. The low rate of occupational mobility among manual laborers has often been noted. Among Japanese leaders of 1960, only 1.3 per cent had fathers and 1.1 per cent had grandfathers who were skilled or unskilled laborers, whereas over one-fourth (26.3 per cent) of the population in 1920 was engaged in these occupations.[25] The low rate of movement of laborers into non-manual occupations is outstanding and it implies a correspondingly lower degree of social mobility. The low rate of movement of laborers is, however, in all probability exceeded by that among the outcastes (who are today most frequently called in Japanese *tokushu burakumin,* "residents of the special communities," or by the abbreviation *burakumin*), and the two groups doubtless overlap somewhat. Although the outcastes were given full legal rights of ordinary citizenship in 1871, they are still the subjects of discrimination. Traits that characterize depressed ethnic minorities in other nations—high rates of crime and juvenile delinquency, poverty and heavy dependence upon aid from agencies of social welfare, relatively poor health, and low levels of education and skills—also characterize the outcastes.[26] Looked upon by ordinary citizens with discomfort as a blemish to national virtue, the outcastes have been a subject which most people prefer to forget. Probably for these reasons, sociological study of these social pariahs has been scanty until very recent years. The size and occupational distribution of the present population are uncertain. Maintaining census statistics on a group which has no legal existence is not in keeping with Japanese ideas of propriety. As in former times, the outcastes live today principally in segregated communities, rural and urban, of central Japan and are concentrated most heavily in and near the neighboring cities of Kyoto, Osaka, and Kobe. The outcastes long gained their livelihood principally from farming (mostly as tenant farmers), various handicrafts such as leatherworking and basketry, and other menial occupations, and they continue today to hold occupations of the lowest prestige.

Recent studies of certain individual communities of outcastes[27] tell us a good deal about conditions of life, which may be described as generally deplorable. Available information also makes clear that this traditional social class has increased in relative as well as absolute numbers during the past century. The population of outcastes today is variously estimated as being between one and three million persons. At the time of their emancipation in 1871, the various categories of outcastes were officially reported to total 383,500 people.[28] DeVos and Wagatsuma state that during the past century the outcaste population "increased seven times faster than the Japanese population."[29] Although this is probably an over-statement, there seems to be little doubt that the group has grown, partly from natural increase, partly from drawing members from the society out-side, and in part from redefinition of outcastes to include some lowly peoples not so designated at the time of emancipation.

The outcastes of Japan are in certain respects a remarkable example of the persistence of a social group long after the end of the circumstances which brought it into existence. In other nations, castes have often been readily distinguishable by physical features or other visible traits. The out-castes of Japan are not so distinguishable. Despite a national attitude of democracy and the relative social mobility that exists among other seg-ments of the population, this social class will probably persist for many years. Individuals among the outcastes now and then acquire wealth and consequent high status in their own group, but elevation in social position in the society at large requires the loss of identity as a member of the out-caste group. Factors that inhibit economic improvement and social eleva-tion of the outcastes are complex, involving psychological considerations of motivation and self-image, and discussion of them is beyond the scope of this paper.[30] Various factors relating to the persistence of the outcaste group also relate, however, to the subject of occupational and social mobility among the general population of Japan, and these will be touched upon later.

Paternalism, Personal Ties, and Group Affiliation

Accounts of life in Japan in times gone by and even recent writings about rural life and the urban underworlds of criminals bring out the importance of kinship and personalized relations with those who are not kin. As in peasant societies elsewhere, the role of kinship was pervasive, and ties with kin were vital to a satisfactory existence. When ties of kin-ship did not exist, the family or other relations of kinship often served as the model for structures of fictive kinship. Social relations in general were strongly personalized and cooperative effort in behalf of the family or other group was the ideal.

The conception of industrial society prevailing in the Western world presents a different picture—one of impersonality, the strongest opposition to nepotism and paternalism, and fierce competition for individualistic gain. As many scholars have noted, the history of Japan illustrates that industrialization does not imply one invariable pattern of human relationships. Scholarly opinion has fairly often maintained that one of the major factors contributing to the speed and ease of Japan's industrialization was the effective use of traditional social relationships of kinship and quasi-kinship in industry and commerce.[31] It was primarily through personalized ties of kinship or friendship that occupational and social movement, as well as social stability, were made possible during the first several decades of Japan's modernization. The national trend of industrial development has, however, been toward conditions which make personalized relations increasingly difficult to maintain in the world of industry and commerce. The rapid increase in very recent years in numbers of families in the nation is an acceleration of a trend beginning in the nineteenth century toward reduction of the size and composition of the family, and serves as one illustration of the dwindling scope of kinship in the nation. Industrial and commercial concerns of the early period of industrialization were principally small, thus fostering personalization. Japan's road to successful survival today depends increasingly upon its success in international competition in trade and industry, upon thrift and efficiency of production and marketing, and these are best achieved by mass production. A trend toward ever-larger business concerns has existed for decades and has grown with accelerated speed in the past several years. This trend was accompanied by the failure, also at an accelerating rate, of small business establishments at least until 1966, the latest date for which information is available.[32]

Today the old and the new co-exist in the employment practices of Japanese industrial concerns. American observers, who see sharp contrasts with practices in their own country, may be impressed by the strength of paternalism and other traditional customs. Japanese scholars are also well aware of the continued existence of traditional practices, which they have most frequently regarded as harmful to efficiency and progress. Odaka summarizes ideas on this subject, describing the "preindustrial employment practices" as including "lifetime employment relations, a wage and promotion system based primarily on age and length of service, sharp status distinctions between superior and subordinate, great stress placed on personal loyalty toward the employer rather than on efficient work, emphasis on intragroup harmony rather than on individual competition, and paternalistic care of the employee, even in his private life."[33] Odaka's concern is primarily with the validity of opposing theories concerning the harmful and helpful effects of these traditional practices. Although this issue does not directly relate to the question of social mobility, Odaka's discussion and conclusions are inferentially relevant. He criticizes both views, pointing out among other things that turnover in labor in Japan is high among the lower echelons of industrial employment and concludes that "the traditional Japanese practices . . . have become less common in recent years, and . . . Japanese industry is now showing unequivocal signs of making progress toward an industrial democracy comparable to those of the free nations of the West."[34]

Odaka's conclusions seem sound enough, but the traditional practices to which he refers are far from extinct. They are strongest where the social goals are the most desirable and where sheer force of numbers does not make personalization impossible—that is, with relationship to the most prestigious occupations. Lifetime employment, paternalism, and other traditional practices are common in large industrial concerns with relation to administrative and professional employees. In certain sectors of employment outside of the giant industrial concerns, these practices also appear to retain great vitality. Small enterprises and Japanese colleges and universities appear to be strongholds of traditionalism in these respects.[35] The several large new religious sects among the many that have come into existence since the end of World War II provide outstanding examples of a partially opposing trend for their staffs of salaried administrators. Soka Gakkai provides opportunities that are probably unparalleled elsewhere in the nation for rising swiftly in position and—within the sect if not in the general society—in prestige, on the basis of individual efforts. Other traditional customs—notably the requirement of loyalty to the group—nevertheless apply also to Soka Gakkai.

Whom one knows remains an important factor in occupational and social mobility, but another factor, individual ability, rises increasingly in importance. Even under the scheme of social stratification of Tokugawa times, individual talent required recognition to allow social life to continue without disorder or collapse, but recognition was then generally given in roundabout ways that preserved the ideal structure and did not nominally dislodge the incompetent from their ascribed statuses.[36] It is significant that although the business elite of modern Japan are drawn from various social backgrounds, they show remarkable homogeneity in educational history. Nearly all are college graduates,[37] and it is probably safe to assume that they possess talent in business affairs.

One of the forms of traditionalism implied by customs of lifetime employment and emphasis on group harmony rather than individual competition merits special note. These customs relate to the traditional importance in Japan of identification with a group and the subordination of the interests of the individual in favor of those of the family or other groups. Early Western writings on Japan stressed familial and community ties but also laid emphasis on the hierarchical nature of interpersonal relations. But hierarchy and kinship were not the only important organizing principles of society. A network of egalitarian social groups—identified variously in modern writings under the names of "associations," "voluntary associations," or "common interest associations"—with instrumental and expressive goals also existed and were important to the maintenance of life.[38] As the strength of ties of kinship and community have weakened during the past century, common interest associations have grown as one of their functional substitutes. What is important to note here is that identification with groups, hierarchical or non-hierarchical, remains important affectively and also has bearing on social mobility. Earlier discussion of group affiliation referred to familial background and identification with social class as factors influencing social mobility. Identification with groups in a psychological sense relating to motivation—and, in Japanese eyes, to character—is also important. It is important in many occupations, perhaps especially those of high prestige, to "identify" in this sense, to give evidence of "sincerity" and "loyalty" that denote dedication to the goals of the group and only secondarily to goals of the self as an individual.

Recent field investigations of the training of administrative and professional employees—the cadre rather than the workers—of large business enterprises in Japan bring out the importance with which such identification is regarded by the executives in charge. Planned programs of indoctrination are conducted to bring about identification, which resembles in some respects religious conversion. New graduates of universities are said to be unsuited for effective employment before indoctrination because they are too individualistic. In order to climb the occupational ladder, the individual must regard himself as a member of the group and others must regard him in the same way, that is, as a loyal member of the group devoted first and foremost to organizational objectives.[39]

Rationales

Some of the foregoing discussion has touched upon the subject of rationales for existence, goals and values that make human life worthwhile. Various of the Japanese ideals and attitudes have important bearing on the subject of social mobility and may properly be regarded as essential for such movement or even as mechanisms that make it possible. One of the most important ingredients of national success is incentive to gain such success. Japan is a nation dedicated to progress and achievement. On the level of the individual, it may be described as a nation composed of people dedicated to personal but not individualistic achievement. Thrift, hard work, and selflessness are Japanese ideals that have long been noted and have often been seen as analagous with the Protestant ethic of the Western world. A recent study seeks principally to determine whether or not such a set of values exists in fact in Japan today and, on the basis of responses to questions regarding attitudes toward work and achievement, concludes: "The answer would plainly seem to be 'yes.' "[40] This conclusion is one that few persons even slightly acquainted with Japanese culture are likely to doubt, especially in view of the nation's remarkable economic recovery after World War II and its subsequent expansion of trade and industry.

Attempts to explain the genesis of this ethic have dealt with religious beliefs and other values, such as Bushido, the code of ethics of the samurai, and with various social and economic circumstances including interpersonal relations of the family.[41] Our concern here is not with the origins of the drive toward achievement but rather with its relationship to occupational and social mobility. In a general way, the relationship seems obvious: adequate resources or potential resources in materials, technology, and manpower must be accompanied by incentive before any nation develops economically or before individuals better themselves economically and rise socially. Particulars of the relationship applying in Japan have not been obvious. It may well be true as many Japanese and foreign observers have contended that the goal of upward social movement for most of Japan is limited to reaching the modest status of the "salary-man," the white-collar worker, but this alone is regarded as a movement upward. There is no doubt, however, that achievement is highly valued today, as it was in Meiji times. The social order has changed, but there has been no diminution in the drive to succeed. The term *namakemano* (customarily translated as "lazy" or "lazy person") still implies a judgment of general moral inferiority rather than merely lack of industry. We see here not only continuity but, as the economic and social rewards for industriousness and personal achievement have become richer in modern times, probably a heightening of the intensity with which the ideal is pursued. High social status continues to be valued, and paths toward it for most people are far easier to travel than in former times.

The principal route to higher social status has become higher education, which is also necessary for successful competition on the part of the nation in international trade. The growth of programs of formal education in Japan during the past century has been phenomenal, and the recent growth of colleges and universities is striking. The efforts of parents to secure for their children the best possible education are no less striking, involving great expenditures of money, time, and effort that are probably seldom regarded as personal sacrifices. A song popular in the 1930s, when students in colleges and universities numbered less than one-fifth of their present enrollment, tells of the ideal marriage: "I'll give my daughter's hand to a university graduate." Since World War II the demand for higher education has grown to the point where it may be called a national mania. A period of national crisis, documented in detail by radio and other news media, arises annually when the results of university entrance exams are announced. Candidates for admission to college today far outnumber facilities available despite an increase in the number of four-year colleges and universities from 201 in 1950, enrolling about 225,000 students in day and night classes, to 346 in 1966, enrolling over 1,000,000 students.[42]

The influence of traditional values is evident in other ways in connection with achievement. Success ideally is not to be won by selfish, individualistic competition with others. Evidence from current field research to which we have already referred indicates that, in actuality, success in at least certain large business firms cannot be gained by those who give evidence of, or are regarded as, selfish seekers for personal gain.[43] These circumstances appear also to apply elsewhere in Japanese society. The wants and needs of the individual in Japan have traditionally been expressed through group membership and group goals, thus providing a rationale for one's existence and efforts that is unselfish, honorable, and attractive. Group participation and striving toward group goals, in turn, provide firm identification with the group and an atmosphere of psychological warmth. The success of a commercial or non-commercial enterprise in modern

Japan continues to depend strongly upon its organizational success, the skill with which it achieves a balance between the interests of the individual and of the total organization. Much of the success of the several large new religious sects of Japan—Soka Gakkai, Rissho Koseikai, Seicho no Ie, and P L Kyodan—can be understood from this viewpoint. Preliminary field research[44] shows interesting parallels between these new religious sects and successful, large business concerns in modes of incorporation of employees or members, internal organization, and rationales. The stated goals of business concerns are not merely or primarily profit but refer to national and even international welfare. We may note in passing that conditions of childhood training in Japan appear to foster psychological attitudes of strong dependence upon other human beings, a circumstance that might partially explain, and is at least congruent with, the Japanese tendency toward group effort and group identification.[45]

Summary and Conclusions

The past century has seen Japan change from a backward country based economically on small-scale agriculture into one of the greatest industrial powers of the world. Accompanying these changes has been a social transformation from a firm structure of hierarchical classes to a condition of modern social flux in which some class distinctions are discernible. These changes may be called a transformation when conditions at the two end points in time are compared. Although the changes have been rapid, they have never been truly revolutionary. The pace of change has heightened since World War II, but traditional customs and attitudes that condition social mobility are still evident. Among these are tendencies toward paternalism and personalization of relationships associated with an emphasis on the ascribed social status of individuals as derived from familial backgrounds, and an emphasis on group efforts and loyalty to the group as opposed to individualistic competition. Although some of these circumstances do not necessarily or always inhibit upward social movement, it is clear that the social milieu in which an individual is reared continues to influence in various ways his prospects of social movement. As elsewhere in the world, a tendency is evident in Japan toward preservation of the old classes, particularly the highest and lowest strata. Upward movement is thus greatest among individuals coming from backgrounds of middle rather than low social prestige. Upward movement is very slight among members of the outcaste group, a traditional class that continues to be sharply distinct and the subject of discrimination.

Reasons for movement or lack of movement in social status are doubtless multiple and, in kind if not in relative forcefulness, appear to be much the same as those existing in other industrial or industrializing nations. As related to backgrounds of family and class, they include differences in opportunities for gaining education in the skills required for positions of prestige and, very likely, differences in motivation and self-image. One of the requisites for upward social movement—a dedication to work, achievement, and progress—is a firmly established value and represents another of the important continuities from the past. Formal education is looked upon as the primary tool that makes achievement possible, and the quest for higher education increases annually in intensity.

Prospects of future developments appear to be toward increasing social mobility and continued waning of traditional customs and attitudes that helped to define and maintain the old social order. The importance of individual talent rises ever more to national consciousness as a prerequisite for recruitment to positions of high status, even though other requirements for eligibility retain some measure of the old characteristics. All indications point to the growth of a huge middle class composed of several substrata which follow occupational lines. Attempts to formulate any simple quantified scheme of social stratification in modern Japan face several problems, however. One of these is social mobility itself, which allows no precise description to remain accurate for any length of time. As elsewhere among industrial nations of the world, science and technology have brought to Japan new occupations and associated "new" social statuses that replace or alter the old. In describing modern Japan, the problem of definition of classes seems acute because of the speed of change in very recent times. Another problem, which again applies to conditions in other nations, is to formulate appropriate criteria of class affiliation. As economic conditions improve generally and as new occupations come into existence, the attributes of social class change correspondingly—and social classifiers seldom seem to be correspondingly mobile in their classifications. Farmers and white-collar workers in Japan are cases in point. Assignments of social status that might appropriately be given them in 1867, 1967, and various points of time between these dates are surely not identical. White-collar workers did not exist as a class in 1867, and the category "farmer" has covered a wide and shifting range of statuses of social prestige.

Whether the social continuities we have discussed are desirable or undesirable is a question with several facets. Traditionalism as it has applied in Japan has obviously worked; it has allowed successful industrialization and the development of a fair degree of social mobility. There is probably much merit in the idea prevailing among American and European scholars of Japan that the rapid course of Japan's modernization was made possible in considerable part by reliance upon and gradual adaptation of traditional ways. It seems certain that the remarkable domestic tranquility which accompanied the cultural changes of the past century may be attributed to the lack of abrupt and drastic departures from tradition. Whether the future welfare of Japan would be better served by rooting out traditionalism, as some scholarly opinion in Japan holds, is another question. The very fact that this idea has risen to consciousness is, of course, an indication of changing attitudes—and very likely reflects the fact that developments toward the expressed goal have already occurred. If we look at the general outlines of change in Japan during the past century in social relations and social classes, a trend is evident toward increasing similarity to the West. This may be described simply in the statement that similar circumstances bring similar results. The conditions under which industrialization began in Japan were not the same as those of the United States, and the social correlates were far from identical. Technological conditions of industrialization have since grown increasingly similar, and these favor certain social arrangements and disfavor others. The full range of social arrangements that is possible is as yet uncertain, but Japan will doubtless long continue to be recognizably distinct despite the apparent trend toward increasing similarity.

NOTES AND REFERENCES

1. See, for example, Ezra F. Vogel, *Japan's New Middle Class* (Berkeley and Los Angeles, 1963).

2. See Nihon Shakai Gakkai Chosa Iinkai, *Nihon Shakai no Kaisoteki Kozo* (Tokyo, 1958); Kunio Odaka, "The Middle Classes in Japan," *Nihon Rodo Kyokai Zasshi* (January 1961); Kunio Odaka, *The Middle Classes in Japan* (mimeographed, undated, about 1963); and other works cited in these notes.

3. Kunio Odaka, *The Middle Classes* (1963).

4. Ibid.

5. Yuzo Yamada, compiler, *Nihon Minzoku Shotoku Suikei Shiryo* (Tokyo, 1951), p. 152.

6. Consulate General of Japan, *Japan Report* 13 (February 15, 1967), 4.

7. *Japan Report* 7 (February 28, 1961), 2–4.

8. *Japan Report* 12 (October 31, 1966), 4.

9. Ibid.

10. Minoru Tachi, *The Japan Times* (January 1, 1966), p. 3.

11. S. M. Lipset and Reinhard Bendix, *Social Mobility in Industrial Society* (Berkeley and Los Angeles, 1959), p. 25.

12. Nihon Shakai Gakkai Chosa Iinkai, op. cit., p. 160.

13. Kenichi Tominaga, "Occupational Mobility in Japanese Society: Analysis of Labor Market in Japan," *The Journal of Economic Behavior* 2, no. 1 (April 1962), 16–17.

14. Alex Inkeles and Peter H. Rossi, "National Comparisons of Occupational Prestige," *American Journal of Sociology* 61, no. 4 (January 1956).

15. Hiroshi Mannari, *Business Leaders in Japan* (Ann Arbor, in press).

16. Ibid., concluding chapter.

17. See, for example, writings in H. D. Harootunian and Bernard S. Silberman, eds., *Modern Japanese Leadership: Transition and Change* (Tucson, 1966).

18. Makoto Aso, "Kindai Nihon ni okeru Eriito Kosei no Hensen," *Kyoiku Shakaigaku Kenkyu* 15 (1960), 154.

19. Hiroshi Mannari, op. cit.

20. Ibid.

21. See, for example, Gogo Fujita, *Nihon Kindai Sangyo no Seisei* (Tokyo, 1948) and Johannes Hirschmeier, *The Origins of Entrepreneurship in Meiji Japan* (Cambridge, Mass., 1964).

22. *Japan Report* 13 (February 15, 1967), 5.

23. Hiroshi Mannari, op. cit.

24. Ibid.

25. Ibid.

26. George DeVos and Hiroshi Wagatsuma, *Japan's Invisible Race* (Berkeley and Los Angeles, 1966).

27. See bibliography of DeVos and Wagatsuma, op. cit.

28. Hiroshi Wagatsuma, "The Pariah Caste in Japan: History and Present Self-Image," in A. V. S. de Reuck and Julie Knight, eds., *Ciba Foundation Symposium on Caste and Race: Comparative Approaches* (London, 1967), p. 121.

29. DeVos and Wagatsuma, op. cit., p. 12.

30. For a detailed discussion of this subject, see DeVos and Wagatsuma, op. cit.

31. See, for example, Iwao Ishino, "The Oyabun-Kobun: A Japanese Ritual Kinship Institution," *American Anthropologist* 55, no. 5, pt. 1(1953), 695–707; James C. Abegglen, *The Japanese Factory: Aspects of its Social Organization* (Glencoe, Ill., 1958); Solomon B. Levine, *Industrial Relations in Postwar Japan* (Urbana, Ill., 1958); and William W. Lockwood, *The Economic Development of Japan: Growth and Structural Change, 1868–1938* (Princeton, 1954).

32. See *The Japan Times* (December 25, 1966), p. 10.

33. Kunio Odaka, "Traditionalism, Democracy in Japanese Industry," *Industrial Relations* 3, no. 1 (1963), 95–103.

34. Ibid., 99, 103.

35. See *The Japan Times* (December 15, 1966), p. 5, for a discussion of the circumstances in Japanese universities.

36. See R. P. Dore, *Education in Tokugawa Japan* (Berkeley and Los Angeles, 1965).

37. Hiroshi Mannari, op. cit.

38. Edward Norbeck, "Common Interest Associations in Rural Japan," in R. J. Smith and R. K. Beardsley, eds., *Japanese Culture: Its Development and Characteristics* (Chicago, 1962).

39. Hiroshi Mannari, personal communication. See also his "Bijinesu wa ika ni Ningen wo Tsukuru ka," *Chuo Koron Keiei Mondai* (Spring 1966).

40. James Allen Dator, "The 'Protestant Ethic' in Japan," *The Journal of Developing Areas* (October 1966), p. 35.

41. See, for example, George A. DeVos "Achievement and Innovation in Culture and Personality," in Edward Norbeck, Douglas Price-Williams, and William McCord, eds., *The Study of Personality: An Interdisciplinary Symposium* (New York, 1968), and Robert N. Bellah, *Tokugawa Religion* (Glencoe, Ill., 1957).

42. *Japan Report* 13 (May 31, 1967), 8.

43. Business enterprises under investigation include Sumitono Electric Manufacturing Co., Inc., Osaka (with over 8,000 employees), and Matsushita Electric Manufacturing Co., Kadoma City, Osaka Prefecture (about 20,000 employees).

44. By Hiroshi Mannari and the author.

45. See, for example, Betty B. Lanham, "The Psychological Orientation of the Mother-Child Relationship in Japan," *Monumenta Nipponica* 21 (1966), 322–32, and George A. DeVos, "Achievement and Innovation in Culture and Personality," previously cited.

The Politics of Marriage
in Changing Middle Eastern
Stratification Systems

I

When, a few years ago, I went to carry out a field study in some Arab-Moslem villages in the Middle East, I was immediately struck by the intensity of public activity over issues concerning women and their marriage. The arrangement of almost every marriage involved political maneuvering on the village level. On the other hand, there was hardly a political dispute or alliance which did not involve in one way or another, at least at some stages of its development, a number of marriages. Often, purely domestic issues between spouses and their immediate kin caused political repercussions which involved a number of political groups. The stability of marriage, therefore, was greatly interconnected with political arrangements in the village. Later, extensive census surveys and intensive analysis of cases showed, for example, that the rate of divorce in marriages contracted outside the political group was twice that in marriages contracted within it. Thus, while women carried out their daily domestic activities, in their institutionalized seclusion, rights to these women were dis-

I am grateful to the Department of Anthropology, University of Pittsburgh, for inviting me to give this paper and for the valuable criticism and comment offered by many of its members.

cussed, negotiated, exchanged, and disputed by men, in the men's guest houses. The women were never mentioned by their personal names but were referred to as the sister or wife of Ego, or simply as the daughter or wife of a certain group.

These villages are not unique in this prominence of public activity in connection with marriage. The overwhelming part of Middle Eastern populations live in similar villages, within the same cultural area, and most scholars who have studied such villages have reported the same kind of phenomena. The villages are predominantly Islamic, and, in accordance with Islamic law, the *Shari'a,* a woman is a legal minor and she cannot directly marry herself off to a man. A woman can be given in marriage to a man only by another man who will act as her guardian.[1] In the ceremony of solemnizing the marriage contract,[2] the bride will not herself be present but will be represented by her guardian, usually her father, brother, or a more remote patrilineal kinsman. Only men will be present in the ceremony. Before contract is signed, the *Shari'a* judge[3] will be taken into the interior of the house and from behind a screen will ask the bride not whether she agrees to marry the bridegroom, but whether she agrees that her father, brother, or another specified man should act as her guardian.

Part of the negotiations for a marriage may be conducted by women, but it is for the men to make the final decision.[4] This decision is governed by two norms or principles. The first emphasizes that a woman should be married within her own patronymic group,[5] to a son either of her actual father's brother, or of her classificatory (that is, a more remote) father's brother. The second principle is derived directly from a *Shari'a* injunction to the effect that a woman should be given in marriage only to a man who is of the same social, political, and economic status as that of her father and her brothers.

Occasionally, these two principles support one another so that the son of the father's brother, whom a woman can marry, has the same social status as that of her father and brothers. More frequently, however, the two principles have been in conflict so that the man who wants to marry her qualifies in terms of one principle but not the other. Thus one of the most frequent kinds of dispute in many Middle Eastern villages is caused by the refusal of a father, actual or classificatory, to give his daughter in marriage to one of his brother's sons when the latter is regarded inferior in social status. In my own study I recorded many cases in which men involved in such disputes were torn between conflicting norms, each of which was supported by custom.[6]

It is obvious from all this that marriage in these villages is directly involved in the system of the distribution of power (political and economic) and prestige, and in the processes whereby this system is maintained or changed. In other words, the pattern of marriage—that is—the pattern of the movement of women in marriage between social groups, is a crucial part of the system of stratification in these villages. An analysis of this pattern of marriage is essential for any understanding of the system of stratification in these villages, where an overwhelming part of the Middle Eastern population lives.

The analysis of interconnections between the pattern of marriage and system of social stratification in these villages is a complex problem in which many social variables are involved. In most of these villages, patrilineal descent, whether actual or putative, is one of the most important principles of social organization. On the basis of this principle the villagers are affiliated within patronymic groups, i.e., groups whose members claim descent in the male line from a common ancestor. These groups are known by different terms in different parts of the Middle East: '*Āila*, '*Ashīra*, *Kabīla*, *Ḥamūla*, and '*Ahl*. Some writers have used the terms *clan* or *lineage* for this kind of grouping, but these terms have acquired in anthropological literature of recent years connotations which are not appropriate to these groups. I shall, therefore, refer to them simply as *patronymic associations.*[7]

The form and functions of these patronymic associations vary widely from society to society, and from time to time within the same society, in relation to major economic and political variables. In some areas, the patronymic associations of a village are landholding units and in others they are not. In still other areas, members of the patronymic association hold some land collectively, in addition to plots of land which are owned separately by individual members.

There are also wide variations in the political roles of these associations, depending largely on the degree of effectiveness of the central government institutions (like police and courts) in the maintenance of law and order in the villages. Where governmental control is weak, the patronymic association assumes fundamental political functions, under the principle of collective responsibility. Where governmental control is strong, the patronymic association is of little political significance. Thus in some areas the patronymic association is mainly political, in other areas mainly economic, while in others it is both.

There are villages which tend to be egalitarian but many others which are sharply stratified. In some of the stratified villages, class boundaries coincide with patro-associational boundaries, so that the different patronymic associations are at the same time status groups which are ranked differently on the scales of wealth, power, and prestige. In other stratified villages class lines cut across patro-associational boundaries so that within every patronymic association there is differentiation in terms of wealth, power, and prestige.

In yet other areas, the patronymic association has ceased to have any major political or economic function but has persisted in the form of a number of households, which are intimately interrelated by patrilateral, matrilateral, and affinal relations, most of which were created by a large proportion of marriages which were contracted in the past, within the patronymic association, and which have not yet run their full courses. These households often continue to live in the same quarter in the village, so that neighborly sentiments and co-operation reinforce other relations. Such a group of households continues to be known by the old name of the association. In some such cases new interests may weld the group together again under new conditions, and thus make use of the various domestic and moral relations which exist between them for new social purposes.

In all these cases, the patronymic association is given form and a measure of internal structure by the myth of patrilineal descent, as expressed in the idiom of a genealogy the depth and shape of which depends on various organizational circumstances. I need not dwell here on the various processes by which genealogies are continually modified to accomodate the myth to changing realities.[8] In some villages there are expert, learned genealogists who are always ready to help individuals and groups to tailor special genealogies which are suited to particular purposes and circumstances. These genealogies are thus, truly, charters for social action in the contemporary situation rather than historical documents.

II

The Middle East is a vast area, with wide ecological, and cultural variations and with great differences in political and economic circumstances. And the variables discussed so far can be found in different combinations and permutations. It is clear, therefore, that it will be very misleading to talk in terms of generalizations about stratification in the Middle East as a whole. Even within the simple, so called traditional, rural areas, the complexities and variations are great. It is true that the Middle East forms a more or less uniform cultural area, particularly if we confine ourselves to the predominantly Arab-Moslem populations. But one of the elementary lessons we learn from social anthropology is that the function, or the social significance, of an institution depends, not on the formal aims of that institution, but on the way the institution is interconnected with other institutions within the same society. The same institution may have different social functions under different circumstances. Thus, for example, while it is true that parallel cousin marriage is widely practiced in villages in almost all parts of the Middle East, its significance may be mainly political in one place, economic in another, and domestic in a third place—or it may be mainly a matter of ranking in terms of prestige.

Sociological and methodological problems of this sort could be overcome if intensive monographic studies for different areas in the Middle East existed. Unfortunately there are very few such studies. The Arab-Islamic Middle East is often said to have developed in the full light of recorded history, and indeed there is a vast literature on the history and cultural institutions of the whole area. But the fact remains that there are today far fewer detailed monographic studies on Middle Eastern societies than on some of the remotest areas of Africa.

Thus, instead of presenting a general, abstract, and inevitably conjectural discussion for the whole area, I shall consider the interconnections between the pattern of marriage and social stratification, within the context of my own field study in a number of Arab-Moslem villages in Israel, along the Jordanian border, within a region known as the Triangle. These villages are in many respects typical of villages in other areas of the Arab Middle East. The intensive part of the work was carried out in two villages, but I also had at least one research assistant in each of the other villages. Although these villages are from a small area and are culturally homogenous, they exhibit various types of combinations of the variables which I have mentioned. My study was concerned mainly with the contemporary situation in the villages, but because of the cataclysmic changes which took place in the area as a result of the Arab-Israeli war of 1948, it became necessary to compare the contemporary situation with the situation obtaining during the Mandatory Period. To push the possibilities of comparison and analysis further I also collected, from various types of records, information on villages in the same area at the threshold of the nineteenth century.

In this way I tried to consider the interconnections between the same variables, within the same local cultural tradition, at three different points in historical time: the year 1959, which is the ethnographic present; the year 1948, to which I refer as the Mandatory Period; and the beginning of the nineteenth century, to which I refer as the Joint Estate Period. In processing the material, I considered each period separately, as if it were a system on its own. In this way I used historical data experimentally and not in order to provide explanations in terms of precedents. My aim from this comparative perspective was to examine variables in different combinations.

During the Joint Estate Period, Palestine was part of the Ottoman Empire. But the country was so poor, so far from the central seat of the empire, and so difficult topographically to control that law and order in the villages could not be maintained effectively by the official central institutions. For centuries the country was the thoroughfare of foreign invaders who continually brought it destruction and poverty. In times of peace there was the continuous danger of the bedouin. When local rule was weak, strong bedouin tribes raided the villages, looted their crops and animals, and inflicted damage on people and property. Malaria epidemics and frequent dry years added more death and starvation to the villages. Thus decimated, the population reached its lowest level.

As a result, land was abundant and individuals and groups could establish rights to unused land simply by settling on it and cultivating it. In the villages, almost all land was state land[9] and was held by the members of each village collectively, in a form of joint ownership called *Mushā'*. Land was redistributed among the villagers periodically, usually every two years. Different methods for this redistribution were used, but the prevailing one was to distribute the land among the patronymic associations of the village, letting the elders of each association distribute its share among the members.

This system of landholding necessitated close cooperation between holders of adjacent plots of land, who had to follow the same time table, rotation of crops, and methods of cultivation. Thus the men of a patronymic association held the land jointly and cooperated closely in cultivating it. At the same time they formed a political unit with collective responsibilities in disputes involving their members and those of other patronymic associations.

At this period there was little differentiation in terms of wealth and prestige among the village households, as land was held jointly and agriculture, which was the major source of livelihood, supplied the bare necessities for subsistence. Within the village, power, both economic and political, was evenly distributed and was usually exercised by the seniors of households or of patronymic associations.

Thus, the dominant cleavage in the village during the Joint Estate Period was on patro-associational lines. Law and order in the villages were maintained by means of a balance of power between the patronymic associations and were regulated by institutionalized forms of collective self-help.

During the latter half of the nineteenth century, and well down to the Mandatory Period, economic and political conditions changed drastically. The country became the center of interest for European powers. A large number of missionaries came and established institutions of various sorts and spent a great deal of imported capital. The number of traders, pilgrims, scholars, and travelers visiting the country increased. The administration was reorganized, and social order became more stable. The population grew substantially as a result of natural increase, of immigration from the neighboring countries, and of the settlement of bedouin in permanent villages. These developments were associated with the breakup of the joint estate in many villages and the conversion of most of it to private property. In the process, a large proportion of peasants became landless and lived as tenants on the land of others.

With the conversion of a great proportion of joint estates to private ownership, the patronymic association lost its economic basis. The new lines of stratification cut across patro-associational boundaries and tended to disrupt these associations. This does not mean that the development of sharp social stratification always disintegrates descent groups. Freedman shows that in the Chinese lineage, which bears many similarities to the traditional Arab patronymic association, differences in wealth between members strengthened, rather than weakened, the lineage.[10] But, in the Chinese lineage, all the members participated periodically in rites of solidarity which, in Freedman's words, "bound the unequal," and they also held some property collectively.[11] In the patronymic association among the Arabs, on the other hand, none of these links existed. More important, the Arab patronymic association suffered from the disintegrative consequences of the developing conflict between the principle of in-patro-associational marriage and the principle of equality of status between the spouses in marriage. The Chinese lineage, being exogamous, was free from such a subversive process.

The Arab patronymic association is organized on two main bases: first, the myth of common descent—of the members being "of the same blood," as the villagers put it—and, second, the principle of parallel cousin marriage. If, for the sake of the discussion, the link of patriliny is ignored for the moment, the patronymic association appears to be a group of men who are intimately linked together through their marriage to one another's sisters or daughters. These patronymic associations are not totally endogamous groups. The ratio of in-group marriage to total marriage varies from one association to another. In my marriage census the ratio varied from 82 per cent for some patronymic associations to 46 per cent for others. But even if these patronymic associations are not totally endogamous, the substantial proportion of the internal marriages in each link its members together intensely and, to some extent, mark the association off from other associations in this respect. Thus, in one specific association with a relatively low ratio of in-group marriage, 34 out of a total of 72 marriages were contracted within the group (which numbered 314 people), while 25 marriages were contracted with women from the rest of the village (with a population of 1,915 people), and another 13 marriages with women from many villages in the area, in a population totaling many thousands. While relationships created by 38 marriages outside the group are with people who are scattered among a large population, the relationships formed by the 34 marriages within the relatively small group created a closely knit network which linked the various domestic units of the association together. These relationships were very intense and complex because they overlapped and also cut across each other. The men of a patronymic association were linked together in a variety of ways which imposed on them different obligations towards each other. Through the recurrence of in-group marriages over a period of time, men who were related matrilaterally by one marriage also became affines by virtue of another marriage, and so on.

Links created by in-group marriage became more intense through the practice, common in most areas of the Middle East, of patrilocal residence. This means that when a girl is married, she simply moves to the next house or to another house within the same quarter. Indeed, in some cases she may not have to move to another house at all. In this way a man may have patrilineal and matrilateral relatives as affines as well as neighbors.

Thus, the political unity of the patronymic association which formally hinges on the principle of unilineal descent is highly consolidated, indeed at some periods made possible, by these in-group marriages. Often it is expressed in terms of such marriages. The material from the Triangle villages suggests that there is a close correlation between the ratio of in-patro-associational marriage and the unity of the association as it manifests itself in actual political action. The villagers themselves sometimes explain their preference for parallel cousin marriage in political terms. They say that children born of such marriages experience no divided loyalties because they have the same men as their father's brothers and mother's brothers, and their loyalty, therefore—as they put it—"remains within their camp."

These parallel cousin marriages also give the Arab patronymic association a greater potentiality for survival in the face of modern changes than is evidenced by many exogamous descent groups. When the Arab patronymic association loses its political function, it can still survive as a discrete social group for some time because of the network of relations created by in-associational marriages contracted during the period when the association functioned as a political unit.

Thus the principle of parallel cousin marriage forms a fundamental part of the structure of the Arab patronymic association. But during the Mandatory Period in the Triangle villages this principle came into sharp conflict with the principle of equality of status between the spouses contracting marriage. The growing disparity in wealth in the villages created links between households across the lines of patriliny. From the census covering marriages contracted during this period in some of these villages, it is evident that some kind of alliance developed between the wealthy households from different patronymic groups and that this alliance involved the exchange of women in marriage across the lines of patriliny. The wealthy from one patronymic association married into the wealthy from other patronymic associations.

The principle of the equality of status of spouses is sometimes also expressed in the form of a principle of hypergamy. A current proverb in the villages says: "Take from the inferior but never give him"—meaning that men may marry women from groups inferior in status but should not permit their sisters or daughters to marry into such groups.

If a woman marries into a status group which is inferior in wealth to that of her father, she is likely to alienate property from her father's group to that of her husband, thus ultimately lowering the status of the former and raising that of the latter. Hence, a status group which gives women in marriage to economically inferior groups runs the risk of losing property and ultimately reducing the group's social status and political power. Such a loss of power is not likely to be offset adequately by exchanging women between the two groups in question, since less power will pass from the poorer group to the richer group.

Again, in village society anything affecting the honor of a married woman affects the honor of her father's group and not her husband's. If she commits adultery, it is the duty of her brothers and parallel cousins— not her husband's group—to kill her. The very fact that a woman is given in marriage to a group considered inferior in status involves loss of prestige to her father's group. Thus, to safeguard the honor of a woman—and hence that of her father's group—efforts should be made for her to be married within her father's group because her own brothers and her parallel cousins are, in any case, the normal guardians of that honor. If, however, she is given in marriage to a man from another group, his status should be equal to, or higher than, that of her father so that the husband's group will be equally capable of protecting her honor.

Evidence from other parts of the Middle East suggests that most villages today are passing through a stage similar to that of the Mandatory Period in the Triangle.

In the Triangle villages, however, this stage came to an abrupt end when political and economic conditions, created by the events of 1948–49, changed drastically and led, at least for a number of years, to a revival of the principle of political patriliny and to the renewed mobilization of the patronymic association in political action. The wealthy in these villages lost a great deal of their land, and the landless sought employment in Jewish towns and agricultural settlements where they obtained union-controlled high wages. As the wealthy were inhibited in many ways from exploiting the new opportunities for wage employment, a new egalitarianism in the level of income emerged. Parallel to these changes in economic opportunity and economic status were changes in the order of ranking in terms of life style. The villagers say: "Today it is the laborer who resides in the high buildings." Among the wage laborers in nearly every village home, there has been a great revolution in housing, furniture, clothing, and food. Radios, for example, have become a necessity and many laborers carry small transistor sets on their way to and from work. Developed further with the institutionalization of election by ballot as a means of recruitment for positions of authority both inside and outside the village, this new egalitarianism, among other things, halted the disruptive processes which had been brought into the patronymic association during the Mandatory Period.

At the same time, some political conditions stemming directly from the long-standing Arab-Jewish dispute created new conditions in these border-villages, conditions which favored political groupings on the basis of the old patronymic association.

I do not intend here to go into a detailed discussion of the complex processes involved in these developments. The point which I want to emphasize is that the revival of the patronymic association as a political unit has entailed, among other things, a stricter control exercised by the patronymic association as a collective over the transfer of its women in marriage. The degree to which this control is effectively exercised is, ultimately, an index of the political unity of the association. The principle underlying this control is that a man has a customary priority right over any outsider to marry a woman from his patronymic association. With this priority over the outsider goes also the customary right to make a smaller marriage payment than an outsider.

If a girl cannot be married within her patronymic group simply because no parallel cousin is available to marry her, her marriage to an outsider will still require the approval of the group's seniors. Thus, when the father of such a girl is approached by mediators, who are asking the hand of his daughter on behalf of the outsider, his usual reaction will be a brief reply: "I shall seek counsel." He will then formally inform the gathering of the seniors, in the association's guest house, of the request and wait for their answer. If any of these men is interested in marrying the man's daughter to some of his patri-kinsmen, he will say so and thus veto the marriage of the girl to the outsider. But if no such wish is expressed and if none of the seniors raises any objection to the proposed marriage, the seniors will wish him luck and permit him to marry off his daughter to the people who have asked for her hand. Even if no man is available to marry the girl within the association, the seniors may sometimes, nevertheless, prevent the proposed match on the ground that the patronymic group of the man seeking the girl in marriage is lower in status to that of the girl.

III

I have discussed the material from the Triangle villages in some detail in order to draw attention to the close sociological interconnections between the pattern of marriage and the system of social stratification in Arab villages under different historical circumstances. By the term *stratification* I have been referring to the system whereby households within a village are differentiated and ranked on three major scales: the economic, the political, and that of social prestige. The pattern of marriage in these villages forms a fundamental part of that system and plays a crucial role in its functioning.

On the economic scale, women can be instrumental in alienating property from one household to another, in accordance with Islamic law. Where, as in these villages, land is the principal form of wealth and the major source of livelihood, the movement of women in marriage between groups can seriously affect the economic fortunes of households and thus alter the position of men on the economic scale of ranking.[12] During the Joint Estate Period in the Triangle villages and in villages in other parts of the Middle East, land—or, rather, the right to the use of land—was, until the middle of the nineteenth century, held collectively by whole patronymic groups and was thus inalienable, through inheritance, to outsiders. But when common land was very rapidly converted to private property, the picture altered drastically.

On the political scale, the marriage of women in Arab villages, as in many other societies, often serves as an instrument for actual or potential political alliance between households. But, in many of the simple societies that have been studied, women must be married exogamously, outside the recognized descent group, and the political impact of marriage is, therefore, confined to intergroup relations. Among the Arabs, on the other hand, women can be—and are—also married within the descent group, and this kind of marriage can affect both the cohesion of the group and the political relations between that group and other groups in the village, depending on the ratio between marriages within the patronymic associations and marriages across patronymic associations. A child born of a marriage between spouses from different patronymic associations has his father's brother in one camp and his mother's brother in another. And in cases of political disputes between the two groups, the child's loyalties are divided. On the other hand, the child born of marriage within the patronymic group has the same man as his classificatory father's brother and as his classificatory mother's brother. Within feuding villages, this can mean a greater chance of peaceful settlement in the second case and violent, prolonged disputes in the first.

Also, in many Middle Eastern villages, the political strength of a patronymic association is measured by the number of its males, and the very biological continuity of the group depends on the continued replacement of dying generations by newborn ones. In exogamous patri-descent groups, men are compelled to bring outside women into the group through marriage in order to acquire rights in their reproductive capacity, but among the Arabs this can be best achieved by marrying their own women. Arab villagers say: "Why give our fortune to strangers?" Thus, the transfer of women in marriage can in the long run affect the distribution of political power between households and between patronymic associations.

On the scale of prestige, it is well known that in most Arab villages (as well as among bedouin and settlers in Arab traditional towns) a most complicated code system is observed in matters relating to the honor of women.[13] In many other peasant and non-peasant societies, groups are differentiated and ranked on the scale of prestige in terms of life style. In Arab villages, however, the most crucial criterion of prestige is the intensity of the jealousy that men publicly show in guarding the honor of their sisters and daughters. An adulterous woman, or even an unmarried woman having a sexual affair with a man, must be killed by her brothers or her father's brothers' sons. If she is killed, as is often the case in these villages, the group not only reasserts its position but also rises in the prestige scale.[14] If she is not killed, they suffer a great loss of prestige, and their social status drops.

These three scales of ranking—the economic, the political, and that of prestige—are sociological isolates forged for analytical purposes only. In actual social life, the scales are very highly interconnected, and ranking in terms of one scale affects ranking in terms of the other scales.

Thus, the transfer of women in marriage between households affects the ranking of men in many ways. For this reason marriage in Arab villages is of crucial political significance and is attended by much political activity. It is the men who are directly involved in the stratification system, and it is the men who, therefore, regulate the transfer of women in marriage.

Underlying this whole arrangement is the ideology provided by the *Shari'a* injunction that women are legal minors and that men are their guardians. Despite the grounding in law, however, this is not only a matter of legal or ideological formulation. In many Moslem countries today various direct and indirect modifications in the *Shari'a* are being introduced to meet changing social conditions.

The question of the legal equality of women with men is involved in many economic, political, and other social processes. Social conditions are rapidly changing, but the new patterns have not yet been fully investigated. As governmental institutions for the maintenance of law and order become more effective and as the economy becomes more developed and more diversified, nation-wide associations which cut across villages and towns are emerging, and the patronymic association in the village may soon lose its social significance. With increased urbanization and with continuous migration of populations from the villages to the towns, women may achieve a degree of economic independence and may succeed in securing for themselves legal equality with men. When they succeed finally in winning the right to give themselves in marriage, the whole pattern of stratification in traditional Middle Eastern society will change.

NOTES

This paper was given in 1966 and therefore does not deal with changes that have taken place in the area since then.
1. *Wali.*
2. *'Ak̲d nikāḥ.*
3. *Ḳāḍī.*
4. If a marriage proves unsuccessful, men invariably put the blame on women, saying in sarcasm: "This was a marriage arranged by women!" (*Hādha kān zwādj niswān.*)
5. *Ḥamūla.*
6. See, for example, the detailed case which I discuss, in Cohen (1965: 71–93).
7. For a more detailed discussion of this point, see ibid., pp. 2–3.
8. For a detailed discussion of these processes, see Bohannan (1952); Fortes (1953); Peters (1960 and 1963).
9. Known as *mīri.*
10. Freedman (1958:136–37).
11. Ibid., p. 91.
12. This point is competently discussed, for a Moslem village in Lebanon, by Peters (1963).
13. Known as *masā'il 'arḍ wa s̲h̲araf.*
14. This is shown in a case discussed in Cohen (1965:126).

REFERENCES

Bohannan, L. (1952) "A Genealogical Charter," *Africa* 22:301–15.

Cohen, A. (1965) *Arab Border-Villages in Israel: A Study of Continuity and Change in Social Organisation*. Manchester, England.

Fortes, M. (1953) "The Structure of Unilineal Descent Groups," *American Anthropologist* 55:17–41.

Freedman, M. (1958) *Lineage Organisation in Southeastern China*. London.

Peters, E. (1960) "The Proliferation of Segments in the Lineage of the Bedouin in Cyrenaica," *Journal of the Royal Anthropological Institute* 90:29–53.

———— (1963) "Aspects of Status and Rank in a Lebanese Village," in *Mediterranean Countrymen,* ed. J. Pitt-Rivers. Paris.

Chapter 9/ Sydel Silverman

Stratification
in Italian Communities:
A Regional Contrast

In recent years, anthropologists have recognized Mediterranean Europe as a meaningful unit of cultural taxonomy, as an area
throughout which there are many social and cultural uniformities (e.g.,
Arensberg 1963). A central place among these uniformities is held by the
patterns of stratification common to Mediterranean Europe as a whole—
patterns that have historical depth of millenia and that are familiar and
evident to the casual observer. Yet an emphasis on cultural commonalities
can be dangerous, not only because it may obscure lines of very real and
important diversity within the area, but because it may lead us to believe
that we know more than we really do.

   Various students have called attention to some dominant themes of
Mediterranean stratification in the course of segregating the area as a cultural entity. Still, how much do such themes tell us about the nature of
the stratification systems of the area? And—just as important—how
much do we understand of the bases and the consequences of Mediterranean stratification patterns? I believe the problem can best be approached
at a regional level, taking units less broadly defined than the culture area.
Therefore, I intend to look at two major regions of Italy, concentrating on
contrasts rather than commonalities in their systems of stratification. My
purpose in doing so is to show, first, the different foundations of the two

stratification systems—above all, their foundations in agricultural organization—and, second, the different implications they have for other aspects of culture.

By the term *stratification* I mean a structure of regularized inequality that differentiates people hierarchically on the basis of their social roles. In this definition, I follow sociologists such as Barber (1957), but I qualify the definition by specifically excluding from the domain of stratification those roles based solely on age, sex, kinship, and personality. It is my assumption (perhaps an unjustified one) that dominant social roles represent an approximate summation of several dimensions of stratification: access to strategic resources, capacity to claim deference, capacity to initiate action, and life style. My special concern is with stratification structures in the context of communities. The main reason for this emphasis is that the community provides a useful field of observation for tracing relationships between stratification and other aspects of culture.

At the outset, we may ask what uniformities exist in stratification in Italy south of the Po (the usual boundary of "Mediterranean" Italy). At least three general characteristics emerge at once. First, this is a two-class world. The stratification structure is disjunctive, although some persons, having escaped the lower world of *la miseria,* yet not belonging in the upper stratum, make up a middle level and, lacking an identity and life style of their own, they emulate those of the upper class.

A second general characteristic is the crucial role of control of land. Control of much land is the ideal distinguishing feature of the upper stratum, and control of any land at all is a criterion for separating the near-lowest ranks from the lowest ones. The point here is *controlling* the land—as distinct from working it or loving it or improving it. High rank is associated with the controller himself remaining inactive while the land is worked by others or left unproductive. Land is, of course, still the strategic resource in this society and the most reliable line of retreat in times of difficulty. Yet the emphasis on control of land and the symbolic value of land go beyond its economic worth.

A third characteristic of Italian stratification is the universal emphasis on the civilized and the urbane. The upper-class world consists of those who represent civilization and conform to values flowing from the city. Ideally, this distinction coincides with that of control of land, for "civilization" is the rationale of the land-controllers and urbanity is their style. However, since the nineteenth century, when alternative paths to "civilization" opened up, the two criteria have begun to diverge. Civilized families lacking land have moved into the upper stratum, while control of land has frequently passed to families who are outside the upper-class world.

This very general statement leaves much unanswered: the nature of the strata, the structuring of uniformities and differences within them, the kinds of relationships between them, as well as—of course—the factors that account for the forms. One way of working toward such answers is to look at patterned variations beneath the surface homogeneity of the culture area. I have followed this procedure in the course of comparing my own field data from central Italy with accounts of southern Italy.[1]

While the stratification systems of both these regions conform to the general statements about Mediterranean Italy as a whole, several points of difference appear. In the first place, the structure of the lower class contrasts markedly in central and southern Italy. Secondly, the criteria that mark off strata and substrata are different in the two regions; while control of land, whether or not one works the land, and conformity to urban patterns are everywhere significant, the ways in which they are spelled out and interwoven differ. Third, the regions contrast in the form and quality of relationships between upper and lower strata.

In addition, when one follows out the implications of stratification patterns for other aspects of culture, other dimensions of contrast emerge. In particular, some of the most frequently discussed characteristics of southern Italian culture stand in contrast to those of central Italy, as correlates of a different stratification system. The political incapacity of southern Italy is the most striking of these. This phenomenon, which Banfield (1958) described as "amoral familism," is significant, on the one hand, in the local community—where it takes the form of a resistance to cooperation beyond the nuclear family or indeed any kind of association for achieving common ends—and, on the other hand, at the level of regional and national politics. Central Italy not only has cooperative affiliations of various kinds, but there is a potential for political activism. A related but somewhat different peculiarity of southern Italy is the absence of organization in the community—in the sense of locally maintained formal groups or even stable alignments. Again, central Italy affords a contrast. Finally, there is the constellation of attitudes of the southern Italian agriculturalist that contradicts many of the assumptions once held about "typical" peasant values. For instance, Redfield found it necessary to modify his statement about peasant world-view after considering evidence from southern Italy

(1956:60–79). The values of southern Italian cultivators appear to be "anti-peasant" because of the emphasis on civilization and urbanity. This same emphasis exists in central Italy; the point is that it takes a quite different form there.

These several contrasts between central and southern Italy can, I believe, be accounted for by differences in the organization of agriculture in the two areas. I see agricultural organization as the basis of stratification patterns and related features of social structure and ideology. The causal relationship between agricultural and social organization is, of course, a two-way street. However, I take the view that there are priorities in the order of causation. It is the existence of such priorities that makes it possible to hypothesize predictive statements about change. For example, I would expect that the social structure would respond to changes in the agricultural system, but I would not expect that agricultural organization would be altered fundamentally by manipulation only of the social structure.

The two areas I am considering may now be identified more precisely, defined on the basis of gross distributions of agrarian characteristics. "Central Italy" refers essentially to the middle altitudes and interior plains of Tuscany, Umbria, and the Marches, as well as adjacent parts of the regions immediately to the north and south. (The Apennine strip running through this zone and the Tuscan coastal plain are excluded.) "Southern Italy" for present purposes consists of most of continental Italy from Campania and Molise southward, excluding a number of littoral areas. To distinguish this zone from the geographic entirety of southern Italy, I borrow the term "Deep South."[2] For both the Center and the South, the situation that I am describing pertains to a "traditional" time period. In central Italy this period extends backward for several centuries, but in the south it was crystallized only in the latter part of the nineteenth century. In both areas the period continues until about the late 1940s; while the traditional systems are still essentially intact, significant changes have occurred since the end of World War II.

I propose now to give a brief description of agricultural organization in the two regions, then to point up the major contrasts in their stratification systems, and finally to explore some of the further implications of these contrasts. In describing agricultural organization—and by this term I mean the organization of resources for agricultural production, including land, capital, and human resources—I am concerned with underlining the most striking characteristics of each region. Thus, the description will necessarily deal in generalizations. In order to clarify the most predominant patterns, those that appear less frequently will be minimized.

In central Italy, the unit of agricultural production is the farm, on which a family of cultivators is settled. Each farm includes the whole range of crops and livestock in the productive complex; thus each farm comprises a variety of different kinds of land and other resources, that are exploited in a closely integrated manner. The land may be situated within a single bounded entity, or if it is divided into nonadjacent plots, all plots are within easy access of each other and of the farmhouse.

There is a one-to-one correspondence between families and farms, and the size of farms corresponds to the size of families: each farm must be large enough to support the family without major dependence upon outside staples, yet it must be within the labor capacity of that family. The actual range of farm size is from two or three to thirty or more hectares, with an average size of ten to fifteen hectares; the corresponding range of family size is from three or four to twenty or more individuals.

The integrity of the farm is maintained over the course of time. It is the farm unit as a whole that is valued and sold on the market, consigned to other peasant families, and passed on to heirs. This stability is a consequence of the fact that an effective unit of production requires a combination of different resources and equipment; the parts of a farm cannot readily be separated and recombined.

Most farms in central Italy are cultivated under a system of share-farming, the *mezzadria*. The farm with its stock and permanent equipment is consigned to a family of cultivators who provide the labor. In principle, the *mezzadria* is an association between a landowner and a peasant family, in which both investments and products are divided, half and half. It constitutes a special type of sharecropping arrangement, characterized by a combination of elements: the integrated farm, the family labor unit, and the participation of both landowner and cultivators in investment and operations. A further characteristic of the *mezzadria* is the high degree of stability of the arrangement.

The *mezzadria* contract binds a whole peasant family, and family labor cannot ordinarily be diverted to other enterprises. These provisions are feasible because the diversity of crops, combined with intensive animal husbandry, provides a fairly equal distribution of labor the year round. The major exception to this statement occurs at a few peak periods. At these times, labor needs that exceed the capacity of the family are filled by a reciprocal work exchange among the families occupying several nearby farms. Within certain limits, large family groups are an advantage to the peasants. Expanding families have access to larger and better farms, and a sizeable group working a big farm usually has greater unit productivity than the same number of persons working several small farms. Thus, the ideal family type for the *mezzadri* (the *mezzadria* peasants) is the patrilocal extended family, in which all sons bring their brides into the household and in which peripheral unattached relatives can also find a place. The labor of the family members is closely co-ordinated; all work is under the direction of the formally designated family-head, who has economic and legal authority over and responsibility for the family as a whole.

While the possibility for families to change farms provides a mechanism for maintaining an adjustment between farm size and family size, a family's occupancy of a particular farm tends to have considerable duration. The *mezzadria* contract is renewed tacitly from year to year, and usually it continues for decades, sometimes for generations.

Under the *mezzadria* system, the landowner, or *padrone,* is defined as the director of the enterprise. He may perform this function either alone or with the aid of a *fattore,* who acts as his technical advisor, agent, and foreman. Major decisions are ultimately the landowner's, but the *mezzadro,* the peasant, is consulted on many matters, and in practice as well as theory both parties to the contract share in decision-making. Both also share in the provision and reinvestment of capital; the landowner is responsible for the more costly equipment, the peasant for the tools and smaller equipment, and both—in equal shares—for the operating expenses. The landowner advances all capital as needed, including the *mezzadro's* part, which is then debited to his account. In addition, the *padrone* is obliged to feed the peasant family in lean years. Beyond the formal provisions of the contract, the landowner ideally is supposed to give protection, economic assistance, and guidance to the *mezzadri,* who are expected to reciprocate with loyalty and various gifts and services. While the reality falls short of this ideal, the landowner-peasant relationship is frequently one of wide-ranging patronage. One reason for this is that the two families do, in fact, interact continuously, as a result of their mutual participation in the agricultural enterprise.

It should be made clear that while the relationship is a complementary one and while both landowner and peasant share a concern for the productivity of the farm, there is nevertheless a fundamental opposition of interests between them. This is manifested in a continuing, though carefully phrased, struggle over the specific division of contributions and returns. Moreover, landowner and peasant are in fundamentally different positions. The peasant's concern is with his own farm only, and his activity on the farm is limited to production. The landowner's interest encompasses several farms and a much broader scope of activity—buying and selling on the market, accounting, long-range planning, perhaps conversion of the agricultural products, and sometimes nonagricultural economic enterprises.

The pattern of land ownership in central Italy approaches a polarization of propertied and landless groups. According to comprehensive surveys of land distribution in Italy, this area exhibits the highest degree of concentration of landed property in the nation (INEA 1956:140). The holdings of the central Italian landowners tend to be moderately large, ranging from a few family farms to estates of several hundred hectares. Small holdings have been of secondary importance in this region, at least until recently (INEA 1956:137); however, there is a small but significant group of peasant proprietors. (In 1946–48, this group worked 23 per cent of the cultivable land area in central Italy, as compared to 59 per cent of the area that was cultivated by *mezzadri* [INEA 1956:190, 199].) In general, these peasant proprietors work self-contained family farms similar to those of the *mezzadri;* in fact, many were originally *mezzadri* who had succeeded in purchasing the farms they were occupying. A very large proportion of the population owns no land at all. These include—of course—the *mezzadri,* as well as the less numerous artisans and other nonagricultural workers.

The position of the various categories of the population with respect to the agricultural system may be summarized by a look at the settlement pattern of the central Italian rural community. The focal point of the community is a nucleated village or town, around which the farms are dispersed. The nucleated center is inhabited by the nonagriculturalists. Dominating the population are the landowners, typically a group of families who have for generations held most of the land of the community. Their active participation in the agricultural enterprise, which is often matched by a broad interest in agrarian technology, is reflected in their residence near their land. Some landowners live in the cities of central Italy, leaving their farms to be managed by resident *fattori,* but they frequently retain part-time residences in the rural community, where they spend the harvest period and holidays. The farms around the community center are occupied by *mezzadri,* peasant proprietors, and a few cultivators working under other kinds of contracts.

Southern Italy presents contrasts with this description in several dimensions. In the first place, the range of products raised by a particular cultivator or family is much narrower than in central Italy. The Deep South, as defined here, can be described in terms of two major, discontinuous agrarian-economic zones. One is the zone of "diversified peasant agriculture," in which peasant entrepreneurs raise a number of crops on small, scattered holdings. "Diversification" in this context is a relative term; each cultivator raises wheat, combining it with one or more additional products—grapes, olives, or figs, and usually a legume or another cereal for rotation. The second zone is the "peasant latifundia," areas of extensive agriculture that are divided up and parcelled out to owner-operators and to other cultivators on short-term contracts. Most of these plots are devoted to wheat. In both zones, livestock raising is of minor importance, generally of a kind that involves little human labor or capital expenditure. (It should be noted that the Deep South by definition excludes those coastal areas in specialized, intensive cultivation and those that are predominantly in commercially run estates.)

Throughout the Deep South, land is divided into parcels, each of which is treated essentially as an independent unit. For instance, land is bought and sold piece by piece rather than in some combination. A cultivator may work several parcels, but there is minimal integration of these units, and they are generally widely scattered. The plots are typically small and irregular. In general, there is great variation among cultivators in the number, size, distribution, and quality of land units they work. Resident farms are unusual, and most cultivators live in large agglomerates, the so-called agro-towns, frequently at a considerable distance from their land.

In contrast to the stability and integrity of the *mezzadria* farm, the land units of the south are unstable over a period of time. Not only do they change hands often, but they change in dimension. Parcels tend to be continually subdivided into fragments of diminishing size. This process is the result of the emphasis in inheritance upon equal shares to all offspring (which may involve not only division of the total property but also splitting up each plot in order to equalize the quality of the shares).

The land is cultivated under a rather bewildering variety of titles and contracts. Typically, a particular cultivator works a number of plots on several different bases simultaneously. The most common form of relationship to the land (in terms of the amount of arable land involved) is peasant proprietorship. Next in frequency is tenancy; the essential criteria of these contracts are the fixity of rental payments and the fact that the cultivator bears full responsibility for costs and operations. Wage labor and sharecropping are about equally common. The category "sharecropping" includes a wide variety of contracts, but most leave the main entrepreneurial functions to the cultivator. Any of these arrangements may apply to a whole plot of land, or to only a specific crop on the plot, or even to only certain operations on a crop. Thus, not only is the cultivator's activity fragmented in the sense that he works separate, unintegrated parcels, often under a variety of terms, but his work may be only on a part of the plot or on a part of the crop's cycle. Moreover, contracts are of short duration, generally for a year or less. Thus, the typical agricultural enterprise of the Deep South consists of a cultivator who combines and recombines different pieces of land of his own and other proprietors, changing the combination continually. Furthermore, the individual cultivator's combination of means as often as not includes casual labor for others and nonagricultural pursuits as well.

Under any of the different arrangements, a cultivator may utilize his own labor exclusively, that of his family, or sporadically, hired labor for which he pays either in wages or in shares. To the extent that the family forms a labor unit, it tends to remain small and loosely organized. In the first place, a family's access to land is restricted to what they can acquire or work on a short-term basis. Moreover, even if they have large holdings, this property is rarely integrated into an entity which can absorb the labor of a large group; for one thing, the emphasis on wheat and only a few other crops minimizes the labor requirement and concentrates it seasonally. As a rule, if a family has more land than they can work, they contract some or all to other cultivators and become rent-collectors themselves. Thus, regardless of the size of the holding, the economic activity of family members tends to be dispersed—among scattered pieces of their own land, in labor on other people's land, in nonagricultural tasks, and so on.

The southern cultivator typically is on his own in carrying on the agricultural enterprise. Whether or not he owns the land, he is responsible not only for labor but for capitalization and decision-making. Noncultivating landowners generally avoid any active involvement in their own properties, and they remain detached from agricultural concerns in general. They may rent their land to subcontractors, or they may hire agents to look after their interests; such middlemen also limit their role to rent-collection. If the proprietor has direct dealings with the peasant who works his land, this relationship tends to be brief and restricted to the business of the enterprise.

The distribution of land ownership is broad, and small holdings are predominant. Contrary to the usual picture of southern Italy as an area of a few large landowners and masses of landless, land surveys have repeatedly shown that large properties account for a very minor proportion both of land area and of agricultural income in the south (Serpieri 1947: 42, 61, 301; Medici 1951:33). Rather, land is widely distributed among a large number of proprietors. However, the most significant characteristics of southern landholding are more subtle ones. First, there is the broad range of variation in holdings, with all degrees from landlessness to large properties represented. Second, there is the intermingling of holdings of different size, for in most areas properties of various sizes occur together. Third, there is the continual circulation of property, as individual holdings are constantly increased or diminished.

As in central Italy, settlement pattern mirrors the agricultural system. Throughout southern Italy, the "rural" population tends to be clustered into large towns. The population of the so-called agro-town is diverse, including agricultural workers of all categories, landowners of small to medium scale, and the nonagricultural provincial elite. Owners of large properties generally succeed in attaining the common goal of all—to live in the cities. The more modest noncultivating landowners are forced to live physically in the rural community, along with the agriculturalists. But they, and the rural elite as well, remain essentially dissociated from the locality and rather look outward to the cities, with which they identify themselves and to which they aspire.

Several differences between the agricultural systems of central and southern Italy should be underlined. First, the extent of consolidation of the economic activity of the central Italian cultivator contrasts with the fragmentation of the southern Italian's. The same point may be made about the economic activity of the agricultural family in each region. In central Italy, the entire family concentrates its labor full-time and year-round on the single enterprise of the farm. In the Deep South, the activity of the nuclear family, as well as that of the individual members, is distributed among a variety of separate agricultural and nonagricultural pursuits.

A second crucial contrast is the long-term persistence of the central

Italian cultivator's activity, as against the instability of the southern Italian's. The central Italian peasant family typically works the same farm for years, even for generations; if a *mezzadria* family changes farms, it is for another that differs mainly in size. In southern Italy, short-term activity is the rule. Tenancy and sharecrop arrangements are of brief duration, while wage labor is casual and irregular. Peasant proprietorship represents a more enduring relationship to the land, but even in these instances, holdings fluctuate a great deal—in overall size and quality as well as in the specific plots involved. In general, the southern Italian continually moves in and out of the various activities that make up the combination of his sources of sustenance.

A third contrast is in the relationship of cultivators to other participants in the agricultural enterprise. The central Italian peasant belongs to a large and highly co-ordinated labor unit. The family, in turn, forms part of a network of equivalent, neighboring families, within which there is a recurrent pooling of labor, as well as continuous mutual aid. In addition, the *mezzadria* family is linked to superordinates—landowner and *fattore*—who provide direction, information, and capital. The southern Italian cultivator is essentially isolated. Individuals or small family groups make their own way. Any impetus toward reciprocal work exchange is obviated by the abundant availability of temporary hired labor. Moreover, landowners and agents have only tenuous connections with the cultivators and are sources of neither capital nor guidance.

A fourth contrast between central and southern Italy is in the distribution of landed property. In central Italy, land is concentrated among a relatively small number of persons, whose ownership tends to be stable over time. Most of these owners fall into two separate categories: the *mezzadria* landowners, who generally have substantial holdings, and the peasant proprietors, who own their single farms. In southern Italy, land is distributed among a large number of owners, ranging from the near-landless to the proprietors of huge estates. In further contrast to central Italy, ownership here is unstable over time.

A fifth important difference between the two regions is in the nature of the involvement of major landlords in the local agricultural system. The central Italian large-scale landowner has a local base in the agricultural community; he is actively involved in the operation of his farms and in the life of the community, whether or not he is a year-round resident there. In contrast, the large landowners of southern Italy do not take an active part in the agricultural enterprise, and they remain detached from the local community—physically, if possible, and, in any case, in spirit.

These differences in agricultural organization are the bases of contrasting patterns of stratification in central and southern Italy. Consider, first, the theme of the two-class world. While this theme is accurate as an initial description of both regions, at closer examination they are quite different, particularly in the structure of the lower class—that is, in the way persons included within this class are ranked with respect to each other. In central Italy, the lower class consists of discrete, ranked categories. Most families are clearly and permanently identified with a particular category, for their occupation and their relationship to the land are full-time and long-term. The fundamental distinction within the lower class is based on the separation of town and countryside: all families associated with the nucleated center are ranked above those of the country. Furthermore, the population of the countryside consists of distinct groups: peasant proprietors, *mezzadri,* and the few agricultural laborers. At the same time, because of the one-to-one correspondence between family and farm, there is little basis for any major differentiation within each group of the countryside.

In contrast, the lower class in southern Italy cannot be described in terms of discrete subgroups. First of all, the settlement pattern provides no basis for division of the population, for all are townsmen alike; nor are residences in the town arranged so that families of common economic position are in exclusive, close proximity. Moreover, families' occupations and the arrangements under which they work land overlap and change continually: the same man may be simultaneously an owner-operator, a sharecropper, and a wage laborer, or he may assume these different statuses in rapid succession; a man may be at once or in sequence a peasant and a nonagriculturalist; a family's members may be involved in a variety of work arrangements. Similarly, the broad range and flux in the distribution of landed property mitigate against the formation of distinct groups in terms of land ownership. Under these conditions, there can be no sharp boundaries between economic or social categories. Rather, there is a continuous ranking of families determined by the particular combination of circumstances at any given time: the quantity of land they own, the specific occupations they practice, the success of their various enterprises, and so on.

It is apparent that the criteria that define strata must also differ in the two regions. Ownership of land is important in both places, and in both, large properties symbolize upper-class status. However, the role of land ownership in differentiating the lower class varies: in central Italy it distinguishes the highest category of the countryside from the lower ones, while in southern Italy it is only one of several criteria that together define rank.

Similarly, the kind of work one does is an indicator of class status in somewhat different ways in the two regions. In central Italy, the significant question (for the lower class) is whether or not one works the land. In the first place, such a distinction generally coincides with the contrast between townsman and countryman, perhaps the most critical line of differentiation in central Italy. Moreover, agriculturalists and nonagriculturalists form distinct and separate groups. Such a distinction would be difficult to make in the south, where the agricultural worker is likely to be simultaneously or successively a nonagricultural laborer as well. Here, the separation is more easily made between manual and nonmanual worker. Thus, whether or not one works with his hands emerges as the crucial status distinction within the diverse population of the Southern agro-town. In central Italy, where town and country divide the population, and where the commonfolk of the town are numerically few, this group includes not only manual workers but also white-collar workers, merchants, policemen, and so on. The mark of working with the hands becomes submerged by more critical differences.

A further contrast between the two regions is in the form of relationships between upper and lower classes. In central Italy, the agricultural organization provides the basis for personalized patronage relationships between the classes. On the one hand, there are potential patrons in the community, for the nucleus of the local upper class consists of landowners who are prosperous and who are concerned with local activities. On the other hand, the *mezzadria* system is conducive to patron-client ties. It involves landlord and peasant in regular contact and close association over a period of years, and it defines a series of mutual obligations between them, extending beyond the essential business of the farm. Since the landlord-peasant relationship is the dominant interclass tie in the central Italian community, it tends to become a model for relationships between the classes as wholes. Thus, many elite members of the community, including those who are not *mezzadria* landowners, assume patronage roles in relation to lower-class families. Typically, these patronage relationships cover a wide variety of functions, and they have considerable continuity in time.

In the Deep South, relationships between the elite and the lower class are more sporadic. In the first place, the upper class tends to avoid local involvements. Moreover, the agricultural system offers no model for inter-class relationships. Ties between landlords and cultivators require only brief and casual contact, and the particular combinations of individuals involved in such ties are constantly changing. Patronage relationships are formed on bases other than agricultural roles, but they tend to be less stable and more functionally specific than those of central Italy.

I turn now to some of the implications of these contrasts between the two regions. I am particularly interested in the issue of the political inca-pacity of the southern community, as opposed to the degree of activism found in central Italy. I am referring to the so-called amoral familism ethos of southern Italy—Banfield's thesis that people act only in the short-run material interest of their nuclear family (1958:85). It seems to me that this ethos is in fact a reflection of the absence of stable group alli-ances in the south and the temporary, contingent nature of political align-ments there. The complex of attitudes and behaviors summarized by the concept of amoral familism is alien to central Italy. In this area there are group political alliances that are stable over time. The reason lies in the fact that the population is divided into discrete socioeconomic strata and substrata. Each has interests peculiar to itself and divergent with respect to each other; many have, in fact, potentially opposing interests (as in the case of landlord and peasant, agriculturalist and nonagriculturalist, peasant proprietor and *mezzadro,* and so forth). Because families' identifications with particular substrata tend to be permanent, alignments continue over a period of time. Political conflicts of local origin revolve around the diver-gent interests of these categories, and issues introduced from outside the community are readily translated into the terms of local class interests.

Because substrata in central Italy are discrete and because their mem-berships have continuity, the divisions within a community correspond to equivalent divisions in other communities, and their equivalence is clearly recognized. Thus, local groupings can develop into organized class move-ments of whole regions. Historically, this has been the case. For example, the *mezzadri* and other categories of central Italy have played an active and quite militant part in the Italian labor movement since the late nine-teenth century. This pattern is important also in the contemporary political situation. Today, national political parties phrase their bids for support in terms of the local divisions, and in fact, voting patterns in the rural com-munities conform fairly closely to these lines.

In contrast, political behavior in southern Italy is related to the absence of discrete substrata with interests distinctive to themselves and opposed to those of others. Here, political alignments cannot follow distinct categorical lines. Rather, they form about particular issues or about particular powerful persons. Such alliances are conditional, and they are shifting; when new issues arise or when other powers are involved, realignments readily occur. Moreover, under these circumstances, it is difficult for a common identification to be made among persons of equivalent position in different communities. Affiliations form locally, on local issues, and they are not easily extended to a regional level or beyond. For these reasons, voting patterns of southern communities often appear erratic to the observer. They are, in fact, quite explicable, although it is essential to recognize that they reflect the flexibility of political alliances, their fluidity over time, and the priority of local terms.

For the same reasons, the Deep South has not historically participated in organized class movements to any great extent. As others have pointed out, the traditional reaction to economic difficulty in the Deep South has never been class-based militancy, but rather individualistic and familistic strategies, above all migration (e.g., MacDonald and MacDonald 1964b: 115). In those instances where migration was followed by return, its result was to further not class-oriented purposes but rather more private ones—to raise the nuclear family a few notches on the local rank scale.

Another aspect of the southern syndrome of political incapacity is the difficulty of initiating or sustaining formal groups or organized community activity. In central Italy, there is a degree of formal organization in community life, largely as a result of the class structure. Of primary significance is the nature of the local upper class and the quality of their relationships with the lower class. The local elite in central Italy are actively identified with the agricultural community; yet, their values and life style are those of the city. They resolve the dilemma by attempting to re-create in the local community the social activity and elegance of urban life. At the same time, their role is one of patronage—not only toward their own clients, but often, by extension, toward the community as a whole. Partly in the effort to bring "civilization" to their rural outposts and partly in the tradition of patronage, members of this class initiate, lead, and support various community associations and activities. There are a number of voluntary organizations that are initiated and maintained at the community level by the local upper class—bands, dramatic societies, recreational clubs, charity organizations, and so forth. In addition, there are recurrent events in the ceremonial cycle that represent a considerable degree of formally organized activity; here too, initiative and economic support stem from the local elite.

In recent years, formal associations of extralocal origin have been introduced into the rural communities. The majority of these are national organizations focusing around class or special-category interests—labor unions, political-party groups, and the like. These associations have been relatively successful at the local level in central Italy. The class structure, marked by discrete divisions each with fairly uniform interests, lends support to such groups.

In contrast, the Deep South lacks both those elements that are the bases of community organization in central Italy: a leadership group and stable substrata. The elite members of the community are dissociated from local affairs; moreover, patronage traditions offer no impetus for organized community activity, for patronage consists of only temporary ties with individual clients. To the extent that there is formal organization in the southern community, it is initiated from the outside, principally from the national political organizations and the Church. However, because lower-class persons have nonexclusive, overlapping socioeconomic interests, few can readily identify with national associations oriented to special interest groups. Church sponsorship is somewhat more effective in achieving a limited degree of formal organization.

I have several times referred to the central place of urbanity among the criteria of Italian stratification systems and in the values system as a whole. In both central and southern Italy, the city is ultimately the source of all that is most highly prized; in fact, "civilization" means "citified." In both regions, conformity to urban patterns serves as an external measure—perhaps the single most useful measure—of one's position among the social classes. However, the particular meaning that urban values have and the way in which they operate in the stratification system vary in the two regions.

Initially, it is useful to distinguish between having urban values and acting them out. Urbanity may be valued by all, as indeed it is throughout Italy, yet not all persons may live in urban-like ways. One of the striking features of the Mediterranean world is that the city provides models for even the smallest settlements. The towns and nucleated villages of central Italy and the agro-towns of southern Italy in many ways replicate in miniature the culture patterns of the city. Yet there is a difference. In the southern community, all persons—elite, petty landowner, and landless cultivator alike—play out the major part of their lives in the piazza, the marketplace, the café, in short, in an urban-like setting. Even those of the lowest ranks are directly involved in town life, although, of course, not in all aspects of it. In central Italy, the city stops at the village walls. The cultivators, a major part of the population, live beyond the walls and are outsiders in the nucleated center. They come in to the village or town mainly on special occasions, and, even then, they do not fully belong there. Their activity and their interest focus on their farms and on the circle of farms surrounding their own. Nevertheless, they know of urban life indirectly and recognize its value, through their close tie with the local upper class. In fact, the patronage relationship in central Italy may be viewed as a mode of communicating values from one class to the other while preserving the enactment of those values to the upper class.

Another significant aspect of urbanity as part of a values system is the question of whether values flow in one direction only—that is, from the city to the countryside—or whether there is a reverse flow as well. Or to put it somewhat differently, is the flow of values exclusively downward through the class structure, or is there a return flow of values upward? Here again, the two regions of Italy contrast. In the South, all things of value to the society as a whole originate in the city; as is often said, southern Italy lacks a soil-bound tradition. (The one value of true lower-class origin is that of the ambivalent *la miseria* itself—which, in its positive aspect, pertains to the common human bond among all those who live in poverty. Yet it cannot be said that this value is shared by the upper class.) In central Italy, however, there is a two-way flow. Although urban values have priority, there are others that stem from the countryside, from both lower and upper strata of the rural zones. The land and the round of life of the peasants are the focus of a distinctive folk tradition, which is appreciated and romanticized by people of the higher strata and of the city. Furthermore, the landlord class contributes to the total society its own values and traditions, in which the land, the peasants, and the sojourns in the country all figure importantly.

The significance of urban values differs in still another way in the two regions, namely in their relation to social mobility. The course of social mobility is somewhat different in central and southern Italy. In central Italy, upward mobility through the substrata of the lower class requires the discarding of former roles and attributes and the assumption of new ones: the *mezzadro's* hired hand takes on a *mezzadria* contract of his own, the *mezzadro* terminates his contract and purchases his own farm, the country-dwelling peasant acquires a nonagricultural occupation and moves into the village. Each step involves, in addition to a change of roles, the acquiring of somewhat different life styles. Because of the sharp demarcation between town and country, those styles that represent *civiltà*—the "civilized" life—are the hallmark of the townsman. It is only at the higher levels of the lower class that they become attainable goals and thus personal aspirations. At this point, the upwardly mobile countryman must bridge the gap to urbanity, a process that requires the learning of patterns that are familiar but unpracticed.

In the Deep South, mobility within the lower class consists of moves along a continuous rank scale. Such moves may result from some advance in any or several of the dimensions that together determine rank: the acquisition of a little more land, a more favorable land-tenure contract, more steady wage work, moderate success in a commercial venture, and so on. Old roles need not be abandoned and new ones assumed; rather, familiar roles and attributes are improved or recombined. Among the attributes that can be bettered by degree are the urbane styles of living, for the basic requirement of "civilized" life, residence in town, is a given. Thus, each small family attempts—within its own possibilities—to emulate ever more closely the urbane, "civilized" ideals of the society. The petty peasant proprietor may achieve a degree of success by becoming an inactive rentier. For many, the best opportunities are in emigration and return. I am not suggesting that upward mobility is easier or more common here than in central Italy. What is significant is that for the cultivators of the south, urban values are more attainable and more readily become personal goals. I am suggesting that it is not enough to know that Mediterranean agriculturalists look to the city for their values. It is equally important to know to what extent they adopt such values as aspirations and what is involved in the process of incorporating them into their behavior patterns.

In contrasting the two regions of Italy, I have in fact been proposing some ways of looking at different kinds of peasant societies, suggesting some of the questions that I think we ought to ask about stratification in such societies. The comparison of adjacent areas within a single cultural tradition has made it easier to focus on what I consider the central issue— the functional interdependencies between productive arrangements and social forms. Yet the same questions might be revealing for the comparative analysis of peasant societies in other times and places.

NOTES

1. Field work was carried out in a rural community in Umbria, from August 1960 through September 1961, with the aid of a National Institute of Mental Health fellowship (MF-11,068) and grant (M-3720). The discussion of southern Italy is based on diverse sources in the historical, agrarian-economic, and anthropological literature (see Silverman 1968).

2. MacDonald and MacDonald (1964a; 1964b) have used this term to refer to continental southern Italy exclusive of the compartment of Apulia and the Naples conurbation. This definition of the area differs slightly from mine.

REFERENCES

Arensberg, Conrad M. (1963) "The Old World Peoples: The Places of European Cultures in World Ethnography," *Anthropological Quarterly* 36:75–99.

Banfield, Edward C. (1958) *The Moral Basis of a Backward Society.* Glencoe, Ill.

Barber, Bernard (1957) *Social Stratification.* New York.

Istituto Nazionale Di Economia Agraria [INEA] (1956) *La Distribuzione della Proprietà in Italia: Relazione Generale,* ed. Giuseppe Medici, vol. 1. Rome.

MacDonald, John S., and Leatrice MacDonald (1964a) "A Simple Institutional Framework for the Analysis of Agricultural Development Potential," *Economic Development and Cultural Change* 12:368–76.

———— (1964b) "Institutional Economics and Rural Development: Two Italian Types," *Human Organization* 23:113–18.

Medici, Giuseppe (1951) *I Tipi d'impresa nell'Agricoltura Italiana.* Rome.

Redfield, Robert (1956) *Peasant Society and Culture.* Chicago.

Serpieri, Arrigo (1947) *La Struttura Sociale dell'Agricoltura Italiana.* Rome.

Silverman, Sydel (1968) "Agricultural Organization, Social Structure, and Values in Italy: Amoral Familism Reconsidered," *American Anthropologist* 70:1–20.

Chapter 10/ Aidan W. Southall

Stratification in Africa

Traditional Africa: Stateless Societies and Ritual Differentiation

In Africa, as in other comparably great regions of the world, we are confronted with great cultural diversity. However, the effective diversity in Africa is perhaps greater than anywhere else at the present time. Before they were cut short by the nineteenth-century onslaught of the Western imperial powers, the indigenous societies and autonomous polities of Africa had to be counted in the thousands. These very numerous indigenous traditional systems remain potently influential today, despite the great transformation which has occurred and despite the fact that they are now incorporated in the much larger, and fewer—yet still rather numerous—new states of Africa. These states number over three dozen. Given the vast number of the traditional societies of yesterday, which are still an important factor, and the relatively great numbers of new states in which they have been incorporated, Africa would seem to offer a unique laboratory of social stratification, both in the number and variety of traditional systems and in the number of contemporary experiments being conducted to incorporate them in larger entities, necessarily involving the evolution of new and all-embracing stratification systems in each new state. It must be added that the experiment is still proceeding and that the new stratification systems have not crystallized sufficiently to be very adequately studied.

231

The consideration of Sub-Saharan Africa separately from the north of the continent is coming increasingly to be recognized as an anomaly. We shall abide by it, however, having regard to the fact that Muslim countries are dealt with in other chapters, and the North African countries are Muslim in a sense in which the Sub-Saharan countries are not, despite the presence of millions of Muslims in them. Since the issue of pluralism in stratification is dealt with elsewhere, we shall also avoid direct confrontation with it, although it is at least a residual factor in most African countries.

There are thus two major contributions which the study of Africa should make to a consideration of social stratification. One, already mentioned, is the laboratory situation provided by many new national systems of stratification coming into being at the same time in diverse circumstances. The other is the example, offered in the older traditional societies of Africa, of almost the complete range of stratification systems historically known to man. Every continent has, at one end of the scale, modern nations and, at the other, some remnants of hunting and collecting peoples, but Africa demonstrates a unique degree of typological continuity from one extreme to the other. Furthermore, the documentation of this range by social anthropology is more representative than in any other region.

Since we cannot attempt any comprehensive survey of stratification in traditional African societies, we shall have to concentrate on those features which seem most interesting and important for a general theory of social stratification. The most important general issue which emerges is the relation of stratification systems to the symbolic representation and ritual co-ordination of society. By a strange paradox this issue may be most important at either pole: in the very small-scale traditional societies where political specialization is slight and ritual co-ordination is certainly wider in scope, and then in modern mass societies where the politico-economic basis of stratification, having been fully worked out and recognized, is no longer acceptable and raises problems of legitimacy and consensus. It is also at the two opposite poles that the question of egalitarianism is present. Nor is this the only aspect of the deepening analogy between the one pole and the other. Political scientists, disillusioned with idealist philosophy, with the straitjacket of the state and the limitations of conventional institutional analysis, are turning to the social anthropology of stateless societies for inspiration in conceptualizing international and supranational contemporary political behavior (Barkun 1964). Computer programmers

looking for models of social systems are taking stateless segmentary societies as classical instances of abiding significance. We therefore feel justified
in looking at the foreshadowing of stratification in stateless societies, not
just for the sake of comparative coverage or of the history of human society, but actually for the unsuspected light which it may ultimately throw
upon our own contemporary problems of stratification.

The distinction between states and acephalous or stateless societies
(Southall 1968) is familiar and will be taken for granted in this discussion.
I have also argued for the empirical importance, in terms of sheer frequency, of intermediate forms which I call segmentary states (Southall
1956). This category will also be used here. But the political dimension is,
of course, not the only significant one. There is a general correlation
between the level of technology, habitat, economy, and society. The most
straightforward distinctions which can be made briefly, for the sake of
their relevance to questions of stratification, are the time-honored ones
between hunting and gathering peoples, pastoralists, and agriculturalists.
None of these compartments are watertight; possible subdivisions are
legion. To many agriculturalists hunting is of extreme importance. Most
pastoralists practice some agriculture. Agriculturalists vary enormously in
productivity, and many are also profoundly attached to pastoralism. Nonetheless, hunting and gathering peoples and pastoralists are characteristically
stateless, and the pastoral societies include some extensive segmentary
systems. Agriculturalists also include many stateless peoples as well as
members of the segmentary states, but these are, on the whole, the least
sedentary and least productive agricultural economies. The most sedentary
and productive economies, combining relatively favorable natural resources
and relatively advanced technologies, include the largest mobilized surpluses, the greatest concentrations of population, the most specialized
political structure, and the most elaborate stratification.

Bearing these preliminary and ultimately unsatisfactory generalities in
mind, we may proceed to illustrate their main dimensions.

From the anthropological point of view it is necessary to consider
stratification as one form of that elusive dual organization which has been
most recently and brilliantly treated by Lévi-Strauss (1963:132). This
may not seem so farfetched if we remember that all stratification theory
starts from the proposition that it is an evaluation of higher and lower,
that "men in society are divided by Marx into two strata" and that the
Marxist emphasis "contributed one of the essential foundations for all sub-

sequent stratification theory" (B. Barber 1968:289). Neo-Marxist writers continue to stress the dual, two-faced, or dichotomous aspect of society not only in the perspective of actual or potential conflict, but in the images of society held by the masses of the people. They argue further that this is true of the most advanced industrial societies, whether capitalist or communist (Dahrendorf 1959). Of course, it is also rightly argued that a mere dichotomy is much too crude a term to cope with the empirical realities of complex stratification, but we must retain it as the fundamental starting point. It is essential simultaneously to keep track of stratification at the dimension of symbolic representations or "images of society," as Western sociologists frequently put it, and the dimensions of social action and institutional structure. Both are equally empirical in their dependence upon verifiable behavioral data, verbal or otherwise. Dual symbolic representations frequently stand for much more complex relationships, just as the actual confrontations of social conflict ultimately align the parties dichotomously, although they comprise much more complex coalitions of sectional interests. Lévi-Strauss remarks of the Winnebago that "they have an apparently diametric dualism of 'upper' and 'lower,' which masks imperfectly a system with three poles. The upper might be represented by one pole—the sky—while the lower must have two poles—earth and water" (1963:153). This diametric dualism, resting at the same time on three poles, represents not only the relation of cosmic symbols but also kinship and marriage arrangements, political structure, and the actual residential arrangements of the Winnebago village. So also Dahrendorf, in speaking of the Western democracies, remarks that the chief of government in many contexts represents his country as a whole and expresses the unity and integration of a nation, yet in other contexts he represents only the majority party and is an exponent of sectional interests (1959:169–70). Again, there is a dichotomy with three poles. In fact, this paradigm turns out to have very far-reaching implications.

Although this argument deserves further exploration at a general level, we must return to Africa. It is important to resist reading dualism into everything and reducing it to banality. It is not merely its pervasiveness which is significant but rather the extent to which there is a valid structure of dualities linking various levels and modes of thought and action into a coherent whole. We shall endeavor to illustrate the extent to which this is true for hunters and gatherers, pastoralists, and agriculturalists and for stateless societies, segmentary states, and centralized states of varying degrees of complexity. We only suggest that this is very widespread; the data would not as yet permit any consideration of its universality for any particular type of social system.

The paradigm in which sets of binary oppositions mask asymmetrical ternary oppositions is relevant to the theory of social stratification in that it is found not only at the symbolic level of cosmology, myth, and ritual but also in the relations of groups and of leadership within groups. Leadership at its simplest leads on to social stratification. There can be no leadership without stratification in its simplest form of an evaluation of higher and lower positions.

Hunting and gathering peoples in Africa are best represented by the Bushmen and the Pygmies. Among the *!Kung* Bushmen there is a marked dualism in religious belief, which is less certainly expressed in dominant social roles. The *!Kung* believe in a greater and a lesser divinity; the greater created the lesser, as well as the world of man and nature, and yet in a shadowy way is held to have been once human himself. On the other hand, the greater divinity is remote from men and usually sends the lesser as his emissary. Both have seven identical names, but only the greater one also has a human name. The name by which the lesser is usually known (although it is also an attribute of the greater) signifies in some closely related cultures "the destroyer and the black chief, who sends death, disease and misfortune" (Marshall 1965:270), but among the *!Kung* this is less clear-cut. Nevertheless, the name of the lesser appears closely linked to the term for the spirits of the dead, who—as the frequent channel of communication between the greater divinity and human beings—seem very similar to the lesser divinity itself. (It should be remarked that, among a number of African and other peoples as well, the concept of divinity comes very close to an identity with the concept of the collective ancestor spirits.) Two important specialized roles seem to exist among the *!Kung:* the headman and the medicine-man. The headman is the unique leader of the band, whereas anyone can be a medicine-man and evidently many are. Leadership as headman confers no rewards except the right of first choice to fireplace and camp site after the site for the whole band has been selected. The leader "carries his own load and is as thin as the rest" (Marshall 1965:267). The leader has the courage to stand out and assume the burden of responsibility. Many other stateless societies at the hunting and gathering level stress leadership as the recognition of physical or moral prowess voluntarily practiced and voluntarily recognized. The duties and obligations seem almost heavier than the rights and rewards, unless a high valuation is put upon the mere position of superordination itself. This is surely significant. The medicine-men cure sickness through communal singing and dancing, ritually drawing evil and sickness out of the congregation into themselves and releasing it through trance. The medicine-men commonly "see" the lesser divinity and thus seem closely linked to him, although only the very greatest of medicine-men have ever seen the greater divinity. The headman's acknowledged dominance seems to be the only analogy in Bushman society to the cosmic dominance of the greater divinity, but this is not made explicit. In these two roles we have elementary approximations of political and ritual leadership, respectively.

The duality which dominates the lives of the Mbuti Pygmies is that between their own forest and the Negro villages with which they are in varying degrees of ambivalent symbiosis (Turnbull 1959:58). The forest stands for the natural, the normal, and the good, the place of peace, harmony, and plenty. The village stands for the supernatural and for evil and trickery. The "two kinds of individual fitted for special responsibilities" (Turnbull 1965:303–04) would appear to be quite clearly, even if not explicitly, related to this duality. One is the young unmarried man who is a great hunter and also a clown, who can mediate disputes by ridicule or even, through his fooling, take them upon himself for resolution. Clearly he is maintaining the ideal norms of the forest. The other specialization is that of headman in relation to the Negro village. He should be a past master of trickery, willing to be subservient to Negro villagers because he can laugh it off in the forest yet with a taste for village life and food, for its palm wine, tobacco, and hemp (marijuana). These two roles have obvious points in common and can even be played by the same individual, but they belong to two distinct yet overlapping worlds.

The pastoral Dinka, with their social system already on a much larger scale than those of Bushmen or Pygmies, display a set of binary oppositions which are much more explicit, more multi-faceted, and quite clearcut at both the mythological and sociological levels (Lienhardt 1961). All Dinka descent groups belong either to "fishing spear" or to "war spear" clans. The former are clearly senior and supply the figureheads and leaders of territorial groups. Their leadership is essentially ritual and priestly. But all territorial groups contain a majority of persons descended from "war spear" lineages, and they provide leaders in time of war. All persons and groups are thus aligned to one of two essentially complementary functions. What may be regarded as the more clearly political function of the war leaders is definitely subordinate in rank to the predominantly ritual function of the "fishing spear" priests, and all ordinary members of war spear and fishing spear clans share the same relative ranking vis-à-vis one another. The superordination of the fishing spear "moiety" of the society is further emphasized at the mythological level, for the whole symbolic order of Dinka society is originally derived from the primeval first "master of the fishing spear." Every major division of the Dinka people is regarded as belonging to its central fishing spear subclan. There is at least as much justification for referring to these two categories of Dinka, by analogy, as aristocrats or nobles and commoners as there is in the case of their Nuer neighbors. Of the latter Evans-Pritchard (1940:215) has written:

We have called them aristocrats, but do not wish to imply that Nuer regard them as of superior rank, for the idea of a man lording it over others is repugnant to them. The aristocrats have prestige rather than rank and influence rather than power. If you are an aristocrat of the tribe in which you live, you are more than a simple tribesman. You are one of the owners of the country, its village sites, its pastures, its fishing pools and wells. Other people live there in virtue of marriage into your clan, adoption into your lineage, or of some other social tie. You are a leader of the tribe and the spear name of your clan is invoked when the tribe goes to war. Wherever there is an aristocrat in a village, the village clusters round him as a herd of cattle clusters round its bull.

Dichotomous complementary distinctions running through stateless societies have been widely reported in Africa, such as the Namoos and Talis of the Tallensi, Jopiny and Jodak of the Kenya Luo, or the numerous and cross-cutting symbolic dualisms of the age-organized Cushites and their Bantu and Eastern Nilotic neighbors. While the higher rank attaches to the most original group in the case of Dinka, Nuer, Kenya Luo and many more, this is not necessarily so. The higher-ranking Namoos among the Tallensi were later arrivals with the august aura of the Mamprusi state about them (Fortes 1945:39). Yet the essential complementarity is retained, for the well-being of the Tallensi could be assured only through the harmonious ritual co-operation of both Namoos and Talis (ibid.:108–14). Likewise, Alur nobles depend on more aboriginal groups for certain rituals.

Among the pervasively age-organized Cushites, Nilotes, and Bantu of North Eastern Africa, there is often a whole array of dualisms and multiple extensions of them which seem to reflect some profound dualistic tendency inherent in these cultures. Characteristically, there is the confrontation of adjacent age sets, age grades, and age generations. This may be rendered explicit in short- medium- and long-term cycles, but even when it is not explicit, it can still be detected as imbedded in the system. The confrontation of adjacent sets is another instance of a binary masking a ternary opposition, as in the case of the Masai, where junior warriors confront senior warriors, senior warriors confront junior elders, and junior elders confront senior elders, but in each case the junior party to the confrontation is backed against the group above by its allies in the group one higher still. The Masai have the further binary oppositions of the left and the right, of the red and black cattle, and of the Masai and Kikuyu "guilds." Such symbolic identifications, among the Masai and others, are sometimes passed on from father to son, sometimes alternate between father and son. That the dualism inherent in age organization is often part of a comprehensive ordering of the whole of human and natural experience is made particularly evident in the case of the Teso, where "the whole sphere of natural existence was methodically divided between the eight age-sets, so that each set had religious or ritual powers over a series of associated objects or activities" (Lawrance 1957:78–79). The Arusha express dualism in their families, lineages, clans, age groups, and territorial divisions, not so much as a philosophical principle as a means of structuring support, opposition, and neutrality in social life (Gulliver 1961).

We have so far been dealing with peoples who have usually been characterized, somewhat imprecisely, as essentially or even fiercely egalitarian. In large degree this is a cultural expression of their poverty in natural resources, exploited by limited technologies. Their supposed egalitarianism is further exemplified in the fact that they have no specialized full-time or hereditary political roles and often give the impression that they would not easily or willingly tolerate any. Yet the hunters and collectors have leadership roles, and the pastoralists, who are even more fiercely egalitarian in outlook, have radical dual distinctions of hereditary ritual rank. Our claim is that, partly because of their relative simplicity, all these peoples reveal—in the sense of their visibility as small-scale observable systems—important aspects of the nature and sources of stratification. All recognize moral evaluations of higher and lower positions, however unstable and informal, despite the lack of any sanctioned authority roles outside the domain of kinship.

Traditional Africa: Segmentary and Unitary States

We may pass on from here to systems which have hereditary roles of some political content yet are still dependent for their integration on elaborate sets of symbols frequently expressed in ritual practices. The Fipa of Southwestern Tanzania are a striking case. The intricate dualism is focused upon two groupings which tradition represents as of different ethnic origin. Once again, the earlier component is ritually senior while the later one is politically dominant. It is impossible to do justice to the extensive and delicate articulation of binary oppositions in a brief statement which can only list the main conceptual associations. The symbolic opposition between the earlier component, which is ritually senior but politically dependent and territorially inferior, and the later component, which is politically dominant and territorially superior but ritually junior (recalling the Dinka situation), is matched by an analogous set of binary discriminations focused upon the symbolism of head and loins respectively. The head is linked with the qualities of being senior, male, intellectual, light, few and weak, while loins are correspondingly linked with balanced opposite qualities of being junior, female, sexual, heavy, many and strong (Willis 1967:530). Once again, the issue that concerns us is the presence of clear evaluations of higher and lower, which are balanced in a complementary, alternating series, instead of in a hierarchy of superordination and subordination. Can this situation occur only in a highly ritualized system with a low level of political and economic differentiation? Furthermore, can such systems of binary discrimination, balancing complementary opposites at a conceptual level, which is also implemented by ritual participation, survive or have much significance where the rewards of the system of social stratification are manifestly unequal? How far can such inequality be compensated by intensity of participation?

The Alur, with their segmentary state, express dualism in their complementary attitudes towards chiefship and leadership (Southall 1956). With regard to his ultimate political sanctions, the Alur chief was described with admiration as a leopard or carnivorous beast which tears people to pieces, yet in his capacity as a sacred ritual personage he "cooled the country," guaranteed rain, fertility, harmony, and peace. The ambivalence towards prominent and dangerous roles was expressed in the fact that, when a group of commoners went to petition an Alur chief to give them one of his sons to live among them as a chieflet, the chief conventionally bade them to kidnap one of his sons for this purpose (ibid.:182). Among the closely related Acholi neighbors of the Alur an heir frequently exhibited fear and reluctance to succeed to the office of chief for which he was qualified by birth.

The mystical danger of leadership and political office is further expressed in the mysterious connection between power and witchcraft which is common among African peoples. For the Alur, witchcraft epitomizes the antisocial and the unspeakable horror which the thought of antisocial acts such as nudity, incest, necrophagy, and cannibalism inspire. In a number of African cultures such perverted acts have been found to be symbolically *inverted* (Middleton 1960:16, 236). Bohannan's analysis of Tiv witchcraft (1957:2–4) makes this particularly plain with its equivalence of "talent or witchcraft substance." For Tiv witchcraft is not only the unspeakable antisocial force which kills, sickens, and frustrates; it is also the indispensable source of authority which maintains order in society. The same point has been made for Nyakyusa, Thonga, and Azande (Wilson 1951:97). Power not only corrupts but it is dangerous; therefore, those born to wield it, or born capable of grasping it, need courage. They are afraid as well as fascinated, repelled as well as attracted, and the use of power arouses both horror and admiration. In Nyakyusa society not only is there an age dichotomy, with separate villages for the old and for the young, but every chiefdom is segmented into two in every generation. There is a certain corresponding dichotomy of ritual and political functions, with elders of the old village retaining the ritual duties while secular authority and warfare is handed over to the new young chiefs (Wilson 1951:31).

As there are two sides to authority, so also are there to subordination. The Okebo people, who lived among the Alur and, in addition to ordinary subsistence activities, served as ironworkers to Alur society (Southall 1956:173) were regarded as definitely socially inferior; yet they prided themselves on the indispensability of their contribution, arguing that Alur society would collapse without the hoes and weapons which they made.

In the Nyoro system, which positively values inequality and is ordered in a firmly established hierarchy of effectively sanctioned and differentially rewarded political offices, a very extensive set of binary oppositions also appears to exist (Needham 1967:447). It would seem, however, that there is no genuine balance, alternation, and complementation, as in the examples above; the left-hand set of qualities is uniformly inferior and pejorative, except for a few obscure anomalies (earth, hunting, sun). Most significant of all, mystical office is associated with the left, political rank with the right. Perhaps there is here a measure of the transition from ritual to political supremacy. However, in most African states the politico-ritual balance remained essentially ambivalent, often retaining the same contrived symbolic counterpoise of "ritual:senior::political:junior" as in the case of the Yoruba, where most of the great rulers were almost completely secluded after installation. The Alafin of Oyo appeared in public only three times a year at great festivals; the Awujale of Ijebu-Ode was never seen in public and was communicated with only through a screen. As a result a secular, political counterpart to these secluded figureheads tended to emerge. The Alafin was actually called "celestial chief" while his Bashorun (or head of the council of chiefs) was called "terrestrial chief" (Forde 1951:19–22). In Bunyoro the king and heaven belong to the right-hand classification, while the queen (presumably queen sister and queen mother) belonged to the left. In neighboring Buganda, the king, queen mother, and queen sister all shared the same supreme title of *Kabaka,* providing yet another case of dualistic asymmetry in the complementary balance of the one male against two female rulers.

The structure of kingship in Rwanda is described as "bipolar" (d'Hertefelt 1965:423) in the sense that "although the king was considered a sacred person, and played a role in the court rites, he was not a Pontifex Maximus nor a rainmaker" (ibid.). The Swazi are referred to as having a "dual monarchy" and " 'twin' rulers—mother and son" (Kuper 1965:499, 483). The Rwanda king's office was essentially political whereas "the most important—and probably the oldest—ritual offices were allocated to three *reges sacrorum;* these ritual kings, whose office was hereditary, governed freeholds and had drums and cyclical royal names" (ibid.). Note again the asymmetry in the polar balance of one political against three ritual figures. The reference to cyclical royal names is important, for in the kingdoms of both Rwanda and Burundi the kings bore a series of names which rotated in the same repeated sequence of four as the reigns passed. Two phases of the cycle prescribed the ideal behavior of warrior kings conducting military expeditions, while the other two phases called for peaceful reigns generating harmony and prosperity throughout the country. Here in this temporal polarity is another dimension of the ineluctable dualism in kingship. Another extremely widespread form which it takes in Africa is the presence of a hereditary political office, derived from conquest or from infiltration and assimilation, complemented by one or more hereditary ritual figures, supposedly representing the former owners of the country and often entitled "owners of the soil," whose ministrations are essential to the well-being of the whole community. Unfortunately, anthropologists have not always been very good at identifying common features of structure from one region to another, so that when we come across figures referred to as "War Chiefs" and "Peace Chiefs" among the Iroquois and other American Indians, the significance is missed.

Rwanda is the best-known example of caste stratification in Africa, although many of its neighbor states (Burundi, Buha, Bugufi, Rusubi, Karagwe, Ankole, Mpororo, Toro, Bunyoro) had essentially similar structures. In Rwanda, political power was concentrated in the hands of the king and the pastoral aristocracy (Tutsi), constituting only about 10 per cent of the population. The lower caste of agriculturalists (Hutu) formed the vast majority of the population, but the small minority of Twa potters, court jesters, and hunters were the lowest caste of all. These castes were distinguished by marked differences of physical type perpetuated by endogamy and by functional and ecological specialization on differing basic activities, and their relative positions were validated by ritual and belief. There was a pervasive "premise of inequality" (Maquet 1961). However, the cult of Ryangombe united all categories of society—Tutsi, Hutu and Twa—within it, while still clearly expressing their distinctness. More remarkably, the somewhat anomalous Rwanda clans each included members of all three castes, although the Tutsi, Hutu and Twa of a particular clan were each in separate lineages which did not intermarry. The caste state of Rwanda was maintained by an effectively monopolistic political and military hierarchy, but the ritual integration of society and the ritual element in the duality of kingship were strongly maintained. It was probably the breakdown of this integration and dualism, before the onslaught of Christian and secular belief, as well as the changed political and economic circumstances, which permitted the whole edifice to crumble so rapidly from 1959 to 1961.

Another very interesting expression of dualism, relevant to the theory of stratification, relates to the complementarity of overt rulers and secret societies, most notably manifest in West Africa where the Poro Society of Liberia, Sierra Leone, and other neighboring countries is best known, but also appearing in parts of the Congo and East Africa. Because these organizations are indeed secret, no adequate account of them has ever been given. Poro covers a very wide area and, because there is no evidence that it is completely unified, must be regarded as polycephalous. Poro offices "involve a fusion of secular and ritual roles" (Gibbs 1965:220), and some may have been hereditary. A Poro official could even depose a secular chief if he was of lower Poro rank (ibid.). The Poro council was said to be the court of highest appeal, "even higher than that of a political chief" (ibid.). The source of sanctions and authority in Poro was undoubtedly ritual. The supreme role consisted of a mask, a voice, distinctive music, and an incumbent elected by his high official peers. The mask is a repository of spirits—ancestral, animal, or totemic (ibid.; Harley 1950:3, 11, 43). The rule of secrecy and the collective decisions of the high officials were ruthlessly enforced by infliction of the death penalty. The Poro hierarchy certainly involved achieved as well as ascribed elements. Entry was only by long series of initiation schools, held in the bush with the utmost secrecy, firmly implanting the ongoing collective authority of the organization through the infliction of physical pain and mystical terror. The ultimate definition is uncompromisingly ritual and supernatural, yet it sanctioned a political order extending far beyond the jurisdiction of any secular chief or even of a single cultural or linguistic community. It provided the dominant system of rank and stratification; yet there was also a hierarchy of secular chiefs, at the three levels of paramount, district, and town (Gibbs 1965:216–17), elected by their peers from among those who had won prominence in those characteristically African ways of acquiring wealth and many wives and children (all closely interlocking factors), dispensing hospitality and largesse, and hence commanding the services of a large body of loyal clients, thus demonstrating the admired ability to manage and manipulate successfully the relationships of men and women. Here again achievement occupies an important place. This secular hierarchy of chiefs exercised control and authority over much of the ordinary day-to-day life of society but only within the limits of obedience and subordination to the ultimate rules and sanctions of Poro, between whose official hierarchy and that of the secular chiefs there was an important but unknown degree of overlap in incumbency. "Political power and Poro power tend to be lodged in the hands of the same individuals, and it is not unlikely that chiefs utilize Poro mechanisms to underscore their political decisions" (Gibbs 1965:221).

Not only, then, were large areas of Africa subject to a kind of asym-

metrical dyarchy, or "polycephalous associational state" as Gibbs chooses
to call it (1965:216), but in the superordinate system of the Poro there
was a fundamental dualism, comparable to those we have found in other
systems, with the ritual aspect taking precedence over the political. "One
of the most crucial attributes of Poro officials" was "their dual sacred-
secular role . . . they are both chiefs and priests, and control material and
non-material affairs" (221).

We have so far dealt with a few straightforward themes: the relation
between polarities and dualisms in the ritual and political sources of leadership, power and rank; at the level of belief (in myth and symbol), in the
formal systems of rank and stratification, and in the empirical pattern of
social interaction. These have been related to broad contrasts in the territorial and numerical size of African societies and their associated levels of
complexity in role differentiation and technology. We must now introduce
further distinctions of status, together with the fundamental question as
to whether all such distinctions are consistently integrated and ordered in a
single hierarchy, a unified overall system. The case of the Hausa illustrates
this very well.

The numerous Hausa states were ruled by emirs, each with a subordinate, hierarchical bureaucracy at such levels as district, village, and ward.
At all levels a strong emphasis on hereditary occupational status was combined with considerable scope for achievement. The emirs belonged to
hereditary royal houses, but several competing houses, or several lineages,
were able to secure the supreme office in some alternating sequence, so
that the effective field of recruitment for the ruler was rather wide. The
heads of districts and smaller subdivisions—although some were hereditary
fiefs—were usually appointed from above, yet qualified by hereditary
status combined with successful achievement.

At all levels there was a great clustering of titles, not only in the
administrative field but in the organizations which structured most specialized occupations, whether of high or low status. Thus even an incomplete list of traditional male occupations specifies hunters, fishers, builders,
thatchers, butchers, tanners, leatherworkers, saddlers, weavers, dyers,
woodworkers, blacksmiths, brass- and silversmiths, calabash-workers, potters, drummers, various musicians, praise-singers, barber-surgeons, tailors,
embroiderers, washermen, porters, commission agents, traders of many
kinds, makers of sweetmeats, baskets, and mats, tobacco grinders, herbal-
ists, clerics, officials, rulers (Smith 1965:124–25). Most of these were also

farmers except for the few at the top of the hierarchy. Most were also of low status, such as butchers and smiths, yet the Head Butcher or Head Smith was obviously a personage of some importance and such offices existed not only at the capital for the whole state but were repeated at every local headquarters of the lower levels of the hierarchy.

Hausa ordered their view of society by various dichotomies, such as rulers and ruled, nobles and commoners, Fulani and Hausa (ethnic groups). These pairs did not coincide although they did overlap considerably. But "the most appropriate model of Hausa stratification is that based on occupational class" (Smith 1965:139). This, however, consists of convenient approximations since there are many cross-cutting hierarchies and divergent roles can even be played by the same individuals. Sometimes the rulers and officials, the learned Koranic scholars, and the more successful traders are viewed together as a composite upper class, while the majority of farmers, traders and craftsmen form a middle class and certain definitely low-ranking occupations, together with the poor farmers, make up the lower class (Smith 1959:249; 1965:139). But there are many anomalies, of which the most striking is the position of slaves.

In some Hausa states half the population may have been slaves, in others less than a quarter (Smith 1959:242). While it may be presumed that they occupied many of the lowest positions in society, they could also occupy almost the highest; only the post of the ruler himself seems to have been absolutely barred to them. In 1906 a new chief of Daura "was selected and installed by the royal slaves without any free officials being consulted" and, "during the last century, the slave officials were sufficiently powerful to have chiefs dismissed and appointed as they pleased" (Smith 1959:242). Slaves themselves could also own slaves. One is irresistibly reminded of the Janissaries and Mamluks of Turkey and Egypt, but the Janissaries, although of captive origin, were actually freed. This is the universal problem of protecting the office of supreme power from the constant threat of qualified rivals.[1] Democratically elected offices should, in this sense, be the most secure since, with an elective presidency, it is in principle impossible for any rival to succeed unless he can contrive to get himself qualified by election. In Hausa Zaria, Fulani rulers "appointed slave generals to command standing armies, as much through fear of internal revolt as for defense against invaders" (Smith 1959:242). Thus hardly any correlation existed between slavery and occupational status.

The occupational status model in the Hausa case is somewhat misleading since it "owes its currency to the fact that it incorporates such ascriptive factors as descent and ethnicity" (Smith 1959:251). It also distinguishes sharply between status and prestige, leading Smith to argue that "the tendency to equate status and prestige in complex modern societies, such as Britain or the U.S.A., may perhaps indicate the lack of general consensus for any simple positional model which may serve as a general guide to social behaviour" (ibid.). He suggests that comprehensive systems of social classes or stratification, "such as Lloyd Warner seeks in America and Talcott Parsons claims to be universal," require the very special conditions of "legal and political equality of the sexes, bilateral kinship, lifelong monogamy, neolocal family organization, high rates of occupational mobility, and the dominance of one or other of the current status variables" (ibid.).

Although Hausa societies lie at the upper end of the range of complexity found in traditional Africa, they are certainly not unrepresentative for the purposes of this analysis. Many millions of Yoruba, Akan, and other West African peoples enjoyed institutions with many of the same features: the combination of ascription and achievement, descent and election in succession to office; multiplicity of interlocking institutions, diversity of specialized craft and occupational roles, great proliferation of titles, and in some cases the use of slaves in positions of importance.

Hausa slaves could themselves own slaves, as well as employing free servants. Their children were both slave and free, according to type of union and relative status of spouses. Second-generation slaves were usually Muslims and could not be violently punished by their owners or sold. It was much the same in Bornu to the northeast and Nupe to the southwest. Nupe slaves were also important at court; they could be landowners; they were employed in crafts such as glassworking. But the status converges with that of whole conquered tribal communities who were simply rural subjects of the Nupe state (Nadel 1947:197–98, 278). Among the Yoruba most slaves were farm laborers. They were, as elsewhere, usually of captive, criminal, or debtor origin. They could always redeem themselves, or be set free, but without this their children were still slaves; they could be sold or even sacrificed[2] (Forde 1951:26). However, the children of slave women by their masters were free and had full rights as heirs. With minor variations of detail, much the same obtained in many other African states, such as the Zande, Mangbetu, Buganda, Bunyoro, and Kongo kingdoms.

Slavery and Stratification

The problem of slave and serf in relation to stratification is, however, of much wider relevance in Africa. Only the smallest and simplest African societies, lacked any concept of serf or slave. Naturally, these included the hunters and collectors and some of the stateless societies on an agricultural or pastoral base. In some cases the institution of unfree status is a very ancient one; in others it is due to the penetration of Arab and European slave trade, and in still others it owes something to the influence of both.

However, the Ituri Pygmies were themselves regarded as serfs by the Bantu in neighboring villages, and some self-recognition of this status clearly existed, although the more independent Pygmy bands, such as those studied by Turnbull, are said to have played along with the idea as an absurdity from which they could profit (Turnbull 1965:294). Similarly, many Bushmen became serfs to Bantu Tswana, and many remnants of hunting and collecting peoples in eastern and northeastern Africa remained in part independent and in part subject to agricultural or pastoral neighbors in some complementary symbiotic relationship. This is clearly part of the early history of ethnic stratification in Africa. We have seen that the Twa in Rwanda were also, in effect, serfs of the Tutsi and clowned for them as the Pygmies did for the forest Negroes.

Among many East African peoples, metal workers formed an endogamous, low caste of apparently distinct ethnic origin, although elsewhere, as in the Congo, this occupation had very high status. There is often some ambiguity in the acceptance by a low status group of various restrictions which symbolize their low status to the rest of society while they themselves may regard their special functions (such as ironworking or hunting) as superior to those of the supposedly higher status groups (as we noted in the case of the Okebo). Such ethnically and functionally based status stratification is found even in some stateless societies, such as those of the Nilo-Hamites.

The personal serfdom and slavery of traditional Africa derives mainly from the capture of foreigners or the punishment of criminals. This implies some development of specialized political institutions, although this may be at quite a simple, small-scale level. The more elaborate forms of servitude are certainly associated with the more complex states and in some cases, such as the Hausa, may also reflect the influence of Islamic practices. In the smaller scale societies the first generation captive was certainly in servitude, although often of a fairly humane, domestic kind. In subsequent generations their status approximated more and more closely that of their masters. In many societies slaves were slain and buried with the ruler, but often this was also the privilege of high status persons.

The case of the Nuer makes this very plain: "Nuer scorn Dinka and persistently raid them" and "persons of Dinka descent form probably at least half the population of most (Nuer) tribes" (Evans-Pritchard 1940: 221). These are captives and immigrants whose children are adopted and incorporated into Nuer lineages. *Jaang,* the Nuer name for the Dinka, can be used for any people whom the Nuer habitually raid and take captive, but to call an already incorporated Dinka *Jaang* is an insult which his own family of adoption would fight to avenge. There are three distinct categories of social rank among the Nuer: *Dil* ("aristocrat"), meaning a member of a landholding lineage who lives within its territory; *Rul* ("stranger"), a Nuer outside his home territory; and *Jaang,* an incorporated person of ultimately foreign origin, nearly always Dinka. The disabilities of *Jaang* are few and situational, mainly of a ritual kind. The basic owner-settler distinction is extremely widespread, even in stateless societies, but particularly in the context of land rights. It is perhaps the most fundamental category of incipient stratification (Southall 1968). The more "kin bound" a society is—as stateless societies usually must be—the more fully strangers and captives have to be incorporated and the fewer their practical disabilities.

In the absence of complementary functions of some advantage to both parties, it is only with a degree of political centralization that the status of captives or serfs can be effectively maintained in practical and material as opposed to ritual and ceremonial affairs. This is the kernel of truth in the otherwise misleading Marxist-evolutionist hypothesis on slavery. In many African hereditary chiefdoms also the overlapping royal-commoner and commoner-foreigner distinctions give rise to two, sometimes three social categories, as among the Tswana (Schapera 1955:31). In the huge expansion and migration of the Ngoni peoples from Natal to the shores of Lake Victoria, two thousand miles to the north, the basic issues of conquest and the incorporation of captives were not essentially different but were on a numerical and territorial scale unprecedentedly vast (Barnes 1954:chaps. I and II). Even among the Suku, in the outlying areas of the Kongo state but too far east to be affected by Portuguese and too far west for Arab slaving (Kopytoff 1965:458), it is argued that persistent thieves and adulterers who were sold, or children and adolescents who were given in compensation for homicide, were usually adopted into the lineage community and were not even really domestic slaves, let alone a distinct class. Thus even in hereditary kingdoms the vertical distinctions of lineage may still override incipient horizontal divisions.

Not only was slavery axiomatically associated more with autocratic and hierarchic societies, but, especially when the influence of foreign slavers began to be felt, there was a certain polarization between the powerful states—which joined in the game and further increased their power and their stratification—and the stateless societies which formed their chief prey. In many cases, involvement in slave trading itself led to concentration of power and state formation where none had been before. The early phases are lost in obscurity. The mysterious Jagas were connected with the founding of many important ruling dynasties throughout the whole vast area from beyond the Congo River in the north to the southern borders of Angola (Edwards 1962:1–5; Vansina 1968:180). The Jagas assimilated captives in thousands but put to death their own children to avoid handicaps on the march (again echoing the Janissaries). Andrew Battell reported that, in the Jaga camp where he lived at the beginning of the seventeenth century, of the sixteen thousand people only twelve men and fourteen or fifteen women were original Jaga (Vansina 1968:67). The slave trade absolutely dominated political, social, and cultural developments in this region for nearly three hundred years, so it is quite impossible to speak of traditional African stratification. Kings' armies came to depend entirely on slaves. But slaves who were pressed too hard could escape to a rival ruler. Not being free, they could not be taxed, and freemen were so oppressed that many societies became polarized into the exploiting nobles on the one hand and the slaves on the other, with ordinary freemen squeezed almost out of existence. Power and status depended on the number of slaves owned. Domestic slaves were distinguished from those for export, yet the whole scheme of things was ultimately geared to the latter.

In Angola the Portuguese councils of Luanda, Masangano, and Benguela pressed the governors to make war for slaves. The governors in turn pressed the captains of local regions, who themselves pressed the local chiefs, who depended upon them for their share in the gains, and "Angola was sheer terror" (Vansina 1968:146–47).

On the East African coast neither Arab nor European slaving became firmly established very far inland until the middle of the nineteenth century. The West African coast was badly affected, but in the powerful states further inland, where slavery was a long established custom, as we have seen, it was not to such an extent the driving force of whole societies. As for the acephalous peoples within reach of the coast, some were mainly preyed upon and decimated, while others endeavored to turn slaving to their advantage and were quite transformed in the process. Thus new polities came into being with centralized institutions and stratification based primarily upon the slave trade and the arms traffic which was its complement. The dramatic increase of political power generated by the first appearance of firearms and the powerful motive to expand it which the slave trade provided were a potent source of new and more stratified societies. "The wealth and power to which this gave rise led to the growth of considerable communities and of miniature but fiercely competitive trading empires in such centres as Bonny, Brass, and later Opobo, on the Niger Delta, and in Old Calabar" (Forde 1956:vii). "Able and enterprising men could build up huge fortunes so that marked social inequality developed between the rich men and poor men in various conditions of dependence on them, and Efik society became partially stratified into overlapping divisions of free-born and slaves, rich men and poor" (Jones 1956:124). While these were still autonomous societies, the European officers of the merchant ships, the missionaries, and the British Consul were crucial influences in their lives. Acephalous segmentary lineages produced hereditary kings who established expanding slave plantations. King fought king, and lineages and segments competed for the throne, but the Egbo society ran across many of these polities providing at least occasional co-ordination and order between them. There is a certain formal similarity with Kpelle and the Poro society. Egbo had grades, through which—to some extent—men bought their way to the top. Petty kings endeavored to use Egbo as an executive arm but could themselves be restrained by it. Egbo delineated an elite of power and wealth on which poorer free men depended, but the majority of the population were slaves (by as many as ten to one, as legend goes). Egbo actually stimulated the development of a rival organization of plantation slaves in self-defense against its exactions. The members of this movement were called the Blood Men after their membership oath. Representing the majority, they were often able to curtail the headlong slaughter of slaves in honor of a dead ruler. Even living rulers tended to ally with the Blood Men over the heads of Egbo. Peculiar and transitory as this historical situation was (lasting from the seventeenth to the end of the nineteenth century, according to available information), it almost caricatures certain aspects of the relation between power, wealth, and status classification which are of much wider relevance.

In many societies of the interior of Africa, under hereditary rule but apparently uninfluenced by foreign conceptions of slavery or slave trade, the role and status of serf, subject, and servant was terminologically fused. In Acholi all who did not belong to the royal lineage of a particular chiefdom were *"lobong,"* a term covering both subject and serf. They were in fact free commoners, although recognizing obligations of service and tribute to their rulers. In most of the Interlacustrine states the term for the agricultural masses of the subjects connoted servant or serf. In many cases there is no historical evidence that their status derived from conquest rather than from more complementary types of assimilation. In most African chiefdoms of moderate size the major distinction of stratification lay between the mass of commoners on the one hand, and, on the other, the members of the ruling lineage, who could sometimes be very numerous, since they were able to practice polygyny on a larger scale than the rest. In the larger and more elaborate systems, such as Bunyoro or Rwanda, there was a further distinction within the aristocratic caste between the royal house itself and the other noble lineages with which it could intermarry.

Obviously, slavery is ancient, highly diverse, and pervasive—although not ubiquitous—in traditional Africa. Its relation to stratification is by no means consistent, since it often cuts across status categories rather than simply forming the lowest stratum of them. It is clearly necessary to distinguish among the various forms of slavery and to separate all of them from serfdom, service, adoption, capture, and immigration. There is no evidence that indigenous forms of slavery did not exist in Africa from time immemorial. But by the time they received any objective study most of them had been influenced by Arab and Islamic forms of slavery coming across the Sahara from the north or down the east coast, and later they were even more radically influenced by the impact of the Euro-American overseas slave trade. Large areas and populations in the interior of Africa were unaffected by the latter until late in the nineteenth century.

Nowhere did slaves, in the stricter sense, form a distinctive stratum of the population, for either they were quickly absorbed into kinship structure, as in the less elaborated traditional systems, or they were found at almost all status levels, as in the more elaborate and foreign-influenced systems. On the other hand, in the indigenous systems of serfdom there was often a fairly clear-cut stratum, inviting formal comparison with the categories of immigrants or foreigners in stateless societies, although the latter faced few of the material disabilities and restrictions of serfdom. The effective distinction between slavery and serfdom in this account lies in the degree to which slaves are subject to actual sale, or at least alienation, but by themselves legally unable to change masters, whereas serfs have more limited obligations, are not subject to sale or alienation, and in principle can usually change masters or patrons. African cultural taxonomies do not necessarily express or follow this distinction, nor does much of the foreign literature upon them.

It is too simple to regard sale as referring to the legal person as a whole, since many kinds of rights over a person may be recognized and treated as saleable or heritable property. As is well known, this is very frequently an aspect of the transfer of women from group to group in marriage. Anthropologists have always insisted that this must be confused neither with the idea of commercial sale in a market economy nor with slavery. However, Laura Bohannan (1949:273) compares that form of Dahomean marriage in which the woman is free-born yet tied to an office (so that her children also belong to the office, and her daughters are married in the same way although her sons are often left to their genitors) to the common African custom of lending cattle to a client and then dividing the calves. Among the Ibibio, although this group lacks the centralization of Dahomey, the persons called *osu* were those bought and dedicated to the owner's cult or descendants of such persons. They were feared and despised, they could not be redeemed, and no free person would marry them. Although, otherwise they had few legal or economic disabilities, they were ostracized, whereas slaves (*ohu*) were not (Forde and Jones 1950:23). Among the neighboring Afikpo Ibo, although "theoretically classless," the *ibe osim* were not allowed to own land and its females were "supposed to be available sexually to any man of another clan" without redress (Ottenberg 1965:20). Although this status was officially abolished many decades ago, Chinua Achebe presents a harrowing case of its strength even after the acquisition of Christian mission education (1960).

The concept of pawnship has often been used for practices in which the loss of a full status of free commoner is temporary and redeemable. Mary Douglas (1964) has described the importance of a variety of pawnship among sparse populations of matrilineal cultivators with little or no fixed property. Such populations stretch in a huge belt across Central Africa from the mouth of the Congo on the Atlantic to the Mozambique coast of the Indian Ocean. The data are incomplete, but already show some two dozen different peoples who exhibit this complex. The salient facts are that matrilineages can pawn their members in settlement of debts and claims. A male pawn is a free man but does not have the rights over his sisters and their children that others do, because these rights have been transferred by contract to his owner. The latter must pay his pawn's marriage and cult dues and settle his debts. Obviously it is a status which can be advantageous to a poor man and was voluntarily accepted. A female pawn could be given by the men of the matrilineage owning her to men who came to live with them. The children would belong to the owning lineage. Pawnship solved some of the conflicting interests of men in a matrilineal system by abrogating matrilineal claims, yet in the long run it strengthened the system because the ownership of pawns was itself transmitted matrilineally. It channelled motivations of power and wealth by providing an attractive arena of competition for followers, their support, labor, and children, within the framework of the matrilineal system.

All authorities insist that pawnship was not slavery. Indeed, pawns were frequently called by a term also meaning "grandchild" and were commonly approximated to this congenial status. Whole pawn lineages thus developed and have often been noted to flourish (Ndembu, Pende, Suku) while their masters' lineages decline, even to the point of extinction. Kopytoff uses the term slavery in speaking of the Suku (1965:458–59) but suggests that "adoption" might be closer to the truth. "A slave was, for all practical purposes, a full-fledged member of the lineage." But if a lineage had been forced to sell one of its members, it would have chosen a slave member, other things being equal. "Slaves, then, did not represent a 'class' in Suku society. . . . In some lineages all the members are 'slaves' in the sense that true blood membership has entirely died out and only the descendants of slaves are present; such a lineage continues to operate in the same way as before vis-à-vis the lineages and the clan to which it was originally related."

In the light of contemporary class and status group theory, it may be said that traditional African pawnship and slavery (excluding cases like Calabar and Bonny which were direct adjuncts of the overseas trade) were legal statuses but not distinct social statuses, for most traditional slaves and serfs had no domestic autonomy but formed part of their owner's domestic economy. They could not, therefore, have any distinctive status grouping or style of life. On the other hand, where there were large serf groups, such as the Okebo among the Alur, their distinctive status and style of life derived from their ethnic and functional rather than their serf position. In the great slave states like the Hausa there could again be no distinctively slave status group or style of life since slaves ran the whole gamut of socioeconomic status from top to bottom of the society.

We have noted the opportunity for achievement and hence a degree of social mobility in a number of cases. Indeed, the importance of achieved positions in traditional African societies is not fully realized. Complex, centralized societies like the Yoruba and the Hausa allowed great scope for achievement not only in the field of marketing and trade but also in the competition for titles and in the extraordinary rise of slaves to high office and wealth. Titles and offices might often be held within a lineage, but this still gave a wide field of opportunity. This was common in West Africa, not only in state systems, but also among large acephalous peoples such as the Ibo. In East Africa the same phenomenon appeared in the leadership of the higher governmental councils of the Kikuyu, and very generally in the leadership of East African age-sets. Most segmentary lineage systems depended a good deal on achieved leadership motivations within prescribed limits of descent. In general, the broad rank and status categories were ascribed, usually at birth, but there was a good deal of scope for achievement within them. Ascribed status looms larger in the ritual field, yet there are achieved positions with ritual implications and ascribed, ritual positions which also have secular implications. But it is important to bear in mind this range of variation between two types since modern studies of stratification concentrate so heavily on the secular and the achieved. It is quite possible for the two types to be represented in the status position of the same individual, with opposite effects, as when the slave achieves high office and great wealth or when the person of high ritual status fails in other basic social objectives such as the maintenance of many wives, the founding of a large family, the achievement of wealth and influence in land, cattle, foodstuffs and hospitality.

Up to a point high status of one type may compensate for low status in the other. But frequently there are complementary requisites, as is indicated by the case of the otherwise wealthy or successful man who is doomed to social oblivion and failure because he has no son to succeed to his status and perform the requisite rituals or by the extreme unpopularity and possible downfall of a chief who is ungenerous. At least, it is an axiomatic characteristic of modern secular society that the compensatory strength of ritual and ascribed status is greatly weakened, although it remains rather vital to the conception of an upper class.

Having adumbrated the main conceptual contributions which seem to be implicit in the variety of traditional African stratification systems, we must at this point in our analysis recapitulate the organizing ideas with which we are concerned. Although ideas about stratification and class can be traced back in the Western tradition to Plato and Aristotle or counterparts briefly found from China to Peru, most influential writing is implicitly related to nineteenth- and twentieth-century Euro-American history and a very great deal of it recently relates to the United States of America. This is a very narrow perspective on the broad expanse of human history and culture. Current anxieties and disillusionments, more poignantly than ever before, prompt the question as to whether the particular formulations found or envisaged so far within the world's most powerful technological system are necessarily those most pertinent to humanity in the long run. A wider look is, therefore, very much in order, particularly with respect to the ritual and symbolic issues raised by the African examples, and to their immediate relevance in an Afro-American context. The possibly ineluctable need of man in society for ritual harmony, going beyond rational arrangements, becomes a burning and topical question in our day.

Since ritual has so far been neglected in the study of stratification, the tracing of this theme in the African material becomes a relevant background. We have endeavored to relate this to the range of territorial and numerical size, social scale and complexity of specialization, and role differentiation. When political specialization centralizes authority effectively, binary and ternary complementarities are partly turned into hierarchy, but some asymmetries remain. These have to do with the ritual-political balance, which survives as long as kingship and almost certainly beyond. In England the lords spiritual remain officially higher in rank than the lords temporal. The Archbishop of Canterbury is the highest ranking commoner, and the sovereign is the fount of honor because both sources are combined in him. The complementary balance of Pope and Emperor in medieval Europe was an alternative form. These solutions are no longer adequate, but effective new ones have not been clearly recognized.

It is obviously impossible to do justice in this brief space to the vast literature on stratification, but we must always bear in mind the fundamental distinctions which have been made between subjective and objective social class and between realist and nominalist studies. Also essential is the question of the degree of legitimacy of class and stratification ideologies and their possible pluralism. Accounts of traditional societies often give us the ideology of an elite which favors the system and omits any other viewpoint. Yet we must concede that many traditional systems of inequality were, to a considerable degree, granted legitimacy by those at the bottom as well as the top. It is in the contemporary scene that conflicting views of legitimacy may develop in different sectors of society. Sometimes these feed into violent changes of regime and attempts at secession.

The Contemporary Scene

It is a commonplace that change in Africa has been recent and rapid. But it has also been very uneven. Traditional Africa was always changing. Individuals, groups, and whole peoples migrated over long distances and long periods, causing radical changes in cultures and social systems, causing new societies to spring up and old ones to disappear. Yet most societies remained rather closed and isolated, varying only within a limited and recognizable compass. Some were more in touch with the outside world and thus were subject to more violent change and fluctuation. Thus, empires rose and fell over a thousand years in the western Sudan. Arab influence had a shallow penetration over as long a period all down the East Coast, doubtless causing many more profound chain reactions which cannot be reliably documented. From the sixteenth century onwards, the Portuguese, followed by other Europeans, had a powerful effect on most coastal peoples, and some further inland where rivers gave access, as to the Kongo Kingdom, or where minerals called, as in the route from Sofala on the Mozambique coast inland to the Monomotapa Kingdom. Many African peoples are known to us only in the form which their society and culture assumed after absorbing these foreign influences.

With the crescendo of partition among the Western Powers in the 1880s came a new dimension of change which can be tritely characterized as being largely exogenous, by contrast with the mainly endogenous change which preceded it. From then on, African peoples were subjected, much more directly and with no real choice, to new institutions and ways whose very framework was and remained external to their own societies. These societies were, at the same time, frequently cut to pieces by imposed frontiers which took no account of them, and amalgamated into much larger units with many other peoples very unlike one another. There are many apparent paradoxes in this process. Many of those who were first proselytized by Christian missions from the sixteenth to the eighteenth century are those who show the greatest resistance or indifference to Christianity today. Those who achieved the most endogenous change are those who now survive best as distinct cultures.

The imposition of larger-scale political systems through amalgamation obviously also entailed imposition of new stratification systems. From this moment all African societies became, to some extent, plural. Naturally enough, colonial authorities—political, economic, or religious—were not always aware of the implications of their actions for emerging systems of stratification. When they had views on the subject, their actions often wittingly or unwittingly belied them. Their views reflected those of particular milieux in their home countries; when they lived abroad, they did not necessarily see the principles applying to them as applicable to their African subjects. By the same token, the Africans learned both from what was preached and what was practiced. Under these circumstances, it is difficult to see how the situations and attitudes of any African people could fail to be fraught with ambivalence and confusion over questions of stratification. This does not mean that Africans are not as skillful as other people in manipulating status situations to personal advantage, even when the principles applicable to one situation must contradict those of another. Rather, it is the overall system and policy towards it that is characterized by ambivalence and confusion.

We have seen that traditional African systems of stratification were diverse, sometimes even minimal, and although the Europeans obviously had much in common, it is nonetheless equally obvious that the attitudes of sixteenth-century Portuguese or eighteenth-century British or French differed markedly from those of any group in the nineteenth and, again, in the twentieth century. In any case, educated Africans were bound to pick up ideas of equality and brotherhood with which they could denounce their masters for betraying their own inspiration.

Colonial rule necessarily involved certain features of a caste system everywhere even though they were not fully legitimated or ritually sanctioned and not even wholeheartedly defended when they came under heavy attack. Portugal, the Republic of South Africa, and Rhodesia are, of course, glaring exceptions, but even here one must note the desire, wherever possible, to dispute the facts but not the principles. With these exceptions, all African colonial territories were under fairly rapid transformation. It is impossible to characterize this transformation briefly from the point of view of stratification except by saying that education has been taken as the key factor, with economic change, religious influence, and political power closely intertwined. We shall therefore pass to a consideration of the contemporary scene, still kaleidoscopic in its variety and constant movement.

The nineteenth- and twentieth-century Europeans who partitioned and colonized Africa were already living in a different age of stratification from those who had discovered Africa and established trade around its coasts. We shall call this the age of the premise of equality. The crucial feature was that the most respected intellects had lost their faith in the inequality of man. This, of course, took some time to affect society. Hexter sees hierarchy as a cosmic and sociological principle shattered for the more acute men of the seventeenth century in Western Europe by developments in science and philosophy alike (1962:115–16). But this was still an intellectual minority. By the end of the eighteenth century the American Republic proclaimed that all men were created equal and the French Republic adopted liberty, equality, and fraternity as its motto.

Maquet, in writing of the Rwanda social system as it was at the beginning of this century, summed it up with the phrase "premise of inequality" (1961:26, 160). As we have seen, the more complex traditional societies of Africa were the most unequal, and there was by contrast an aggressive egalitarianism about some stateless societies. Yet the latter did not necessarily preclude recognition of differences in rank and ritual status. It is generally agreed that in most African societies access to subsistence and to the culturally esteemed good things of life in general was not subject to great inequalities. There were widespread levelling mechanisms which tended to disperse accumulated wealth rapidly. Extended kinship obligations and corporate ownership provided a general right of access to use and to consumption which transcended incipient inequalities between individuals. The more hierarchical polities certainly diverged from this somewhat, yet a high sense of general, participational access usually remained, for these societies were highly ritualized. While ritual distinctions of rank and stratification are certainly not immune to the arguments of Marx, the productive system was such that these arguments, even where true, were much less important. Ritually integrated systems of stratification did not directly reflect differences in access to wealth and material resources. Legitimate power, wealth, and ritual status were multidimensional, as they were to some extent in the oriental empires and in medieval Europe. Indeed, vestiges of this still remain.

In the old Africa, ritual inequality did not necessarily spell great inequality of access to power and wealth. In the old Europe both forms of inequality were present, though not always perfectly in step. The change from the premise of inequality to the premise of equality in Europe was, in effect, a change from ritual inequality to ritual equality of status. But, as we know, while ritual equality certainly has majority acceptance in twentieth-century Europe and America, it does not spell equality of access to power and wealth.

In the recent struggle for independence, African leaders used the premise of equality, which in its modern form they had learned from Europeans, as an effective weapon. They thereby became considerably committed to it themselves and raised popular expectations accordingly. But with the battle for political, if not economic, independence won over most of Africa, the relevance of the premise of equality has changed. The difference between the societies of Europe and America and those of Africa is that, in the former, much greater inequalities of wealth have been generated which so far have proved impossible to break down to equal shares, whereas in the latter, it has not yet proved possible to generate extra wealth per head to raise the masses out of the equality of their shared poverty.

There is here a profound syndrome of factors which must surely be central to any consideration of stratification in comparative perspective or historical depth. In traditional Africa, as in medieval Europe, there was the counterpoise of the ideological order and of the socioeconomic order. The former was associated with ideas of a sacred, moral, and legal order and with differences and inequalities which were seen as ineluctable, ethical, and somehow just and functionally complementary. The latter was expressed in levels of objective material well-being and the style of life and nexus of social relationships built upon it. The two orders need not coincide, but they cannot diverge beyond a certain critical point in any system without radical change.

As we have seen in the case of Bushmen and Pygmies, in social situations which can justifiably be described as the simplest—because the numbers of persons, of differentiated roles, and of specialized tools involved are all few—the coincidence of the two orders is almost complete.

But usually this is not so. It is somewhat misleading to argue that there is a tendency towards consistency between them, because, although this may in a sense be true, in the real world there is usually a continuous interaction between them. If changes in population, role differentiation, or technology led to marked transformations in the socioeconomic order, some corresponding accommodation was likely in the ideological order. No doubt it was also possible for innovative ideas to lead to changes in the ideological order and to some corresponding accommodations in the socioeconomic order, but it is realistic to envisage continuous changes occurring in either order, as well as interaction and accommodation between them, so that some divergence and inconsistency between the two is always likely to remain. If there are tendencies to equilibrium, they never fully catch up with the changing situation. We have documented many instances of this divergence. The phenomena of stratification and social change cannot be understood unless these two orders are kept conceptually distinct. This problem seems to have bedevilled the historians, as is amply illustrated by Hexter's devastating criticisms of Pollard, Tawney, Trevor-Roper, and others in their faulty analysis of the changing place of the aristocracy and the emergence of the middle class (1962).

In the great transformation of the last few centuries, which we have had to oversimplify as the change from the "premise of inequality" to the "premise of equality," there has been an erosion of the ideological by the socioeconomic order, so that the former seems to have lost much of the autonomy it once possessed. Many writers have shown how the ideological order has come to be determined more and more by economic interests, contractual arrangements, and the cash nexus, rather than by any accepted legitimate ideological expression of social differences.

When the idea of the subjection of the sovereign himself to a superior moral order failed to carry conviction, that moral order was bound to collapse. When the sovereign himself was no longer subject, his justification disappeared. Justice could no longer depend upon complementarity but only upon equality. The divergence of the ideological order, based upon the premise of equality, from the accompanying socioeconomic order is perhaps greater than ever before. Its legitimating expression must be sought in the secular rituals of voting, electoral participation, and stated equality before the law, whether in so-called liberal or popular democracies.

A conceptual framework which serves to unravel the confusion over the rise of the middle class in Europe will do the same in Africa. The case of eighteenth-century France, the period of crescendo in the transformation, is a striking illustration (E. G. Barber 1955:4–16). In the accepted ideological and legal structure of France there were only two classes, noble and commoner (*roturier*). Yet, in the socioeconomic order there was an important differentiation between the ancient feudal nobility (*noblesse d'épée*) and the *noblesse de robe* promoted from the wealthy higher bourgeoisie. The bourgeoisie, although it included some of the wealthiest people in the land, remained commoner from the ideological and legal point of view, and of course there are parallels to this in Japan, China, and India. In the socioeconomic order there was considerable confusion between the *noblesse de robe* and the higher bourgeoisie from which they had been drawn. In England the same kind of confusion existed as to whether a wealthy knight was upper or middle class. In our view such confusion need not be reflected in analysis, for there are two different answers, equally valid—one in terms of the legal-ideological, the other in terms of the socioeconomic order. The French bourgeoisie took pride in many generations of separation from the socioeconomic status of peasants or workers, although this separation did not affect their legal-ideological status. *Roturiers* were excluded from army commissions and from high ecclesiastical office. The Catholic Church sanctioned the moral legitimacy of the inegalitarian structure and the denial of recognition to the middle class despite the lurking equality of all men before the Christian God, which eventually burst through. Barber's illuminating analysis seems implicitly to recognize the dual counterpoise which I regard as fundamental. However, she phrases this in terms of the polarity of caste and open-class systems, never empirically realized but approximated by India in the one case and the United States in the other. I would rather insist that this polarity expresses itself in the dual counterpoise which I have noted as common to most societies, one aspect of which is the universal problem of mobility on the one hand and solidarity on the other.

A number of important conceptions relevant to stratification must be distinguished in Africa today. They are inconsistent with one another, and some are held more strongly by one section of the population than another, but many people hold them all with reference to different situations. The first is the premise of equality, already mentioned, an idea derived from Europe that all men should be—and in some sense intrinsically are—equal. This is strongly reinforced by another idea which is newly formulated, yet derived from the old Africa, to the effect that in fact all men empirically are equal. They are equal by virtue of African kinship and family systems which, it is asserted, can continue to guarantee this even in a modernizing society. African kinship does indeed soften and mitigate economic inequality. It still provides the only system of social security in Africa today. But it has its limits. Blessed by the receiver, it is cursed by the donor, even though donor and receiver may sometimes be the same person at different times. In short, it mitigates, but no longer can transcend, increasing economic inequality. In the old Africa anyone who accumulated wealth and power greatly above the average, or above that appropriate to the status ascribed to him, was guilty of a sin analogous to the Greek ὕβρις. He was the butt of witchcraft and sorcery, hatred and disapproval. In any case his success was bound to express itself also in the accumulation of large numbers of wives, children, and dependents, among whom his wealth would be dispersed at his death. Modern forms of investment and testation begin to evade these levelling mechanisms. But belief in the equality guaranteed by African kinship has been particularly important in enabling ruling elites to insist that the new African societies are classless and will remain so, thus shielding themselves from feelings of guilt and responsibility for the increasing gap which divides them from the masses. It is here that there seems to be the greatest faith in the survival of traditional virtues. This has sometimes been misplaced, as in Nigeria, where increasing fury at the needless luxury and display of the governmental elite was one of the factors contributing to the collapse of the civilian federal government. Indeed, it is a pervasive factor in the new African nations.[3]

The third idea of stratification is derived from traditional systems and may, therefore, vary somewhat for each locality in a new African nation. These traditions are weakened but not broken. In principle, people can escape from them by moving out of their traditional communities to towns, or places of modern employment, or by gaining a modern education and achieving a modern occupational role even within the geographical limits of the traditional community. All those who are most influential in political and economic life, as well as many others, do escape. Yet, one must conclude that the majority of Africans still receive their initial socialization in the context of these traditional ideas, tempered somewhat according to the degree of radical change which has occurred in the local power structure, the local basis of subsistence, and the degree of local penetration of modern education. All of these things vary widely from one locality to another.

Even those who escape to work elsewhere still spend much of their lives, especially their later lives, mainly under the influence of the modified traditional stratification system.

The next factor contributory to contemporary ideas of stratification is that of ethnic stereotypes. The greatly accelerated spatial and social mixing of members of different ethnic groups brought about by colonial rule and continued under independent rule—even when the majority still retain ultimate ties with their traditional localities—has brought about a confrontation between numerous ethnic groups which were formerly widely separated and has induced a certain hierarchical stereotyping. Despite the numerous exceptions and the dwindling relevance of some of these stereotypical associations, there is a widespread tendency to lump together whole ethnic groups for their association with local dominance, land ownership, former military prowess, high level of education, monopoly of higher bureaucratic posts or of clerical jobs, muscular strength and effective physical labor, or poor physique and unskilled work, or even with continued resistance to the forces of change and hence the maintenance of rural isolation or nomadism. Since traditional African cultures were as ethnocentric as cultures elsewhere, it is the valuations by each ethnic group of all the others, rather than of itself, which may approximate to some consistent hierarchy. It does not amount to a unilinear ordering, but to a rough conception of relative collective statuses. The very fact that class consciousness as such is inhibited strengthens, perhaps even necessitates, hierarchical ethnic stereotyping. (I would argue the same in relation to the United States as opposed to Latin America.)

The sampling of ethnic attitudes is subject to many pitfalls, both because of the extreme ambivalence, known to be present but not revealed by formal interview, and also because of the multiplicity of possible interpretations. Exploration in 1963 by a market research firm in East Africa suggested some interesting tendencies (Burke 1966:232–35). The most unequivocal result was the demonstration of the great prestige of the Ganda people, not only in Uganda but also in Kenya and Tanzania. In Uganda, when asked with whom they would prefer to live if compelled to leave their own people, the sample of Toro, Nyoro, and Soga, centralized Interlacustrine Bantu neighbors of the Ganda, together with the acephalous Bantu Gisu, all expressed an overwhelming preference to live with the Ganda. The Nilotic Lang'o and Teso samples from north Uganda also expressed preference for the Ganda by a narrow margin over one another or their Nilotic Acholi neighbors. Only the Acholi put another people (the Teso) slightly above the Ganda. The Ganda themselves expressed a clear preference for living outside Uganda altogether, rather than with any other Ugandan people, thus conforming to the general idea of their superior feelings towards their Ugandan neighbors. The Ganda call members of all other neighboring African groups *bannamawanga,* which means "gentiles," as the Romans used *gentes* and the Greeks ἔθνοι. The preference for Ganda came out in Kenya and Tanzania also. There was a tangle of asymmetrical dislikes and preferences among Kenya peoples which would require further refinement: Kikuyu was low in the preferences of Luyia, Luo, and Kamba, but high in those of the coastal Bantu. In Tanzania, nearly all groups preferred to live among a non-Tanzanian people, thus perhaps negatively giving correct expression to the fact that no ethnic group is pre-eminent and that national unity is much greater on the ethnic plane in Tanzania than in the other East African countries.

Mitchell's results from the study of Central African peoples on the Copperbelt were somewhat similar (1956). The ranking of other peoples depended a good deal on geographical proximity and cultural similarity, with a tendency to negatively value those distant in these respects. But, as in East Africa, certain peoples had special prestige transcending these factors, especially the Ngoni, Ndebele, and Bemba, whose past military prowess still put them high, while certain other peoples were put correspondingly low, at least in part because of their willingness to do work involving contact with human excreta. Mitchell argues cogently that these ethnic identities, in nontraditional, urban contexts, are no longer systems of social relationships but categories of interaction within a wider system (ibid.:30). As such, they organize and facilitate the superficial and transitory relationships so characteristic of modern contexts, which are qualified by other criteria on further acquaintance. It must be remarked that the type of ethnic stratification—which forms one element in the evolution of most contemporary African societies, where the number of ethnic groups is large and the reciprocal ratings vary asymmetrically from group to group —has received very little scholarly attention so far (e.g., Shibutani and Kwan [1965]; H. S. Morris [1968]).

Although general recognition of class distinctions as such is inhibited by several factors, it does appear in appropriate contexts, whose importance is increasing. In towns and all large centers of polyethnic employment and interaction, there is not only the somewhat imprecise ethnic stereotyping usually accompanied by formal courtesy in social intercourse, but in personal dealings there is a concrete recognition of the general criteria of an open class system. Housing and neighborhood, friends and even kinsfolk, hence all places and contexts of voluntary association—hotels, restaurants, bars, clubs, etc.—are rated according to the usual criteria of occupational prestige, power, income, and education. Moreover, there is an insistence upon the recognition of such distinctions in the provision of appropriately different facilities, with cost as the mediating factor. The concept of "first class gentleman" was used in this context by urban Africans asserting status rights in Uganda as long ago as the late 1940's.

Africa has, in fact, until now been passing through a period in which all the usual diagnostic criteria of an open class system could be approximated and subsumed in the single factor of education, as far as non-traditional contexts were concerned. Literacy and knowledge of the appropriate European language were, and still are, prerequisites for any advancement in major commerce, industry, or government in the broadest sense, essential keys to the new technology and bureaucracy. The large part played by foreigners in the development of commerce and industry, the continuing weakness of African entrepreneurship in establishing large and lasting enterprises—despite the ubiquity and importance of petty trading in West Africa and the large number of personal fortunes made—resulted in what many writers have called the politicization and increasing bureaucratization of the whole development process. The rapid expansion of these new institutional structures during the present generation, combined with the progressive turnover of higher posts from foreigners to Africans at Independence and after, has meant that the new school systems of African countries have hardly yet trained the first complete body of personnel to occupy all these posts. Promotion has been unprecedentedly rapid, but inevitably it has already begun to slow down. Twenty years ago a high school education was a passport to eventual eminence in most African countries, but a university degree very soon became essential and now no longer suffices to catapult the holder rapidly to the top as it did ten years ago. But it is impossible, humanly speaking, to gear an educational system perfectly to institutional development, especially in the context of a liberal education which prevailed hitherto. Bottlenecks here and surpluses there inevitably appeared.

Degree holders now have increasing anxiety, and even a paradoxical sense of relative deprivation, that their rate of promotion is already bound to be much slower than that which their immediate predecessors enjoyed. Meanwhile at the other end of the system, primary education is disqualifying hundreds of thousands of Africans for rural life, at least in their own estimation, and is driving them to the towns where no acceptable jobs exist to absorb their ever-increasing numbers. The transition from gross shortage to effective surplus has been painfully rapid. Already it is reported that school expansion is no longer keeping pace with population growth, and the absolute number of illiterates is actually expected to increase. If this continues, it will tend to impose a new barrier between urban literate and rural illiterate masses, a barrier which it was hoped the progress of education would eliminate. Such dynamic forces, combined with the medley of presuppositions about stratification derived from the past and the present and from inside and outside Africa, make for inevitable lack of coherence in stratification, although some consistency in underlying trends may be discerned.

Perhaps it might be argued that at least the objective factors of stratification are of their nature consistent, however inconsistent the subjective attitudes towards them may be. But even this distinction is somewhat slippery. The traditional distinctions which remain, and newer ideas derived from them, with respect to the influence of kinship or ethnic origin, must to a large extent be considered as objective social facts, not mere subjective attitudes. They are not just statistically frequent but have a certain publicly accepted legitimacy, which is still sanctioned by many ritual practices. The extreme rarity of interethnic marriage is one of the most widespread negative demonstrations of this. The capacity for local survival of traditional prestige roles under new names is a more positive one. Yet the tide is certainly running against the higher positions of hereditary status. No African monarchs survive as heads of state except in Ethiopia and Morocco in North Africa and the small countries of Lesotho and Swaziland. Their future is uncertain, but the overall trend is indisputable. It is otherwise with such traditional positions in the local communities to which the masses of Africans belong. They have a much longer lease on life, surviving through various transformations.

The ultimate question is, of course, the form which African societies will take in the course of the development programs which they have set themselves. It is now clear that the normal pattern of Western capitalistic laborsaving development is impossible because of the explosive demographic factor which will dominate the scene for at least a generation to come. Defining a modernized society as one that is capable of self-sustaining growth over the long run, Lerner (1967:21–22) does not believe that modernization is "either desirable or feasible in every society of the contemporary world" since "a generation or two hence, some types of society will be able to modernize more effectively at lower human cost." He believes that Africa is especially favored by being able to wait and see, avoiding the mistakes of others (ibid.:38). We hope this view is correct, but it seems to arise from a naively static view of the African situation, which in fact is already beginning to suffer from that "decoupling of the twin processes of urbanisation and industrialisation" which Lerner deplores.

This problem has far-reaching implications. The most likely guess is that urban populations, and most of all those of the primate capital cities, will continue to grow fast, even though much of this future growth may be in the form of an expanding, volatile, lumpen proletariat of unemployed and semi-employed. With the best success that can be hoped for in industrial development, the vast majority of people will be left tied to rural agriculture, on a subsistence base with a cash crop surplus. These vast rural populations may well remain somewhat marginal to any emergent system of stratification embracing the society as a whole. On the other hand, the urban and wage- or salary-earning population will be drawn into a more integrated national system, highly differentiated in wealth and status, in which the premise of equality and the levelling mechanism of African kinship will be strained to the breaking point. Traditional and ritual status differentiations will have little relevance, and ethnic differences will gradually be transcended by the elite but will remain strong for the proletariat. The system may well take the form of classes as status groups, hierarchically arranged, but not clearly divided from one another, with an "ideology of non-equalitarian classlessness" (Lloyd 1966:59), maintained by the elite through control of the mass media, aided by the insecurity of the urban proletariat and the marginality of the rural masses. The style of life achieved by the present elite, partly in emulation of their colonial predecessors and their privileged access to expensive education, is likely to perpetuate them as a semi-hereditary group. But they will always be able to recruit talent from outside where necessary and to maintain the fiction of an open class system.

There are two further possibilities to consider. Given the prevalence of effectively one party systems, together with the intractable nature of the fundamental problems of development which they face, it is somewhat unlikely that any ruling clique can retain popularity or power indefinitely, as the constant coups d'état of recent years amply indicate. Will there be a rapid circulation of power cliques, largely from within the same civil and military, bureaucratic government elite, with most of the bureaucrats remaining more stable than the rest? Or will there be a circulation of elites, in which the fabric of society is more profoundly stirred and new leaders, from outside the incumbent elite, ride violently to power on the rising discontents of urban unemployed and hopeless rural masses? There is likely to be a mixture of both processes, in which the more purely political incumbent elite, whether civilian or military in individual background, is bound to provide the focal target for hostility and to be swept away when violence comes, whereas both military and civilian bureaucracies, apart from their top figureheads, will have to be retained with substantial continuity for some time to come.

Anyone who reads newspapers knows how important armies have suddenly become in Africa. Only six years ago Coleman and Brice could write "African armies are perhaps the least developed in the contemporary world. Indeed, in many of the new states they are quite literally in the process of being established" (1962:403). Recent events in at least a dozen tropical African countries, not to mention Egypt and Algeria in the north, remind us of the political importance of armies, however new or small. The change from moderate independence movement to more revolutionary independence movement, to one party autocracy, to military dictatorship, has become so frequent as to seem an almost normative pattern for the circulation of elites. This inescapable political power of African armies strengthens the element of bureaucratic hierarchy combined with a degree of open recruitment in African stratification systems. Since African economic policy depends more on politics and planning (interacting with external pressures) than on the outcome of individual entrepreneurship, the discipline and professionalism, which must to some extent prevail in any army, appear as strategic virtues with which few other institutional structures can compete. It is indeed surprising that military regimes appear as amenable to a return to civilian government as some of them do. The officer corps has great growth potential as a key elite component, as Ethiopia has already shown (Lloyd 1966:9).

As Dahrendorf (1959) and Djilas (1957) have applied neo-Marxist theory to industrial and communist society respectively, so can it also be applied to Africa, most of which is neither industrial nor communist. The conflict between African independence movements and colonial ruling elites was clearly a case of class conflict conforming with Marxist theory in form but not in content. So was the revolution in Rwanda of Hutu against Tutsi, the overthrow of the Kabaka and Ganda traditionalist forces by the national government of Uganda, the early coups in Nigeria before the secession of Biafra, the coups in Congo Brazzaville, Sierra Leone, Ghana, and the unsuccessful coup in Ethiopia. Where Africans hold effective economic power, it is through political office; therefore class conflict must focus upon the latter. But the presence of class conflict in the Marxist sense does not prove the existence of classes in the most prevalent meaning of the term in non-Marxist western sociology. Bendix argued sixteen years ago that "class differences have come to be subordinated to the much more decisive conflict between the underdeveloped areas and the industrialized West" (1953:598). From the perspective of the present it would seem that this is another dimension of conflict, still of enormous importance, but that the conflict of groups in African countries for power and the economic control that is tied to it is quite decisive in the short run, at least from the internal point of view, and is not subordinated to the international dimension. While foreign colonial rulers were actually present in a country, they could be used effectively by independence movements to heighten solidarity by the principle of complementary opposition. Now that they are no longer present and visible they cannot be used so effectively, however much African leaders see foreign, neo-colonial economic influence as their main enemy.

So far, writers on Africa have found it most appropriate to speak of elite and masses rather than classes, while recognizing that classes may emerge more clearly in the future (Lloyd 1966:60; Southall 1966:342). The Marxist view stresses conflict between self-conscious interest groups, while the prevalent Western view stresses mobility between status groups. Traditional Africa stressed the symbolic and ritual meaning of publicly accepted status differences. If African countries do not progress rapidly in raising the real income-per-head of the masses, and if the channels of upward mobility become clogged, there will be constant risk of conflict through rival factions finding support from the masses. The combination of economic inequality, low mobility, and the premise of equality is an awkward one. It would seem intolerable unless some meaning can be found in persisting inequalities, which can be convincingly conveyed to the masses. Such is the endeavor of some leaders to mobilize the whole society into a vivid and intense awareness of its common participation. They see this, with some justification, as a valid continuation of the collective and corporate aspects of traditional African society.

The lesson of traditional Africa is that difference can be made meaningful, that it can be made complementary and contrapuntal, through an inequality in one dimension being matched against an inequality in another, so that the possible sense of relative deprivation of one group or section of society vis-à-vis another is to some extent compensated by the symbolic and ritual meaning which provides a genuine sense of fulfillment and satisfaction. This is certainly a dangerous idea in the modern context, amply confirming the Marxist interpretation of the contribution of religion to society. Among the crucial differences in traditional Africa were the usually low degree of entrenched difference of access to subsistence and material goods and the high level of general participation in an integrated social process, facilitating the generation and maintenance of stable and satisfying symbolic meanings. Whether comparable meanings can be established and expressed—when the means of exploitation of one group by another are so much more highly mobilized and centralized—is debatable. Can such satisfactions be enjoyed without sapping the very forces which must be unleashed for the emancipation of man in the underdeveloped world? The search for meaning in society certainly seems to be one of the most pressing tasks of our time, both in Africa and the West, although for different reasons. It is perhaps the most neglected aspect of the modern study of stratification, which the study of traditional African systems brings back forcibly to our attention.

NOTES

1. See the detailed discussion of this point in Goody (1966), introduction.
2. They appear to correspond to what some writers would call pawns.
3. The premise of equality and the collective and co-operative virtues of African kinship and family systems are fused in the potently evocative idea of African Socialism (Friedland and Rosberg 1964), which is actually thought of as "a continuation of the traditional way of life" (Grundy, in ibid.:177).

REFERENCES

Achebe, Chinua (1960) *No Longer at Ease.* New York.

Barber, Bernard (1968) "Stratification, Social," in *International Encyclopaedia of the Social Sciences,* vol. 15. New York.

Barber, Elinor G. (1955) *The Bourgeoisie in 18th Century France.* Princeton.

Barkun, M. (1964) "Conflict Resolution through Implicit Mediation," *Journal of Conflict Resolution* 8, no. 2:121–30.

Barnes, J. A. (1954) *Politics in a Changing Society.* Oxford.

Bendix, Reinhard (1953) "Social Stratification and Political Power," in *Class, Status, and Power,* ed. S. M. Lipset and R. Bendix.

Bohannan, Laura (1949) "Dahomean Marriage: A Revaluation," *Africa* 19:273–87.

Bohannan, Paul (1957) *Justice and Judgement among the Tiv.* Oxford.

Burke, F. G., and S. Diamond, eds. (1966) *The Transformation of East Africa.* New York.

Coleman, J. S., and B. Brice (1962) *The Role of the Military in Underdeveloped Countries.* Princeton.

Dahrendorf, Ralf (1959) *Class and Class Conflict in Industrial Society.* Stanford.

d'Hertefelt, Marcel (1965) "The Rwanda of Rwanda," in *Peoples of Africa,* ed. J. Gibbs. New York.

Djilas, Milovan (1957) *The New Class: An Analysis of the Communist System.* New York.

Douglas, Mary (1964) "Matriliny and Pawnship in Central Africa," *Africa* 34:301–14.

Edwards, Adrian (1962) *The Ovimbundu under Two Sovereignties.* Oxford.

Evans-Pritchard, E. E. (1940) *The Nuer.* Oxford.

Forde, C. Daryll (1951) *The Yoruba-Speaking Peoples of South-Western Nigeria.* London.

————, ed. (1956) *Efik Traders of Old Calabar.* Oxford.

Forde, C. D., and G. I. Jones (1950) *The Ibo and Ibibio Speaking Peoples of South-eastern Nigeria.* London.

Fortes, M. (1945) *The Dynamics of Clanship among the Tallensi.* Oxford.

Friedland, William H., and Carl Rosberg, eds. (1964) *African Socialism.* Stanford.

Gibbs, James, ed. (1965) *Peoples of Africa.* New York.

Goody, Jack, ed. (1966) *Succession to High Office.* Cambridge.

Gulliver, P. H. (1961) "Structural Dichotomy and Jural Processes among the Arusha of Northern Tanganyika," *Africa* 31:19.

Gutkind, P. C. W. (1967) "The Energy of Despair: Social Organization of the Unemployed in Two African Cities: Lagos and Nairobi," *Civilisations* 17, no. 3:186–214; no. 4:380–405.

Harley, G. W. (1950) *Masks as Agents of Social Control in Northeast Liberia,* Papers of the Peabody Museum of American Archaeology and Ethnology, vol. 32, no. 2. Cambridge, Mass.

Hexter, J. H. (1962) *Reappraisals in History.* Evanston, Ill.

Jones, G. I. (1956) "The Political Organization of Old Calabar," in *Efik Traders of Old Calabar,* ed. C. D. Forde. Oxford.

Kopytoff, I. (1965) "The Suku of Southwestern Congo," in *Peoples of Africa,* ed. J. Gibbs. New York.

Kuper, Hilda (1965) "The Swazi of Swaziland," in *Peoples of Africa*, ed. J. Gibbs. New York.

Lawrance, J. C. D. (1957) *The Iteso*. Oxford.

Lerner, Daniel (1967) "Comparative Analysis of Processes of Modernisation," in *The City in Modern Africa*, ed. H. Miner. New York.

Lévi-Strauss, Claude (1963) *Structural Anthropology*. New York.

Lienhardt, Godfrey (1961) *Divinity and Experience: The Religion of the Dinka*. Oxford.

Lipset, S. M., and R. Bendix (1953) *Class, Status and Power*. Glencoe, Ill.

Lloyd, P. C., ed. (1966) *The New Elites of Tropical Africa*. Oxford.

Maquet, J. J. (1961) *The Premise of Inequality in Rwanda*. Oxford.

Marshall, Lorna (1965a) *The Harmless People*. New York.

————— (1965b) "The !Kung Bushmen of the Kalahari Desert," in *Peoples of Africa*, ed. J. Gibbs. New York.

Middleton, John (1960) *Lugbara Religion*. Oxford.

Miner, Horace, ed. (1967) *The City in Modern Africa*. New York.

Mitchell, J. C. (1956) *The Kalela Dance*. Rhodes-Livingstone Papers no. 27. Manchester, England.

Morris, H. S. (1968) "Ethnic Groups," in *International Encyclopaedia of the Social Sciences*, vol. 5. New York.

Nadel, S. F. (1942) *A Black Byzantium*. Oxford.

Needham, Rodney (1967) "Right and Left in Nyoro Symbolic Classification," *Africa* 37:425.

Ottenberg, Phoebe (1965) "The Afikpo Ibo of Eastern Nigeria," in *Peoples of Africa*, ed. J. Gibbs. New York.

Parkin, D. J. (1966) "Urban Voluntary Associations as Institutions of Adaptation," *Man* 1, no. 1.

Schapera, I. (1955) *A Handbook of Tsana Law and Custom*. Oxford.

Shibutani, T., and K. M. Kwan (1965) *Ethnic Stratification*. New York.

Smith, M. G. (1959) "The Hausa System of Social Status," *Africa* 29, no. 3:239.

————— (1965) "The Hausa of Northern Nigeria," in *Peoples of Africa*, ed. J. Gibbs. New York.

Southall, A. W. (1956) *Alur Society, a Study in Types and Processes of Domination*. Cambridge.

————— (1968) "Stateless Society," in *International Encyclopaedia of the Social Sciences*. New York.

————— (1970) "Rank and Stratification Among the Nilotes," in *Social Stratification in Africa*, ed. Arthur Tuden and Leonard Plotnicov. New York.

Turnbull, Colin (1959) "Legends of the Bambuti," *Journal of the Royal Anthropological Institute* 89, no. 1:45.

————— (1965) "The Mbuti Pygmies of the Congo," in *Peoples of Africa*, ed. J. Gibbs. New York.

Vansina, Jan (1968) *Kingdoms of the Savannah*. Madison, Wis.

Willis, R. G. (1964) "Traditional History and Social Structure in Ufipa," *Africa* 34:340–52.

————— (1967) "The head and the loins: Lévi-Strauss and beyond," *Man* 2, no. 4:519.

Wilson, Monica (1951) *Good Company*. Oxford.

Chapter 11/ Reinhard Bendix

Tradition and Modernity Reconsidered

Introduction

Modernization is a term which became fashionable after World War II. It is useful despite its vagueness because it tends to evoke similar associations in contemporary readers. Their first impulse may be to think of the "modern" in terms of present-day technology with its jet travel, space exploration, and nuclear power. But the common sense of the word "modern" encompasses the whole era since the eighteenth century when inventions like the steam engine and the spinning jenny provided the initial technical basis for the industrialization of societies. The economic transformation of England coincided with the movement of independence in the American colonies and the creation of the nation-state in the French Revolution. Accordingly, the word "modern" also evokes associations with the democratization of societies, especially the destruction of inherited privilege and the declaration of equal rights of citizenship.

These changes of the eighteenth century initiated a transformation of human societies which is comparable in magnitude only to the transformation of nomadic peoples into settled agriculturalists some ten thousand years earlier. Until 1750 the proportion of the world's active population

This essay was originally published in *Comparative Studies in Society and History* 9 (1967):292–346 and is reprinted by permission of the Cambridge University Press.

engaged in agriculture was probably above 80 per cent. Two centuries later it was about 60 per cent, and in the industrialized countries of the world it had fallen below 50 per cent, reaching low figures like 10 to 20 per cent in countries with a relatively long history of industrialization. In Great Britain, the country which pioneered in this respect, the proportion of the labor force engaged in agriculture reached a low of 5 per cent in 1950.[1]

Wherever it has occurred, the modernization of societies originated in social structures marked by inequalities based on kinship ties, hereditary privilege, and established (frequently monarchical) authority. By virtue of their common emphasis on a hierarchy of inherited positions, pre-modern or traditional societies have certain elements in common. The destruction of these features of the old order with the consequent rise of equality are one hallmark of modernization; hence the latter process shows certain uniformities. These changes in the social and political order were apparent before the full consequences of the industrial revolution were understood. As a result, most (if not all) thinkers of the nineteenth century ". . . exhibit the same burning sense of society's sudden, convulsive turn from a path it had followed for millenia. All manifest the same profound intuition of the disappearance of historic values—and, with them, age-old securities, as well as age-old tyrannies and inequalities—and the coming of new powers, new insecurities, and new tyrannies."[2] And, as Professor Nisbet adds, "sociology in Europe was developed almost wholly around the theses and anti-theses cast up by the two revolutions and their impact upon the old order."[3] We owe many insights to this intellectual tradition. Yet today there are indications that this perspective gave an oversimplified view of traditional societies, of modern societies, and of the transition from the one to the other. This oversimplification resulted from heavily ideological interpretations of the contrast between tradition and modernity, and from undue generalizations of the European experience. Today, a more differentiated and balanced interpretation of modernization should be possible; the following discussion is presented as a contribution to that end.

Its first part deals with an aspect of the history of ideas. The rise of industrial civilization in Europe engendered a new conception of society, invidious contrasts between tradition and modernity, and a theory of social change culminating in the work of Karl Marx and most recently in a revival of theories of social evolution. My effort will be to show how our conceptual vocabulary in studies of modernization developed. The second part offers a methodological critique of this intellectual tradition and proposes an alternative conceptualization of the contrast between tradition and modernity. In the third part I shall attempt to develop a comparative approach to the study of modernization and illustrate it by a tentative application to the field of social stratification.

Persistence and Change of Ideas about Modern Society

A New Perspective

The sense that the late eighteenth century represents a hiatus in intellectual perspective as well as a new departure in the history of Western civilization is as common among scholars as is the related connotation of the term "modern" among people at large. Before the seventeenth and eighteenth centuries, the world of nature and of man was conceived as an emanation of Divine Providence. Since then our thinking has been restructured in all fields of learning. As the idea of God became fused with that of Nature, the concept of the universe created at the beginning of time was gradually replaced by the idea of an infinitely various and endlessly active process of evolution. The idea was applied in parallel fashion to our understanding of the growth of knowledge, to a new conception of God as in Schelling's *Naturphilosophie,* and to an ethical interpretation of world history, as in Kant's view, that "all the excellent natural faculties of mankind would forever remain undeveloped" if it were not for man's nature with its quarrelsomeness, its enviously competitive vanity, and its insatiable desire to possess or to rule.[4] Here was one of many schemes by which thinkers of the late eighteenth and early nineteenth centuries linked the fractious qualities of individual men with the concept of a self-contained regularity or lawfulness attributed to the social world. While Kant used a teleological construction in this respect, classical economists like Adam Smith asserted that man's propensity to truck, barter, and exchange one thing for another gave rise to actions obeying an impersonal law, like the law of supply and demand. By their actions in society individuals conform to a regularity or higher principle without intending to do so. Phrases like the "end of nature" or the "invisible hand" by which Kant and Smith referred to such a higher principle may be considered a survival of an earlier belief in Divine Providence or a harbinger of later concepts of society and economy. In any case, they helped to usher in a new view of the social world as an impersonal structure possesssing attributes or principles of its own.

The following discussion presents an historical sketch of ideas about the new industrial society in the making—with special emphasis upon the effects of that society on different social classes. My purpose is to show that the invidious contrast between tradition and modernity is the master-theme which underlies a great diversity of topics and influences our under-standing of modern society to this day.

In his *Essay on the History of Civil Society,* first published in 1767, Adam Ferguson attributed the progress of a people to the subdivision of tasks (Adam Smith's division of labor) which at the same time improves the skills of the artisan, the profits of the manufacturer, and the enjoyment of consumers.

Every craft may engross the whole of a man's attention, and has a mystery which must be studied. . . . Nations of tradesmen come to consist of members, who beyond their one particular trade, are ignorant of all human affairs, and who may contribute to the preservation and enlargement of their commonwealth, without making its interest an object of their regard or attention.[5]

Ferguson's discussion formulates ways of looking at modern society which have become commonplace. The division of labor necessarily restricts the understanding of those who specialize. In so doing it also increases their productivity and the wealth of the country. Hence, private ends, a lack of conscious concern for public welfare, and public benefits go together. This laissez-faire doctrine is joined, as Marx already noted, with a theory of social action, at least in rudimentary form. By attending only to his own business, each man is distinguished by his calling and has a place to which he is fitted. In Ferguson's view the differences among men are a direct outcome of the habits they acquire in practicing different arts: "Some employments are liberal, others mechanic. They require different talents, and inspire different sentiments."[6] In his assessment of these corollaries of specialization, Ferguson combines the older conventional wisdom with insight into the emerging problems of modern society. The old division of society into a leisured, ruling minority and the bulk of a working popula-tion is reflected in his view that social rank depends on the work men do. Those who must eke out a mere subsistence are degraded by the "objects they pursue, and by the means they employ to attain it." Those who belong to the superior class are bound to no task and are free to follow the disposition of their mind and heart.

At the same time, Ferguson is well aware that increasing division of labor exacts a price. The ends of society are best promoted by mechanical arts requiring little capacity and thriving best "under a total suppression of sentiment and reason."[7] Another Scotch philosopher, John Millar, points out that art and science improve with the division of labor but produce in the worker, who is employed in a single manual operation, a "habitual vacancy of thought, unenlivened by any prospects, but such as are derived from future wages of their labor, or from the grateful returns of bodily repose and sleep."[8] The human cost of manual labor under modern conditions of production is thus a theme from the very beginning of industrial society.

At that time, and ever since, it has been argued that this human cost is inevitable. The burdens of the laboring classes under the new conditions are simply a new form of the ancient division of society into masters and servants. Attempts to relieve these burdens only decrease the wealth of a country and hence ultimately aggravate the lot of the workers themselves.[9] Yet this advocacy of the traditional rank-order under new conditions did not in the long run match the significance of another, much more critical body of opinion.

Conservative and Radical Critiques of Industry

In many parts of Europe men of letters viewed the discrepancies between rich and poor with alarm and with a feeling that the destitution of the people represented a new phenomenon and an increasing threat to the social order. The ideas of a growing bifurcation of society into two opposed classes as well as the doctrine of pauperization—both of which are familiar to modern readers from the writings of Karl Marx—were in fact beliefs spelled out by many European writers during the seventeenth and eighteenth centuries.[10] Their sense of crisis is reflected in ideas about social rank which sought to take account of the changes occurring in industrializing societies. To exemplify these ideas, indicate something of their ubiquity, and show how strongly they have influenced modern social thought, I shall take examples from Germany, France, and the United States. These judgments about social ranks in a period of transition reflect something of both the experience and moral sense of men of different social ranks and the moral sense with which the writer himself regards the role of different groups in that transition.

The first example contrasts a conservative and a humanist critique of commercialization in late eighteenth century Germany. In 1778 the publicist Justus Möser complained in an article on "genuine property" that in his day the German language had lost its capacity to designate an owner's inalienable relationship to his property.[11] At one time ownership of land included associated rights in addition to those of proprietorship, such as the right to hunt, to vote in the national assembly, and others. These rights had been known by distinctive terms which gave a clue to the specific rights an owner enjoyed in perpetuity. He could sell or otherwise dispose of the land itself, but he could not divest himself of these rights any more than a purchaser of the land could acquire them. Möser's critique of the change of language is thus at the same time an indictment of moral decay resulting from an easy transfer of property. The relationship between an owner and his property is in his view a source at once of personal identification and social stability. These are ensured only as long as ownership of land confers on the proprietor rights and privileges which give him status in the community and can be obtained by inheritance only, not by purchase.

The humanist critique of commercialization looks at first glance very similar to that of Möser. Trading as well as the ownership and care of property undermine an individual's integrity, because his every act and thought turns on considerations of money and economic expediency. Man is ruled by that which should be at his service. In his novel *Wilhelm Meisters Lehrjahre,* originally published in 1796, Goethe expresses this view when he writes: "What can it avail me to manufacture good iron whilst my own breast is full of dross? Or to what purpose were it to understand the art of reducing landed estates to order, when my own thoughts are not in harmony?"[12] But Goethe's hero goes on to relate this anticommercial view to the conflicting personal values of the *Bürger* and the aristocrat. The latter, he claims, has polished manners in keeping with his lofty social position, but he does not cultivate his heart. The *Bürger* cannot make such pretensions. For him the decisive question is not "who he is" but what "discernment, knowledge, talents, or riches" he possesses. "He must cultivate some individual talent, in order to render one talent useful, and it is well understood that in his existence there can be no harmony, because in order to render one talent useful, he must abandon the exercise of every other."[13] Thus, to Goethe's hero, the aristocrat has high social standing but a cold heart, the *Bürger* may gain distinction by his attainments, but only the artist is in a position to pursue the "harmonious cultivation of his nature."[14]

The resemblance between these views does not go beyond their common rejection of commerce. Möser looks backwards towards a society characterized by a rank-order of privilege and subordination based on land and the rights associated with landownership. He attributes to that society not merely stability, but ideal qualities of mind and feeling such that man's relations to his fellows are in harmony and his work an adequate outlet for his capabilities. Against this mythical image of the past, the commercialization of property appears as a decay of civilization. During the century and a half which followed, Möser's praise of inalienable, prescriptive rights was associated again and again not only with the benevolence of paternalistic rule but also with the warmth of personal relations and the sense of personal belonging made possible by a closely knit, hierarchic community. Against this benign view of tradition Goethe's hero defines his own position by referring to the empty cruel heart which goes together with the polished manners of the aristocrat. Bourgeois man stands forth by virtue of his individual achievements, which represent greater personal worth than the ease and poise which are an unearned, and hence unmerited, by-product of inherited privilege. The *Bürger* may lack manners, but at least his individual attainments establish his personal worth. Yet, like Ferguson and Millar, Goethe's hero decries the stultifying effects of specialization. The merit of achievement is only relative, for in the ordinary man it is the result of a one-sided development; all his other capacities are sacrificed so that he may be useful. This praise of man's protean capacities—here put as the artist's many-sided cultivation of his personality—has been associated ever since with the radical critique of bourgeois civilization. An emphasis on achievement as an attribute of that civilization entirely misses this inherent ambiguity of the value of individual striving and creativity.

The two opinions from late eighteenth century Germany reflect a provincial setting in which economic change was slow but from which imaginative men witnessed more rapid changes taking place in England and France. The classic document portraying this response is Goethe's epic poem *Hermann und Dorothea* in which the upheavals of the French revolution are commented on from afar and in eloquent contrast to the well-being and contentment of an average, small-town *Bürger* family.[15] Under these circumstances reflections about the effects of commerce on the ranks of society tended to be abstract, whether they consisted of nostalgic references to the past or humanistic celebrations of personal values.

With the advance of commerce and industry during the first decades of the nineteenth century, critical reflections on the impact of these changes continued. Invidious contrasts between tradition and modernity, and between one-sided utility and individual creativity, were elaborated and reiterated, but with more direct attention to the nature of work. Across an interval of more than two generations one may compare the contrast between Möser and Goethe's hero in Germany with the contrast between de Bonald and Proudhon in France. According to Bonald, industry has increased the material wealth of the country, but it has also produced civic unrest and moral decay. Members of families employed in industry

work in isolation and frequently in different industries. They have no more acquaintance with their master than what he commands and what little he pays. Industry does not nourish all ages nor all sexes. True, it employs the child, but frequently at the expense of his education or before he is sufficiently strong for such work. On the other hand, when a man has reached old age and can no longer work, he is abandoned and has no other bread than that which his children may provide or public charity bestow. . . .

The [industrial laborer] works in crowded and sedentary conditions, turns a crank, runs the shuttle, gathers the threads. He spends his life in cellars and garrets. He becomes a machine himself. He exercises his fingers but never his mind. . . . Everything debases the intelligence of the industrial worker.[16]

In this critique of industry emphasis on the incapacities resulting from specialization are related to the industrial worker and his family. To eke out a subsistence, members of the family are dispersed, they work in isolation, and have no human relationship with their employer. In addition, industry as a whole abuses the child and gives no care to the aged.

In all these respects agricultural work is superior. On the land the different classes work alongside each other and at the same tasks; hence there is no social isolation between them. Children and old people are cared for and productively employed at tasks commensurate with their capacities. Agricultural work is not only healthy in contrast with industrial; it also furthers the intelligence of the peasant or farm laborer. Cultivation of the land demands attention to varied tasks, furthers neighborly cooperation, and through contact with natural processes lifts thought "to that which endows the earth with fertility, gives us the seasons, makes the fruit ripen."[17] Where Möser emphasizes the social stability and moral worth achieved by inalienable property rights, Bonald emphasizes that similar values are inherent in the nature of agricultural work. For Bonald as for Möser, the material benefits of commerce and industry are not worth the price in human values they exact. For both, the traditional social order represents sociability, meaningful human relations, proper security, care for young and old, and man's opportunity to develop his capacities to the full. In all these respects industry is said to fail; its sole accomplishment is the increase of wealth.

This critique of industry is not very different at points from Proudhon's radical attack upon the new industrial order (1846). Proudhon also believes that specialization has a destructive effect upon the individual. Like Bonald he deplores the helplessness of industrial workers and feels that the advance of technology turns men into machines.[18] But their common critique of industry and praise of agriculture shows that Proudhon and Bonald see the same facts in entirely different terms. For example, both agree that agricultural work is many-sided, not one-sided and stultifying like industrial work. Yet Proudhon finds this praiseworthy as the foundation of individualism not, like Bonald, as the foundation of neighborliness and cooperation. Proudhon sees the agricultural proprietor as the solitary man who tills the soil for his family and does not depend upon the assistance of others: "never have peasants been seen to form a society for the cultivation of their fields; never will they be seen to do so." This ability to maintain his family by his own efforts makes the peasant into the ideal anarchist. By contrast Proudhon emphasizes that certain industries "require the combined employment of a large number of workers" involving subordination and mutual dependence. "The producer is no longer, as in the fields, a sovereign and free father of a family; it is a collectivity."[19] Thus, for Proudhon, industry is the locus of an enforced collectivism, mutual dependence, and subordination, whereas agriculture enhances freedom and individualism. He favors agriculture, because he rejects the "hierarchy of capacities" as a "principle and law" of social organization.[20] By contrast, Bonald accepts inequalities among men as a fact of nature which is merely recognized by society. For him the distinction between industry and agriculture turns on the question of which activity furthers the community, not the individual; and in this respect industry enhances human isolation, while agriculture promotes human solidarity.

Clearly, each writer structures the evidence to suit his purpose. For Proudhon neighborly assistance disappears from the agricultural community because he searches for a personification of the individualism which is his ideal; for Bonald the harshness of the peasant's struggle with nature, and the human abuse which is endemic in close neighborly relations, disappear in the roseate image of the community modeled on the familial pattern. Much the same is true of the two views of industry. For Proudhon the relative freedom of the industrial worker does not exist, and he ignores the fundamental subordination of the farm laborer in agriculture. Bonald, on the other hand, sees the worker's freedom only in its negative side, as human isolation in contrast to a benign solidarity in agriculture. One man idealizes agriculture as the bulwark of traditional society; the other, however mistakenly, sees it as the principal means of leveling social differences, decreasing mutual dependence, and enhancing individual freedom. Transparent as they are, such ideological constructions have had a profound influence upon the contrast of tradition and modernity down to the present.

To these examples I wish to add a brief reference to similar arguments on this side of the Atlantic. They will show something of the persistence of the intellectual tradition I am characterizing, even under quite divergent conditions. In the United States conservative views like those of Bonald had been openly expressed during the first decades following the Declaration of Independence. During the 1830's the public disclosure of these views became politically inexpedient, even among New England conservatives.[21] At the same time, the belief in inequality became a matter of deep conviction in the southern states. In this regional context, conservative views became linked with an attack on northern industrialism, on the one hand, and a defense of slavery, on the other. In his *Sociology for the South,* George Fitzhugh denounced men of property who are masters without the feelings and sympathies of masters, engaged in the selfish struggle to better their pecuniary condition and hence without time or inclination to cultivate the heart or the head.[22] Fitzhugh reiterates the theme which is already familiar to us: that the division of labor may make men more efficient, but that it also confines the worker to some monotonous employment and makes him an easy prey of the capitalist, who considers him solely in monetary terms.[23] In this setting the standard argument against the division of labor, which Marx emphasized so much, is used in a defense of slavery! Fitzhugh contrasts the moral destitution of the free laborer, hated by his employer for the demands he makes and by his fellow workers because he competes for employment, with the moral attainments and domestic tranquillity of the South, which is founded upon the parental affection of the masters and child-like obedience of the slaves.[24]

This view is strangely echoed by Orestes A. Brownson, a New England cleric and radical Christian who had identified himself with the workers in the 1830's and later became converted to Catholicism. Brownson contrasts the moral degradation imposed on both employers and workers with the benign features of paternalism:

Between the master and the slave, between the lord and the serf, there often grow up pleasant personal relations and attachments; there is personal intercourse, kindness, affability, protection on the one side, respect and gratitude on the other, which partially compensates for the superiority of the one and the inferiority of the other; but the modern system of wages allows very little of all this: the capitalist and the workman belong to different species, and have little personal intercourse. The agent or man of business pays the workman his wages, and there ends the responsibility of the employer. The laborer has no further claim on him and he may want and starve, or sicken and die, it is his own affair. with which the employer has nothing to do. Hence the relation between the two classes becomes mercenary, hard and a matter of arithmetic.[25]

This language is not essentially different from that of the *Communist Manifesto;* it culminates in the contrasting images of exploiters and exploited, of haughty indifference, on the one hand, and injured hostility, on the other. Brownson even uses Marx's symbol of the worker as an appendage to the machine, although the phrase may have been common among social critics of the mid-nineteenth century.

The examples I have cited suggest that, from the late eighteenth century on, men of letters were made deeply anxious by what they considered the moral crisis in human relations, brought on by the coming of industry. Karl Mannheim has pointed out that critics like Möser and Goethe or Bonald and Proudhon were deeply divided in their political views but nonetheless based their opposition to industrial society on grounds that are similar to quite a striking extent.[26] Industry depends upon the division of labor and, as that division progresses, men cease to be masters of the machines they use and instead become their victims. As labor becomes more monotonous, workers are increasingly deprived of the opportunity to develop and apply their human faculties. More generally, the specialized development of one capacity in the interest of productivity and commercial success entails the atrophy of many or most other capacities. Industrial man appears as the counterimage of Renaissance man at all levels of the social structure. At the same time, commercialization loosens the ties which bind men to each other. Freedom from paternal rule and the hierarchy of rank is obtained for the individual—but only at the price of fraternity. The ties among men lose their basis in sentiment and the sense of moral obligation and come to depend on economic interest alone. As equals, men compete with one another rather than cooperate; and as employers and workers, they strike bargains solely in terms of material advantage.

These themes have been standbys of social thought for almost two centuries.[27] They owe their profound emotional appeal to the invidious linkage between the transition to an industrial society and the decline of the two ideas of individual creativity and human fraternity. Obviously, conservatives attribute both of these values to a largely symbolic, hier-archic order of the past, but implicitly (and sometimes explicitly also) radical critics of industrial society use the same clichés. By their incorpora-tion in the work of Karl Marx these clichés have become a dominant influence on modern thought because of the unique way in which Marx combined the sense of moral crisis described above with his claim that his approach represented a scientific study of society. Reflections on Marx's theories are legion; here they will be pursued only to the extent that the reader can form an independent judgment of the differences between the presentation which follows and this most influential treatment of social classes in the process of modernization.

The Marxian Perspective

"The history of all hitherto existing societies is the history of class struggles." The *Communist Manifesto* begins with this sentence, yet Marx's work as a whole does not contain a sustained analysis of social classes. The third volume of his lifework, *Das Kapital,* breaks off after four para-graphs of a chapter which was to be devoted to this topic. The paradox has drawn much comment, but it is more apparent than real. Probably Marx had said what he had to say about social classes, since it is not diffi-cult to summarize his views.[28]

For Marx, classes are but the agents of social change, and their ulti-mate determinant is the organization of production. His reasons for this assumption go back to early philosophical considerations. Today these would be considered existentialist in the sense of inferences derived from basic exigencies of human experience. Men cannot live without work; they also propagate their kind and hence enter into the social relations of the family. Men use tools to satisfy their needs; as basic needs are satisfied, new needs arise and techniques of production are improved. The prolifer-ation of needs and improved techniques put a premium on cooperation based on some division of labor, for divided labor increases productivity. How labor is divided depends on the organization of production, specifically on the distribution of property in the means of production. It is, therefore, the position which the individual occupies in the organization of production with regard to that distribution of property which indicates his social class.

In the unfinished chapter on class mentioned above Marx distinguishes between wage-laborers, capitalists, and landlords (who form the three great classes of capitalist society) and the "infinite distinctions of interest and position which the social division of labor creates *among* workers [as well] as *among* capitalists and landowners."[29] In a complex society, individuals are distinguished from one another in a great many ways, even when they belong to the same class. Thus, individuals who depend entirely upon wage-labor may still differ greatly in terms of income, consumption patterns, educational attainment, or occupation. Efforts to ascertain class membership by grouping people in terms of their similar share in the distribution of material goods, skills, and prestige symbols, in Marx's view, produces only statistical artifacts. For him "class" refers to a process of group formation in which people are united despite the "infinite distinctions of interest and position" which divide them.[30] To be sure, a shared position in the organization of production is the necessary condition of a social class. But only the experience gained in making a living, and particularly the experience of economic and political conflict, would prompt workers, capitalists, or landowners to develop a consciousness of class and become united in action. Marx specified a number of conditions that would facilitate the process. Where communication of ideas among individuals in the same class position is easy, repeated economic conflicts will lead to a growth of solidarity and a sense of historic opportunities. Profound dissatisfactions arise from an inability to control the economic structure in which the ruling class curtails the economic advance of the group and subjects it to exploitation. In Marx's view a social class becomes an agent of historical change when these dissatisfactions lead to the formation of political organizations so that a fully developed class is a politically organized group, capable of overcoming in action the distinctions of interest and rank that divide it.

This interpretation of social class was based in the first instance on Marx's detailed observations of the English labor movement which he himself systematized in the following words:

Large-scale industry assembles in one place a crowd of people who are unknown to each other. Competition divides their interests. But the maintenance of their wages, this common interest which they have against their employer, brings them together again in the same idea of resistance—*combination*. Thus combination has always a double aim, that of putting an end to competition among themselves, to enable them to compete as a whole with the capitalist. If the original aim of resistance was that of maintaining wages, to the extent that the capitalists, in their turn, unite with the aim of repressive measures, the combinations, at first isolated, became organized into groups, and in face of the unity of the capitalists, the maintenance of the combination becomes more important than upholding the level of wages. This is so true that English economists have been astonished to observe the workers sacrificing a substantial part of their wages in favour of the associations, which in the eyes of the economists were only established to defend wages. In this struggle—a veritable civil war—all the elements for a future battle are brought together and developed. Once arrived at this point the association takes on a political character.[31]

This conception of class as a group gradually emerging to self-consciousness and political organization in the course of economic and political struggles was at once analysis and projection: analysis insofar as Marx systematized his observations of emerging working-class movements in England from the late eighteenth to the middle of the nineteenth century;[32] projection insofar as Marx generalized from this analysis, both with regard to the formation of classes in the past (for example, that of the bourgeoisie under feudalism) and with regard to the development of a revolutionary working class in the future. The latter views applied not only in England but in all countries undergoing a capitalist development such as England had experienced since the eighteenth century. We should understand what gave Marx confidence in predicting that the struggle he analyzed would eventuate in a revolutionary overthrow and reconstitution of society.

The first point to be mentioned is Marx's acceptance and dramatic elaboration of the ideas briefly described above. Like Ferguson, Millar, Möser, Goethe, Bonald, Proudhon, Fitzhugh, Brownson, and a host of others, Marx was deeply impressed by the moral crisis which capitalism had wrought in man's relation with his fellows and his work. To cite Marx's views on alienation at this point would be to repeat many of the moral reflections cited earlier (albeit in more Hegelian language) and what has been elaborated in a thousand ways by critics of modern society since his day.[33] But Marx's elaboration of widely shared beliefs assumed special significance. The reason is, I believe, that for him the mounting alienation of men was part of an economic process in which repeated and severe depressions together with the capitalists' restrictive practices would create an ever-increasing discrepancy between the forces and the organization of production, or, in simpler language, between the economy's capacity to satisfy human needs and the satisfaction of needs which is actually achieved. Marx's economic analysis seeks to support this interpretation, and in view of the importance he attached to it, he had no reason to feel that he had neglected the analysis of social class. His analysis is distinguished from the many other writers who developed similar themes by the belief that he had proved man's alienation to be a symptom of the *final* phase of "pre-history."

Secondly, Marx welcomed the technical and economic changes which were revolutionizing the old order, but he saw the difference between then and now in a very special way. Earlier epochs were marked by "manifold gradations of social rank," but the modern era tends towards a simplified antagonism between bourgeoisie and proletariat. While this prediction has not stood the test of time, it is of a piece with his view that all previous history is pre-history. Never before had the social world been stripped of all its traditional practices and religious beliefs; only now had it been revealed as it really is, capable of a rational ordering by men who have come within reach of satisfying all their desires. Eventually, the classless communist society of the future would establish both a true fraternity among men and, on that basis, an opportunity for each to develop and apply his capacities. Though he refused to speculate about this new order, Marx was emphatic that world history was nearing its decisive turning point. In his view, man's productive potential had become so great that the deprivations of inequality and hence the substitute gratifications of religious beliefs had become obsolete. For the same reasons human relations have become transparent so that the social order is now capable of being "consciously regulated by freely associated men in accordance with a settled plan."[34] Marx believed that this equalitarian society of the future would bring about a complete break with the past, leading to a cessation of class struggles and freeing men from being at the mercy of circumstances not of their own choosing. For the first time in history, men had the opportunity to establish a rationally planned society. To cope with this turning point in world history, Marx devoted his life work to an analysis of those cumulative conditions, endemic in the capitalist organization of production, which would bring about the final revolutionary struggle.

The third point to be noted is the famous paradox of Marx's determinism. On the one hand, he predicted that the contradictions inherent in capitalism would inevitably produce a class-conscious proletariat and a proletarian revolution. On the other, he assigned to class-consciousness, to political action, and to his own scientific theory a major role in bringing the inevitable about. The paradox is resolved once it is remembered that for Marx the eventual revolution—as well as the subjective actions and ideas which help bring it about—are consequences of the mounting contradictions between the potential for productivity and the actuality of exploitation. Marx explains the eventual political maturity of the proletariat and the constructive role of "bourgeois ideologists" as well as his own scientific theory as creative responses to contradictions which are the product of capitalism.

For Marx "all hitherto existing societies" encompass the "pre-history" of class struggles as contrasted with the classless society of the future. All his attention is focused on analyzing the last phase of that pre-history. Accurate, scientific understanding of this phase is ultimately indispensable for choosing and guiding political action, but capitalism also jeopardizes all constructive and undistorted use of intelligence. Between these two positions there is a fundamental ambivalence. Marx wants to *know,* accurately and dispassionately; but, since his own theory of the socio-historical foundation of knowledge casts doubt upon the possibility of a science of society, he also wants to make sure that the knowledge gained will play a constructive role in human affairs. Science shows that alienation must get worse, and the worse alienation gets, the more it will function as the historical precipitant of the truth which will make men free. Accordingly, his lifelong work on economic theory, cast in a scientific mold, and his moral vision of an ultimate revolt against alienation support each other. In his view a moral and world-historical crisis is upon us because we face the prospect of immiseration—relative deprivation and the loss of fraternity and creativity—just when an era of plenty has become possible. Marx's confidence in the contribution of his own theory was greatly re-enforced by this coincidence—as he saw it—of a moral and an historical crisis. But at the same time we should note that this combination of a moral concern, a world-historical perspective, and a scientific stance greatly re-enforced the invidious contrast between tradition and modernity as the foundation of a scholarly understanding of modernization.

Critique of an Intellectual Tradition

The interpretations of modernization which I have reviewed established an intellectual tradition which has remained predominant down to the present. By their frequent reformulations of the contrast between tradition and modernity, such writers as Ferdinand Toennies, Emile Durkheim, and, among American sociologists, Charles Cooley, Robert Park, Robert Redfield, and Talcott Parsons have strongly re-enforced that tradition. For all their diversity, these and related writers have the idea in common that "traditional society" and "modern society" constitute two systems of interrelated variables. The tendency is (1) to treat societies as "natural systems," (2) to search for the independent variables which—if altered initially—will cause changes in the related, but dependent variables in the process of transition from one type to the other, (3) to conceive of the transition as one of declining tradition and rising modernity, and, finally, (4) to assume that social change consists of a process that is internal to the society changing.

Marx was probably the most prominent expositor of this approach. England was the first country to industrialize. In Marx's view she exemplified the laws of capitalist development which he had analyzed in *Capital*. Writing in 1867, in his preface to the first edition of that work, Marx declared England to be the classic ground of the capitalist mode of production. He explained his analytic procedure in the following terms:

The physicist either observes physical phenomena where they occur in their most typical form and most free from disturbing influence, or, wherever possible, he makes experiments under conditions that assure the occurrence of the phenomenon in its normality. In this work I have to examine the capitalist mode of production, and the conditions of production and exchange corresponding to that mode. Up to the present time, their classic ground is England. That is the reason why England is used as the chief illustration in the development of my theoretical ideas. If, however, the German reader shrugs his shoulders at the conditions of the English industrial and agricultural laborers, or in optimist fashion comforts himself with the thought that in Germany things are not nearly so bad, I must plainly tell him, *"De te fabula narratur!"*
Intrinsically, it is not a question of the higher or lower degree of development of the social antagonisms that result from the natural laws of capitalist production. It is a question of these laws themselves, of these tendencies working with iron necessity towards inevitable results. The country that is more developed industrially only shows, to the less developed, the image of its own future.[35]

Marx made these predictions on the assumption that the same organization of production generates everywhere the same or similar transformations of social classes and the political structure. As an empirical proposition, this assumption is misleading because it treats societies as if they were entirely self-contained structures, each evolving in terms of given, internal tendencies. Actually, once industrialization had been initiated in England, the technical innovations and the institutions of the economically advanced country could be used as a model to move ahead more rapidly than England had while mitigating or even avoiding the problems encountered by the pioneering country. I shall consider this possibility in more detail below; Marx himself also noted it but did not think it significant. Instead, he declared that his analysis of the advanced country could help to "shorten the birth-pangs" of similar developments in other countries. By making social change in the long run entirely dependent upon the economic structure, Marx precluded recognition of the importance which international emulation and governmental initiative, nationalism, and the diffusion of ideas could have in countries that followed in the wake of English industrialization. It is a measure of the surpassing influence of the intellectual tradition culminating in Marx that basically similar assumptions still inform many recent and empirical studies of development. Some of these studies will here be considered in brief review in order to substantiate this statement.

Studies of social change typically operate with a "before-and-after" model of the society under consideration. The earlier and the later social structure are distinguished by two sets of dichotomous attributes, and one has great difficulty in resisting the view that each set constitutes a generalizable system of interrelated variables. On that assumption societies can be classified according to the degree to which they exhibit one set of attributes rather than another, resulting in a rank-ordering of countries in terms of their relative modernization. An example of this procedure appears in Daniel Lerner's well-known study *The Passing of Traditional Society*.

The great merit of Lerner's study consists in its candid use of Western modernization as a model of global applicability. For Marx, England, as the country that is "more developed industrially," exemplified universal "laws of capitalist development"; for Lerner, Western modernization exhibits "certain components and sequences whose relevance is global."[36] He recognizes that the North Atlantic area developed first and rather gradually, while other countries came later and sought to develop more rapidly;

but, like Marx before him, he dismisses this as a secondary consideration.[37] As Lerner sees it, the central proposition is that in the process of modernization, then as now, four sectors or dimensions are systematically related to one another: urbanization, literacy, media participation, and political participation. The author appears to regard the following statement as central to his purpose:

> The book seeks to explain *why* and show *how* individuals and their institutions modernize together. It denies a unique role to "human nature" or to "social determinism." Having no taste for beating dead horses, we do not even acknowledge these as issues, but go directly to a "behavioral" perspective. To wit: social change operates through persons and places. Either individuals or their environments modernize together or modernization leads elsewhere than intended. *If new institutions* of political, economic, cultural behavior *are to change in compatible ways, then inner coherence must be provided* by the *personality matrix* which governs individual behavior. We conceive modernity as a participant style of life; we identify its distinctive personality mechanism as empathy. Modernizing individuals and institutions, like chicken and egg, reproduce these traits in each other.[38]

This vigorous assertion of a behavioral perspective rejects a psychological as well as a social determinism, but is still beholden to the conventional contrast between tradition and modernity.[39]

Professor Lerner puts the case in a conditional form which is hard to reconcile with his emphasis on behaviorism. He says in effect that either new institutions change in compatible ways (meaning, presumably, ways similar to the Western model), or modernization leads elsewhere than intended (meaning, presumably, in directions differing from the Western model). He believes that the high association between urbanization, literacy, media participation, and political participation in modern societies points to an underlying, systemic coherence (which Lerner calls "the participant style of life") such that societies can be ranked in accordance with their degree of tradition, transition, or modernity. Yet I do not believe there is any assurance that once initiated economic growth will be self-sustaining or that new institutions will change in compatible ways. Professor Lerner himself asserts that "traditional societies exhibit extremely variant 'growth' patterns; some are more urban than literate, others more media participant than urban."[40] Such "deviations from the regression line" are due to the fact that "people don't do what, on any rational course of behavior, they should do"[41]—hardly a consistent, behaviorist position. And although Professor Lerner recognizes that in the emerging nations people have not done what according to his model they should have done, he still considers his model validated by events.[42]

In recent years Lerner's work has been followed by a whole series of studies which compile attribute-checklists on which the countries of the world are ranked by the degree to which they approximate the characteristics of Western industrial societies.[43] Such an approach rests on an application of evolutionary theory to very short time-periods despite earlier warnings that this is highly questionable, even from the standpoint of evolutionism.[44] If the earlier and the later social structure constitute two generalizable systems of interrelated variables, it may be logical to infer that the transition from one to the other is characterized by admixtures of attributes from both and, over a period of time, by a decline of attributes from the first and a rise of attributes from the second. Despite cautionary comments, the tendency is to substitute a horizontal compilation for the vertical dimension of history.[45] Yet attribute-checklists of the relative modernization of countries do not easily avoid the implication that change, once initiated, must run its course along the lines indicated by the Western model, and that in the transition to modernity all aspects of the social structure change in some more or less integrated and simultaneous fashion. Only on these assumptions is it reasonable to ignore the timing and sequence of modernization of countries in their several and distinct aspects. However, just this timing and sequence can make a crucial difference for the success or failure of the effort to modernize. In his introduction to Lerner's book, David Riesman notes that the transitional individual is defined as one who attends to the mass media, but cannot read—to which he appends the disturbing question: "What will a society look like which is dominated by such 'post-literate' types?"[46] This question points to the possibility of a transition of long duration, a contradiction in terms which arises from evolutionist assumptions and leads to a questionable nomenclature about "developing" or "transitional" societies which may never become developed enough to be called modern. Related questions are raised as efforts at modernization in these so-called developing countries have led, or are leading, to changes of sequence and timing as compared with the Western model. For example, in many European countries the franchise was extended rather slowly, while in many newly independent countries universal suffrage has been adopted all at once.[47] Such a difference is ignored where countries are merely ranked at one point in time in terms of the degree to which the franchise has been extended to the adult members of their populations. The matter is not necessarily improved by the addition of another index, say that of literacy, because such data—even if they were reliable—would not reveal the level of education attained by the population. More generally, checklists of attributes of modernization are not likely to yield reliable inference, if—without regard to sequence and timing—their several items are interpreted as indexes of approximation to the Western model.[48]

Nevertheless, comparative studies of modernization necessarily rely on the Western experience when they construct developmental sequences. This practice becomes hazardous only when past experience is used to extrapolate to the future of industrializing societies. In their book, *Industrialism and Industrial Man,* Clark Kerr and his associates explicitly emphasize that the "logic of industrialism" they have constructed involves abstractions on the assumption that the "transition stage of industrialization" has passed. Indeed, they emphasize that tendencies *deductively* arrived at (albeit by illustrative reference to the experience of developed societies) are not likely to be fully realized in the *actual* course of history. Yet, throughout the volume phrases recur which betray a confusion between these two levels of analysis. On the same page tendencies are alternately called logically constructed and inherent (33–34); emphasis on the contrast between abstraction and history is followed by the assertion that "the empire of industrialism will embrace the whole world" (46); industrialization is called an "invincible process," while the uncertainties of the future are relegated to variations of length and difficulty in the transition or to the several types of past industrializations (19–20, 47 ff.). Perhaps the most arresting feature of this deterministic view of the future is that the industrialism of the whole world is predicated, not on the organization of production as in Marx, but on the initiating or manipulating actions of five different elites whose capacity to industrialize whole societies is simply assumed. Exceptions, delays, and what not are seen as deviations which "cannot prevent the transformation in the long run,"[49] while neither the possibility of failure nor that of unprecedented types of industrialization is given serious consideration. Seldom has social change been interpreted in so managerial a fashion, while all contingencies of action are treated as mere historical variations which cannot alter the "logic of industrialism." Although the recognition of alternate routes to industrialization is a distinct improvement over the unilinear evolutionism of the study by Lerner, the authors abandon the gain they have made when they predict one sys-

tem of industrialism for all societies in much the same way as Marx predicted the end of class struggles and of history for the socialist society of
the future.

An Alternative Approach to Tradition and Modernity

The studies cited above may suffice as examples of the persistent
influence of an intellectual tradition which originated with the emergence
of industrial society in western Europe. Necessarily, studies of social
change rely on historical experience. But the preceding review of ideas
about social change has suggested that Western modernization has been
accompanied throughout by a particular intellectual construction of that
experience, prompted by moral or reforming impulses often presented in
the guise of scientific generalizations. Theories of social evolution have
had a particularly important influence in this respect in that they tend to
use historical experience to construct contrasting ideal types of tradition
and modernity and then use that contrast to make contingent generalizations about the transition from one to the other. In the following section,
I turn to a critical assessment of this approach as well as to the proposal
of an alternative.

Ideal Types are not Generalizations

At a minimum, considerations of change involve two terminal conditions so that the word "change" refers to the differences observed before
and after a given interval of time. Without knowing in what respects a
later social structure differs from an earlier one, we would not know what
changes to look for and explain. Accordingly, we are obliged to characterize the earlier (pre-modern) and later (modern) social structure by two
lists of mutually disjunctive attributes.

The abstract formulation of such contrasts can be as seriously misleading, however, as the moral evaluations reviewed earlier. The point may be
illustrated by using Talcott Parsons' contrast between universalism and
particularism as attributes of modernity and tradition, respectively. In Europe traditional society, though particularistic in many respects, involved a
major element of universalism through the Christian faith and the institutions of the Catholic Church; in China traditional society involved other
universalist elements through Confucianism and the examination system; even in India, where Hindu religion and the caste system fostered an

extreme particularism, the basic cultural themes of that particularism spread throughout the subcontinent. Evidently, "particularism" characterizes traditional societies only in some respects, while in others it is combined with a "universalism" which may be as different as Catholicism, Confucianism, or the ideas of reincarnation. Hence, the disjunctive characterization of tradition and modernity by such abstract terms as "particularism" and "universalism" exaggerates and simplifies the evidence, as Max Weber pointed out in his discussion of the ideal type. Such characterization says nothing about the strength or generality with which any one attribute is present. Also, the use of one or several abstract terms to characterize either tradition or modernity tends to mistake labeling for analysis, since apparently societies vary not only in the degree but also in the kind of their universalism or particularism. And at this abstract level it is quite probable that no society is without some elements from both ends of the continuum, leading some writers to use phrases such as "the modernity of tradition" or "the tradition of the new."[50]

These problems are compounded when we turn from the contrast between social structures "before and after" to a consideration of change from the one to the other. In this respect we can be guided by Max Weber's discussion of this problem: "*Developmental* sequences too can be constructed into ideal types and these constructs can have quite considerable heuristic value. But this quite particularly gives rise to the danger that the ideal type and reality will be confused with one another."[51] Accordingly, ideal-typical constructs of development must be sharply distinguished from the actual sequence of historical changes, but Weber notes that this distinction is "uncommonly difficult" to maintain. For in *constructing* a developmental sequence we will use illustrative materials in order to make clear what we mean and hence will be greatly tempted to confuse the sequence of ideal types with an historical course of events.

The series of types which results from the selected conceptual criteria appears then as an historical sequence unrolling with the necessity of a law. The logical classification of analytical concepts on the one hand and the empirical arrangements of the events thus conceptualized in space, time, and causal relationship, on the other, appear to be so bound up together that there is an almost irresistible temptation to do violence to reality in order to prove the real validity of the construct.[52]

The hazards referred to by Weber have not gone unnoticed. Following the tradition of Maine, Durkheim, and Toennies, Robert Redfield compared four contemporary communities in Yucatan. He emphasized that his method was not to be recommended to those wishing to raise questions "as to whether changes in any of the characters are related to or conditioned by changes in any of the others, and as to how they are interrelated. . . ." But while Redfield clearly stated that he had not answered such questions, he nevertheless supposed that "there is some natural or interdependent relation among some or all of the characters in that change with regard to certain of them tends to bring about or carry with it change with respect to others of them. . . .[53] In thus seeing his problem as one of causal "relations among variables" Redfield unwittingly disregards his own warning concerning the disjunction between ideal types and historical sequences. We should try to understand why this confusion is as widespread as Weber already suggested.

In operating with a "before-and-after" model of the society under consideration, one has difficulty in resisting the view that the two sets of attributes characterizing the earlier and the later social structure constitute generalizable systems of interrelated variables. But in adopting this view, we entirely ignore that the specification of a list of attributes is ideal-typical and hence simplifies and exaggerates the evidence. If we are to avoid mistaking ideal types for accurate descriptions, we must take care to treat the clusters of attributes as hypothetically, and not actually, correlated. We need these clusters to distinguish between social structures, we illustrate them by historical examples, but these are still abstractions, constructs that can only be used as tools of analysis. Redfield, for example, suggested that the relative isolation and the occupational homogeneity of communities coexisted in many instances and was perhaps causally related. No doubt there are many isolated communities with relatively little division of labor, but degree of isolation and occupational differentiation are correlated very imperfectly, and over a period of time communities have varied independently in both dimensions. If one wishes to get away from the artificiality of ideal types one can visualize two overlapping frequency distributions in which either isolation or occupational heterogeneity are treated as the dependent variable. Such distributions would approximate historical reality more closely, whereas the ideal type of an isolated and homogeneous community is best employed as a suggestion for the investigation of isolated communities with considerable division of labor or nonisolated communities that are relatively homogeneous.[54]

That these cautions are often ignored may be illustrated by reference to two related and quite common lines of reasoning. One of these has to do with the notion of prerequisites. Beginning with the contrast between tradition and modernity (in one of its many versions), the analyst takes all the basic traits of modernity to be prerequisites of modernity, a procedure which implies that regardless of time and place all countries must somehow create all the conditions characteristic of modernity before they can hope to be successful in their drive of modernization. But

obviously, some of the factors listed are not prerequisites at all, but rather something that developed in the course of industrial development. Moreover, what can be reasonably regarded as a prerequisite in some historical cases can be much more naturally seen as a product of industrialization in others. The line between what is a precondition of, and what is a response to industrial development seems to be a rather flexible one.[55]

Such a distinction could be made only if the specific processes of industrialization are analyzed. However, causes and consequences tend to become confused with one another, if it is assumed that the process of industrialization is uniform and that countries entering upon this process at a later time will repeat in all essentials the previous industrialization of some other country.[56]

Another line of reasoning involves an undue generalization from a limited historical experience (rather than working back from present characteristics to necessary prerequisites). For example, the decline of kinship ties and the concomitant rise of individualism were an aspect of Western modernization. Today we are learning how many meanings and exceptions were, in fact, compatible with this overall tendency, although these are quite properly ignored when we construct an ideal-typical sequence. But, rather than using that sequence to show how and why actual historical developments deviate from it, we use it to make contingent predictions about the future of developing societies. To be sure, no one is likely to say simply that these societies will develop; he states instead that they will not develop unless kinship ties decline. There are at least three things wrong with this procedure: (a) it ignores the exaggerations and simplifications which went into the formulation of the ideal type in the first place, hence blinding us to the role which kinship ties and collectivism played in the modernization of Western Europe; (b) it also blinds us to the possible ways in which kinship ties and collectivism might be, or might be made, compatible with the modernization of other areas since, tacitly, we have misused the ideal type as a generalization; and (c) it diverts attention from the very real possibility that modernization may never arrive at modernity, so that terms like "development" or "transition" are misnomers when applied to societies whose future condition may not be markedly different from the present.

These considerations do not stand alone. Several writers have examined critically the assumptions of the intellectual tradition which I have characterized and have also found it wanting. Elkan and Fallers have examined specific local developments, like the mobility of wage labor in Uganda, and have shown in what respects this experience differs from the mobilization of a work force in early industrial England.[57] In his discussion of the changing craft traditions in India, Milton Singer has questioned the assumption of a uniform recapitulation of the process of industrialization and the tendency to employ the concept of tradition as a generalization rather than an ideal type.[58] Similar questions have been raised and systematized by Neil Smelser, who distinguishes clearly between ideal-typical constructs of, and generalizations about, social change, and who emphasizes that the latter are difficult to achieve. Even if the "vicious circle of poverty" is broken, subsequent changes of the social structure will vary according to the pre-industrial conditions of the country, the particular impetus to development, the path which modernization takes, the significant differences that persist in developed economies, and finally the impact and timing of dramatic events.[59] As Wilbert Moore has pointed out in a similar context:

The manner in which history prevents its own replication creates difficulties in generalizations that will unite historical and contemporary experience and deal with the diversity that optional paths of change introduce. . . . In addition to minimum, required sequences and results, what is needed, and is mostly not at hand, is the construction of limited-alternative or typological sequences where total generalization is improper.[60]

Strictures of this kind are of rather recent date, though Gerschenkron expressed them in 1952. They have not replaced the dominant evolutionary approach to the comparative study of modernization. The impetus to generalize even where generalization is improper derives not only from the intellectual tradition I have traced. It derives also from the desire to put policy directives on a scientific basis, and from the indispensability of ideal types in studies of social change. The fact that time and again the distinction between tradition and modernity has been oversimplified does *not* mean that we can dispense with that contrast entirely. Studies of social change are not possible without a "before-and-after" model of the social structure in question.

The Contrast Restated

I shall start with the rejection of ideal types that are mistaken for generalizable systems of interrelated variables. The contrasts between premodern and modern social structures may be formulated along the several dimensions that are conventionally distinguished in the analysis of social structures. The problem of the causal interrelation among these dimensions is one of empirical research which cannot be replaced by logical deductions, as long as the evidence argues against the assumption of one uniform process of modernization. Nor is it proper to turn the two attribute-checklists by which we may distinguish tradition from modernity into two systems to which certain properties are imputed. For in this way a set of separate or separable attributes is transformed into the structural propensities of a collective entity. Such reification is closely related to the moralism and scientism that has characterized many reactions to industrialization, as we have seen.

Smelser has suggested the concept of "structural differentiation" as a basic analytical tool for the study of modernization. He sees the transition between tradition and modernity as involving changes in several spheres of life. In technology there is a change from simple techniques to the application of scientific knowledge, and in agriculture from subsistence farming to the commercial production of agricultural goods. In industry human and animal power are replaced by power-driven machinery. And with industrialization the population shifts increasingly from the farm and the village to the city and the economic enterprises located in it. These processes of change consist of, or are accompanied by structural differentiation in the sense that in each case an earlier structure that combines several economic functions is eventually replaced by a later one characterized by greater specialization or by a greater division of labor, as the older writers called it.[61] Smelser is careful to point out that, while these processes may occur jointly, it is also true that each has occurred independently of the others. He emphasizes that structural differentiation in such other realms as the family, religion, and stratification is not simply a consequence of industrialization alone; it has occurred in pre-industrial areas, for example, as a result of colonialism.[62] In this way, "structural differentiation" provides us with a summary designation of the contrast between tradition and modernity without prejudging the systemic character of either term. The designation allows us to investigate the causal relation between different processes of structural differentiation.

Such investigations are needed, if we are to employ the indispensable, ideal-typical contrasts between "before" and "after" without imparting a spurious, deductive simplicity to the transition from one to the other.[63] A case in point is the cultural ramifications of changes in economic institutions which are properly conceived as instances of structural differentiation. The German historian Otto Brunner has shown that in the pre-modern societies of Europe the facts of economic life were typically incorporated in treatises on estate or household management, in which instructions concerning agriculture and the keeping of accounts occurred side by side with advice on the rearing of children, marital relations, the proper treatment of servants, and related matters. Technical and economic considerations were very much a part of the moral approach to human relations, a juxtaposition which belongs to a world in which the household or estate typically constituted a unit of production, consumption, and social life, whereas the separation of morals from economics belongs to a society in which the family household is typically separated from the place of work.[64] In this case, the change in economic institutions and in intellectual outlook may be considered related instances of "structural differentiation," but it should be clear that this relationship is complex and requires detailed investigation.

Such investigations can help us avoid the ambiguities which remain at the abstract level because terms like "differentiation" are not as neutral and unequivocal as one would wish. Following Durkheim, Smelser notes that modernization involves a "contrapuntal interplay" between differentiation "which is divisive of established society, and integration which unites differentiated structures on a new basis."[65] In interpreting this statement certain cautions are needed in order to avoid the value-implications of the conventional evolutionary model. Thus, a traditional economy tends to be characterized by little differentiation between economic and familial activities *within* more or less self-sufficient households or estates. *Within* the family and the community there is likely to be a high degree of integration in the sense, say, that the authority of social rank and religious norms are accepted without question. But at this point we must take care not to commit the romantic fallacy which is so prominent a part of the intellectual tradition I have surveyed.

First, lack of differentiation and high integration *within* the family and community go together with a high degree of fragmentation *between* them. Second, within families and communities everyday life is one of "proud and cruel publicity," as Huizinga puts it. Since all activities occur within the household or estate, there is a high degree of interdependence which is not only benign but also extremely coercive, which fosters sentimental attachments but also the most intense personal hatreds, which encourages fraternity but also mutual surveillance and suspicion. Accordingly, when we say that structural differentiation is divisive of the established family households, we should be aware that not only their group solidarity and stable norms (integration of established society) are disrupted, but also their lack of privacy, their personalized cruelties and oppressions from which no member of the household could previously escape. We should be aware that this disruption of the household as one form of integration goes hand-in-hand with overcoming the fragmentation between households. By the same token, integration *between* "differentiated structures on a new basis"—increased interdependence—is accompanied by increasing differentiation *within* these structures: increased privacy and freedom from personal coercion. A modern economy is characterized, therefore, by the separation of family household and workplace (structural differentiation) and by increased interdependence of the family with the market or of workers in the factory (integration on a new basis). Thus, only assiduous attention to the liabilities and assets of each structure can avoid the ideological implications of the ideal-typical contrast between tradition and modernity. Otherwise, we merely nurse the discontents of industrial society by contrasting the liabilities of the present with the assets of the past.

To avoid this pitfall, it is useful to summarize the preceding discussion in explicit contrast to the received conventions of sociology. Social structures may be distinguished by the magnitude and the psychological implications of the solidarities they achieve. Typically, traditional societies achieve intense solidarity in relatively small groups that tend to be isolated from one another by poor communication and a backward technology, and that also tend to create for their individual participants an intensity of emotional attachment and rejection which modern men find hard to appreciate and which they would probably find personally intolerable. Typically, modern societies achieve little solidarity in relatively small groups, but, by virtue of advanced communication and technology, these groups tend to be highly interdependent at an impersonal level. In this setting individual participants experience an intensity of emotional attachment and rejection at two levels which hardly exist in the traditional society—namely, in the nuclear family at its best and its worst and at the national level where personal loyalties alternate between being taken for granted in ordinary times and moving up to fever pitch during national crises or other direct confrontations with alien ways of life.

Analogous considerations apply to the invidious personification of modernity and tradition. We saw that the stultifying effects of the division of labor became a major theme of social philosophers from the beginning of industrialization. Generation after generation of writers have reiterated the theme with the same critical note, varying it merely to accommodate different contrasting images of man which have ranged from "the aristocrat" and "the medieval craftsman" to the several versions of "the Renaissance man" of protean capacities who has been the daydream of intellectuals from Goethe's Wilhelm Meister and Baudelaire's *Dandy* to Herbert Marcuse's "Multi-dimensional Man."[66] This romantic utopia of intellectuals in an era of industrialization must be taken seriously, indeed, since the ideal images of a culture affect the changing social structure in a thousand ways, but the idea of unlimited creativity by "the individual" or "the people" is as much a chimera as is that of a womb-like security and warmth in human relations attributed to a bygone age. These are projections of the discontents of intellectuals with a civilization that induces in them an intense ambivalence between elitism and populism—a point to which I return in the following discussion.

The contrast between tradition and modernity may be recast accordingly. It is probably true that traditional societies are characterized by universally accepted cultural norms, but this goes together with the subservience of men of letters to the church and to private patrons, and with the prevalence of illiteracy in the general population. It is, therefore, not accidental that terms like "ideology" and "intellectuals" originated in Europe during the eighteenth century, when traditional beliefs were challenged, men of letters were emancipated from previous subservience and literacy increased along with printed materials and a market for literary products. The universal cultural norms of traditional society also go together with a low level of productivity and communication and with a consequent fragmentation of the social structure in economic, legal, and political terms. One implication of this fragmentation is the prevalence of force and fraud and of jurisdictional disputes among a large number of solidary groups which depend for their cohesion not only on common norms but also on the imperatives of self-help and defense.[67] In each of these solidary groups and in the polity as a whole, society tends to be divided sharply between rulers and ruled. Those of gentle birth have a disproportionate share of the wealth and privileged access to positions of formal authority, and they enjoy sociability, leisure, and culture, whereas the bulk of the population lives in the drudgery of physical labor and in poverty, without access to literacy, culture, or positions of influence, and without recognized means of airing their grievances. In this setting the term "society" is applied only with difficulty since the people themselves live in fragmented subordination while their rulers constitute "the society" because they are the persons worthy of note in the country. Still other attributes could be listed, but those mentioned may suffice as a contrast-conception for a reformulation of modernity.

It is probably true that modern societies are characterized by relatively few cultural norms that are universally accepted and strongly adhered to, and this goes together with a relative emancipation of men of letters and a nearly universal literacy in the general population. Structural differentiation in technology and communications has led to high levels of productivity and a high degree of impersonal interdependence. Associated with this interdependence are the attributes of the nation state: the adjudication of legal disputes, the collection of revenue, the control of currency, military recruitment, the postal system, the construction of public facilities, and others have been removed from the political struggle among competing jurisdictions and have become the functions of a national government. Another and related characteristic of modern society is the process of fundamental democratization by which, in Karl Mannheim's phrase, "those classes which formerly only played a passive part in political life," have been stirred into action.[68] The old division between rulers and ruled is no longer clear-cut, since the ruled have the vote and the rulers are subject to formal controls at many points. Status distinctions no longer coincide with hereditary privileges. In this setting the term "society" is appropriately applied to all people in a country who constitute that society by virtue of their interdependence and equality as citizens.

The foregoing discussion has attempted to "de-ideologize" the conventional contrast of tradition and modernity. At this general level the contrast holds good for many societies that have undergone a process of modernization. Most "traditional societies" lack means of rapid communication so that the bulk of the population lives in relatively small enclaves isolated from one another. However, if one goes beyond such generalities, one is often obliged also to go beyond the simple contrast discussed here because what is true of *all* traditional societies is by the same token not very illuminating about any one of them. For example, a key feature of the European experience was the tie-in of universal cultural norms with the organization of the Church and hence with the enduring, if rather unstable, balancing of centralizing and decentralizing tendencies of government which culminated in the development of representative institutions.[69] In countries like Russia and Japan universal cultural norms came to prevail in a manner that is quite different from this western European pattern. The study of social change in these societies would, therefore, require a more specific conceptualization of the contrast between tradition and modernity in order to be analytically useful. The general contrast here discussed should be only the beginning of analysis, although often it has been mistaken for analysis itself.

Another limitation of the conventional contrast becomes apparent when one applies these concepts to colonial and post-colonial societies outside Europe. Can any colonial society be said to have the characteristics of "tradition"? Does it have universally accepted norms? And since the prevailing norms surely do not apply to the subject population, in what sense can one in fact speak of one society? Chances are that one should take account of at least two traditions if one wishes to contrast the past and present social structure of these countries: the native tradition and the tradition of a dual society created by the colonizing country. Analogous questions apply to the European frontier settlements abroad, as in the United States, Canada, Australia, and New Zealand, but here the native populations were not strong enough to create the problem of a dual society, while the imported culture of the European settlers already represented a major break with the medieval tradition. The point of these comments is to suggest that, in actual analysis, more than one model of change is needed and that the construction of several such models is preferable to any attempt to force all types of social change into the Procrustes bed of the European experience.

The suggestion that ideal types of social change are frequently of limited applicability is made in the belief that this makes them more, not less, useful. Once the weakness of the most general formulation as well as the limitations of the western European model are observed, it is then appropriate also to recognize the utility of focusing attention on the area in which the breakthrough to modernity was achieved first. The following analysis attempts to spell out the implications of this breakthrough and to interpret the process of modernization in the light of the foregoing discussion.

Modernization in Comparative Perspective

Theoretical Orientation

As European societies approached the modern era, men of letters came to think about differences of social rank with an awareness of a new society in the making. Although political and ideological rather than scholarly, these ideas about modern society have strongly influenced the concepts with which social scientists have approached the study of modernization. At this point it is useful to state the common denominator of this intellectual tradition in terms of three related tenets.

(A) The industrial revolution in England and the contemporary political revolution in France had a profound cultural impact, frequently leading men of letters to formulate pervasive and invidious contrasts between the old and the new social order. As a result tradition and modernity came to be conceived in mutually exclusive terms, not only as a conceptual aid but also as a generalized, descriptive statement about the two contrasting types of society. Related to this approach is a conception of each type of society as a social system, characterized by the functional interdependence of its component parts and a balance of forces among them. Hence, traditional and modern societies appear as two types of societies, each with its own, built-in tendency towards self-maintenance or equilibrium.

(B) From the vantage point of Europe in the late eighteenth and early nineteenth centuries, both revolutions and much of the social change that followed appeared as phenomena that were internal to the societies changing. This mode of explanation goes back to influences emanating from Plato and characteristic of Western philosophy down to the present.[70] In the late eighteenth century this intellectual tradition was reflected in interpretations of the growth of commerce and industry. Specifically, many writers of the period considered the division of labor a major factor in promoting social change. To a man like Ferguson, that growth depended ultimately on the subdivision of tasks, which determines the ideas and actions of men, provides the basis for the difference between social classes, and gives rise to political actions.

The view that social change is the product of internal social forces has a certain basis in historical fact, difficult as it obviously is to separate facts from reflections upon them. Most observers of early industrialization thought economic change the primary factor, whether they believed that governmental measures reflect that change, as the radicals did, or that these measures were needed to avert its worst consequences, as the conservatives did. In England, the work of the classical economists enhanced this consensus, because opposition to mercantilist policies argued for less regulation of economic affairs and hence for a secondary role of government. As governmental controls over the economy were reduced, as guild regulations were abandoned, as labor mobility increased along with population, trade, and manufacture, it became very plausible to consider that society and economy possess a momentum of their own, while government merely responds to the impact of social forces. At this time, office-holding was still a form of property ownership so that the idea of authority as an adjunct of ownership partly described the society. In addition, the industrial revolution first occurred in England. As opposed to continental countries England (along with Holland) lacked an absolutist tradition with its basis in a standing army, and she was also characterized by a more permeable upper class than the countries of the continent. It was indeed a unique constellation of circumstances which gave new emphasis to the old view that social change is internal to the society changing, that social change originates in the division of labor, and that, consequently, government or the state are products of the social structure. It may be suggested that this intellectual perspective unduly generalizes from a very limited phase of the English experience.

Accordingly, both the intellectual tradition of Europe and the specific historical constellation at the end of the eighteenth century encouraged explanations of social change which emphasize the continuity and interconnectedness of changes *within* society, a tendency which was re-enforced when modern nationalism came into its own. As a result a certain lawfulness was attributed to the social structure, while the relative autonomy of government and the impact of external factors upon every society were ignored or minimized. Paradoxically, this perspective also prevailed during a period of absolutist regimes, of European overseas expansion and of worldwide industrialization, when societies were increasingly subject to influences from abroad in contrast to the relative integrity of national societies in western Europe. This cultural and historical background may help to account for the prominence of explanations which attribute change to a society's internal functional differentiation, such as the increasing division of labor, an observation that can alert us to the limitations of this intellectual perspective without questioning its analytic utility in the proper context.

(C) The third tenet asserts that ultimately industrialization will have the same effects wherever it occurs. This follows, or appears to follow, from a combination of assumptions rather loosely linked with the preceding points. Where the causes of social change are conceived as intrinsic to a society, industrialization (and, more vaguely, modernization) is considered to have certain necessary and sufficient prerequisites without which it cannot occur. Conversely, once these prerequisites are given, industrialization becomes inevitable. The same reasoning is applied to the consequences of the process. Once industrialization is under way, it has certain inevitable results. In the long run, modernity will drive out tradition and fully industrialized societies will become more and more alike.

The three tenets mentioned here are closely related. Their common basis is the conception of society as a structure arising from a fixed set of pre-conditions and characterized by mutually re-enforcing attributes which makes the change of the structure appear as an inevitable modification of interrelated variables. This conception of society is closely related to the theory of social evolution, although that theory is not of direct concern to the present discussion. But the three assumptions of social system, internal differentiation, and developmental inevitability form a coherent approach to the study of industrialization from which the approach to be discussed below will now be distinguished.

(A) Against the view that tradition and modernity are mutually exclusive, I wish to maintain that even the two revolutions of the eighteenth century are best understood as culminations of specific European continuities, that is, that "modern" elements were evident long before the modern era. (By the same token, the European tradition, and English society particularly, had distinctive attributes not found in other civilizations.) The point may be illustrated with regard to the bases of social action. Kinship ties, religious beliefs, linguistic affiliations, territorial communalism, and others are typical forms of association in a traditional social order. None of these ties or associations have disappeared even in the most highly industrialized societies; to this day the relative decline of "traditional" and the relative ascendance of "modern" solidarities remain or recur as social and political issues. But some of the old ties or associations were weakened by the ascendance of Christianity, others by the Renaissance and Reformation, and others still in the course of the struggles between absolutist rulers and the estates. It may be recalled the Max Weber's lifework documents the proposition that Christian doctrine and the revival of Roman law militated against familial and communal ties as foci of loyalty which compete effectively with the universal claims of legal procedure and the Christian faith. The ethical universalism of the Puritans and its subsequent secularization were later links in this chain of pre-conditions. By these prior developments in western Europe men were freed very gradually for such alternative solidarities as those of the nuclear family, social class, and national citizenship. In my view there was indeed a breakthrough to a new historical era, but this was the result of continuities reaching back to classical antiquity, which came to a head in a specific time and place owing to the very particular conditions of English society in the seventeenth and eighteenth centuries. This element of continuity was neglected by men of letters who interpreted the emerging industrial society in terms of a cultural conflict between tradition and modernity. However, in other respects continuity was emphasized.

(B) Against the conception of change as intrinsic, I wish to maintain that, following the breakthrough in England and France, every subsequent process of modernization has combined intrinsic changes with responses to extrinsic stimuli[71] and has involved government intervention as a prominent feature of that process. The modernization of societies is *not* to be understood primarily as a result of internal changes in which governments play at best a secondary role. The great lacunae of the interpretations here opposed is their failure to account for the diffusion of ideas and techniques, the prominent role of government, and the rising tide of nationalism, all of which have accompanied the process of industrialization throughout.

The point is a general one. All complex societies have an internal structure and an external setting. Likewise, all complex societies possess a formal structure of governmental authority which differs from, and is relatively independent of, the group formations arising from the social and economic organization of society. For analytic purposes it is legitimate to separate these dimensions and to neglect one or another of them, if this seems indicated by the problem under consideration. But in the comparative study of modernization, and especially one that focuses attention on problems of social stratification, such neglect seems inadvisable. The influence of modernization on the means of communication is international in scope so that we should attend to the external setting of societies even where our primary focus is on changes internal to their social structures. Moreover, the secondary or dependent role of government resulted from very particular historical circumstances, as noted earlier, and should not be considered a general theoretical proposition. The facts are that intellectuals have played a major role in helping to transform the social structure of backward societies and have done so more often than not in reference to prior economic and political developments abroad. Likewise, government officials have played a major role in the development of economic resources or have supported and implemented an institutional framework in which such a development became easier. To be sure, these are possibilities, not certainties. But to neglect the rather independent role of intellectuals or governmental officials in the process of modernization is to subscribe to the Marxian view that the international setting, the political structure, and the cultural development of a society depend in the long run on its organization of production.

(C) Against. the concept of industrialization as a largely uniform process of structural change, I wish to emphasize the importance of diffusion and of government "intervention" for an understanding of this process. England was the first country to industrialize and in Marx's view she exemplified the "laws of capitalist development." Writing in 1867, in his preface to the first edition of *Capital,* Marx had declared England to be the classic ground of the capitalist mode of production. England was more developed industrially than other countries. As they enter upon the path to industrialization, these other countries will undergo developments comparable to those of England because of the tendencies inherent in the capitalist organization of production. Marx made this prediction on the assumption that the same organization of production generates everywhere the same or similar transformations of social classes and the political structure. As an empirical proposition, this assumption is misleading. Once industrialization had been initiated in England, the technical innovations and the institutions of the economically advanced country were used as a model in order to move ahead more rapidly than England had and also as a warning so as to mitigate or even avoid the problems encountered by the pioneering country. Marx himself noted this possibility, but he did not consider it seriously. He declared that his analysis of the advanced country could only help to "shorten the birthpangs" of similar developments in other countries, for the capitalist mode of production is governed by the same laws or inevitable tendencies wherever it occurs.

Again, the point is a general one. Industrialization itself has intensified the communication of techniques and ideas across national frontiers. Taken out of their original context, these techniques and ideas are adapted so as to satisfy desires and achieve ends in the receiving country. Certainly, such adaptation is affected at every point by the resources and economic structure of the country, but Marx tended to make necessities out of contingencies. He did not give full weight to the historical traditions which affect the social structure of every country and with it the capacity of a people to develop its opportunities. Nor did he consider that this structure is modified materially by the international transmission of techniques and ideas and by attempts to control the process and repercussions of industrialization politically. Against the view that industrialization has the same effects wherever it occurs, I wish to maintain the importance of timing and sequence as crucial variables. Once industrialization has occurred anywhere, this fact alone alters the international environment of all other societies. In one sense it is true to say that because of timing and sequence industrialization cannot occur in the same way twice.

Accordingly, studies of modernization should be guided by two considerations which have been neglected in the past. Although it is true that certain consequences follow from an increasing division of labor, these are embedded in the *particular* transition from a pre-industrial to an industrial structure which distinguishes one society from another. The social structure of a country's transitional phase should, therefore, be a primary focus of analysis rather than be dismissed as a survival of the past. In addition, modernization, once it has occurred anywhere, alters the conditions of all subsequent efforts at modernization so that "the late arrivals cannot repeat the earlier sequences of industrial development."[72] Both considerations, the significance of the transition and the demonstration effects of earlier sequences, preclude an evolutionary interpretation of the process of modernization.

The reorientation I propose considers the industrialization and democratization of western Europe as a singular historic breakthrough, culminating a century-long and specifically European development. But modernization brings about special discontinuities by virtue of its expansive tendencies so that the relation between the intrinsic structure and external setting of societies assumes special significance. Thus, the internal, historically developed structure of a country and the emulation induced by economic and political developments abroad together affect each country's process of modernization.

Towards a Definition of Modernization

My objective is to define the term so that it refers to change during a specific and limited historical period. I want to show that throughout the designated period the process of change has certain overall characteristics. But at the same time I re-emphasize the distinction between "modernization" and "modernity." Many attributes of modernization like widespread literacy or modern medicine have appeared, or have been adopted, in isolation from the other attributes of a modern society. Hence, modernization in some sphere of life *may* occur without resulting in modernity. It is well to emphasize this uncertainty if we wish to compare past and present developments. Such uncertainty concerning their future existed in the past history of all presently industrialized countries, just as it exists at present in the so-called developing countries. Recognition of this uncertainty provides a better basis for the comparative study of modernization than the alternative assumption that industrialization has the same prerequisites and results wherever it occurs.

In thus preferring uncertainty to a generalizing, systemic analysis, we deal in effect with two approaches to the study of social change. The *retrospective* approach employs a "before-and-after" model of society, that is, some variant of the contrast between tradition and modernity. Such models are indispensable aids in an analysis of social change, which can start from a knowledge of past changes, even though they should still be employed with the cautions suggested earlier. The *prospective* approach cannot employ such a model directly because it seeks to deal with future contingencies rather than changes that have occurred already. This second approach may still employ the available "before-and-after" models, but its emphasis will be on the diversity of modern societies in the search for clues to the process of transformation. This is the approach I adopt for the remainder of this discussion.

By modernization I refer to a type of social change which *originated* in the industrial revolution of England, 1760–1830, and in the political revolution in France, 1789–1794. One can set the inception of the changes here considered differently, and this is in fact advisable for certain purposes. The expansion of Europe, for example, antedated the late eighteenth century; some aspects of modernization like the diffusion of modern weapons can be traced back to the fifteenth century.[73] Also, particular antecedents of modernization can be traced back very far, as in the instance of printing or of representative institutions or ideas of equality, and many others. Nevertheless, there are reasons of scale which make it advisable to separate the transformations of European societies and their worldwide repercussions since the eighteenth century from earlier economic and political changes. Reference was made at the beginning to the massive transformation of agriculture: the changes leading to a declining proportion of the labor force engaged in agricultural production were initiated in the eighteenth century. Similarly, the fundamental elitism of societies prior to the eighteenth century has been replaced, albeit gradually, by a "fundamental democratization" (Mannheim), and this change may again be traced to beginnings in the eighteenth century. Also, the distinction between rulers and ruled had coincided roughly with the distinction between the literate and the illiterate. That distinction was beginning to break down in the course of the eighteenth century with the slow spread of both literacy and printed matter.[74] These three transformations of the economic, political, and social order may suffice as an indication that it is useful to treat the eighteenth century as a breakthrough to a new historical era, at any rate in studies of modernization.

The economic and political breakthrough which occurred in England and France at the end of the eighteenth century put every other country of the world into a position of backwardness. Indeed, the same may be said of the two pioneering countries. The economic transformation of England provided a model for France, while the political revolution of France instantly became a major focus of political debate in England. Ever since, the world has been divided into advanced and follower societies. With reference to the eighteenth and early nineteenth centuries, it is appropriate to have this formulation refer to England and France as the advanced countries and all others as follower societies, although even then the statement would have omitted earlier pioneering countries such as Holland or Spain. But since that time the process has ramified much further. Follower societies of the past such as Russia or China have become advanced societies, which are taken as models by the satellite dependencies of eastern Europe or by some African and Asian countries that have won their independence since World War II. Each of the countries that have come to play the role of pioneer with regard to some follower society has a history of externally induced changes, although with the success of modernization the emphasis on this extrinsic dimension may become less salient than it was at an earlier time. Accordingly, a basic element in the definition of modernization is that it refers to a type of social change since the eighteenth century, which consists in the economic or political advance of some pioneering society and subsequent changes in follower societies.[75]

This distinction implies a shift in intellectual perspective. The traditional posture of sociological theory conceives of change as slow, gradual, continuous, and intrinsic to the societies changing. This view is more or less appropriate as long as we confine ourselves to the enduring characteristics of a social structure which may aid or hinder the modernization of society. As suggested earlier, it is quite appropriate to the interpretation of change in European civilization, and this was the intent of Max Weber's question concerning the combination of circumstances to which the rationalism of Western civilization can be attributed. However, once the two eighteenth-century revolutions had occurred, subsequent social changes were characterized by a precipitous increase in the speed and intensity of communication. Ideas and techniques have passed from advanced to follower societies, and to a lesser extent from follower to advanced societies. Within a relatively short historical period there are few societies which have remained immune from these external impacts upon their social structures.[76]

Diffusion of ideas and techniques may be a byproduct of expansion by advanced societies, but it occurs even in the absence of expansion because of the economic and political breakthrough in eighteenth century Europe. As Gerschenkron has pointed out, leading strata of follower societies respond to this breakthrough by introducing the most modern, capital-intensive technology, in order to close the gap as rapidly as possible.[77] This tendency is part of a larger context:

One way of defining the degree of backwardness is precisely in terms of absence, in a more backward country [or "follower" society as I have termed it here], of factors which in a more advanced country serve as prerequisites of development. Accordingly, one of the ways of approaching the problem is by asking what substitutions and what patterns of substitutions for the lacking factors occurred in the process of industrialization in condition of backwardness.[78]

Such substitutions may be adopted in the belief that they represent shortcuts to modernity. They are part of the effort to avoid the difficulties encountered in the modernization of the advanced country. It is interesting that this idea of the advantages of backwardness did not originate with Leon Trotsky (as has sometimes been supposed) but was expressed already in the late seventeenth century.[79] The implication of this perspective is that all aspects of modernity are up for adoption simultaneously, and priorities depend upon available resources, the balance of forces in the follower society, and the relative ease of transfer. The fact that such items as medication, printed matter, educational innovations, and political practices like the franchise are more easily transferred than advanced technology requiring heavy capital investment is another aspect of the divergence of processes of modernization.

Many writers have observed that in this setting of follower societies, governments play—or attempt to play—a decisive role. The special utility of this perspective for comparative studies of modernization is evident from a recent comprehensive analysis of English, French, and German industrialization since the eighteenth century. In that context, David Landes states that for the governments of Europe "industrialization was, from the start, a political imperative."[80] Governments may be more or less successful in meeting the imperatives confronting them, and their attempts to do so will be affected throughout by the structural attributes of their societies. Generally speaking, governments attempt to play a larger role in the modernization of relatively backward than of relatively advanced societies. Since this generalization applies to "follower societies" after the eighteenth century, and since most societies of the world are (or have been) in that category, the proposition is perhaps only another aspect of modernization, that is, of the distinction between the two types of societies. The difference can be of strategic importance for modernization, since follower societies are by definition lacking in some of the elements of modernity found in advanced societies. Where governments manage to provide functional equivalents or substitutes for these missing elements, they may succeed in reducing the backwardness of their societies, but this presupposes a relatively effective government which is an attribute of modernity or advance.[81]

Here again a major shift in intellectual perspective is implied. The view that government is an integral part of the social structure, but may have the capacity of altering it significantly, is not in the mainstream of social theory. More common is the opposite view that formal government and its actions are epiphenomena, the product of forces arising from the social and economic structure of society. This view, related to the emanationist and evolutionary intellectual tradition, was re-enforced (as noted earlier) by a particular historical constellation in early nineteenth century Europe. Writers of quite incompatible political views agreed, nevertheless, that government is an epiphenomenon, and this uncommon agreement still influences modern social thought. Yet in studies of the modernization of complex societies it is more useful to consider social structure and government, or society and the state, as interdependent but also relatively autonomous spheres of thought and action.[82]

The gap created between advanced and follower societies and the efforts to close it by a more or less ad-hoc adoption of items of modernity produce obstacles to successful modernization.[83] In his discussion of the new states that have come into being since World War II, E. A. Shils has characterized these obstacles as a series of internal, structural cleavages: "It is the gap between the few, very rich and the mass of the poor, between the educated and the uneducated, between the townsman and the villager, between the cosmopolitan or national and the local, between the modern and the traditional, between the rulers and the ruled."[84] Although such tensions exist in advanced states as well, they are far more pronounced not only in the new states of today but also in the follower societies of the past which can be ranked, albeit roughly, by their degree of backwardness.[85] The analogy between backward or underdeveloped social structures then and now should not be pressed too much, since the continental countries possessed many cultural and economic attributes that were relatively favorable to modernization. But it is also true that during the nineteenth century there was a gradient of backwardness within Europe such that the countries to the east paralleled the gaps found in the new states of today more closely than did the countries of western Europe.[86]

The analogies or parallels noted here are especially close at the cultural level, for the gap created by advanced societies puts a premium on ideas and techniques which follower societies may use in order to come up from behind. Educated minorities are, thereby, placed in a position of strategic importance, while the always existing gulf between the educated and the uneducated widens still further. In a world marked by gradations of backwardness, the comparative study of modernization must attend to the reference society that becomes the focus of attention in the follower society, especially for the educated minority that seeks to utilize advanced ideas and techniques in order to catch up.[87] Here one can see at a glance that ideas about social change focusing on the internal division of labor necessarily made much of standard social classes like workers and capitalists, whereas a focus on the distinction between advanced and follower societies, and on the communications-effects of modernization, necessarily gives prominence to the role of intellectuals and of education. It is as typical of backward countries to invest heavily in education in order to bridge the gap as it is for an intelligentsia to develop and engage in an intensified search for a way out of the backwardness of their country.[88] A typical part of this search consists in the ambivalent job of preserving or strengthening the indigenous character of the native culture while attempting to close the gap created by the advanced development of the reference society or societies.[89]

Four aspects of the process of modernization have been distinguished in the preceding discussion:

(A) Reasons of scale suggest that since the eighteenth century the external setting of societies, and especially the gap created by the early industrialization of England and the early democratization of France, have imparted to the degree of backwardness the special significance of an obstacle and a challenge to modernization.

(B) In their endeavor to bridge this gap follower societies typically search for substitutes to the factors which were conditions of development in the advanced countries. Within the limitations imposed by nature and history, all aspects of modernity (as developed abroad) are up for adoption simultaneously, and the problem is which of the adoptable items represents a shortcut to modernity. Since the achievement of modernity is not assured, it is part of this process that the adoption of items of modernization may militate against modernity, or may be irrelevant to it.

(C) This common setting of follower societies in turn imparts special importance to government. Typically, governments attempt to play a major role in the modernization of the society at the same time that they seek to overcome the sources of their own instability which arise from the special tensions created by backwardness.[90]

(D) The division of the world into advanced and follower societies, together with the relative ease of communication, puts a premium on education as a means to modernization which is more readily available than the capital required for modern technology. Education and modern communications also encourage the development of an intelligentsia and a cultural product which—as Wilhelm Riehl had noted already in 1850—is in excess of what the country can use or pay for.[91] This recurrent phenomenon is reflected in a mushrooming of efforts to overcome the backwardness of the country by attempts to reconcile the strength evidenced by the advanced society with the values inherent in native traditions.

Comparative Aspects of Social Stratification

This concluding section outlines a program of comparative study dealing with social stratification in relation to modernization. In the past that study has been approached in terms of the either-or contrast between tradition and modernity and an emphasis on continuous changes, internal to the society studied and largely determined by the division of labor. The present analysis seeks to reorient this intellectual convention. It emphasizes the continuity of social change, since the contrast between a social structure then and now is an artifact of conceptualization, needed to comprehend changes in a society which appear over a time span of centuries. At the same time, the process of modernization may have a peculiarly disrupting effect on changing patterns of social stratification, due to the hiatus created between advanced and follower societies. Governmental intervention is another possible source of discontinuity, since authority structures are here conceived as relatively autonomous. In other words: although social change is a continuous process, it is often affected by factors conventionally considered extrinsic to the social structure. In societies undergoing a process of modernization relations among social groups are peculiarly exposed to such extrinsic influences, although changes in other aspects of the social structure (for example, the family) may be less affected in this manner. Typically, the modernization of societies is accompanied by a nationwide redefinition of rights and duties on the part of individuals and groups, involving governmental action at many points. This redefinition frequently involves conflicts in which actors and onlookers alike respond not only to the actions and beliefs of others, but also to the images of such group relations derived from prior developments in their reference society. The following discussion attempts to show that these general points bear directly on the study of social stratification.

The simplified contrast between tradition and modernity shows us that medieval society was ruled by a landowning aristocracy and capitalist society is ruled by a bourgeoisie owning the means of production. If one conceives of the transition from tradition to modernity as the decline of one set of attributes and the rise of another, one gets the simple picture of a declining aristocracy and a rising bourgeoisie. Possibly Marx has contributed more than anyone else to this conception. His interpretation of the bourgeoisie as the collective historical agent which created the revolutionizing effects of modern industry has produced a tendency to read a "rising bourgeoisie" back into the last thousand years of European history.[92] The broad effect of this tendency has been to make the merchants of pre-eighteenth-century Europe into direct precursors of nineteenth-century industrial entrepreneurs—without benefit of evidence, to fasten upon them a corresponding degree of striving and social protest when in fact they fit quite well into the social structure of feudal Europe, and hence to antedate the decline of the aristocracy by some centuries in order to provide room for the rising bourgeoisie.[93] But the evidence concerning changes of social stratification in the course of industrialization does not present the simple picture of a declining aristocracy and a rising bourgeoisie. In most European countries there is evidence rather of the continued social and political pre-eminence of pre-industrial ruling groups even when their economic fortunes declined, as well as of the continued, subordinate social and political role of the middle classes even when their economic fortunes rose. In Europe this pattern applies rather generally to the period of transition to an industrial society. Here is how Joseph Schumpeter puts the case with reference to England, while pointing out that in modified form the same applies elsewhere:

The aristocratic element continued to rule the roost *right to the end of the period of intact and vital capitalism.* No doubt that element—though nowhere so effectively as in England—currently absorbed the brains from other strata that drifted into politics; it made itself the representative of bourgeois interests and fought the battles of the bourgeoisie; it had to surrender its last legal privileges; but with these qualifications, and for ends no longer its own, it continued to man the political engine, to manage the state, to govern. The economically operative part of the bourgeois strata did not offer much opposition to this. On the whole, that kind of division of labor suited them and they liked it.[94]

In the modernization of Europe, aristocracies retained political dominance long after the economic foundations of their high status had been impaired and after alternative and more productive economic pursuits had brought bourgeois strata to social and economic prominence. The capacity to rule obviously varied among the several aristocracies, as did the degree to which other strata of the population tended to accept their own subordinate position. In Europe, these legacies were eroded eventually, but only after the transition to an industrial society was affected by the general pattern to which Schumpeter refers. This pattern of a continued political dominance by traditional ruling groups, even under conditions of rapid modernization, reflects an earlier condition of the social structure, when families of high social and economic status had privileged access to official positions while all those below the line of gentility were excluded. Pre-modern European societies were characterized by a vast number of status differences and clashes of interest of all kinds, but by only "one body of persons capable of concerted action over the whole area of society;"[95] that is, a tiny, possessing minority of the well-born was capable of concerted action and hence constituted a class, while the whole mass of unorganized and—under these conditions—unorganizable persons were set apart by their common lack of access to positions of privilege. Accordingly, European societies conformed at one time to a pattern in which class and authority were more or less synonymous terms, but this identity diminished in the course of modernization and was replaced eventually by the principle of separation between office and family status.[96]

This equalization of access to public employment is an aspect of modernization which makes sense of the assumptions we bring to this field of study. In modern sociology government employment is not considered a basis, or an index, of social stratification. Rather, government employment (even in high positions) is seen as a dependent variable, for example, when we examine the distribution of public officials by social origin. Yet this perspective presupposes the separation of government office from the claims a family can make by virtue of its social status and economic position. These assumptions were less applicable in an earlier phase of European societies, and today they are less applicable in the follower societies that are economically backward. There, governments play, or attempt to play, a major role in the process of modernization, as we have seen. Under these conditions government employment provides one of the major bases of social mobility, economic security, and relative well-being. In fact, in economically backward countries the government is one of the major economic enterprises. Hence, government officials partake of the prestige of ruling, even if their positions are humble. And in view of the power at the disposal of government, access to government office and influence upon the exercise of authority are major points of contention—in the personalized sense characteristic of societies in which interaction is kinship-oriented.[97] While this importance of government employment is associated with economic backwardness and the weakness of middle strata in the occupational hierarchy, it can also divert resources from uses which might overcome these conditions. In the absence of viable economic alternatives, government employment itself becomes a major basis of social stratification,[98] although these new polities frequently institutionalize plebiscitarian, equalitarian principles in the political sphere. This identification of class with authority differs fundamentally from the elitism of medieval European societies, in which only a privileged minority had access to positions of authority.

The preceding sketch suggests several perspectives for the comparative study of ruling classes in the process of modernization. Within the European context it focuses attention on the continued importance of traditional ruling groups throughout the period of modernization. In this respect, further study would have to differentiate between the relatively accommodating development in England and the much more conflict-ridden development of other follower societies. At the same time, I have suggested that the modernization of Western societies generally shows a gradual separation between governmental office and family status. The continuity between tradition and modernity remains a characteristic of social change throughout, for even the increasing differentiation between office and family in Western civilization reveals a variety of historically conditioned patterns. There is no reason to assume that future developments elsewhere will be more uniform. The comparative study of ruling groups in the process of modernization can thus combine the three themes, mentioned above: the continuity of change, the effect of extrinsic influences on the changing role of ruling strata, and the relative separation between government and social structure. The same themes may be combined in the study of other social groups.

In this sketch no attention has been given to the patterns of action and reaction which characterize a society's changing structure and have obvious relevance for an understanding of its ruling groups. This aspect of changes in social stratification comes most readily into focus as one moves from the top to the bottom ranks of the social hierarchy. Here one may use the simplified contrast between tradition and modernity as a point of departure, because the rise of political participation by the lower strata is a generally characteristic feature of modernization. In medieval Europe lower strata fragmented in household enterprises of a patriarchal type existed side by side with a ruling class characterized by wealth, high status and high office. Karl Marx has analyzed this condition effectively with regard to the French peasantry:

The small peasants form a vast mass, the members of which live in similar conditions, but without entering into manifold relations with one another. Their mode of production isolates them from one another, instead of bringing them into mutual intercourse. The isolation is increased by France's bad means of communication and by the poverty of the peasants. . . . Each individual peasant family is almost self-sufficient; it itself directly produces the major part of its consumption and thus acquires its means of life more through exchange with nature than in intercourse with society. The small holding, the peasant and his family; alongside them another small holding, another peasant and another family. . . . Insofar as there is merely a local interconnection among these small peasants, and the identity of their interests begets no unity, no national union and no political organization, they do not form a class. They are consequently incapable of enforcing their class interest in their own name, whether through a parliament or through a convention. They cannot represent themselves, they must be represented. Their representative must at the same time appear as their master, as an authority over them, as an unlimited governmental power, that protects them against the other classes and sends them the rain and the sunshine from above. The political influence of the small peasants, therefore, finds its final expression in the executive power subordinating society to itself.[99]

Probably Marx would have agreed that this analysis of peasants in nine-teenth century France applied *mutatis mutandis* to the small craftsmen of the towns, to the manorial estates as well as to the independent peasant freeholds in medieval Europe. The family-based enterprise fragmented the lower strata into as many units of patriarchal household rule over family, servants, and apprentices. On the other hand, the heads of households would join with others in guilds, exercise authority in official capacities, join in the deliberation of representative assemblies, and thus constitute a class or classes in the sense of groups capable of concerted action.

In this setting fundamental democratization refers not only to the extension of the franchise but to the whole process of class formation by which the fragmentation of the lower strata is gradually overcome. Geo-graphic mobility increases, literacy rises along with the diffusion of news-papers, patriarchal rule and household enterprises decline as conditions of work lead to an aggregation of large masses of people in economic enter-prises providing opportunities for easy communication.[100] As Marx noted, these conditions gave rise to trade unions, political organizations, and a heightened class-consciousness due to repeated conflicts with employers. He was too preoccupied with industry to note that groups other than workers and means of communication other than direct contact at the place of work might come into play.[101] He was also too committed to an evolutionary perspective with its emphasis on the eventual decline of the aristocracy to note the importance of the beliefs which upheld the legitimacy of the tra-ditional ruling class even in an industrializing society. Large masses of people at the bottom of the social hierarchy retained their loyalty to the established order, even in the face of the physical and psychological deprivations so suddenly imposed upon them.[102]

This loyalty is evident in the numerous references to the real and imaginary rights enjoyed under the old order. Populist protest based on such references meant, among other things, the demand for equality of citizenship. That equality was proclaimed by the legal order and by the appeals to national solidarity in an era of well-publicized empire-building, but in practice it was denied by the restriction of the franchise, the dominant ideology of class relations, and the partisan implementation of the law. The rising awareness of the working class in this process of fundamental democratization reflects an experience of *political alienation,* a sense of not having a recognized position in the civic community of an emerging industrial society. During the nineteenth century nationalism was so powerful in part because it could appeal directly to this longing of the common people for civic respectability, a longing which was intensified by acute awareness of development in other countries. When this quest was frustrated and as ideas of the rights of labor spread during the nineteenth century, people turned to the socialist alternative of building a new civic community to which they, too, could belong.[103] This general interpretation of working-class agitation in Europe may be contrasted with the problems encountered today under conditions of greater economic backwardness and greater advance abroad.[104]

In employing the English development as the prototype of later developments in other countries, Marx mistook the exception for the rule, a consideration which also applies to his analysis of an emerging working class. As English workers attained a level of group-consciousness in the late eighteenth and early nineteenth century, they necessarily became aware of England's pre-eminent position as a world power. In follower societies the lower strata necessarily rise to an awareness of the relative backwardness of their society. Also, early working-class agitation in England occurred in an anti-mercantilist context which militated against protective legislation during a transitional period of greatly intensified deprivations. In follower societies the greater reliance on government makes social legislation a natural concomitant of early industrialization.[105] In England the work force in the early factories was separated effectively from the land, and population increase in the countryside as well as the city roughly corresponded to the increasing demand for labor, whereas the work force in many follower societies retains its familial and economic ties to the land,

and population increase in city and country is well in advance of the demand for labor.[106] This contrast has many ramifications, which vary with the degree of industrialization achieved locally and the degree of governmental control over internal migration, to mention just two relevant considerations. The permanent separation of workers from their ties to the land obviously facilitates the growth of class-consciousness and of political organization in Marx's sense of the word. On the other hand, a continuation of these ties may result in a weak commitment to industry (and hence weak group solidarity), and/or in the emergence of segmental peasant-worker alliances in urban and national politics. Where this latter alternative exists, one can begin to appreciate how important it is to consider such phenomena in their own right rather than treating them as transitions that are expected to disappear with increasing modernization. We do not know, after all, what forms modernization might take where separation between town and countryside fails to occur, at least for a considerable period of time.[107]

Having considered ruling and lower strata, I wish finally to turn to a brief analysis of education and intellectuals, again using the guidelines of the preceding discussion. In the case of England, education had been a privilege associated with high status until, in the course of religious controversies, several sectarian groups instituted private school systems so as to preserve the integrity of their beliefs. The idea of making education available beyond these narrow circles immediately raised the question of danger to the social order because workers and peasants would learn to read and write. This apprehension is quite understandable when one considers that the basic dividing line between those who officially ranked as gentlemen and the vast majority of the people coincided exactly with the division between the literate and the illiterate. Still, the social mobilization of the population due to commerce and industry undermined the old hierarchy of ranks and posed the problem of ensuring that the people would retain their old regard for rank, and this led to the gradual spread of education with a strong emphasis on religion. The ambivalence accompanying this spread of education was not unlike the parallel problem of military conscription: both were aspects of a fundamental democratization which gave unprecedented political importance to people who could read and—in times of emergency— had guns.[108] These issues are transformed in follower societies which seek to achieve the benefits of an industrial society, but, if possible, by a speedier and less costly transition than occurred in England. In these societies popular and higher education seem to provide the easiest shortcut to industrialization since by this means the skill level of the population is raised while the highly educated increase their capacity of learning advanced techniques from abroad. Under these conditions governments in follower societies usually push education, even though in so doing they also jeopardize their own political stability. They may attempt to avert such dangers through restrictions of the franchise, censorship, control of associations, etc., and one can differentiate between follower societies of the nineteenth and the twentieth centuries in terms of their respective degrees and types of control over a mobilized population.

Such contrasts in the role of education are paralleled by contrasts in the role of intellectuals. Many educated persons engage in intellectual pursuits from time to time, but the term "intellectuals" is usually (if vaguely) restricted to those persons who engage in such pursuits on a full-time basis and as free professionals rather than "hired hands."[109] Intellectual pursuits occur in all complex societies, but intellectuals as a distinct social group emerged as a concomitant of modernization. In western Europe men of letters underwent a process of emancipation from their previous subservience to the Church and to private patrons because industrialization created a mass public and a market for intellectual products. The whole process was one of great complexity, but it can be simplified for present purposes. Intellectuals tended to respond to their emancipation by a new cultural elitism, and to the new mass public by responses which vacillated between a populist identification with the people and a strong apprehension concerning the threat of mass-culture to humanistic values.[110] Because these responses were quite incongruent with the dominant materialism of advanced industrial societies, intellectuals experienced a social and moral isolation. During the nineteenth century the great economic and political successes of advanced European societies re-enforced, rather than assuaged, the isolation of those intellectuals who took no direct part in that success and questioned the cultural and personal worth of those who did. To the extent that this estrangement resulted from the emancipation and consequent elitism of intellectuals, as well as from their ambivalent reaction to a mass public, it must be considered a concomitant of modernization.[111]

The response of intellectuals, briefly sketched here, was largely internal to the most advanced societies of Europe. At the same time, the breakthrough achieved by the industrial and political revolutions of England and France made other countries into follower societies. The economic advance of England and the events of the French Revolution were witnessed from afar by men to whom the backwardness and autocracy of their own country appeared still more backward and autocratic by comparison. Under these conditions cultural life tends to become polarized between those who would see their country progress by imitating the more advanced countries and those who denounce that advance as alien and evil and emphasize instead the wellsprings of strength existing among their own people and in their native culture. Both reactions were typified by the Westernizers and Slavophils of Tsarist Russia, but the general pattern has occurred again and again. It has been a mainspring of nationalism and of movements for national independence. In this setting intellectuals do not remain estranged witnesses of a development carried forward by others; they tend to turn into leaders of the drive towards modernization.[112]

Epilogue

This discussion has endeavored to provide a framework for the comparative study of modernization and inequality. Much work along these lines remains to be done, so that a proper conclusion seems premature. But in closing it may be useful to point up the relevance of the reorientation here proposed to the comparative study of stratification as an aspect of modernization.

For too long, such studies have been influenced by a stereotype derived from the Marxian tradition. According to this stereotype, history is divided into epochs, characterized by a predominant mode of production and, based upon it, a class structure consisting of a ruling and an oppressed class. Each epoch is further characterized by a typical sequence of changes in the relations between the two major classes. In the early phase of such an epoch the dominant mode of production is being established under the leadership of a class in its period of revolutionary ascendance. For a time this class is progressive. Its economic interests are identical with technical progress and human welfare, and hence on the side of liberating ideas and institutions. Eventually however, such an ascending class becomes a ruling class, like capitalists or feudal lords. The interests of such a class, which favored technical progress originally, now call for opposition to it. From a champion of progress in its period of ascendance the class has turned into a champion of reaction in its period of dominance. Increasingly, the ruling class resists attempts to change the social and economic organization of society, because now change would endanger its position. But meanwhile, within the structure of the old society, a new class has gradually been formed from the ranks of the oppressed, who have no such vested interests and who in due time will overthrow that old structure in order to make way for a full measure of the material progress which has become technically possible. Within the European context this grandiose simplification appeared to account for the feudal powers of resistance, the progressive, rising bourgeoisie and its gradual transformation into a reactionary ruling class, and finally the class of the oppressed proletariat which has a world to win and nothing to lose but its chains.

It is quite true, of course, that Marx modified this scheme to allow for all kinds of leads and lags in interpreting the actual historical developments of his time. These modifications may have appeared all the more persuasive because of the passionate moral and intellectual conviction with which Marx adhered to the basic assumptions of the scheme itself. This conviction, I have suggested, was part of the European intellectuals' response to the crisis in human relations brought about by the rise of an industrial society, a response which suggested an either-or confrontation between tradition and modernity with its many ramifications.

A critical awareness of this intellectual heritage can assist the reorientation needed in the comparative study of stratification. It prompts us to recognize that the contrast between tradition and modernity is itself part of the evidence we should consider. This intellectual response to the rise of industry has been an aid or hindrance (as the case may be) in each country's modernization, typically marked by the emancipation of men of letters and by the manner in which they assessed their country's backwardness relative to the advances of their reference societies. Once the unwanted legacies of this intellectual response are discounted, as I have attempted to do in this essay, a rather different approach to the study of stratification emerges.

The division of history into epochs, like the distinction between tradition and modernity, is a construct of definite but limited utility. These constructs will vary with the purpose of inquiry. While we have found it useful to consider late eighteenth century Europe as an historical turning point, it is recognized that the process of modernization which reached a crescendo since then is coextensive with the era of European expansion since the late fifteenth century or, as Carlo Cipolla has called it, the "Vasco da Gama era." If our interest is in accounting for the cumulative causes for this historical breakthrough in Europe, our emphasis will be on the continuity of intra-societal changes. If we wish to include in our account the worldwide repercussions of this breakthrough and hence the differential process of modernization, our emphasis will be on the confluence of intrinsic and extrinsic changes of social structures. Both emphases are relevant for the comparative study of stratification.

Within this broad context the rise of new social structures as of technical innovations appears as a multifaceted process, not exclusively identifiable with any one social group. Typically, the pioneers of innovation seek the protection of ruling groups rather than defying them—provided, of course, that such groups exist and can provide protection. The outcome of this process varies with the pressure for innovation and the degree to which given ruling groups themselves participate in innovation or feel (and are) jeopardized by it. At any rate, the emphasis upon the continuity of ruling groups in the era of modernization is a first corollary following from the rejection of the either-or image of tradition and modernity.

A second corollary involves what Karl Mannheim has called the "fundamental democratization" of modern society. The contrast between the monopoly of rule by a tiny minority of notables and the principle of universal suffrage in modern nation-states is striking and unquestioned. But the growth of citizenship, which occurs in the transition from one to the other, involves highly diverse developments in which the relative rights and obligations of social classes are redefined as the political process interacts (more or less autonomously) with the changing organization of production. In the era of modernization this interaction can be understood best if proper attention is given to the international setting as well as the internal differentiation of social structures.

In the end it may appear—from a mid-twentieth century viewpoint—that the growth of citizenship and the nation-state is a more significant dimension of modernization than the distributive inequalities underlying the formation of social classes. In that perspective Marx's theory of social classes under capitalism appears as a sweeping projection of certain temporary patterns of early nineteenth-century England. Not the least argument favoring this conclusion is the growth of the welfare state in the industrialized societies of the world, which in one way or another provides a pattern of accommodation among competing social groups as well as a model to be emulated by the political and intellectual leaders of follower societies. My object has been to provide a framework which can encompass these contemporary developments as well as the modernization processes of the past.

NOTES AND REFERENCES

1. See Carlo M. Cipolla, *The Economic History of World Population* (Baltimore, 1964), pp. 24–28. By focusing attention on the technical and economic effects of the process, Cipolla provides a comprehensive formulation of what is meant by industrialization. Nothing like that clarity can be achieved with regard to modernization, which is more inclusive and refers, albeit vaguely, to the manifold social and political processes that have accompanied industrialization in most countries of Western civilization. The following discussion contains contributions towards a definition of modernization.

2. See Robert A. Nisbet, *Emile Durkheim* (Englewood Cliffs, N.J., 1965), p. 20.

3. Ibid., p. 21*n*.

4. Immanuel Kant, "Idea for a Universal History with Cosmopolitan Intent," in Carl J. Friedrich, ed., *The Philosophy of Kant* (New York, 1949), p. 121. Note the relation of this view with the intellectual tradition traced in Arthur Lovejoy, *The Great Chain of Being* (New York, 1961), passim.

5. Adam Ferguson, *An Essay on the History of Civil Society,* 5th ed. (London, 1782), pp. 302–03.

6. Ibid., pp. 308–09.

7. Ibid., p. 305.

8. See John Millar, "Social Consequences of the Division of Labor," reprinted in William C. Lehmann, *John Millar of Glasgow, 1735–1801* (Cambridge, 1960), pp. 380–82. This volume contains a reprint of Millar's *Origin of the Distinction of Ranks,* first published in 1771.

9. Edmund Burke, "Thoughts and Details on Scarcity (1795)," in *Works* (Boston, 1869), 5:134–35. Burke himself used the laissez-faire doctrine to support his argument by showing that the law of supply and demand governed the wages paid to labor and that interference with that law would merely aggravate the condition of the poor. The traditional argument against the injustice of this system is exemplified by William Godwin, *Enquiry Concerning Political Justice and its Influence on Morals and Happiness,* ed. F. E. L. Priestley (Toronto, 1946), 1:15–20.

10. See the survey of these opinions by Robert Michels, *Die Verelendungstheorie* (Leipzig, 1928), passim.

11. Justus Möser, *Sämtliche Werke* (Berlin, 1842), 4:158–62. I owe this reference to the article by Karl Mannheim cited below.

12. J. W. Goethe, *Wilhelm Meister's Apprenticeship,* tr. R. Dillon Boylan (London, 1867), p. 268. See also Baron Knigge, *Practical Philosophy of Social Life* (Lansingburgh, 1805), pp. 307–08.

13. Goethe, op. cit.

14. See Werner Wittich, "Der soziale Gehalt von Goethes Roman 'Wilhelm Meisters Lehrjahre,'" in *Hauptprobleme der Soziologie, Erinnerungsgabe für Max Weber* ed. Melchior Palyi (Berlin, 1923), 2:278–306.

15. For documentation of the social and literary life of the period see W. H. Bruford, *Germany in the 18th Century* (Cambridge, 1939), passim. The literary and philosophical response to the French revolution is analyzed in Alfred Stern, *Der Einfluss der franzoesischen Revolution auf das deutsche Geistesleben* (Stuttgart, 1928), but I know of no comparable summary treatment of the German response to English industrialization. See, however, Hans Freyer, *Die Bewertung der Wirtschaft im philosophischen Denken des 19. Jahrhunderts* (Leipzig, 1921) for some relevant materials.

16. M. de Bonald, *Oeuvres Complètes* (Paris, 1864), 2:238–39.

17. Ibid. Note in passing that this contrast between agricultural and industrial work was made in almost identical terms by John Millar years earlier. The difference between Millar's liberalism and Bonald's conservatism seems to be reflected only in Millar's emphasis on the knowledge of the present and Bonald's greater stress on his religion. Cf. Lehmann, op. cit., pp. 380–82. As Max Weber has pointed out, this emphasis on the piety of the peasant is a distinctly modern phenomenon, related to invidious contrasts between town and country. See Max Weber, *Sociology of Religion* (Boston, 1963), p. 83.

18. P. J. Proudhon, *A System of Economic Contradictions or The Philosophy of Misery* (Boston, 1888), 1:138.

19. P. J. Proudhon, *General Idea of the Revolution in the 19th Century* (London, 1923), p. 215. This work was written in 1851.

20. Proudhon, *A System of Contradictions or The Philosophy of Misery*, p. 132.

21. Cf. Norman Jacobson, *The Concept of Equality in the Assumptions of the Propaganda of Massachusetts Conservatives, 1790–1840* (Ph.D. dissertation, University of Wisconsin, 1951).

22. George Fitzhugh, *Sociology for the South* (Richmond, 1854), pp. 233, 235.

23. Ibid., p. 161.

24. Ibid., pp. 106–07, 253–54. A major analysis of this southern ideology in historical perspective is contained in W. J. Cash, *The Mind of the South* (Garden City, N.J., 1954), passim.

25. Orestes A. Brownson, *Works* (Detroit, 1884), 5:116–17. This passage was written in 1857, after the author's conversion to Catholicism.

26. Karl Mannheim, "Conservative Thought," in *Essays in Sociology and Social Psychology* (London, 1953), pp. 74–164.

27. Different meanings of alienation as a central tenet of anti-capitalistic ideology are examined is Lewis Feuer's essay on this concept in Maurice Stein and Arthur Vidish, eds., *Sociology on Trial* (Englewood Cliffs, N.J., 1963), pp. 127–47. That men of opposite political persuasion have come to employ this concept is analyzed sociologically by René König, "Zur Soziologie der Zwanziger Jahre," in Leonhard Reinisch, ed., *Die Zeit ohne Eigenschaften* (Stuttgart, 1961), pp. 82–118.

28. The following account is based in part on Reinhard Bendix and Seymour M. Lipset, "Karl Marx's Theory of Social Classes," in *Class, Status and Power* (New York, 1966), pp. 6–11.

29. See T. B. Bottomore and Maximilien Rubel, eds., *Karl Marx, Selected Writings in Sociology and Social Philosophy* (London, 1956), p. 179. My italics.

30. Cf. T. H. Marshall's definition of class as "a force that unites into groups people who differ from one another, by overriding the differences between them." See his *Class, Citizenship and Social Development* (Garden City, N.Y., 1964), p. 164.

31. Bottomore and Rubel, op. cit., pp. 194–95.

32. A recent massive study by E. K. Thompson, *The Making of the English Working Class* (New York, 1964), passim, enables us to appreciate this Marxian perspective in that it describes the movements Marx observed with the benefit of another hundred years of scholarship. However, the author faithfully reproduces Marx's own blindness to the strongly conservative elements that were an enduring part of working-class agitation (by treating these elements as a passing phase) as well as to the mounting gradualism of the labor movement (by terminating his study in the 1830's).

33. A convenient compilation of relevant quotations from Marx is contained in Bottomore and Rubel, op. cit., Pt. III, chap. 4. To my knowledge the most penetrating analysis of this complex of ideas is that of Karl Löwith, *From Hegel to Nietzsche* (New York, 1964).

34. Karl Marx, *Capital* (New York, 1936), p. 92. Marx attributed religious beliefs and ideologies which disguise the actual relations of men in society to the conflicts of interest engendered by its class structure. It was, therefore, logical for him to anticipate that the advent of a classless society would coincide with the end of ideology, since the need for ideology would then disappear. Human relations become transparent, Marx believed, once the materialist interest in distorting them vanishes.

35. Ibid., pp. 12–13 (from the preface to the first edition).

36. Daniel Lerner, *The Passing of Traditional Society* (New York, 1964), p. 46. The reasoning in this work (originally published in 1958) is paralleled at many points by that contained in W. W. Rostow, *The Stages of Economic Growth* (Cambridge, 1961). For a critical evaluation of the latter, see W. W. Rostow, ed., *The Economics of Take-Off into Sustained Growth,* Proceedings of a Conference by the International Economic Association, (New York, 1963).

37. Lerner, op. cit., pp. 65–68. See also the 1964 preface to the paperback edition.

38. Ibid., p. 78. My italics.

39. Cf. the discussion of the system of modernity in ibid., pp. 54–65. See also David Riesman's comment on p. 13 of his introduction.

40. Ibid., p. 65.

41. Ibid., p. vii (1964 preface).

42. Ibid., pp. vii–x. The fact that Lerner chooses to ignore what he so clearly recognizes was explained by David Riesman in his introduction to the original edition by "the general belief that there must be a way—a way out of poverty and the psychic constriction of the 'Traditionals'—[which] links the author of this volume with his own national tradition.—But this very American belief that there is a way is a dream. And Professor Lerner, as a student of communications, understands that it is dreams that inspire not only new wants but new solutions—as well as violent gestures toward modernity. What seems required from his perspectives is an allopathic rationing of dreams, enough to spark the religion of progress, of advance, without inciting to riot"—to which Riesman adds the observation that "the emotional and political fluency of newly-liberated illiterates can be quite terrifying," and that "a movie image of life in America . . . is a radical 'theory' when it appears on the screens of Cairo, Ankara or Teheran." Ibid., p. 10.

43. See S. M. Lipset, *Political Man* (Garden City, N.Y., 1950), chap. II and the references cited there. See also Phillips Cutright, "National Political Development," *American Sociological Review* 28 (1963):253–64, and by the same author, "Political Structure, Economic Development, and National Security Programs," *American Journal of Sociology* 70 (1965):537–50, but also the critical contribution by Stanley H. Udy, Jr., "Dynamic Inferences from Static Data," ibid., pp. 625–27. Meanwhile, massive studies along similar lines are under way. See A. S. Banks and R. B. Textor, *A Cross-Polity Survey* (Cambridge, Mass., 1963) and Bruce M. Russett, Hayward R. Alker, et al., *World Handbook of Political and Social Indicators* (New Haven, 1964).

44. See Margaret Mead, *Continuities in Cultural Evolution* (New Haven, 1964), p. 7, where the author cites Franz Boas' acceptance of evolution on a planetary scale, but also his rejection of the application of evolutionary concepts to temporal sequences

of a few centuries since short-run changes can go in any direction—a position accepted by most modern evolutionists.

45. Cf. Raymond Grew and Sylvia L. Thrupp, "Horizontal History in Search of Vertical Dimensions," *Comparative Studies in Society and History* 8 (January 1966): 258–64.

46. David Riesman, in Lerner, op. cit., p. 14.

47. In the countries of western Europe that extension was relatively gradual during the nineteenth century; the establishment of universal suffrage dates only from the first world war or the early 1920's. See Stein Rokkan, "Mass Suffrage, Secret Voting, and Political Participation," *Archives Européenes de Sociologie* 2 (1961):132–52. By contrast, a compilation shows that, of 39 nations that have become independent and joined the United Nations between 1946 and 1962, only seven do not have universal suffrage. The restrictions usually refer to members of Buddhist religious orders, whose rules do not permit them to vote, and to members of the armed forces.

48. Sometimes, as in statistics on economic growth and demographic trends, data of current trends from one country are superimposed onto the past trend-data of another, more advanced country, but the similarity of current with past trends does not resolve the question of sequence and timing. Note the critical analysis of this approach by Simon Kuznets, "Underdeveloped Countries and the Pre-industrial Phase in the Advanced Countries," in Otto Feinstein, ed., *Two Worlds of Change* (Garden City, N.Y., 1964), pp. 1–21.

49. Clark Kerr, John T. Dunlop, Frederick Harbison, and Charles A. Myers, *Industrialism and Industrial Man* (Cambridge, Mass., 1960), p. 49 and passim.

50. The first phrase occurs several times in Lucian W. Pye and Sidney Verba, eds., *Political Culture and Political Development* (Princeton, 1965), passim. The second is the title of a book by Harold Rosenberg.

51. Max Weber, *The Methodology of the Social Sciences* (Glencoe, Ill., 1949), p. 101.

52. Ibid., pp. 102–03.

53. Robert Redfield, *The Folkculture of Yucatan* (Chicago, 1941), pp. 343–44.

54. See the related discussion in Reinhard Bendix, "Concepts and Generalizations in Comparative Sociological Studies," *American Sociological Review* 28 (1963): 532–39.

55. Alexander Gerschenkron, *Economic Backwardness in Historical Perspective* (New York, 1965), p. 33. My indebtedness to Gerschenkron will be evident throughout; in several respects my analysis represents a sociological extension of points first suggested by him in the context of economic history.

56. Ibid., p. 40. Cf. also Gerschenkron's critical discussion of Rostow along similar lines in Rostow, ed., *The Economics of Take-Off*, pp. 166–67. See also for a related discussion Albert O. Hirschman, "Obstacles to Development," *Economic Development and Cultural Change* 13 (1965):385–93.

57. Walter Elkan and Lloyd A. Fallers, "The Mobility of Labor," in Wilbert E. Moore and Arnold S. Feldman, eds., *Labor Commitment and Social Change in Developing Areas* (New York, 1960), pp. 238–57.

58. Milton Singer, "Changing Craft Traditions in India," in Moore and Feldman, eds., op. cit., pp. 258–76.

59. Neil J. Smelser, *The Sociology of Economic Life* (Englewood Cliffs, N.J., 1963), pp. 105–06.

60. Wilbert Moore, *The Impact of Industry* (Englewood Cliffs, N.J., 1965), p. 19. See also the same writer's earlier monograph on *Social Change* (Englewood Cliffs, N.J., 1963), chap. 5. Similar critiques of evolutionism are contained in the writings of S. N. Eisenstadt, especially in two recent essays "Social Change, Differentiation and Evolution," *American Sociological Review* 29 (1964):375–86 and "Social Transformation in Modernization," ibid., 30 (1965):659–73.

61. See Smelser, op. cit., pp. 101–02, 106.

62. Ibid., p. 112.

63. See, for example, the analysis of changes in industrial organization by H. Freudenberger and F. Redlich, "The Industrial Development of Europe: Reality, Symbols, Images," *Kyklos* 17 (1964):372–401.

64. The characterization of pre-modern treatises on economics is contained in Otto Brunner, *Neue Wege der Sozialgeschichte* (Göttingen, 1956), pp. 33–61. Cf. also the analysis by Peter Laslett, *The World We Have Lost* (London, 1965), passim.

65. Smelser, op. cit., p. 110.

66. See Cesar Grana, *Bohemian Versus Bourgeois* (New York, 1964), passim, for a sympathetic analysis of this imagery. Herbert Marcuse's *One-Dimensional Man* (Boston, 1964) appeared too late to be included in Grana's concluding anaylsis.

67. It may well be the present-day absence of a need for self-help and defense which makes the closely knit solidarity of such groups appear oppressive to a modern observer, especially if he discounts the romanticism with which such solidarities have been interpreted in the past. By the same token, it may be the absence of that need for self-help and defense which weakens the solidarity of groups in modern societies and allows for the development of individualism. The older pattern often arose from the imposition of taxes in return for privileges, which necessitated the organization of communities for self-help and defense; Max Weber discussed this device under the concept of liturgy. Cf. Max Weber, *The Theory of Social and Economic Organization* (New York, 1947), p. 312–13. A society like the Russian in which this order pattern was preserved up to the present time may well engender customs and attitudes markedly different from those that are familiar to us today. For an insightful discussion of these customs and attitudes see Wright W. Miller, *Russians as People* (New York, 1961), chap. 5.

68. See Karl Mannheim, *Man and Society in an Age of Reconstruction* (New York, 1941), p. 44. The foregoing discussion develops ideas presented in another context in Reinhard Bendix, *Nation-Building and Citizenship* (New York, 1964), pp. 105–06 and passim.

69. See Otto Hintze, "Weltgeschichtliche Bedingungen der Repraesentativverfassung," in *Staat und Verfassung* (Göttingen, 1962), pp. 140–85.

70. For the link between the theological conception of emanationism with theories of social evolution and functionalism, see Arthur Lovejoy, *The Great Chain of Being* (New York, 1960), Karl Loewith, *Meaning in History* (Chicago, 1949), and Kenneth Bock, "Theories of Progress and Evolution," in Werner J. Cahnmann and Alvin Boskoff, eds., *Society and History* (Glencoe, Ill., 1964), pp. 21–41. The intellectual tradition discussed in these works has been criticized very effectively—and in a manner that corroborates the present discussion at many points—by Ernest Gellner, *Thought and Change* (Chicago, 1964), passim.

71. So, of course, did the initial development of England depending as it did on intense competition with Holland. The point that social structures cannot be understood by exclusive attention to their internal developments is a general one. See Otto

Hintze, "Staatsverfassung und Heeresverfassung," in *Staat und Verfassung* (Göttingen, 1962), pp. 52–83. The essay was originally published in 1906.

72. See Milton Singer, op. cit., p. 262.

73. Carlo Cipolla, *Guns and Sails in the Early Phase of European Expansion, 1400–1700* (London, 1965), passim.

74. See notes 1, 47, and 68 for earlier references to changes in agriculture and political participation. The changes in literacy and the availability of printed matter are surveyed for England in Raymond Williams, *The Long Revolution* (London, 1961), pp. 156–72.

75. The terms of that distinction do not stay put. Before the modern period England was a follower society while Holland and Sweden were advanced, especially in the production of cannons. Cf. Cipolla, *Guns and Sails*, pp. 36–37, 52–54, 87n. In the twentieth century the Russian revolution, the Fascist regimes, and the Chinese revolution have added their own modifications of this distinction as an aspect of modernization. Singer, op. cit., pp. 261–62 refers to the same distinction by speaking of early and late arrivals, but I wish to emphasize the sense of pioneering or backwardness which has animated people in advanced and follower societies. These terms refer to the evaluations of the participants rather than to my own assessment of progress or backwardness.

76. There are those who consider societies closed systems. They would counter this diffusionist argument with the contention that societies are not passive recipients of external stimuli, but select among them in accordance with the dictates of their internal structure. This interpretation is an extension of the equilibrium model and as such a secular version of the original theological belief in pre-established harmony. That older view was as compatible with the existence of evil in a divinely created world as the functionalist interpretation is compatible with the existence of conflict and change. Neither view is compatible with the possibility of a self-perpetuating disequilibrium, or cumulative causation as Myrdal has called it.

77. Gerschenkron, op. cit., pp. 26, 44, and passim.

78. Ibid., p. 46.

79. See the analysis of this complex of ideas in the work of Gottfried Wilhelm von Leibniz (1646–1716), especially the interesting contacts between Leibniz and Peter the Great with regard to the modernization of Russia, in Dieter Groh, *Russland und das Selbstverständniss Europas* (Neuwied, 1961), pp. 32–43.

80. David Landes, "Technological Change and Development in Western Europe, 1750–1914," in H. J. Habbakuk and M. Postan, eds., *The Cambridge Economic History of Europe; The Industrial Revolutions and After* (Cambridge, 1965), vol. 6, part 1, p. 366.

81. Note the frequency with which "political unity" appears as an index of modernity in the several lists of attributes presented in Marius Jansen, ed., *Changing Japanese Attitudes Towards Modernization* (Princeton, 1965), pp. 18–19, 20–24, and passim.

82. For a discussion of this point, see Bendix, *Nation-Building and Citizenship,* pp. 15–29.

83. On the "ad hoc diffusion" of items of modernity, see the illuminating discussion by Theodore H. von Laue, "Imperial Russia at the Turn of the Century," *Comparative Studies in Society and History* 3 (1961):353–67 and Mary C. Wright, "Revolution from Without?," *Comparative Studies in Society and History* 4 (1962): 247–52.

84. E. A. Shils, "Political Development in the New States," *Comparative Studies in Society and History* 2 (1960):281.

85. Gerschenkron, op. cit., pp. 41–44.

86. Cf. Landes, op. cit., pp. 354, 358.

87. The concept "reference society" has been chosen in analogy to Robert Merton's "reference groups." Cf. Robert K. Merton, *Social Theory and Social Structure* (Glencoe, Ill., 1957), pp. 225 ff.

88. Cf. the succinct overview of the intelligentsia by Hugh Seton-Watson, *Neither War Nor Peace* (New York, 1960), pp. 164–87. See also Bendix, *Nation-Building and Citizenship*, pp. 231 ff.

89. The most sensitive analysis of this bifurcation I have found in the literature is the study by Joseph Levenson, *Modern China and its Confucian Past* (Garden City, N.Y.,1964), passim. Cf. also Cipolla, *Guns and Sails*, pp. 116–26.

90. See the analysis of these tensions by E. A. Shils, "Political Development in the New States," cited above.

91. Cf. the chapter on "Die Proletarier der Geistesarbeit" in Wilhelm Riehl, *Die Bürgerliche Gesellschaft* (Stuttgart, 1930), especially pp. 312–13.

92. For a vigorous critique of this tendency, see J. H. Hexter, *Reappraisals in History* (New York, 1963), passim. Note also the cautionary comments regarding the problem of historical continuity in Gerschenkron, op. cit., pp. 37–39.

93. For a more balanced assessment of the European bourgeoisie, see Otto Brunner, *Neue Wege der Sozialgeschichte*, pp. 80–115.

94. Joseph Schumpeter, *Capitalism, Socialism, and Democracy* (New York, 1947), pp. 136–37. See also pp. 12–13 for a more generalized statement. Substantially the same observations were made by Frederick Engels in 1892, but the political primacy of the aristocracy and the secondary role of the bourgeoisie appeared to him only as a survival which would disappear eventually. See Frederick Engels, *Socialism, Utopian and Scientific* (Chicago, 1905), pp. xxxii–xxxiv. For an empirical study, see W. L. Guttsman, *The British Political Elite* (New York, 1963).

95. Cf. Peter Laslett, *The World We Have Lost*, p. 22 and passim.

96. Cf. Ernest Barker, *The Development of Public Services in Western Europe, 1660–1930* (London, 1944), pp. 1–6 and passim.

97. Cf. Clifford Geertz, "The Integrative Revolution," in Geertz, ed., *Old Societies and New States* (Glencoe, Ill., 1963), pp. 105 ff. Cf. my article "Bureaucracy" in the forthcoming edition of the *International Encyclopedia of the Social Sciences*.

98. Cf., for example, the statement that "In Egypt, the middle class has been weak in numbers and influence, and civil servants have comprised a large portion of it." See Morroe Berger, *Bureaucracy and Society in Modern Egypt* (Princeton, 1957), p. 46.

99. Karl Marx, *The 18th Brumaire of Louis Bonaparte* (New York, n.d.), p. 109.

100. See John Stuart Mill, *Principles of Political Economy* (Boston, 1848), pp. 322–23.

101. Cf. the analysis of growing class-consciousness among workers in Karl Marx, *The Poverty of Philosophy* (New York, n.d.), pp. 145–46, but note also the evidence adduced by David Mitrany, *Marx against the Peasants* (London, 1951), passim.

102. To discount such beliefs because they disappeared eventually is no more plausible than to make the aristocracy's role decline in advance of its eventual demise. Cf. the discussion of the "traditionalism of labor" in my book *Work and Authority in Industry* (New York, 1956), pp. 34 ff.

103. For a fuller statement of this interpretation, see Bendix, *Nation-Building and Citizenship*, pp. 61–74.

104. As always, the contrast is not absolute. During the nineteenth century, as one went eastward in Europe, one encountered certain parallels to the underdeveloped syndrome of today, namely an increased importance of government and rather weakly developed middle strata. See the illuminating statement by David Landes: "The farther east one goes in Europe, the more the bourgeoisie takes on the appearance of a foreign excrescence on manorial society, a group apart scorned by the nobility and feared or hated by (or unknown to) a peasantry still personally bound to the local *seigneur."* See Landes, op. cit., p. 358.

105. The debate concerning the deprivations of early English industrialization continues. But whatever its final resolution in terms of the changing standard of living, there is probably less disagreement on the psychological repercussions. The separation of the worker's home from his place of work, the novelty of factory discipline which had previously been associated with the pauper's workhouse, the brutalization of work conditions for women and children merely by the shift away from home, and related matters constitute impressive circumstantial evidence. Note also that the statement in the text makes sense of Germany's pioneering in the field of social legislation as an attribute of an early follower society.

106. Cf. Landes, op. cit., pp. 344–47 for a summary analysis of the labor-supply problem in the English industrial revolution in terms of the current state of research. These findings can be contrasted readily with comparative materials on various follower societies contained in Wilbert Moore and Arnold Feldman, eds., *Labor Commitment and Social Change in Developing Areas*, passim.

107. Note that Marx and others with him considered that separation a prerequisite of capitalist development. Cf. the discussion of the distinctive position of workers in African countries by Lloyd A. Fallers, "Equality, Modernity and Democracy in the New States," in Geertz, ed., op. cit., pp. 187–90. See also Richard D. Lambert, "The Impact of Urban Society upon Village Life," in Roy Turner, ed., *India's Urban Future* (Berkeley, 1962), pp. 117–40.

108. In these respects there are, of course, striking differences between France and England which can be considered symptomatic of the radical and the conservative approach to education and conscription. For a comparative treatment of these issues see Ernest Barker, *The Development of Public Services in Western Europe,* chaps. 2 and 5.

109. The circularity of this statement is unavoidable. In a general sense, pursuits engaging the intellect refer to the creation and maintenance (transmission) of cultural values, but each of these terms (cultural values, creation, maintenance, transmission) is the subject of constant debate, and that debate itself is an important intellectual pursuit. Since this debate involves the pejorative as well as appreciative use of these terms, and by that token the endeavor of speakers to belong to the positive side of the cultural process (in however marginal a fashion), no one set of defining terms will be wholly satisfactory. In view of this difficulty the most reasonable alternative is to set up a typology of intellectual pursuits and leave the group of persons called intellectuals undefined. For one such attempt see Theodor Geiger, *Aufgaben und Stellung der Intelligenz in der Gesellschaft* (Stuttgart, 1949), pp. 1–24, 81–101.

110. See the case study of this process in England by Leo Lowenthal and Marjorie

Fiske, "The Debate over Art and Popular Culture," in Mirra Komarovsky, ed., *Common Frontiers of the Social Sciences* (Glencoe, Ill., 1957), pp. 33–112.

111. I avoid the term "alienation" because misuse has made it worthless. For a scholarly treatment of this intellectual response to bourgeois society in nineteenth century Europe, see Karl Loewith, *From Hegel to Nietzsche*, passim. Cf. also the analysis of the social distance between intellectuals and practical men in Joseph Schumpeter, op. cit., pp. 145–55 as well as the unusual acceptance of that distance by at least one great artist, William Faulkner, who speaks of writers "steadily occupied by trying to do the impossible" while keeping "out of the way of the practical and busy people who carry the burden of America." See Faulkner's speech on the occasion of receiving the National Book Award in *The New York Times Book Review* (February 6, 1955), p. 2.

112. See E. A. Shils, "Intellectuals, Public Opinion and Economic Development," *World Politics* 10 (1958):232–55.

Index

Biographical Notes

Index

Throughout this index, the abbreviation *bib.* indicates *bibliographic reference.*

Biographical Notes

REINHARD BENDIX is Professor of Sociology at the University of California at Berkeley. Acknowledged as one of the foremost contemporary social scientists, he has published extensively in the history of sociological theory, social change, and social class. He is the author of *Max Weber: An Intellectual Portrait, Higher Civil Servants in American Society, Work and Authority in Industry, Social Science and the Distrust of Reason,* and *Nation-Building and Citizenship.* With S. M. Lipset he has published *Social Mobility in Industrial Society* and *Class, Status and Power.*

BURTON BENEDICT is Professor of Anthropology at the University of California at Berkeley, and was formerly of the London School of Economics. He has worked extensively on the theoretical problems of social pluralism, and in this connection has conducted research in Mauritius, the Seychelles, and Malawi. In London and Boston his research covered Chinese, Buddhists, and Muslims. Benedict has authored many articles and titles of his books include *Indians in a Plural Society: People of the Seychelles, Mauritius: Problems of a Plural Society,* and *Problems of Small Territories.*

ABNER COHEN is on the faculty of the School of Oriental and African Studies at the University of London. He received his doctorate from the University of Manchester and has been Visiting Professor of Anthropology at Cornell University. Arab-Muslim villages on the Israel-Jordan border and Southern Nigeria have been the sites of his field research. His work shows a concern with the inter-relations of politics and economics. He has written *Arab Border-Villages in Israel: A Study of Continuity and Change in Social Organizations* and *Custom and Politics in Urban Africa.*

BERNARD S. COHN, considered one of the outstanding young scholars of Indian history and social change, has been a Guggenheim Fellow, and has held appointments in sociology, anthropology, and history. Currently he is Professor of History and of Anthropology at the University of Chicago. He has been

347

Assistant Editor of the *Journal of Asian Studies,* has contributed to *Village India,* and is the author of *Traditional India: Structure and Change.*

PAULA BROWN GLICK has held faculty appointments at Cambridge and the Australian National University. She is now Professor of Anthropology at the State University of New York at Stony Brook. Her research has been with the peoples of West Africa, Australia, New Guinea, the New Hebrides, and the American Indians. Her publications are particularly concerned with kinship and political and ecological aspects of social organization. With H. C. Brookfield she is co-author of *Struggle for Land: Agriculture and Group Territories among the Chimbu of the New Guinea Highlands.*

From an earlier career in law in his native South Africa, LEO KUPER has emerged as one of the country's leading analysts. He has expanded his initial interest in race relations to include investigations in social pluralism. With his wife, Hilda, he has edited *African Law: Its Adaptation and Development,* and with R. Davies, *Durban: A Study in Racial Ecology.* His books include *Passive Resistance in South Africa* and the prize-winning *An African Bourgeoisie.* He is now Professor of Sociology at the University of California, Los Angeles.

ROBERT MARSH, Professor of Sociology at Brown University, is also an historian of Chinese civilization. His numerous articles and books are largely concerned with Chinese history and social organizations, and he has done extensive field research in Hong Kong and Taiwan. Among his books are *The Mandarins: The Circulation of Elites in China, 1600–1900,* and *Comparative Sociology: Toward the Codification of Cross-Societal Analysis.*

EDWARD NORBECK is Dean of Humanities and Professor of Anthropology at Rice University. His firsthand research has been among American Indians, Japanese in the United States and Japan, and Hawaiian Islanders. The breadth of his interests is reflected in the titles of his published volumes, which include *Takashima: A Japanese Fishing Community, Pineapple Town—Hawaii, Religion in Primitive Society, Prehistoric Man in the New World* (co-edited with J. D. Jennings), and *Changing Japan.* He is also Editor of *Rice University Studies,* the journal of Rice University.

LEONARD PLOTNICOV is Associate Professor of Anthropology at the University of Pittsburgh. His research has focused on modern urbanization with particular emphasis on West Africa. He is the author of *Strangers to the City: Urban Man in Jos, Nigeria,* and co-editor (with Arthur Tuden) of *Social Stratification in Africa.*

SYDEL SILVERMAN is Associate Professor of Anthropology at Queens College of the City University of New York. Since 1960 she has periodically carried out field research in Italian peasant communities. A number of articles based on this work have been published.

RAYMOND T. SMITH, one of the foremost scholars of Caribbean societies, is Professor of Anthropology at the University of Chicago. He is a former Professor of Sociology at the University of Ghana and Professor of Social Anthropology at the University of the West Indies. On the basis of his research in Jamaica and Guyana he has written many articles on ethnic plural societies and is the author of *The Negro Family in British Guiana* and *British Guiana*.

AIDAN SOUTHALL is Professor of Anthropology at the University of Wisconsin, Madison. He is a former Director of the East African Institute of Social Research at Makerere University, Uganda. His researches and publications have dealt both with traditional and modern social systems in East Africa and Madagascar, within which he has focused on political and kinship systems, social stratification, and processes of social and cultural change. He is the author of *Alur Society,* co-author of *Townsmen in the Making* (with P. C. W. Gutkind), and editor of *Social Change in Modern Africa.*

ARTHUR TUDEN is Professor of Anthropology at the University of Pittsburgh. His research, mainly in Central Africa, has been centered on kinship, economic, and political systems. He is a co-editor of *Political Anthropology* (with Marc Swartz and Victor Turner) and of *Social Stratification in Africa* (with Leonard Plotnicov).